US Environmental Policy in Action

"The third edition of *US Environmental Policy in Action* addresses the often-overlooked topics of implementing and evaluating environmental policy and includes the voices of state and local officials on the front lines—the rule-writers, inspectors and others who play a critical role in shaping environmental policy. The case studies and 'voices' sections are especially helpful in illustrating how broad policy ideas are put into effect and evolve over time, and explain the difficult choices facing policymakers. The new edition, which comes at a time of intense political and social conflict, offers a welcome inclusion of social justice issues, and how they interact with environmental policy, and is sure to be of great interest to readers. This insightful book is easy to read and accessible to a wide range of audiences."

—Robert Duffy, *Professor of Political Science, Colorado State University, USA*

"*US Environmental Policy in Action* allows readers to explore how policy is developed and implemented in federal and state environmental agencies using clear prose and an engaging writing style. I'm delighted to see this third edition, as it includes additional analysis of how issues of social justice intersect environmental policymaking—something that is essential in moving forward with climate change, clean air, and water programs, among others. Rinfret and Pautz use case studies to illustrate how key actors influence policy implementation, as well as show stakeholders who are left out or largely dismissed from the process. Anyone interested in the practice of environmental policy will want to find a place for this stellar book in their library. Highest recommendation."

—Denise Scheberle, *Clinical Teaching Professor, School of Public Affairs, University of Colorado Denver, USA*

"A flurry of new environmental policy adoption by the federal government and many states in the early years of the 2020s underscores the need for the revised edition of this important text. Sara Rinfret and Michelle Pautz guide readers through the pivotal stages of policy implementation and evaluation, cutting across multiple environmental topics and adding expanded perspective on social justice considerations."

—Barry Rabe, J.Ira and Nicki Harris Family, *Professor of Public Policy, University of Michigan, USA*

Sara R. Rinfret · Michelle C. Pautz

US Environmental Policy in Action

Third Edition

Sara R. Rinfret
Politics & International Affairs
Northern Arizona University
Flagstaff, AZ, USA

Michelle C. Pautz
Political Science
University of Dayton
Dayton, OH, USA

ISBN 978-3-031-17502-2   ISBN 978-3-031-17503-9   (eBook)
https://doi.org/10.1007/978-3-031-17503-9

Cover illustration: the_burtons/Moment/Getty Images

This Palgrave Macmillan imprint is published by the registered company Springer Nature
Switzerland AG
The registered company address is: Gewerbestrasse 11, 6330 Cham, Switzerland

To our students – they hold the keys to our environmental future.

PREFACE

As we finalized the third edition of this book during the fall of 2022, we did so during an extraordinary time in our history in which:

- There have been 6 million global deaths due to the coronavirus;
- The January 6 Congressional hearings continue to unfold revealing unsettling facts;
- The authority of the US EPA to regulate greenhouse gas emissions was significantly curtailed by the US Supreme Court in *West Virginia v. EPA*;
- The lowest water levels to date were recorded for Lake Mead and the Great Salt Lake;
- *Roe v. Wade* was overturned by the US Supreme Court;
- Record hot temperatures affect the US and other parts of the world;
- The nation continues to grapple with gun violence, including attacks at an elementary school in Texas and during a 4th of July celebration in Illinois;
- Congress passed the Inflation Reduction Act;
- Critical race theory curriculum is scrutinized by state legislatures; and
- Beyoncé releases her *Renaissance* album.

For some, the items in aforementioned list may not appear to be connected, but they are indeed. Democracy is messy and societal issues at a given time are necessary to understand and contextualize how and why environmental policy is made (or is not). At its most basic level, environmental issues concern the air we breathe, the water we drink, and the land and resources we live on and use to sustain our lives. Although we both share a passion for these issues we come from different places—Sara is an avid outdoorswoman and Michelle is most definitely not. Much like many of us reading this book, we are collectively committed to understanding complex environmental issues and working with our students to tackle these intractable challenges. Most importantly, we are interested in how policy works on the front-lines—not just in the halls of Congress. This orientation, coupled with our passions for learning and teaching, motivated the first edition of this book.

The third edition of this book continues to find the US at a turning point in addressing environmental issues. Radical swings in our nation's politics have led us to a point where incremental changes are no longer sufficient. Instead, significant action must be taken now to save our planet from challengess like climate change. We believe that we can once again harness the groundwork and energy from the environmental movement in the 1960s and 1970s to once again rise to the occasion and solve the environmental challenges of today.

There are many noteworthy environmental policy texts available, but what sets this one apart and makes it particularly useful in today's world is our emphasis on the "doing" of environmental policy. Often environmental policy texts focus at the highest levels of our government—notably the federal level—and discuss policy from that vantage point emphasizing the politics of it all. Although we discuss environmental policy at the federal level and consider politics too, we take the conversation a step further and discuss implementation on the front-lines. Our focus on this action orientation stems from both our professional experiences working in environmental policy and regulation and also from our academic backgrounds in public administration. It is important to understand how and why Congress passed the Clean Air Act in 1970, for example, but it is equally important to understand how that law is implemented through the work of air inspectors and members of the regulated community and what four plus decades of experience and additional research and data mean for safeguarding the quality of the nation's air. Additionally, we incorporate stories of individuals on the front-lines of environmental policy implementation to enhance our understandings of these issues. With these deeper understandings and richer contexts, we hope to move the conversation forward in a productive manner about what the government should and should not do as it concerns the environment.

More specifically, our third edition addresses key elements that continue to be elusive in existing texts, yet are topics students frequently want to know more about: (1) a detailed discussion about how policy is implemented, including at the subnational level, (2) illustrative case studies explaining foundational concepts, and (3) lived experiences by highlighting an actor or a practitioner in the field so students can move from theory to practice. Many of these elements remain from the first two editions, but we have updated the stories and examples. Added in this edition is an emphasis on social justice. Given the inflection point of our society—not just in terms of environmental issues—adding this perspective to the discussion of environmental policy is essential.

In particular, the US finds itself in a transition period after the Trump administration and the first few years of the Biden administration. These two administrations have demonstrated that while the leadership of the federal government is significant, it is not the only venue for action. This period also signals a profound refocus on environmental policy and the intersection of environmental policy and social justice. It is important that the texts available to students speak to this moment. Environmental issues are social justice issues, but too often they are not framed in such a way and texts leave environmental justice to a small part of a chapter (if at all) at the back of the book. In our third edition, we integrate social justice considerations in challenge questions for the environmental policy classroom. For example, in Chapter 6, when learning about rulemaking, it is essential to discuss and consider which stakeholders are included during pre-proposal and notice and comment stages, and which stakeholders are not.

With this approach to environmental policy in action, this book is intended for readers coming to it from a variety of contexts. For students in environmental studies and sustainability studies programs, this book will aid in an understanding of the governmental and policy side of these issues. For students in political science and public administration, this book will help in applying core concepts in these fields to the environmental realm. For students in the natural sciences and engineering, this book will assist in explaining why seemingly obvious solutions to environmental challenges go unpursued in environmental policy.

Ultimately, our take on environmental policy issues comes from the passion and energy our students have shown us over many years and across institutions when it comes to tackling these very present and intense issues before us. We hope that this book helps advance understanding of environmental issues and charts a path forward because inaction is action, but inaction—particularly in this policy area—can have significant and lasting negative ramifications for us and generations to come.

Flagstaff, USA   Sara R. Rinfret
Dayton, USA   Michelle C. Pautz
August 2022

Acknowledgments

As is the case with the environmental issues we discuss in the following pages, the number of people who contributed to and supported our efforts developing and writing this book is significant. Therefore, while our names adorn the cover of this book, it is essential that we acknowledge a wonderful group of colleagues, friends, and family members that helped bring this book to fruition in its first edition and were equally essential in the revisions and additions for the second and third editions.

First and foremost, we must acknowledge our students who motivate us, challenge us, and keep our passion for this topic and our hopes for future generations alive. We have both taught at a variety of institutions over many years and we continue to be impressed by our students who crave understanding in the hopes of making the world just a little bit better for the future. A number of students have helped us with various aspects over the course of each edition, including Emily Kaylor, Taylor Pair, Susan Weaver, and Jeff Cook. Jeff, a former student of Sara's, was instrumental in reworking Chapter 8. His passion for understanding the next generation of environmental policy should not go unnoticed and we thank him for his willingness to push us to revise and update.

In addition, our respective institutions and colleagues have been supportive of our work. At the University of Dayton, the colleagues in the Department of Political Science have been very supportive and encouraging, especially Dr. Grant Neeley who is a wonderful department chair. At the University of Montana and Northern Arizona University, Sara is indebted to the encouragement and support from her colleagues. And colleagues at other institutions, including Dr. Denise Scheberle, Dr. Bob Duffy, and Dr. Michael Kraft, have been incredibly helpful.

Each of us are supported by wonderful friends and family members who must be mentioned.

Sara could not have written this third edition without mentioning the support of family and colleagues. Her interests and passion for environmental policy come from living in the American West. The support of her parents to move west for graduate school was a life-changing experience, of which she is forever fortunate. Countless hikes and runs with her husband, Bob, provided an appreciation for the natural beauty of Arizona and its importance to the future of environmental policy. He has also supported countless revisions and editions. I am extremely fortunate to have learned from the best and brightest minds in the discipline from Northern Arizona University and Colorado State University—Drs. David Schlosberg, Jacqueline Vaughn, Chuck Davis, Sandra Davis, and Robert Duffy.

Most importantly, my students continue to inspire me. I am unbelievably humbled by and honored to work with so many students over the last decade. Their commitment to providing solutions for environmental problems is insurmountable, yearning to learn more and ask how. To my students that worked numerous hours to write their own plans to meet the University of Montana's carbon goals, thank you. This was not an easy endeavor and you each saw the politics behind policymaking first-hand. To my students at Northern Arizona, thank you for working countless hours to write a climate action plan for a large statewide community. Regardless, our students are the future to our environmental success. As educators, we must continue to push ourselves and our students to discuss a variety of solutions to address the very real and imminent environmental problems of today and tomorrow.

Michelle must acknowledge teachers, mentors, colleagues, and friends and family. My abiding interest in environmental policy regulation started as a young girl interested in marine mammals, and this curiosity led to several transformative experiences as an undergraduate at Elon University. In the same year, I took environmental policy with Dr. Sharon Spray and environmental economics with Dr. Doug Redington. These courses convinced me that there was nothing I wanted to study more than environmental issues. I then had the good fortune to intern with what was then the North Carolina Department of Environment and Natural

Resources thanks to Dr. Chalmers Brumbaugh. My passion for these issues only intensified as Dr. Betty Morgan helped me find my way to graduate studies in public administration at Virginia Tech. There, with the guidance of Dr. Karen Hult, Dr. Larkin Dudley, and the late Dr. John Rohr, I was able to continue my work in this area. Dr. Susan Buck was also an important guide along this journey. I owe these educators and mentors an incredible debt for helping me find my path.

In addition to these individuals, the love and support of my friends and family are essential. Sara and I first met on a panel at a Midwest Political Science Association conference many years ago, and a productive professional relationship as well as a friendship has evolved that I am grateful for. Friends have enthusiastically listened to my ramblings about my research pursuits and writing for more hours than is fair, especially Danielle, Kurt, and Kris. And my mom, who passed away this winter, was also a constant source of support. But through all of it, Steven has stood next to me, challenging me when needed, listening with patience and kindness, and encouraging me always. Being married to an academic is not easy and Steven is the patient and supportive partner I never even knew I needed. Quite simply, I cannot imagine my life without him. His patience, grace, and encouragement are accentuated by the love and support of our wonderful four-legged girls. Sydney, Victoria, and Mackenzie are always tolerant when my hours researching and writing keep me in front of a screen for longer than they would prefer. Their simple presence with understanding eyes and wagging tails is often just what I need. And to Emma and Ellie whose paws are gone from this world, but who are forever in my heart, I owe them so much.

CONTENTS

LIST OF FIGURES

LIST OF TABLES

CHAPTER 1

Environmental Policy in Practice

Introductory Story: Lessons from *the Lorax*
Dr. Seuss's *The Lorax* presents readers with a choice: protect the land for future use or develop the land for monetary gain. The story unfolds as a young boy attempts to understand what caused the extinction of the beautifully colored Truffula Trees. He discovers that the trees were cut down in order to produce Thneed needed for various products. Eventually, Thneed was overproduced, causing the natural landscape to become dark and dreary—a wasteland where no one wanted to live because of all the pollution. This story reminds us what happens when we make environmental choices; cutting down trees has costs and benefits.

The story of *The Lorax* struck a chord with former administrator of the US Environmental Protection Agency (EPA), Lisa Jackson; she hoped that the book, which was turned into a feature film in 2012, would help us understand the importance of protecting the environment (Nakashima 2012). During her time at the EPA, Jackson always kept a copy of *The Lorax* in her desk to remind her of the importance of protecting the environment (Boyle 2010). Even though the *Lorax* is a children's story, it serves as an essential lesson for present-day environmental policymaking—"Unless someone like you cares a whole awful lot, nothing is going to get better. It's not" (Suess 1998).

© The Author(s), under exclusive license to Springer Nature Switzerland AG 2023
S. R. Rinfret and M. C. Pautz, *US Environmental Policy in Action*,
https://doi.org/10.1007/978-3-031-17503-9_1

In 2022, the United States, for the first-time in decades passed the Inflation Reduction Act, which is predicted to make significant strides to combatting global climate change. Despite this noteworthy legislation, the US continues to confront a host of environmental issues that range from protecting the gray wolf in Wyoming and Montana, preventing drinking water contamination to endeavoring to preserve biodiversity and combating climate change. Although the environmental problems we confront are more complex than those in Dr. Seuss's *The Lorax*, the choices they present are no less stark. The following pages demonstrate how addressing challenges through the lens of environmental policy in the US.

We begin our conversation about environmental policy by defining key terms. First, a basic dictionary definition of "environmental policy" is necessary. The word "environment" encompasses our natural surroundings and includes how it is affected (e.g., pollution, water, sanitation). We define environmental policy as one area of public policy that the government is called to address by its citizens. More specifically, environmental policy is government action related to the natural environment.

Environmental policy is also about making tough choices. It is difficult because it can pit individuals against one another. The American public might be opposed to shutting down a coal mining company in Colstrip, Montana that releases harmful pollutants because it means a loss of jobs for the community; however, that same public also wants a clean environment. Environmental policymaking is difficult because it brings together an enormous array of actors—institutional (Congress, the President, and the Courts) and non-institutional actors (media, interest groups, political parties, and the public). All of these actors have their own perspectives and their own agendas.

In addition, environmental decisionmaking is challenging because the information age has brought us a deluge of material. Discerning fact from fiction can be frustrating and overwhelming. Historically, institutional actors, if they did not have the requisite information to decide, relied upon scientific or policy experts to inform and help them make the best, most informed choice. However, the temptation for institutional actors is to bypass outside expertise and advance their own decisions with information readily available from the click of a button from an Internet search or reading Tweets. For politicians, the temptation is to base choices increasingly on how they might help secure re-election (Jacobson 2012). For instance, if an elected member of Congress' congressional district has the highest unemployment rate in the US, the goal is not going to be to shut down the local coal mining facility because jobs are needed; and this takes precedence over protecting the environment. However, what if this coal mining company's chemicals end up in the local water supply and kill thousands of citizens? As this example suggests, environmental policy is about difficult choices.

The focus of this introductory chapter is to first present a few environmental dilemmas (e.g., air pollution, water contamination, garbage disposal, and species protection) in order to examine the choices that the US has made about these issues. Then, we introduce the reader to the central theme of our book: we need to pay attention to the doers of environmental policy, as they are the people on the front-lines of environmental policy, implementing society's choices.

With the term "front-lines," we are referring to the people who implement or carry out environmental policy on a daily basis. These individuals on the front-lines include environmental rule-writers, who translate congressional statutes into actionable policy, and environmental inspectors, who ensure that your neighborhood waste management company is complying with federal law to ensure that your waste is properly stored. They also include members of advocacy groups who urge collective action as well as policy analysts who provide the important facts and analysis we need to make decisions. Furthermore, we cannot overlook those businesses that cooperate with rule-writers and environmental inspectors to protect the environment (Pautz and Rinfret 2013). The argument we make in this book is simple: in order to understand environmental choices made in the US, we need to pay attention to the doers of environmental policy, many of which occupy the so-called fourth branch of government (i.e., the bureaucracy).

Environmental Dilemmas and Choices

We offer a snapshot of environmental challenges (e.g., air pollution, climate change, hazardous and solid waste, etc.) and the choices the US has made to address some aspects of these issues. These choices by no means indicate that these environmental issues have been resolved. Our goal is to introduce our readers to some examples, leaving the remaining pages of the book to fill in the details. Environmental policy evolves daily and with ever-changing balance of power in the White House, House of Representatives, and Senate, there will be even greater need for our institutional actors to bargain and compromise regarding the future of environmental policy.

Clean or Dirty Air?

Prior to the 1970s, the air quality in the US was often defined as unhealthy or dirty because of the pollution that filled the air in many of our major cities, such as Los Angeles (Andrews 2006). Among the culprits of the dirty air were six major toxic pollutants: sulfur dioxide, nitrogen dioxide, carbon monoxide, particulates, lead, and ozone (Andrews 2006). These six pollutants are of concern because of their impact on the health and well-being of humans; but, what are the origins of these pollutants? For instance, carbon monoxide (the most common of the six) is colorless and odorless and is a product of burning fossil fuels (including running your car), and when there is too much of it in the air, it can cause an array of cardiovascular problems and even visual impairment.

To address these concerns, Congress established air quality standards with the passage of the Clean Air Act (CAA) of 1970, which created National Ambient Air Quality Standards (NAAQS). The EPA, in implementing the NAAQS, established limits for the aforementioned six pollutants and continues to enforce these standards across the country (Kraft 2017). Going back to our example of carbon monoxide, the NAAQS standards forced car manufacturers to devise ways to produce cars that are cleaner burning. The EPA suggests that when examining these six areas of pollutants that lead to poor air quality, significant improvements have been made over time. The EPA reports from 1980 to 2020, air quality in the US has improved because the agency set standards that were required to be met; if not, fines resulted (US EPA Air Quality 2020). To demonstrate some of these improvements, the EPA's longitudinal study of carbon monoxide from 1990 2020 to reports a decrease by 73% [US EPA Air Quality 2020]).

Cleaning up dirty skies may appear as a simple choice, but challenges still exist today. Although Congress did pass the Inflation Reduction Act in 2022, lawmakers in the US have yet to pass climate change policy. "Climate change" is the term explaining that the Earth is warming and, according to the EPA, the Earth's temperature has increased by 1.6 degrees Fahrenheit over the last century. Accordingly, the logical question then becomes: What has caused the temperature increases? The vast majority of scientific research supports the conclusion that human activities—through the burning of fossil fuels—have released significant quantities of carbon dioxide, posing a threat to human health. However, some US politicians, including Senator Ron Johnson (R-WI), argue that the warming of the Earth is a natural occurrence, not a human-made one, and scientists should not be trusted to make these determinations. Some members of Congress agree with Senator Johnson and do not see the value in pursuing climate change policy because the consequences will be realized well after their life expectancy. The choices we have available here are to either believe or not believe the science. As President Obama noted in his 2014 State of the Union address: "climate change is a fact." For some, though, the answer is not this simple.

Is It Really Drinkable?

It seems unfathomable that you could not drink the water from your faucet at home because the US does have some of the cleanest tap water in the world, which ensures we do not fill our drinking glasses with chromium or chlordane (Andrews 2006). However, safe drinking water has not always been available in the US—and today there are still concerns with tap water in Flint, Michigan and Jackson, Mississippi. In 1976, Congress passed the Safe Drinking Water Act (SDWA). The SDWA estab lished national standards to protect our drinking water from naturally occurring or human-made contaminants that might be found in drinking water. The US EPA works with state and local governments to ensure safe drinking water from the more than 160,000 public and private drinking water suppliers in the US. The SDWA, however, does not regulate private wells that serve fewer than 25 individuals (US EPA Drinking Water 2014).

Threats to our drinking water still exist (McLendon 2014). One of the problems with the SDWA is that it does not regulate "nonpoint" sources, which include runoff from farms (e.g., cow manure), construction, or stormwater runoff (e.g., you are washing your car and the soap goes into the nearby drain). Therefore, our water can still become polluted from sources that are classified as non-point because the exact origin cannot necessarily be determined. Let us hypothesize that a nearby river necessary for a town's water supply has high traces of fecal matter. The presumption is that the source of the contamination could be from the adjacent yogurt factory that has thousands of cows grazing in close proximity to the river. However, there are also several large farms alongside the river. Therefore, how could someone determine definitively the source of the drinking water contamination? One option would be to blame all of the farms, or at least the one closest to the drinking water facility. We know that contaminants upstream travel downstream, but how do you determine who is responsible? It is not an easy answer.

The SDWA routinely monitors and tracks only 91 contaminants. Yet, there are new chemicals manufactured each day and we are unaware of their effects on our tap water. For instance, methylcyclohexane methanol (MCHM), a black licorice-smelling chemical that is used to clean coal, is not on the list of 91 routinely monitored contaminants. In 2014, a water-treatment plant near Charleston, West Virginia found this chemical in the water (Levitz et al. 2014). Ingesting this chemical can cause vomiting and other flu-like ailments, but much is still unknown about MCHM.

MCHM's scary counterpart, TTHM (trihalomethanes—used in disinfection byproducts) was found in Flint, Michigan's drinking water supply in 2015. The City of Flint's testing showed high levels of lead in the drinking water supply—104 parts per billion. The acceptable EPA rate is fifteen parts per billion. These high levels of lead sparked a state of emergency declaration ordered by then President Obama. Michigan has since attempted to take steps to address what went wrong in Flint (US EPA Flint 2022).

The question driving these incidents is whether or not the US EPA, or state equivalent, should be required to examine and test every single chemical ever manufactured, which would take significant amounts of time and resources.

Taking Out the Trash

No one—except *Sesame Street*'s Oscar the Grouch—likes trash, but few people think about it once the local garbage collector picks it up weekly and drives it away. However, there are safeguards—just as with the air we breathe and the water we drink—to protect us from solid waste through the Resource Conservation and Recovery Act (RCRA) of 1976.

Prior to the 1970s, the customary approach to taking out the trash was to dump it cheaply—often, in the ocean or burning it in a dumpsite (Andrews 2006). Obviously, these practices were not environmentally friendly and, with the creation of RCRA, Congress required the EPA to develop criteria for the safe disposal of hazardous waste. For instance, former EPA administrator William Ruckelshaus tried to implement "Mission 5000" to close 5,000 out of the 14,000 reported dumps across the US and convert into sanitary landfills. Ruckelshaus fell short of this mission, but, over time, all dumps had been closed and converted to sanitary landfills (Andrews 2006). By the 1980s, RCRA became even more stringent because of two horrific stories of hazardous waste disposal in Love Canal, New York, and Times Beach, Missouri. Congress was disappointed with the EPA during these hazardous waste crises and amended the RCRA in 1984 to enact more stringent provisions requiring rapid EPA action (Kraft 2017). More specifically, the Comprehensive Environmental Response and Liability Act (CERCLA) of 1980 was set up to help provide the cleanup of previous toxic dumping sites.

According to the EPA, Americans generated about 292 million tons of trash in 2018 and, of this trash, 94 million tons were either recycled or composted (US EPA Wastes 2022). However, since 1960, these waste totals have increased by almost 70%, which is burdening local landfills that are on the brink of capacity in urban areas such as New York City, where expansion is limited (US EPA Wastes 2022). Many Americans do not consider the disposal of our daily trash as a crisis because we pay a monthly flat fee and it is easily taken away from our homes.

Regardless, the US is facing a solid waste problem because landfills are full and finding new space is problematic—after all, who wants a landfill built next door. But, what are our choices in addressing our overcrowded landfills? One option is to provide incentives or more stringent policies that mandate recycling and composting to help alleviate overcrowding concerns. Another option is to charge Americans based on their monthly use—the less you throw away, the less you get charged. Alternatively, all elementary and high school students could be required to take a class on the best practices of how to reduce the waste we generate. These options could be plausible, but are probably impossible because Americans hate to be required to do something.

Why Should We Care About Plants and Animals?

Apart from assuring that air and water are clean and the land is safe for humans, the US has also been active in protecting the environment for plants and animals. On December 28, 2018, the US celebrated the forty-fifth birthday of the Endangered Species Act (ESA) of 1973. The US is one of the few countries that has national legislation to protect animals and plants from becoming extinct. Under the ESA, the US Fish and

Wildlife Service (USFWS) has the authority to protect and list endangered and threatened animals and plants. To date, the USFWS, through the ESA, has been able to protect approximately 99% of all species and plants that have been placed on the endangered or threatened lists from becoming extinct (Environment News Service 2014). Efforts during the Trump administration weakened the ESA, but President Biden is working to repeal this actions (Grandoni and Fears 2021).

Nonetheless, the ESA, like many other environmental laws, can spark controversy. For instance, what if you want to build a new golf course, but are told you are unable to do so because the building plans would inhibit the nests of the California Condor? Or, what happens when the USFWS determines that a species has met its population threshold and hunters determine in Wyoming that they will shoot and kill gray wolves to protect their livestock? The ESA is a noteworthy piece of legislation, but it has not come without controversy, particularly in western parts of the US (Rinfret 2009).

As noted in the opening pages of this chapter, environmental policy is created through the efforts of various institutional and non-institutional actors. As we have seen in a few of the aforementioned dilemmas, environmental issues can and do result in difficult choices. These choices have become even more difficult because of congressional gridlock—the inability of congressional policymakers to reach a compromise. Gridlock is problematic because many of the lingering challenges, ranging from climate change to what to do with overcrowding landfills, affect the daily lives of Americans; no one wants water that we cannot drink because of a chemical spill. Even with gridlock in Congress, environmental choices and policy are being made through a less obvious approaches.

While it is true the federal government creates environmental law for states and local governments to implement, this does not mean they are unimportant. With any environmental law, states must implement federal policy. States, however, can exceed federal minimum requirements or if there is not a federal policy (i.e. 10th amendment), states can create their own. California routinely sets much stronger environmental policies than the federal government does. In 2013, California created its own cap and trade system to reduce its greenhouse gas emission levels. Although touted by environmentalists as a work in progress, the California Supreme Court ruled it was not an unconstitutional tax on businesses. By way of comparison, the US Congress has failed to adopt a national level cap and trade system.

Environmental policymaking is also made by bureaucrats in government agencies. For example, environmental rule-writers in the USFWS used legislation such as the ESA to designate critical habitat to protect the polar bear in Alaska.[1] There are also thousands of government regulators who work for state-level environmental agencies such as the Montana Department of Environmental Quality. These state-level regulators monitor the local coal company, for example, to ensure the correct scrubber on its smokestack so the company does not pollute the air we breathe.[2]

Inevitably, environmental policy confronts a host of choices with a myriad of actors. Yet, in the third edition of our book, we encourage our reader to consider who has a seat at the table to determine the outcome of environmental policy choices. In particular, we encourage our reader to actively consider and question if those responsible for policy outcomes perpetuate marginalization of specific populations or actively work with communities to address them.

PLAN OF THE BOOK

The chapters in this book are designed around one central theme: to better understand the doing and implementing of environmental policy through the often-unnoticed actors on the front-lines. This is not to say that we disregard the more prominent actors, but we emphasize those actors who are often overlooked or absent from other textbooks. We argue that this focus is especially important in an era of congressional gridlock or lack of policy action for the environment at the most macro levels. Accordingly, this book addresses several elements missing in existing texts: (1) explanations and discussions of policy implementation from an institutional perspective, (2) illustrative case studies explaining foundational concepts, (3) introductory stories of practitioners in each chapter so that readers can connect theory with practice, and (4) end of the chapter challenge questions so we can question who gets to decide policy outcomes and why.

In order to provide a solid foundation for our readers, Chapter 2 focuses on establishing a context in which environmental policy is made. This chapter begins by considering the history of environmental protection in the US, starting with the conservation and preservation movements in the late nineteenth and early twentieth centuries. We focus on the modern environmental movement in the 1960s and overview the social and political movements that culminated in more than two dozen major environmental laws, which continue to provide the backbone of US environmental policy today. Within his conversation, we trace public opinion on environmental matters, past and present.

The final section of the chapter explores the role of scientific knowledge and information in environmental policy discussions. American society is seemingly more skeptical about scientific information than it was in the past; such skepticism impacts public discourse on environmental matters. Transmission of scientific knowledge is important, as the various perspectives on environmental issues increasingly debate the science itself, rather than debating what should be done in response to the science. Many of the insights we can draw contemporarily about environmental issues can be understood by how American society views scientific information. These discussions of public opinion and science help contextualize our consideration of the role Rachel Carson had in spurring a national focus on environmental concerns through her ability to communicate complex scientific information to the general public, notably through *Silent Spring* and the effect Greta Thunberg is having on people around the world. The case study in this chapter considers the still ongoing drama in Flint, Michigan, and the safety and quality of the drinking water in this city.

Chapter 3 builds on these foundations by delving into the process of policymaking in the US. We begin with an overview of public policy and explore the stages heuristic model as a framework for understanding how policy is made. To help illustrate the realities of making environmental policy, we then review the stages model's shortcomings in understanding environmental policy. We use this discussion to demonstrate that environmental policy is not, often, made in the neat, linear fashion many would think; rather, it is a complex process that is often messy, vague, and unpredictable. After demonstrating the complexity of the policymaking process, we consider the various factors that influence the crafting of policy. Our case study in this chapter explores the policymaking process by using single-use plastic policy as an example. For our voices section, we examine the efforts of Michigan Governor Gretchen Whitmer and Los Angeles Mayor Eric Garcetti and how they have tackled climate change in their work.

Chapter 4 delves into the key institutional (or official) actors and their impact on US environmental policy. More specifically, this chapter provides an in-depth discussion of how Congress, the courts, and the presidency have shaped environmental policy in the twenty-first century. In particular, we offer a brief overview of how each of the three branches of government impact the US environmental policy regime and how each of the players' roles has ebbed and flowed in recent decades. These perspectives are captured with our introductory story from White House National Climate Change Advisor, Gina McCarthy, and our chapter case study documents the challenges of US policymaking in gridlock.

Chapter 5 examines the instrumental role that a variety of "unofficial actors" (i.e., interest groups, the media, and lobbyists) have played in shaping environmental policy in the US. To understand the remarkable impact that groups can play in policymaking, the chapter begins with the introductory story of Women's Voices for the Earth, an organization devoted to sound the alarm on harmful toxins in women's feminine products. Detox the Box demonstrates how the work of grassroots interests can affect change on the front-lines of environmental policy. The closing section of the chapter uses the case of Daniel McGowan to determine whether the actions of this unofficial actor should be classified as environmental terrorism.

How vague policy language is translated into rules and regulations for organizations and individuals to follow is the focus of Chapter 6. The rulemaking process is frequently ignored in environmental policy discussions; however, it is through this process that policy is put into action. We begin this chapter with lessons from our introductory practitioner, current US EPA administrator Michael Regan. Then, we provide an overview of the rulemaking process, from the pre-proposal stage to rule finalization in the *Federal Register*. To document the nuts and bolts of the rulemaking process, the case study for this chapter examines corporate average fuel economy (CAFE) standards and how presidential directives and court rulings can engender regulatory rollbacks. As our case study and chapter introduction demonstrate, rulemaking is important, especially environmental rulemaking, but politics can affect progress.

Crucial to understanding environmental policy on the front-lines is investigating how environmental policy is implemented. Chapter 7 turns to the regulatory environment and begins by discussing the nature of command and control regulations and how they are the primary tool of environmental policy. In particular, we draw connections from earlier chapters as we discuss the governing and economic contexts that shape the implementation of environmental policy. As in Chapter 6, we focus on the actors in environmental policy in this chapter by highlighting the role of environmental inspectors, particularly the inspectors at the state level. These inspectors are the government officials who are responsible for the implementation of environmental regulation every day. We look at who these individuals are and what their experiences and challenges are like. For the case study in this chapter, we focus on the story of a regulated facility, its perspective, and the perspective of its environmental regulator. In our introduction, we explore the stories of a state air pollution control inspector, which enables our readers to gain a thorough understanding of what it is like to be an inspector. This discussion helps us understand the individuals who are responsible for protecting the environment on a daily basis.

Figuring out if environmental policy is working is more critical now than ever. Chapter 8 provides an overview of how environmental policy is evaluated and the complexities of its evaluation. Much of policy evaluation has to do with the quantification of various variables, which is understandably complex in this policy realm. We consider how this is done, with a significant portion of this chapter devoted to both understanding how cost-benefit analysis and risk assessment are conducted. Our chapter voice and case challenge the contemporary notions of cost-benefit analysis through an examination of environmental justice. Our introduction notes the important work of the Department of Energy's Shalanda Baker Our case study examines longitudinal research on commercial hazardous waste, defining for the reader, the intricate details of environmental justice in the US.

Chapter 9 explores the natural resource and energy policy nexus that often define environmental policy in the American West. This chapter begins with the story of Deb Haaland, the first Native American to serve as a Cabinet-level Secretary to the US Department of the Interior. This introductory story gets at the heart of the interconnectedness of natural resource and energy policy. The majority of public lands are managed by federal agencies (e.g., BLM, USFWS, USFS, NPS). Yet, within these lands are resources that could be used for energy development in the US The chapter concludes with the case of the Dakota Access Pipeline to the true complexities of the actors involved trying to influence public policy outcomes.

Discussions of environmental policy often focus on pollution, natural resources, and energy. The role of food production and consumption on these areas is significant, so Chapter 10 focuses on food policy. The chapter begins with a look at a group of West Virginia University students working to eliminate food deserts in Ohio. Then the chapter goes on to discuss food production and consumption in the US, along with the role of the government in providing dietary guidance to Americans. Nutrition labels on food products sold in the US are a piece of the government's role in protecting public health and ensuring food safety. The role of food in our society and the cultural trends around the topic are also investigated. The case study in this chapter explores the FDA's updated sodium requirements.

Finally, Chapter 11 looks at environmental policy, past, present, and future. The chapter offers three overarching characteristics of environmental policy today: (1) hyper-partisanship and polarization, (2) debate over government's role in environmental protection leading to paralysis at the national level, and (3) continued persistence of major environmental issues. This synthesis is not meant to persuade readers and students that progress on environmental issues is hopeless; rather, it is intended to contextualize the situation and demonstrate urgency so the future can see action.

CHAPTER WRAP-UP

US environmental policy does not come without obstacles. In 2022, the US mid-term elections, historically have record breaking shifts for the party not in power. However, for the first time in over 40 years, this did not occur. We suggest that Americans used their vote to confront a myriad of social and economic issues that pose challenges for our democracy. Accordingly, our approach here is to focus on *how* environmental policy is implemented and evaluated from the ground up as many traditional environmental policy texts ignore this critical dimension.

Therefore, we examine the processes of implementation and evaluation along with the often-neglected actors who are critical to these aspects of environmental policy (i.e., environmental inspectors and rule-writers). Such an examination is particularly important as congressional policy is implemented by those on the front-lines of public policy. Nevertheless, as the Lorax says, "It is not about what it is. It's about what it can become" (Seuss 1998).

Challenge Question for the Environmental Policy Classroom

Use the USGS water quality tracker https://www.usgs.gov/tools/tra cking-water-quality-nations-streams-and-rivers to make a list of concerns. In examining your list of concerns, which communities are most impacted? What are the demographics of these communities? Are these individuals involved in outcomes? Why or why not?

SUGGESTED RESOURCES

Readings and Websites

Andrews, Richard L. *Managing the Environment, Managing Ourselves: A History of American Environmental Policy.* New Haven, CT: Yale University Press, 2006.
Fifth Assessment Report. "Intergovernmental Panel on Climate Change." Accessed October 15, 2018 http://www.ipcc.ch/report/sr15/.
Seuss, Dr. *The Lorax.* Nashville, TN: Randall House Publishers, 1998.

Films or Videos

Before the Flood. 2016. Directed by Fisher Stevens. Appian Way, Dune Entertainment.
The Future of Energy: Lateral Power to the People. 2016. Directed by Brett Mazurek.
The 11th Hour. Directed by Leila Conners and Nadia Conners. 2007. Appian Way, Greenhour, and Tree Media Group. DVD.
The Lorax. 2012. Chris Renard and Kyle Balda. Los Angeles, CA: Universal Studio. DVD.

REFERENCES

Andrews, Richard L. *Managing the Environment, Managing Ourselves: A History of American Environmental Policy.* New Haven, CT: Yale University Press, 2006.
Boyle, Lisa Kass. "Earth and the Balance of Power What the Citizens United Ruling Means for the Environment." *Huffington Post*, February 6, 2010. http://www.huff-ingtonpost.com/.
Environmental News Service. "Celebrating 40 Years of Endangered Species Success." Accessed January 30, 2014. http://ens-newswire.com/2013/12/31/celebrating-40-years-of-endangered-species-act-success/.

Grandoni, Dino and Fears, Darryl. "Biden Administration Moves to Bring Back Endangered Species Protections Undone Under Trump". *Washington Post*, June 4, 2021. https://www.washingtonpost.com/climate-environment/2021/06/04/biden-endangered-species/?msclkid=f8b91fcfba7611ec8f6dc40010396b20.

Jacobson, Gary C. *Politics of Congressional Elections*. Upper Saddle, NJ: Pearson, 2012.

Klyza, Christopher McGrory and David Sousa. *American Environmental Policy: Beyond Gridlock*. 3rd edition. Cambridge: MIT Press, 2013.

Kraft, Michael E. *Environmental Policy and Politics*. 5th edition. New York: Longman, 2017.

Levitz, Jennifer, Cameron McWhirter, and Valerie Bauerlein. "West Virginia Begins to Lift Water Ban." *Wall Street Journal*, January 14, 2014. http://online.wsj.com/.

McLendon, Russell. "How Polluted Is US Drinking Water?" Accessed January 30, 2014. http://www.mnn.com/earth-matter/translating-uncle-sam/stories/how-polluted-is-us-drinking-water.

Nakashima, Ryan. "The Lorax: Green Commerical Tie-Ins For Dr. Suess Film." *Huffington Post*, February 8, 2012. http://www.huffingtonpost.com/.

Pautz, Michelle C. and Sara R. Rinfret. *The Lilliputians of Environmental Regulation: The Perspectives of State Regulators*. New York: Routledge, 2013.

Rabe, Barry. *Greenhouse Governance: Addressing Climate Change in America*. Washington, DC: The Brookings Institute, 2010.

Rinfret, Sara R. "Changing the Rules: Federal Environmental Rulemaking." Ph.D. Dissertation, Northern Arizona University, 2009.

Seuss, Dr. *The Lorax*. Nashville, TN: Randall House Publishers, 1998.

US EPA. "Drinking Water." Accessed January 20, 2014. http://www.epa.gov/epawaste/nonhaz/municipal/index.htm.

———. "Our Nation's Air: Trends Through 2020." Accessed April 11, 2022. https://gispub.epa.gov/air/trendsreport/2021/#home.

———. "Flint's Drinking Water Response." Accessed April 11, 2022. https://www.epa.gov/flint?msclkid=1a9e7448ba7611eca623896ef17d6b2b.

———. "National Overview: Facts and Figures on Materials, Waste, & Recycling." Accessed April 11, 2022. https://www.epa.gov/facts-and-figures-about-materials-waste-and-recycling/national-overview-facts-and-figures-materials?msclkid=7018d2fdb9c811ec95813939156b608f.

CHAPTER 2

The Development and Context of American Environmental Policy

Introductory Story: Galvanizing Environmental Actions through the Efforts of Rachel Carson and Greta Thunberg
The scale and scope of environmental issues can often seem overwhelming and the ability of an individual to affect them can seem remote. However, there are examples of individuals past and present who influence environmental movements, including Rachel Carson and Greta Thunberg.

Rachel Carson was a marine biologist who worked for the US Fish and Wildlife Service and is widely credited with galvanizing the modern environmental movement with the publication of her book *Silent Spring*. Her role in fundamentally altering the nation's pesticide industry seemed unlikely given her roots and her gender. Born in rural Pennsylvania, not too far from Pittsburgh, in 1907, Carson spent much of her early years exploring her family's farm. She loved to read and write stories about the natural environment. This led to her original intention to study English at the Pennsylvania College for Women (now known as Chatham University), but she changed her major to biology. She graduated in 1929 and then went on to Johns Hopkins University where she studied zoology as a part-time student while working in a lab to earn money for tuition. When she completed her master's degree in 1932, she had planned on continuing her education and earning a doctorate but returned home to help her family during the Great Depression. Carson went to work in a temporary

S. R. Rinfret and M. C. Pautz, *US Environmental Policy in Action*, https://doi.org/10.1007/978-3-031-17503-9_2

position for the US Bureau of Fisheries, writing scripts for a radio program to educate people about marine life. During this time, she also published her own essays on related topics. Over time, her position at the Bureau of Fisheries evolved to where she analyzed data on fisheries and wrote brochures for the public and she eventually came to supervise a small group of writers within the agency, which eventually became known as the US Fish and Wildlife Service.

In 1945, Carson wrote for the first time about the new, revolutionary pesticide, dichlorodiphenyltrichloroethane, better known as DDT. It would be almost two decades before she wrote a book about the subject. During the intervening years, Carson wrote a lot about the ocean and marine life, including the books *The Sea Around Us* and *The Edge of the Sea*. Her writing became prolific enough and spurred enough speaking engagements that Carson was able to resign from the USFWS to write full time. By the late 1950s, Carson was following developments around DDT and its widespread use in agriculture and began writing about it and its harm to the environment and public health. These efforts culminated in the publication in 1962 of *Silent Spring*. The thrust of her book was that pesticides can have negative effects on much more than their intended target through the food chain. She also accused the chemical industry of lying about the effects of its product.

As you might imagine, the book was highly criticized and ignited a firestorm upon publication. She was by no means the first to discuss the dangers of DDT—a pesticide that has been since banned in the US—but her book became a best seller and sold millions of copies. The scientific community reviewed her work and supported her research and analysis, but the chemical industry responded very negatively to the book (as might be expected). Ultimately, Congress was spurred into action. Her book was written in a manner that was accessible to scientists and the general public alike. It was serialized in *The New Yorker* and featured in the Book of the Month program. News media covered the book and the debate it sparked. Carson was already ill from breast cancer and its treatments, and she died in April 1964. Her efforts to convey complex scientific information to the general public are widely credited with leading to the ban of DDT and catapulting environmental concerns to the forefront of the nation's attention in the 1960s.

Greta Thunberg is a Swedish climate activist who is galvanizing people around the world, and especially young people, to take actions to stop the advance of climate change who may be following in Carson's footsteps. Thunberg first learned about climate change as a young student and by the age of 11, she became so distraught about it that she stopped eating and talking. She was eventually diagnosed with Asperger syndrome, obsessive-compulsive disorder, and selective mutism. After struggling for several years, she began her school strike campaign in 2018, when she was 15, after getting the idea from American students who refused to go back to school after a high school shooting in Parkland, Florida. As she continued her school strike, she began writing about climate change and chronicling her actions on social media. Additionally, she began regular protests outside the Swedish parliament.

By the end of 2018, Thunberg had inspired many others by her activism and she was speaking in numerous settings, including the plenary session of the 2018 UN Climate Change Conference. In 2019 to attend a UN conference, she sailed across the Atlantic Ocean in a racing yacht that was outfitted with solar panels and underwater turbines to demonstrate the ability to be carbon neutral. Her activism has brought awareness to climate change as she has garnered audiences with European parliaments, the U.S. House of Representatives, Pope Francis, Malala Yousafzai, among others. The "Greta Effect" has encouraged people—especially school-aged peers— to learn more about climate change and participate in climate activism. *Time* magazine named her Person of the Year in 2019. She continues her activism today as a young adult.

Both Carson and Thunberg have affected how Americans, and people around the world, thought about their relationships to the environment and have compelled attention to key environmental policy issues of their times.

To understand the challenges of environmental policy today, and to place in context the role of Rachel Carson, Greta Thunberg, and many others, we have to start at the beginning. By reviewing the development of environmental policy in the US, we understand better the context of environmental policymaking today. More specifically, this chapter explores the history of environmental policy in the US, examines in greater detail the American public's evolving opinion on environmental issues, and considers how society deals with complex scientific and technical issues. Without this understanding, it would be difficult to understand our present challenges in environmental policy.

As we examine the historical context of environmental policy in this chapter, several important themes emerge. First, notice that the US government, albeit at different levels (e.g., federal, state, and local), has been involved in environmental policy for a long time. Our look at environmental policy's history will begin with Colonial America, despite the common misconception that the US only waded into environmental policy in the 1960s. Second, we focus on how the government's role in environmental matters has ebbed and flowed over time due to the ever-changing mood of the American public and political leadership and this is likely to continue in this policy area. Third, since the 1990s, the traditional means of making environmental policy—notably, congressional action—have largely stalled for reasons we will discuss. But this does not mean that environmental policy action is not happening as there are alternative pathways. These less obvious means of policymaking are growing in their use. The major themes of the development of environmental policy will define environmental policy into the future. Accordingly, we begin by investigating the first efforts of governmental action regarding the environment before turning to public opinion and public discourse on science.

HISTORICAL EVOLUTION OF US ENVIRONMENTAL POLICY

Most people think that the earliest US government involvement in environmental matters came during the 1960s, alongside the other major social movements of the era. This is not the case. Although it was not called environmental policy or thought of in such a manner, colonial Americans passed important local ordinances that grappled with the relationship between people and the environment. In this section, we take a chronological approach to investigating the history of environmental policy and draw some conclusions about each time period.

Colonial America

Even before the US formally existed as a country, its colonial residents demonstrated some concern over the environment and awareness of the need for its health. As early as 1626, colonists in Plymouth (in Massachusetts Bay Colony) passed ordinances limiting the harvesting and sale of timber (Andrews 2020; Nash 1990; Vaughn 2007). This is not to say that these early settlers were environmentalists as we might think of today, because they did try to control nature and fundamentally alter it; however, there is some indication that these early Americans thought overharvesting needed to be curbed along with maintaining natural spaces. In 1681, William Penn set aside lands in Pennsylvania to be kept natural, and Massachusetts followed suit in 1691 (Vaughn 2007). Moreover, other colonies took various steps to preserve some of their own resources. For example, there were hunting bans in Massachusetts and measures to protect coastal waterfowl in New York. Similarly, Connecticut passed laws to protect its game animals. It is also worth noting that many of the nation's founders, including George Washington and Thomas Jefferson, were concerned with the health of the environment on their own estates, as evidenced by their frequent mentions of these matters in correspondence and journals. To summarize, we see some indication that early Americans were concerned with the environment, and that may have led to some limited and local government efforts to address environmental issues about the use of natural resources.

Nineteenth Century

As the eighteenth century gave way to the nineteenth, the US began to establish itself and to grow both in terms of population and territory. The acquisition of new territories spawned quests to explore these newly incorporated lands and the explorers' tales of their adventures captivated Americans. Lewis and Clark began their famous expedition westward in 1804, and trips to explore and settle lands continued throughout the century.

Furthermore, changing landscapes dominated the young country in different ways, particularly toward the end of the century. The late 1800s saw dramatic population shifts as industrialization enticed many Americans to leave rural, agrarian lifestyles for urban centers where jobs in factories offered a way to move up in society. With large numbers of people living in urban areas, concerns arose that anyone might expect when lots of people live near one another in a confined space—garbage, waste, and other sanitation issues. Cities across the country, including Philadelphia, New York, Boston, Chicago, and St. Louis, saw significant rises in their populations and had to confront new challenges. Not only were there concerns about growing numbers of people living together in urban areas, but the reasons many people moved to cities—factory jobs—brought even more environmental challenges. These factories and tanneries contributed to concerns over environmental impacts of these operations (Andrews 2020).

The end of the nineteenth century brought a variety of reform movements, often encapsulated in the broader moniker of the Progressive Era.

Demands for improved working conditions, increased sanitation, prohibition of alcohol, and other social reforms abounded. It was also during this time that the formal, academic study of public administration—the doing of government—emerged, as government was increasingly called upon to address societal ills.

With this foundation, we better understand how concerns about the environment came about in the 1800s because they were often couched within broader movements focused on public health conditions and the increasing desire for outdoor recreation. As germ theory[1] emerged along with new understandings of the need for sanitation, worry over the emissions from factories and their dumping of wastes also surfaced. In addition, as people's lifestyles evolved when they left rural areas for urban ones, there was increasing desire for recreation in open spaces. In particular, hunting and other activities in the natural environment were fashionable, particularly for the well-to-do in society. Magazines such as *The American Sportsmen* and *Forest & Stream* expressed concern over the quality and quantity of game and fish stocks for sportsmen. These instrumental motivations for environmental health parallel other motivations.

Intrinsic reasons also explain the growing focus on environmental issues. The term ecology was first coined in the late 1800s. Published in 1854, Henry David Thoreau's *Walden* details his two years living in a small cabin on Walden Pond in Massachusetts. In his writing, Thoreau describes his observations about nature and the growing disconnect between humans and nature. His book was initially slow to find a wide readership, but over time it did, contributing to the growing focus on nature. George Perkins Marsh wrote *Man and Nature* in 1864, which called for planting measures to thwart erosion and for the protection of songbirds in response to the impact of human activity on the natural environment. Other ways of noting human connection with the environment are exemplified in the First Arbor Day in 1872 and the creation of the Sierra Club by John Muir in 1892.

The federal government took a number of actions to signal that environmental issues—albeit not necessarily characterized as such—were an area of emphasis during this period. Congress passed the Homestead Act in 1862 that offered people 160 acres of public lands (mostly in

---

[1] Germ theory is the idea that diseases are caused by various microorganisms and sanitary conditions can help stem their ill effects.

the west) if they lived on it and worked the land. More than 250 million acres of public lands were converted to private ownership as a result of this law (Kraft 2011, 91). In 1871, the US Fish Commission[2] was created, and it was the first federal agency responsible for the conservation of a specific natural resource (Vaughn 2007, 12). Although George Catlin first proposed the idea of a national park in the 1830s, it was not until the 1870s that the first national parks were created. Two million acres spanning across three states near the upper Yellowstone River were set aside to form Yellowstone National Park in 1872. Sequoia, Kings Canyon, and Yosemite National Parks were created shortly thereafter. Rounding out some of these highlights was the creation of large subsidy programs to ranchers, farmers, and mining companies to encourage resource development.

By the close of the nineteenth century, it would be difficult to define as a movement any of the actions described earlier surrounding the natural environment and its health, but the beginnings of interest in environmental and resource issues are evident. These starts, however, gave way to a more concerted movement in the early 1900s.

Early Twentieth Century: 1900–1930s

The turn of the twentieth century brought with it the definitive beginnings of an environmental movement in the US. The origins of this movement center on the debate between conservationists and preservationists, which is still evident in public discourse today. Accordingly, we begin with an overview of this debate and then continue through the entire century and the birth of the modern environmental movement.

The first few decades of the twentieth century can be encapsulated by the conservation and preservation movements and the tension between the two. Conservationists, led by Gifford Pinchot (among others), who would go on to lead the US Forest Service, embraced the idea that natural resources could be used in a sustainable way that would allow for the growth and development of society. Advocates of conservation emphasized the efficient use of resources for development and took an instrumental view of nature. Such a view indicates that nature is valued because one sees value for human use of it. In other words, one might

---

[2] This commission later became the US Fish & Wildlife Service.

value the well-being of nature because she wants to ensure plenty of healthy fish in the nearby pond for fishing.

In contrast, preservationists sought to preserve wilderness and natural resources from any development other than for recreation and education. An oft-cited preservationist is John Muir who founded the Sierra Club—the first major environmental organization—in 1892. The preservationists believed that the environment had value in its own right—intrinsic value. In other words, the fish in the pond have value because they are fish—unrelated to a person's interest or use of those fish. However, generally speaking, the conservationists dominated government action regarding the environment. President Theodore Roosevelt was a champion of the conservation movement; his passion for the natural environment began as a young man who loved studying nature, and this love was manifested in his desire to better understand it by perfecting his hobby of taxidermy. He was an avid sportsman and spent a good deal of time out West camping, hunting, and exploring.

The debates between conservationists and preservationists are contextualized in the broader social and economic context of the early twentieth century. As noted earlier, in the late 1800s, public health and sanitation concerns emerged, and the first local government laws were passed dealing with pollution, which was increasingly recognized as a public health issue. Chicago and Cincinnati were the first cities to approve air pollution laws and, by 1920, more than three dozen cities had similar laws (Kraft 2011, 92). However, it was not until 1952 that the first state—Oregon—passed state air pollution laws (Kraft 2011, 92; Portney 2000; Ringquist 1993). In addition, the dust bowls of the 1930s brought attention to drought and erosion. These severe dust storms caused major damage to America's prairie and farmlands, particularly in the erosion of topsoil. Finally, a number of environmental organizations continued to emerge, including the National Audubon Society in 1905, the National Parks Association in 1919, the Izaak Walton League in 1922, the Wilderness Society in 1935, and the National Wildlife Federation in 1936 (see Chapter 5 for more information on environmental organizations).

As we already indicated, most of the federal government's actions during these decades were focused on land management and the conservation of the nation's natural resources. In 1903, President Theodore Roosevelt created a Public Lands Commission to help the development of land and, then, in 1905, Roosevelt tapped Gifford Pinchot to run the newly created Forest Service. A few years later, the White House convened a Conference on Resource Management organized by Pinchot that attracted more than 1,000 leaders for a few days in May 1908 (Vaughn 2007, 14). This meeting concluded with the recommendation that the president create a National Conservation Commission to catalog the nation's natural resources, which was done. By the following year, 41 states had created similar state-level agencies. Moreover, this conference discussed forest, soil, and water management issues. In 1916, the National Park Service was created. Subsequent presidents continued to oversee the creation of new national forests and other laws to protect particular species.

As the country grappled with the Great Depression, President Franklin D. Roosevelt was largely concerned with economics and social policy; however, components of the New Deal focused on natural resource issues. In particular, the Tennessee Valley Authority, created in 1933, sought to provide low-cost energy to Americans. Other programs included the Soil Conservation Service and the Civilian Conservation Corps, which addressed a variety of environmental concerns and put Americans to work during the height of the Depression.

Furthermore, there were a number of congressional actions during the 1930s that are notable. In 1934, the Taylor Grazing Act was passed to address overgrazing on America's grasslands and, 2 years later, the Flood Control Act delegated to the Army Corps of Engineers the responsibility for developing and implementing policies to protect watersheds and improve flood control. Federal government actions along these lines were firmly in the purview of government action by the outbreak of World War II (Vaughn 2007, 15).

Mid-twentieth Century: 1940s and 1950s

The end of World War II saw great changes in American society. Success on the war front and emergence from dire economic circumstances from the Great Depression left the American population much more hopeful, optimistic, and proud. Although the Harry Truman and Dwight D. Eisenhower administrations were far more concerned with national security threats and the spread of communism, environmental issues surfaced on the national scene. Eisenhower maintained, however, that pollution issues were a state and local government matter rather than a federal issue (Sussman et al. 2002, 4). With peace and economic growth, Americans began to focus on leisure, recreation, and quality-of-life concerns. Americans flocked to the national parks in pursuit of recreation and leisure. More than 30 million people toured national parks in 1950, compelling the government to grow the parks system (Vaughn 2007, 15).

Although the federal government's attentions were largely focused elsewhere, there are two notable federal environmental laws passed during this time period: the Federal Water Pollution Control Act of 1948 and the Air Pollution Control Act of 1955. Even though neither law was much of a success, these laws signal the first attempts of the federal government to enact legislation aimed at addressing the growing pollution problem in the US. The Federal Water Pollution Control Act tried to prevent and mitigate water pollution, mostly through delegation of responsibilities to the states, as it was widely presumed that states were responsible for water quality. The law did little to stem pollution, as it did not require any direct reductions in pollution to the nation's waterways. Congress largely gutted and rewrote the act in the early 1970s because it was so ineffective, and the new act became the modern Clean Water Act (CWA). In addition to concerns over the quality of water, air quality was also a concern by the mid-1950s. Smog and soot were increasingly problematic in major metropolitan areas, including Los Angeles. Again, Congress responded by passing the 1955 Air Pollution Control Act, which was the first federal legislation to address air pollution. The act stipulated that air pollution was a threat to public health, but it did little to curb air pollution, as the law mostly called for government research into the effects of air pollution and methods of reducing it.

Examining these two decades reveals that the federal government was tepidly entering into the arena of environmental concerns, although its emphases clearly lay with national security threats. What is important to note about the decades preceding the birth of the modern environmental movement is the emergence of a citizenry increasingly able to turn its attention to quality-of-life issues—such as pollution—as the dire economic circumstances of the 1930s and World War II gave way to economic growth and prosperity in the 1950s.

The Birth of the Modern Environmental Movement

The 1960s in America are synonymous with a tumultuous period of significant social change. The increasingly affluent population made significant educational advancements and emphasized quality of life concerns while contending with conflict abroad. The Civil Rights Movement and the Women's Movement, along with many other movements, challenged traditional societal norms. Moreover, conflict in Southeast Asia escalated, and the US soon saw itself embroiled in a war in Vietnam. These events and movements compelled distrust in the establishment, particularly governmental organizations and corporations, and this distrust grew and permeated many aspects of life.

Concerns about the environment mounted as well. In particular, rapidly advancing scientific and technical knowledge led to worries over the effects of seemingly benign, everyday things like pesticides. As discussed in the chapter's opening story, Rachel Carson, a biologist wrote the book *Silent Spring* (published in 1962), which was intended for the lay audience and detailed the dangerous effects of pesticides, dichlorodiphenyltrichloroethane (DDT) in particular, on wildlife and led to a considerable public panic. This book is widely credited with galvanizing the modern environmental movement, as it topped bestseller lists and led to the ban of DDT. Other notable books of this decade underscored the need to re-conceptualize the relationship between society and nature, including Paul Ehrlich's *The Population Bomb*.

Before one thinks that it was only books that changed the public discourse on environmental concerns, rest assured that numerous focusing events spurred the public as well. For example, the Cuyahoga River in Cleveland, Ohio was at one time so polluted that sections of it could not sustain fish life. In addition, there were numerous instances in the 1950s and 1960s when the river literally caught on fire from all the toxic sludge. A fire was so bad in 1969 that the Cuyahoga River was featured in *Time* magazine. Two major oil spills off the coast of Santa Barbara, California, in early 1969—just days into Richard Nixon's administration—captured the attention of the media. These events, featured prominently in the news, helped solidify the public's demand for governmental action.

Although these particular events occurred in the latter part of the decade, the federal government increasingly took action over the course of the entire decade. In 1963, the first Clean Air Act (CAA) was passed, and subsequently amended in 1967; it authorized public hearings on air pollution issues. The following year (1964) saw the passage of the Wilderness Act that set aside tracts of public lands and barred development so as to preserve some lands in their natural condition. Furthermore, in 1964, the Land and Wildlife Conservation Fund Act was enacted, which coordinated local, state, and federal government efforts to acquire and develop lands. Other pieces of federal legislation include the Water Quality Act passed in 1965, the Endangered Species Preservation Act in 1966, and the Wild and Scenic Rivers Act and National Trails Act, both in 1968.

Arguably, the most significant piece of federal legislation came in 1969 with the passage of the National Environmental Policy Act (NEPA). The purpose of NEPA is "to declare a national policy which will encourage productive and enjoyable harmony between man and his environment; to promote efforts which will prevent or eliminate damage to the environment and biosphere and stimulate the health and welfare of man; to enrich the understanding of the ecological systems and natural resources important to the nation; and to establish a Council on Environmental Quality" (NEPA 42 USC § 4321). This statute is a key environmental law that (1) establishes national environmental policy goals, (2) requires the federal government to analyze the environmental impacts of proposed projects and devise ways to mitigate negative environmental impacts, and (3) creates the Council on Environmental Quality within the White House. NEPA is largely a procedural environmental law that requires any federal executive agency to review how proposed agency action may impact the environment. Therefore, if an agency is considering a new program or project, such as building a highway, the agency has to study the environmental impacts it might cause and conduct an environmental assessment (EA) or, if the impacts are more significant, produce an environmental impact statement (EIS). Without delving into a lot of detail about these procedures here, suffice it to say that the research and investigation that coincides with the preparation of such statements can significantly alter an agency's course of action so as to lessen its environmental impact.

The 1960s saw the emergence of the full-fledged modern environmental movement, born of the broader social unrest of the time period, numerous focusing events, and a ramping up of governmental action as it related to the environment. These first steps toward a comprehensive national environmental policy laid the groundwork for the 1970s—arguably, the most productive decade ever of environmental policymaking (and Table 2.1 notes major environmental laws).

Table 2.1 Major environmental laws

Year	Law
1969	– National Environmental Policy Act
1970	– Clean Air Act Amendments
1972	– Federal Water Pollution Control Act Amendments (better known as the Clean Water Act)
	– Federal Insecticide, Fungicide, and Rodenticide Act
	– Marine Mammal Protection Act
1973	– Endangered Species Act
1974	– Safe Drinking Water Act
1976	– Resource Conservation and Recovery Act
	– Toxic Substances Control Act
	– National Forest Management Act
	– Federal Land Policy and Management Act
1977	– Clean Air Act Amendments
	– Surface Mining and Reclamation Act
1980	– Comprehensive Emergency Response, Compensation, and Liability Act (better known as Superfund)
1986	– Emergency Planning and Community Right to Know Act
	– Superfund Amendments and Reauthorization Act
1990	– Clean Air Act Amendments
	– Oil Pollution Act
	– Pollution Prevention Act
1992	– Energy Policy Act
1996	– Safe Drinking Water Act Amendments
2003	– Healthy Forests Restoration Act
2005	– Energy Policy Act
2007	– Energy Independence and Security Act
2009	– American Recovery and Reinvestment Act
	– Omnibus Public Lands Management Act
2021	– Infrastructure Investment and Jobs Act
2022	– Inflation Reduction Act

The 1970s: The Development of Modern Environmental Regulation

The beginning of the 1970s continued the momentum of the previous decade in terms of environmental protection. Most of the major environmental laws that persist today, the federal environmental agencies, and mainstream environmental interest groups came about during this decade. Moreover—and of particular interest contemporarily—most of the governmental action regarding the environment enjoyed broad, bipartisan support from politicians and citizens alike.

Two pivotal events in 1970 demonstrated the nation's determination to protect the environment. The first Earth Day was celebrated on April 22, 1970, by millions of Americans and it continues to be celebrated annually. Rosenbaum (2011) describes the first event as the "Big Bang of US environmental politics" (7). Senator Gaylord Nelson (D-Wisconsin) founded Earth Day by calling for an environmental teach-in. Earth Day events were held across the nation. At the end of the same year, the US Environmental Protection Agency (EPA) was created by President Richard Nixon via executive order. Nixon recognized the need for a single agency to coordinate and oversee a coherent national environmental policy and he appointed William Ruckelshaus as the agency's first administrator. President Nixon was not a passionate environmentalist, but he realized the importance of responding to the public's demand for environmental action and the building of momentum in Congress. These two events in the same year set the trend for the decade and signaled the national emphasis on environmental protection.

Several pivotal focusing events kept the nation's attention on the health of the environment. The 1973 Arab oil embargo brought energy policy center-stage as the Organization of Petroleum Exporting Countries (OPEC) voted to cut oil production by five percent and Saudi Arabia halted oil exports to the US because of US support of Israel, thus leading to gasoline shortages in the US. Toward the end of the decade, a neighborhood in Niagara Falls, New York became the go-to example of what happens when hazardous chemicals are buried beneath ground and, then, an elementary school is built atop the contaminated ground. This environmental disaster, known as Love Canal, led to the passage of legislation designed to clean up environmental hazards. In 1979, the Three Mile Island Nuclear Generating Station near Middletown, Pennsylvania experienced a partial nuclear meltdown, heightening concerns about the safety and reliability of nuclear power. With these events and growing government action, numerous environmental organizations got their start in the 1970s, including the League of Conservation Voters, the Natural Resources Defense Council, Save the Bay, Greenpeace, and Public Citizen.

With the significant focus on the environment, the federal government embarked on its most productive decade of environmental policymaking ever, with many of the laws falling under the purview of the newly created US EPA. In 1970, the Air Pollution Control law, passed 15 years earlier, was dramatically overhauled and became the Clean Air Act (CAA) that is still the guiding federal law on air quality today. The CAA mandated, for the first time, federal air pollution standards and put in place a regulatory structure to ensure that the laws were enforced. Under this law, both mobile (e.g., vehicle) and stationary (e.g., industrial) sources of air pollution would be subjected to emissions limits. In addition, four major regulatory programs were started under the CAA: the National Ambient Air Quality Standards (NAAQS), State Implementation Plans (SIPs), New Source Performance Standards (NSPS), and the National Emissions Standards for Hazardous Air Pollutants (NESHAPs).

Just two years later, a similar overhaul of the 1948 Federal Water Pollution Control law was passed and became the modern Clean Water Act (CWA) in 1972. Much like the dramatic revisions that came with the 1970 CAA, the 1972 CWA completely restructured the federal government's approach to ensuring water quality. Waste could no longer be discharged from a point source (e.g., pipes into bodies of water) without a permit to ensure certain emissions limits were followed. The CWA set national water quality goals and established the National Pollution Discharge Elimination System (NPDES). In addition, a grant program was established under this law to fund the building of wastewater treatment plants around the nation. Similar to the CAA, the CWA included enforcement provisions that would ensure the limits would be followed, unlike the environmental legislation from prior decades. It is worth noting that President Nixon vetoed the CWA, citing economic and inflation concerns, but the Congress easily overrode the presidential veto.

Additional laws enacted during this decade merit mention. In 1972, the Coastal Zone Management Act was passed that gave grants to states to establish coastal zone management plans. The Marine Mammal Protection Act and the Federal Environmental Pesticides Control Act were also passed in the same year. In 1973, the Endangered Species Act was passed that mandated the government list certain species as threatened or endangered in an effort to protect species from extinction. The passage of the Safe Drinking Water Act that provided the first federal standards protecting the quality of the nation's drinking water came in 1974. President Gerald Ford begrudgingly signed this law although it enjoyed broad support in Congress.

In 1976, Congress passed the National Forest Management Act, the Federal Land Policy Management Act (FLPMA), the Toxic Substances Control Act (TSCA), and the Resource Conservation and Recovery Act (RCRA). The last two laws require a little elaboration. The TSCA requires chemical substances to be tested to ascertain their environmental impacts before being sold on the open market, and the Act permits the EPA to regulate or ban any substances that pose "an unbearable risk of injury to health or to the environment." The RCRA continues to be the key law governing hazardous wastes in this country; RCRA requires national standards for the treatment, storage, and disposal of hazardous waste and takes a "cradle-to-grave" approach regarding such hazards.

The last few years of the decade saw the election of the first avowedly environmental president, Jimmy Carter. Unlike his predecessors, President Carter portrayed himself as an environmentalist and expectations for his presidency were high. During his time in the White House, the Surface Mining Control and Reclamation Act was passed in 1977 that established the first federal standards for strip mining operations and required restoration of lands that were mined. Amendments to both the CAA and CWA were passed and, in the last days of his administration, the Comprehensive Environmental Response, Compensation, and Liability Act (CERCLA) was passed. In October 1977, the Department of Energy was created to bring together the disparate energy programs in various governmental agencies.

By the end of the 1970s, the US had an impressive statutory and regulatory framework from which to protect the nation's environment. For the first time, federal agencies were devising environmental standards that, if not met, would have real consequences for those that violated them. Concerns over the environment were, clearly, here to stay and the nation seemed committed to doing what it could to improve and protect the health of the environment. Nonetheless, with more than 10 years of experience trying to ensure environmental protection, Americans began to see the challenges with their regulatory structure and have experience with the costs associated with such protection.

The 1980s: Changing Course with Environmental Protection

The productivity of the 1970s provided the US ample opportunity to gain significant experience implementing an array of environmental protection measures. This familiarity led to growing debates over the best approach to environmental policy in the nation in the 1980s that have continued developing ever since. In particular, key themes include the disintegration of the bipartisan collaboration that produced the major statutes just a handful of years prior, intensification of arguments about costs and economic considerations associated with environmental protection, and debate over the role of government in this policy arena. Although much of the foundation of environmental policy remained intact throughout the 1980s, significant efforts were made to undo policies, and approaches were reassessed during this decade.

For the first time, the environmental movement was put on the defensive with the election of Ronald Reagan as president in 1980, as his administration signaled a major shift in the nation's approach to the environment. Whether one concludes that this was the first administration hostile to the environment or if President Reagan was emphasizing economic concerns before environmental ones or somewhere in between, his administration fundamentally altered environmental policy and debate about it. Several key changes defined his approach, and we will take each in turn.

The Reagan administration emphasized that government should be limited and devolved to the most local level possible and kept closest to the people. This meant that programs were divested from federal government control to the states for administration and in some cases devolved even further to local control. This aligns with a traditional conservative point of view on the role of government. In terms of environmental policy, Reagan determined that, with divestiture to the states, the size and scope of the federal bureaucracy could be cut, particularly the US EPA. During his administration, the EPA's budget was initially slashed 11% and further reductions were advocated (Layzer 2012, 104). Other environment and natural resources agencies were cut too, including the Fish and Wildlife Service, which saw a 28% cut between 1981 and 1983 (Layzer 2012, 105). These budget cuts coincided with significant personnel cuts in agencies. The amount of money the federal government authorized for environment and natural resource programs fell from $17.9 billion in 1980 to between $12 and $15 billion for most of the 1980s (in constant, 1994 dollars) (Layzer 2012, 131). As these cuts persisted, Congress—spurred, in some measure, by outrage among the American public—scaled back some of the proposed cuts.

Second, and related to pushing governmental control to local levels, the Reagan administration embraced a broad view that government's role in society should be much smaller and more limited. More specifically, government regulation should be kept at a minimum and this policy tool should only be employed when absolutely necessary. This foundational view on government was coupled with a belief that economic growth was stifled, rather than enhanced, by government involvement in the market. Therefore, Reagan took various steps to ensure that any government regulation and its effects were minimized. Perhaps the best example of Reagan's policies in action is Executive Order 12,291 that required federal agencies to conduct a regulatory impact analysis on any new regulation and submit it to the Office of Information and Regulatory Affairs for review. This order was designed to ensure that the benefits to society exceeded the costs of any regulatory action taken (Shabecoff 1981). The changes made to the adoption of government regulations formalized the White House's role in the process and allowed it to influence regulatory efforts. This Executive Order remained in effect during the administration of both Reagan and his successor, George H. W. Bush. Subsequent administrations have modified Reagan's executive order, but largely left it in effect.

The efforts to curb the federal government's role in environmental protection were met with resistance, particularly into Reagan's second term in the White House. Americans and environmental groups mobilized to stymie the administration's efforts to curb and repeal environmental protections. Reagan's first EPA administrator, Anne Gorsuch Burford (mother of Supreme Court Justice Neil Gorsuch), who was a champion of Reagan's approach to government, regulation, and its role in the environment, was ultimately forced out of her position. As a result, William Ruckleshaus returned to the helm of the EPA as her successor. James G. Watt was Reagan's selection to head the Department of Interior; he was a controversial figure because he was branded as hostile to environmental protection as he advocated the use of federal lands for timber harvesting, expanded grazing, and various other commercial interests. In addition, several significant events during the 1980s reminded Americans of the destruction being done to the environment. By the mid-1980s, depletion of the Earth's protective ozone layer was front-page news and it galvanized international action to curb the effects of ozone-depleting materials such as chlorofluorocarbons (CFCs). Moreover, in 1984, a gas leak at the Union Carbide plant in Bhopal, India, exposed more than half a million people to methyl isocyanate gas and other chemicals. In 1986, a nuclear power plant in Chernobyl, in present-day Ukraine, suffered a catastrophic nuclear meltdown.

During Reagan's two terms in the White House, every major environmental statute that came up for renewal was, indeed, reauthorized, including the Hazardous and Solid Waste Amendments in 1985, Superfund Amendments in 1986, the Federal Insecticide, Fungicide, and Rodenticide Act Amendments in 1988, along with amendments to the CWA. Additionally, the Emergency Planning and Community Right to Know Act (EPCRA) was passed in 1986 (part of the Superfund reauthorization) that requires local governments and communities be provided information about chemical hazards in the area so the community can plan for emergency situations.

By the end of the 1980s, environmental issues no longer enjoyed the broad bipartisan support that had defined them in past years, as the nation had experienced environmental regulation for several decades, and conflicting perspectives on the role of government in regulation, the economy, and the environment had solidified. Reagan had shaped the foundation of the Republican Party's position on the environment as skeptical and resistant to governmental efforts because of concerns over economic implications and overreach of the government. However, it should be noted that although there were many environmental issues that were not addressed during this time period (e.g. climate change, acid rain, toxic pollution) and the federal government's approach to environmental issues shifted, the government still maintained a clear role in environmental protection and the worst fears expressed with Reagan's election were not realized (Shabecoff 1989). These outcomes were in part the result of the concern of Americans and efforts of environmental groups, which saw their membership rosters swell to record levels. Congress was left trying to strike a balance between governmental protection of the environment without negative effects on the economy. This decade fundamentally changed the nation's approach to the environment as cost concerns gained substantial footing against environmental concerns.

The 1990s: Stagnation

The last decade of the twentieth century saw continued evolution in how the federal government responded to environmental issues. Reagan's vice president, George H. W. Bush, campaigned promising to be an environmental president and, after his one term in office, hopes were high for Bill Clinton's administration, as longtime environmentalist Al Gore was his vice president. Despite hopes and expectations, the 1990s increasingly saw environmental issues take a backseat to other more prominent domestic

and international concerns, as environmental issues was, indeed, reauthorized despite punctuations from a few major events. Consider this decade
in two parts defined by the Bush and Clinton presidencies.

By the early 1990s, our understanding of environmental issues had
grown and developed significantly. In particular, advances in science and
technology helped us understand the global and interconnected dimensions of these issues and, in 1989, the spill of the Exxon Valdez in Prince
William Sound, Alaska, provided a poignant reminder. On March 24,
1989, the Exxon Valdez oil tanker ran aground off the coast of Alaska due
to human error and negligence, spilling approximately 11 million gallons
of oil into the pristine ecosystem—the worst environmental disaster in
the US until the explosion on the Deepwater Horizon drilling platform
in the Gulf of Mexico in 2010. Containment and cleanup of the Exxon
Valdez spill was hindered by the difficulty in accessing the site. Hundreds
of thousands of animals died, and the long-term effects to the environment are still being studied today. This incident led directly to the passage
of the Oil Pollution Act of 1990. Other significant events of this decade
included the US' involvement in the first Gulf War, when Iraqi forces
invaded neighboring Kuwait. The petroleum industry of this region was
significantly impacted by the war, and massive oil-field fires were frequent
and devastating.

During George H. W. Bush's campaign for the presidency in 1988,
he declared that he would be an "environmental president" but, ultimately, he never truly fulfilled that promise. In large part, his four years
in the White House were marred by other events and concerns, including
the aforementioned Gulf War. However, "his administration ended the
pernicious impasse of the Reagan years with important, if episodic, new
policy initiatives" (Rosenbaum 2011, 11). President George H. W. Bush
favored market solutions to environmental issues, just as his predecessor
did; however, he did appoint more environmentally friendly officials to
head major environmental efforts, including William Reilly to run the
EPA. Nonetheless, federal budgets did not align with Bush's campaign
promise to be an environmental president. There were some increases to
some environmental dimensions of the federal budget, but those increases
did not match the statutory mandates for those agencies (Layzer 2012,
184).

There were some notable policy efforts, however. The 1990s saw major
changes and improvements to air pollution with the passage of the CAA

Amendments, including the acid rain allowance trading program. President Bush's leadership was essential to the enactment of the legislation that called for stricter motor vehicle emissions standards and established a market trading program, among others. As mentioned previously, the Oil Pollution Act was passed in 1992 as was the Energy Policy Act, which created a federal energy plan designed to reduce dependence on foreign oil, encourage energy efficiency, and promote conservation. Efforts at preventing pollution also gained traction with the passage of the Pollution Prevention Act.

Internationally, President Bush's leadership on environmental issues was tepid at best. In 1992, there was an Earth Summit in Rio de Janeiro coinciding with the twentieth anniversary of the Stockholm Declaration, which was the first United Nations declaration on the global environment that led to the creation of the United Nations Environment Programme. Bush faced criticism for his plans not to attend the Earth Summit, despite promises for the US to lead globally on environmental issues. Only after pressure did Bush relent and lead the US delegation. The US was a signatory to Agenda 21—a non-binding statement of principles—but it refused to sign the Convention on Biological Diversity.

By 1992, the presidential campaign was in full swing and Bill Clinton ousted Bush after only one term in office. Although the environment did not feature prominently in the campaign, environmentalists were optimistic about this new administration because Al Gore, author of *Earth in Balance*, was the incoming vice president; Gore had previously established himself in the Senate as a champion of environmental issues. This optimism did not last long as the 1994 midterm elections brought Republican control to the Congress and the Republicans signaled their inclinations to oppose additional environmental regulations. Republicans focused their attention on lessening regulatory burdens, reducing paperwork requirements, and incorporating cost into decisionmaking. However, interest in the environment quickly waned as other domestic priorities—particularly healthcare, crime, drugs, and urban infrastructure—dominated the policy agenda. The Clinton administration mobilized to stymie efforts at rolling back environmental laws and slashing budgets, including the use of the veto power. Clinton's re-election in 1996 signaled that his administration's priorities were here to stay, but scandal quickly overshadowed his remaining years in the White House.

Most governmental efforts at environmental protection never gained sufficient traction. Early in Clinton's first term, sweeping changes were proposed to public land policies, including the raising of grazing fees, but those proposals were immediately attacked. By the midterm elections in 1994, two new national parks in California, Death Valley National Park and Joshua Tree National Park, had been created. In 1996, the Food Quality Protection Act was passed that involved the EPA in determining health risks in food and mandating the agency consider all of the ways in which consumers were exposed to chemicals, as well as determine a reasonable risk health standard. The Safe Water Drinking Act was reauthorized and the Sustainable Fisheries Act (also known as the Magnuson-Stevens Act) became law.

Besides legislative action, the Clinton administration did use executive power to focus attention on some facets of environmental concerns. In particular, Clinton's 1994 Executive Order 12,898 was the first federal government action dealing with environmental justice concerns (see Chapter 8 for more about environmental justice). Another notable executive order was 12,866, which Clinton used to replace Reagan's executive order mandating White House Office of Management and Budget review of agency rules. Clinton modified that requirement to mandate review of "significant regulatory actions."

In terms of agency action, Clinton's appointments to federal agencies generally pleased environmentalists. Bruce Babbitt became Secretary of the Interior and endeavored to shift the agency's focus to water conservation and away from dam building. Clinton tried to elevate the EPA to a cabinet-level agency, but that effort was defeated in Congress (Layzer 2012, 199). Carol Browner was Clinton's pick to head the EPA and under her leadership, the EPA promulgated new particulate matter and ozone standards. He pursued increases to the budgets of the EPA, Interior, and other environmental agencies.

In addition to some modest accomplishments at the domestic level, Clinton tried to renew the US' involvement internationally on environmental issues. In 1993, the US signed the Biodiversity Convention, but its ratification stalled in the Senate. Also, the US participated, under Vice President Gore's leadership, in the negotiations and drafting of the 1997 Kyoto Protocol on Climate Change. Although the US did sign the convention, ratification by the Senate was not pursued, as Senate leaders made it clear that it would not succeed.

In the final days of Clinton's tenure, significant executive actions were taken in an attempt to make last-minute efforts to protect the environment. Clinton used his powers under the 1906 Antiquities Act to designate national monuments, but the incoming administration put much of those efforts on hold.

The 1990s saw some renewed focus on environmental concerns; however, these concerns were often overshadowed by other priorities— both domestic and international—and by the trials and tribulations of the American political environment. Both Presidents Bush and Clinton spoke of being environmentally minded, but both presidents failed to meet expectations of their respective elections. Bush only served one term, thereby limiting the timeframe in which to accomplish significant environmental actions. He did help orchestrate major amendments to the CAA that were widely welcomed, but war in the Persian Gulf and the limits of a single term kept his accomplishments at a minimum. With two terms, Clinton had longer to achieve environmental policy objectives, but other domestic pursuits, politics, and the Monica Lewinsky scandal that consumed his last years in office left him with the label of "underachiever" in this policy arena according to environmental interests.

The Early Twenty-First Century: Presidents Bush and Obama

The lack of rhetoric about the environment during the presidential campaign in 2000 proved to be indicative of the lack of emphasis on environmental issues in the US in the first decade of the twenty-first century. Former Governor George W. Bush (R-Texas) and then-Vice President (former senator, D-Tennessee) Al Gore were the major party candidates for president in 2000, and neither candidate mentioned much about the environment during the campaign, as other issues dominated it. After a controversial election that ultimately ended with the Supreme Court's halting of ballot recounting in Florida, George W. Bush became president in January of 2001. Within months of taking office, the terrorist attacks on September 11 came to redefine politics and policy in the country and dramatically change the nation's priorities. Despite two very different presidents in the opening years of the century, the years following the 9/11 attacks saw environmental concerns—along with many other policy pursuits—take a backseat to other issues, namely, national security and economic conditions.

George W. Bush entered office promising to undo much of the Clinton-era policy and adjust the nation's approach to regulation. On his first day in office, President Bush issued a moratorium on regulations in development from the Clinton administration (which is often the case when new administrations take office), including the actions Clinton took under the Antiquities Act. In addition, Bush quickly retracted his campaign pledge supporting regulation of carbon dioxide emissions from power plants. Related to energy production, Bush tried repeatedly to open public lands to drilling and energy extraction, particularly in Alaska's Arctic National Wildlife Refuge (ANWR). He also wanted to open public lands in the West to expedite oil and gas leases to increase US production. In addition to this, he called for stricter cost-benefit analyses and more rigorous risk assessment for any new environmental regulation.

Regarding federal agencies and their activities, Bush took a number of significant steps, both regarding appointments and with his administration's involvement. Bush's appointments to key agencies generally went to individuals from the oil and natural gas industry or individuals who were pro-business advocates, as opposed to environmental advocates. The appointment of former New Jersey Governor Christine Todd Whitman to head the EPA was an exception, but she did not remain in the post long; public clashes between Whitman and the White House led to her resignation in 2003. Subsequent EPA administrators during Bush's tenure included former Utah Governor Michael Leavitt who replaced Whitman and, then, in 2005, Stephen Johnson took over. Spencer Abraham was appointed Secretary of Energy and was a notable opponent of increasing fuel efficiency. Gale Norton was Bush's pick to lead the Interior Department, as she was a protégé of Reagan's Interior head, James Watt. She championed attempts to drill in ANWR.

Additional examples demonstrate the Bush administration's approach to environmental concerns throughout its tenure. The White House meddled rather publicly with the EPA. The much-anticipated 2003 Draft Report on the Environment from the EPA was widely reported to be interfered with, including language changes that suited political purposes, rather than comporting with scientific research and evidence-based information. Bush followed in Reagan's footsteps and sought budgetary cuts to federal agencies working in environmental and natural resources pursuits. His first budget called for an 8% decrease in funding for environment and natural resource programs, including a 6.4% cut for the EPA (Layzer 2012, 266).

The Bush administration ultimately failed in its pursuit of stopping the EPA from regulating greenhouse gases (GHGs) under the CAA. The EPA, under direction from the White House, determined in 2003 that it was not statutorily authorized to regulate carbon dioxide and other

GHGs; and the EPA quickly found this decision challenged in court. The Supreme Court ruled in 2007 in *Massachusetts v. EPA* (549 US 497) that the EPA was indeed authorized to regulate those pollutants under the Clean Air Act and did not have sufficient reasons not to regulate them.

Legislatively, Bush oversaw passage of several major initiatives that purported to be good for the environment. The 2003 Healthy Forests Restoration Act is demonstrative of administration efforts to reframe the debate about the environment and use terminology to suggest one end goal of protecting forests, whereas, in fact, statutorily pursuing other and less environmentally minded ends (Vaughn and Cortner 2005). In 2005, Vice President Cheney oversaw the controversial closed-door meetings that led to that year's Energy Policy Act. The Act was intended to increase the supply of energy, improve efficiency of energy, and accelerate research and development. However, it has been heavily criticized for its over-reliance on increasing US energy production from fossil fuel sources at all costs. Toward the end of his time in office, Bush also signed into law the Energy Independence and Security Act of 2007, which was a follow-up to the 2005 Energy Policy Act, that emphasized energy efficiency and mandated an increase in the corporate average fuel economy (CAFE) standards to 35 miles per gallon by 2020, reflecting a significant increase over standards at the time.

Finally, the US largely removed itself from international environmental protection efforts during the Bush presidency. Citing the Kyoto Protocol on Climate Change as "fatally flawed," the White House formally withdrew the US from the agreement. In addition, international meetings that focused on environmental and natural resource concerns were generally overlooked by the US, and low-level delegations were sent to represent the country. For example, despite criticism, Bush chose not to attend the 2002 World Summit on Sustainable Development in Johannesburg, South Africa.

The nation changed forever because of events that unfolded during Bush's time in the White House. Moreover, with the nation's focus shifting to security concerns and military involvement in Afghanistan and Iraq, environmental concerns—along with many others—were neglected. During the 2004 campaign, environmental concerns were hardly mentioned in the presidential race between Bush and Senator John Kerry (D-Massachusetts). Furthermore, the 2008 campaign that brought Senator Barack Obama (D-Illinois) to the White House to succeed Bush focused little on environmental matters.

The inauguration of President Obama brought with it a sense of optimism and change for the nation that had become deeply divided over many issues, particularly the involvement of US forces abroad in the War on Terror. Many observers looked to the new president with hope that the country's policies on the environment would change, and a renewed focus on environmental protection and fighting climate change might come about. During his campaign, Obama indicated that he would pursue policy goals on the environment, and his initial actions in office fueled optimism, particularly coupled with the short-lived Democratic control of Congress. However, over time, the Obama administration focused its attention elsewhere.

Regarding federal agencies, Obama's appointees and directives of executive agencies marked a change from the previous administration. Lisa Jackson, the former head of the New Jersey Department of Environmental Protection, was appointed to oversee the EPA during Obama's first term. The EPA quickly rescinded a number of regulations from the Bush administration, particularly new source review changes under the CAA. In addition, the EPA set to work on stricter mercury and hazardous air pollutant standards from coal-fired power plants. In 2010, the EPA began tracking, for the first time, the carbon dioxide emissions of large industrial polluters. Gina McCarthy, who had a long history of working in local, state, and federal environmental regulation, replaced Jackson in 2013 as the EPA head when Jackson resigned. McCarthy's tenure in this role followed much of the same trajectory, particularly with regard to carbon emissions. Ken Salazar was appointed to head the Interior Department; his appointment was seen as only a moderate departure from the tenor of the Bush administration (Layzer 2012, 351). The Interior Department removed gray wolves from the endangered species list in Montana and Idaho, but not in Wyoming. Legal challenges were brought, and the courts ruled against the administration, thus forcing the re-listing of the wolves in all the aforementioned states.

Legislatively, Obama was largely focused elsewhere, particularly on the nation's economy and its recovery from the Great Recession, on healthcare, and on national security concerns. The American Recovery and Reinvestment Act of 2009 was signed shortly after Obama came into office and, although its aims had little to do with environmental concerns, the Act provided more than $100 billion of spending on tax incentives and loan guarantees related to energy efficiency, renewable energy, and fuel economy. It remains to be seen if there will be demonstrable effects on the environment from this law, especially given steps the Trump administration has taken. Much of the challenge has been because governmental efforts were focused elsewhere, and an increasingly divisive Congress stalled efforts. In 2010, Republicans regained control of the House, and, although the Democrats maintained control of the Senate through the 2012 elections, they did not have a filibuster-proof majority. Further, environmental issues are increasingly proving to be a litmus test for candidates, as the partisan divide in Washington grows.

Internationally, Obama promised to restore the US as a key actor in international environmental efforts, and, more specifically, to curb the effects of climate change. The 2010 explosion and sinking of the Deepwater Horizon drilling platform in the Gulf of Mexico and the ensuing release of oil for three months brought renewed attention to the extraction of oil from underground sources; however, neither the White House nor Congress championed major legislation in response. Instead, the Minerals Management Service—the federal entity charged with overseeing such drilling operations—was dissolved and reconstituted as the Bureau of Ocean Energy Management, Regulation, and Enforcement within the Department of Interior.

In 2015, Paris Climate Agreement was reached with the goal of keeping the increase in global temperature to below 2°C above pre-industrial levels to reduce the risks and effects of climate change. Each country who is a signatory to the agreement develops and implements their own plan to meet the goals of the agreement. The Paris Agreement is significant because it was adopted by all participating member nations. While there is ample reason to criticize the agreement because of its lack of enforcement mechanisms, the agreement was a huge step in uniting the world to fight climate change together. These efforts, though, met with tepid reception in Congress and then the Trump administration's subsequent withdrawal of the US from the agreement.

In light of Congress's reluctance to engage in environmental matters and the challenges on the international stage, the Obama administration pursued many of its policy goals through non-legislative means. The Clean Power Plan is an example of how the Obama administration, like administrations before it, endeavored to use executive actions to pursue a policy agenda. Recognizing that Congress was unlikely to act on climate change, the EPA began action on climate change per Obama's direction. The CPP required that states meet specific reductions of carbon dioxide emissions, using whatever means they choose to address the concerns and conditions of their states. These plans would be submitted to the EPA for review. Different regions of the country would have different goals based on a host of factors, including its electrical grid and existing fossil fuel power plants. The EPA sought to achieve reductions of 25% by 2030. The administration also expected public health benefits and economic development opportunities from the CPP. Unsurprisingly, the plan quickly found itself the focus of court challenges as the rulemaking process unfolded, with challengers alleging that the EPA overstepped its legal authority. Under the Trump administration, the EPA repealed the plan altogether.

By the conclusion of Obama's second term in office, his record on the environment was mixed. Legislatively, there was little progress on major environmental efforts and even a disaster like the Deepwater Horizon could not compel action. Nor was Congress able to address concerns over the safety of the nation's drinking water after the lead contamination of Flint, Michigan's water supply became widely known. However, administratively, Obama achieved quite a bit through executive action, but much was undone by his successor. And his administration was able to make some progress on the international level. The administration did pursue executive actions and made progress at the international level.

The Trump Administration: The Undoing of Environmental Policy

Whenever the political party that controls the White House changes, we typically see changes to the nation's environmental policy agenda and priorities, especially as views on environmental issues are increasingly a litmus test for politicians to affiliate with one party or the other. This was true when Ronald Reagan became president after Jimmy Carter as well as when Barack Obama became president after George W. Bush. However, the Trump administration demonstrated not just a change in priorities but a fundamental undoing of the nation's environmental policy. Many high-ranking government officials that served in both Republican and Democratic administrations quickly expressed concerns about the dismantling of environmental protections (Kaufman 2018).

Beginning with Donald Trump's campaign rhetoric, there was a clear signal that he wanted a dramatic shift in the nation's approach to environmental issues. Regarding climate change, candidate Trump rejected the scientific evidence that climate change is occurring and caused by human activity. Indeed, he went so far as to say that climate change is a hoax perpetuated by China (Wong 2016). In a Fall 2018 *60* Minutes interview, President Trump changed his rhetoric a bit about climate change, saying "I think something's happening. Something's changing and it'll change back again. I don't think it's a hoax, I think there's probably a difference. But I don't know that it's manmade" (Stahl 2018). He also contended that the EPA was waging a "war on coal" that had to be stopped. Other campaign pledges included approving the Keystone XL pipeline (which is a pipeline bringing tar sands oil from Canada through the US to the Gulf of Mexico that was vehemently debated during the Obama administration and ultimately rejected), "canceling" the Paris Climate Change Agreement, and opening up more government lands to oil and gas development (Beeler 2018).

Upon his election, Trump took the first steps to fulfilling these campaign promises and "Making America Great Again" through his appointments, as well as through his federal budget and policy priorities. Among his appointees, two stand out—his appointment of Rick Perry as Secretary of Energy and Scott Pruitt as EPA administrator. Rick Perry was one of the candidates for the Republican nomination for president in 2016. The former governor of Texas thought that his appointment as Energy Secretary meant that "he was taking on a role as a global ambassador for the American oil and gas industry that he had long championed in his home state" (Shelbourne 2017; see also Lewis 2017). To provide a point of comparison, Perry, who had a stint on *Dancing with the Stars* and majored in animal science at Texas A&M University, replaced Ernest Moniz in the role. Moniz, was a professor at MIT and had earned a Ph.D. in theoretical physics from Stanford. As we will discuss in greater detail (particularly in Chapter 9), the Department of Energy is charged with pursuing the nation's energy interests and security, including research and development, conservation, stewardship of nuclear weapons, and oversight of the wastes generated from nuclear energy.

Trump's first administrator of the EPA was Scott Pruitt. Pruitt previously served as Oklahoma's attorney general and in that role, he directed his office to respond to the "constitutional crisis" being brought on by the Obama administration. Regarding the environment, Pruitt sued the EPA 14 times—collaborating with litigants from industry—but typically had little luck in the court challenges (Talbot 2018). These attitudes and actions guided his efforts at the EPA.

Upon assuming his role, Pruitt announced that he was taking the EPA "back to basics" in an effort to refocus on the agency's work on its "traditional" priorities, such as cleaning up contaminated sites under Superfund, rather than focusing on current environmental threats, like climate change (Talbot 2018). Many observers were concerned that with his previous efforts, Pruitt was fundamentally against the mission of the agency that he headed. The administration's first federal budget proposal included steep cuts to the EPA of more than 25% and Pruitt supported those cuts. He oversaw significant environmental rule roll-backs, supported the administration's efforts to remove the US from the Paris Climate Agreement, favored undoing of the Clean Power Plan, and stood by as the morale and organizational culture of the EPA plummeted leading to nearly 1,000 career civil servants leaving the agency (Roston and Flavelle 2018). Scientific information was routinely suppressed, particularly in the area of climate science (Skowronek et al. 2021, 107). Pruitt also found himself the subject of much controversy while in his role. According to a Quinnipiac Poll in April 2018, 52% disapprove of the job he did as EPA administrator and only a quarter of respondents approved (the remainder were unsure) (Quinnipiac Poll 2018).

In July 2018, Pruitt was compelled to resign as EPA administrator as his tenure with the agency succumb to scandal. Andrew Wheeler was appointed to replace Pruitt as acting administrator, and his leadership raised questions quickly. Wheeler's government career included working for the EPA's Office of Pollution Prevention and Toxics during the George H. W. Bush administration as well as working for the Senate Environment and Public Works Committee and serving as an aide to Senator Jim Inhofe, a prominent climate change denier; and Wheeler has been on record as a climate denier too (Kormann 2018). In addition to these roles, Wheeler was also an energy industry lobbyist, representing electric utilities, coal companies, uranium producers, and even Murray Energy (Friedman 2018). More recently, he acknowledged that humans have some impact on the climate, but says that impact is not completely understood (Kormann 2018).

At the beginning of a new administration, it is common for an agency, such as the EPA, to put a hold on rulemaking that is in progress, but that hold typically lasts for a month or two to allow the new adminis-tration to establish its priorities. Under the Trump administration, these holds lasted for several years. As already indicated, the EPA rolled back dozens of major environmental rules. For example, the Clean Power Plan was repealed and the agency not only stopped efforts to combat climate change but undid a lot of efforts surrounding climate change. Regulations on heavy-duty trucks—known as gliders—which are trucks with new cabs and chassis built on old engines were undone. These regulations, effecting five percent of the truck fleet, were aimed at reducing the more than 300,000 tons of nitrous oxides and 8,000 tons of diesel particulate matter a year that resulted in 1,600 premature deaths (Talbot 2018). Besides the American Lung Association, Volvo Group North America (manufacturer of Volvo and Mack trucks) and the American Trucking Association were against this repeal. Superfund regulations were dismantled so that contaminated sites can be redeveloped more quickly. References to climate change and the science concluding that the climate is changing because of human activity were removed from the EPA's website. The administration also announced reconsideration of the rules around fuel economy that mandated automakers to achieve a fleetwide average of 54.5 miles per gallon by 2025. And seventeen states and the District of Columbia sued the EPA over these efforts (Domonoske 2018). At the conclusions of the Trump administration, more than 100 environmental regulations were rolled back or in the process of being rolled back (Irfan 2021). Additionally, the agency started 30% fewer enforcement cases and collected 60% fewer fines by comparison with the same period in the previous administration; and it has been estimated that the US saw an increase in deaths from air pollution and a rise in greenhouse gas emissions as a result of these actions (or inactions) (Irfan 2021). More than 1,600 EPA employees left the agency and only a few hundred were hired, decimating the workforce and morale (Irfan 2021).

The EPA was not the only federal agency that shifted course on environmental protection. The Bureau of Land Management took steps to rescind rules protecting the environment and public health from the harmful effects of hydraulic fracturing, or fracking, for natural gas. And, the Endangered Species Act (ESA), which has been protecting species for almost five decades, was attacked. While the ESA has often been criticized in the past, even under periods of Republican control, the law has not been attacked the way it was under the Trump administration (Davenport and Friedman 2018). The Departments of Interior and Commerce, at the direction of the administration, announced fundamental changes to the ESA with provisions that would, for the first time, allow economic consequences of protecting species to be considered in deciding whether or not to protect the species. These proposals were adopted, but once the Biden administration took office, these regulations were rescinded. It is worth noting that the ESA is credited with saving the American alligator, bald eagle, and gray whale from extinction, among many others (Davenport and Friedman 2018).

The Trump administration made significant progress in its four years to fulfilling campaign promises of dismantling environmental protections in the US Rules were repealed, enforcement proceedings halted, science was stymied, and the administrative apparatus gutted. These efforts represent a significant departure from the trajectory that the nation has been on for decades regarding environmental issues under leadership from both political parties. This administration brought questioning of science and scientific information into the mainstream and that rhetoric is now commonplace in the Republican Party as it pertains to environmental issues.

The Start of the Third Decade of the Twenty-First Century: The Biden Administration

The tumult of the four years of the Trump administration is subsiding with the Biden administration. Upon taking office, President Joe Biden announced that his administration would focus on four crises, climate change among them (the other three crises are Covid-19, the economy, and racial justice). His administration is also working to restore the environmental rules and regulations that the Trump administration repealed; however, it will take time to do so. Regarding his commitment to climate change, Biden signed an executive order in February 2021 for the US to formally rejoin the Paris Agreement. Additionally, he appointed former EPA administrator under Obama, Gina McCarthy, to be the White House National Climate Advisor and he appointed former Senator and Secretary of State, John Kerry, as US Special Envoy for Climate; both of these positions are new in a presidential administration.

President Biden has also taken action to rebuild federal environmental agencies through his leadership picks and budget priorities. Michael Regan, who had been the head of North Carolina's environmental protection agency, was tapped to rebuild and lead the EPA. Among Regan's priorities is tackling environmental injustices and racism. After all sorts of cuts under Trump, Biden is proposing significant increases to the EPA's budget—upwards of 28%—and major efforts to hire nearly 2,000 new employees (Lee et al. 2022). Deb Haaland was appointed as Secretary of the Interior, the first Native American to serve in the cabinet, and Jennifer Granholm is the Secretary of Energy.

Beyond these structural maneuvers of the Biden administration, numerous actions have taken place signaling the federal government's renewed role in environmental protection. Trump had stripped from the National Environmental Policy Act (NEPA) provisions that required government agencies to assess the environmental impacts of their actions and projects (e.g. construction of highways, bridges) but the Biden administration restored those requirements in 2022 (Bagenstose 2022). Additionally, the power of states to set more stringent auto pollution and mileage rules than the federal government's rules was also restored (Davenport 2022). **The Inflation Reduction Act passed in the summer of 2022 and was signed into law on August 16 of that year by President Biden. It authorizes spending $391 billion on energy and climate change, among a multitude of provisions. The law is projected to reduce the U.S.'s greenhouse gas emissions by 2030 to 40% below their 2005 levels. Time will tell if the law achieves these forecasts.** Other notable actions include reinstating the Migratory Bird Treaty Act, canceling the permits for the Keystone XL pipeline, strengthening the Endangered Species Act, and amending the fuel efficiency standards for vehicles.

It is still too soon to offer an evaluation of the Biden administration's ability to restore the federal government's role in environmental protection as there are signs of both optimism and pessimism. On the positive side, there has been early and vocal support for protecting the environment and addressing climate change and the Inflation Reduction Act is a signal of such efforts. However, on the negative side, movement is slow especially as Congress struggles to pass legislation. The first two years of the Biden administration saw the Democrats control Congress and the results of the 2022 midterms are still being tabulated as this book goes to press. Additionally, the Trump administration appointed more than 200 federal judges and changed the balance of the Supreme Court of the United States; these appointments will have lasting effects on environmental protection for decades to come. In particular, the Supreme Court in June of 2022 significantly curtailed the EPA's authority to regulate greenhouse gas emissions in *West Virginia v. EPA*.

THEMES IN THE US' EXPERIENCE
WITH ENVIRONMENTAL POLICY

As we close our discussion of the historical evolution of environmental policy in the US, several themes emerge. First, at the start of the third decade of twenty-first century, the American government has had decades of experience with environmental policy already. Today, most citizens expect the government to be involved with environmental policy, at least insofar as it concerns protecting the population from the ill effects of pollution and hazardous materials. That said, these expectations do not preclude ongoing conversations about the extent to which the government should be engaged in environmental protection.

With decades of experience with modern environmental policy in the US, it is important to note that how governmental action impacts the environment varies. Put differently, during the first major efforts regarding environmental protection in the 1970s, we saw legislative action to determine environmental outcomes. Over time, however, with the evolving role of Congress, the increasing power of the presidency and its influence on executive branch agencies, and the growing partisan divide, environmental concerns have been crowded out of the legislative agenda of Congress; however, this has compelled the use of non-legislative pathways for the continued development and execution of environmental policy (c.f. Klyza and Sousa 2013). With major environmental legislation unlikely to make its way through Congress, executive agencies are increasingly using powers given to them by Congress and following directives of the White House to ensure ongoing environmental protection. Additionally, states and even local governments are endeavoring to step in and do more and test the bounds of their authorities on environmental matters in response.

Recognizing the length of time that the government has been involved in protecting the environment and the legitimacy that time affords leads to another key point about the government's action in this area: governmental response to environmental concerns is largely reactive. Because we value a democratic system in the US and we want government to act on behalf of what the people want, there is generally only consensus for governmental action in response to events and circumstances. The government does not proactively regulate or limit behaviors until they are proven to be detrimental to the health of its population and the environment. This reactionary nature is as our Founders intended and ensures that government represents the will of the people. The flip side, however, is that the government is often seen to be slow to act and only fixes problems after they arise. It is important to keep in mind that truly proactive governments are, generally, those that Americans do not want to resemble—dictatorships, authoritarian regimes, and the like. However, being reactionary does, often, leave pollution and contamination to happen before the government steps in.

With a governmental structure that is reactive, a third theme emerges: the importance of the public's role in demanding governmental action. The influence of the public extends to undoing or weakening environmental regulations and even inaction. As we have seen, modern environmental regulation in the 1960s and 1970s came about because the public demanded it. By the 1980s and the election of Ronald Reagan, the public insisted that government lessen its regulatory burden, and that happened. Then, the public became concerned as environmental disasters occurred and, through Congress, the public pushed back on regulatory retreats. During the Trump administration, there was mobilization of the public, as evidenced in events like the March for Science on Earth Day 2017 and others. And we continue to see social unrest around environmental issues today and we will see what effect public demand regarding the environment might engender, if any. In the realm of policy, inaction is just as important and significant as action. These trends in America's experience with environmental protection are important to note, particularly when considered in conjunction with the public's sentiment regarding environmental issues over time.

PUBLIC OPINION AND THE ENVIRONMENT

Much of our history with environmental matters in the US is a product of how the public thinks about the issues and whether or not the public wants government to take action. In a country with a democratic tradition, we do ascribe to the ideal of government of the people, by the people, and for the people. Therefore, it is worth exploring, chronologically, how the people have thought about the environment, past and present, and look to the future for signs of what might come before next articulating key trends in public opinion on the environment. Understanding these trends is important as policy scholars, such as Kingdon (2011), emphasize the significance of public opinion in setting the nation's agenda for government action.

Americans have long been obsessed with public opinion data. Nationwide polls began in the mid-nineteenth century, and Alexis de Tocqueville famously noted in his travels in the US and the resulting tome, *Democracy in America*, just how fixated Americans are with public opinion. With regard to the environment, public opinion and support of environmental issues have swung dramatically over time; however, we do not have much public opinion data before the 1970s because public opinion on this category of issues was neglected (Dunlap 1991). Furthermore, Americans' opinions about the environment are complex and, depending on the question, one might draw very different conclusions about their opinions.

As discussed previously, public concern over the environment grew dramatically throughout the 1960s and into the 1970s. By the first Earth Day, 53% of Americans believed that reducing pollution was one of the three biggest national problems; nonetheless, after that April event, public sentiment dropped rapidly by June of the same year (Layzer 2012, 80; Vaughn 2007, 18). However, Americans generally thought the US was making progress in terms of the right balance of environmental laws and regulations. In 1973, 34% of survey respondents said the existing regulations had not gone far enough, whereas 32% said there was the right balance (Dunlap 1987, 9). Moreover, in that same year, only 13% of survey respondents thought the environmental laws went too far (Dunlap 1987, 9). Americans were willing to align government spending with their opinions as well. Throughout the 1970s, survey data reveal that between 48 and 61% thought the government spent too little money on environmental protection (Dunlap 1987, 10). Furthermore, a plurality of Americans thought economic growth should be sacrificed for environmental quality during the 1970s (Dunlap 1987, 11). However, various other challenges and realities in the 1970s often crowded out environmental concerns—in particular, the energy crisis and mounting Cold War tensions often diverted public saliency (Vaughn 2007, 18). Opinions changed, however, by the early 1980s with the Reagan administration.

Our earlier consideration of environmental policy in the 1980s demonstrates that, by the Reagan administration, we had more experience with environmental protection, and opinions seemed to shift. In 1981, a Roper Poll found that 31% of Americans thought environmental regulations had not gone far enough, 38% thought they had hit the right balance, and 21% thought they went too far (Dunlap 1987, 9). After a few years of Reagan-led challenges to environmental protection, the percentage of

Americans who thought more regulations were needed peaked at 48% in 1983 (Dunlap 1987, 9). In addition, during this time, Americans continually expressed concern that the government was spending too little on the environment—as much as 58% of respondents to surveys in 1984, 1985, and 1986 said there was too little spending (Dunlap 1987, 10). For further substantiation that the American public was generally put off by some of the Reagan administration's efforts related to the environment, 58% of survey respondents in 1986 said economic growth should be sacrificed for environmental quality (Dunlap 1987, 11, 22). Indeed, by the close of the 1980s, it was apparent that public support for environmental protection had endured the efforts of the Reagan administration to roll it back. However, public support for environmental protection did not then—and does not now—necessarily translate into political action.

Response to the government's environmental policy efforts in the 1980s led to widespread public support for environmental protection in the 1990s. A Gallup Poll in 1990 found that 76% of respondents considered themselves environmentalists, and a Washington Post Poll found that nearly three quarters thought the environment had grown worse since 1970 (Vaughn 2007, 24). In addition, the saliency of environmental concerns is demonstrated in public opinion data in 1990 that found 71% of Americans thought the government was spending too little on the environment—an all-time high (Dunlap 2002, 11). Moreover, in 1992, 63% of people thought the government had not gone far enough to protect the environment—another record (Dunlap 2002, 11). The early 1990s saw the high-water mark in terms of public support for governmental action regarding the environment.

At the beginning of the twenty-first century, Americans said more was needed in terms of environmental protection, but other major issues and debates over, arguably, the dominant environmental issue—climate change—have caused some significant alternations to the sentiments Americans express about the natural environment. For example, a March 2001 Gallup Poll indicated that 42% worry "a great deal" about the health and quality of the environment, but only 27% thought "immediate and drastic" action is needed (Saad and Dunlap 2001, 6).

By 2008, a decidedly different trend of public opinion and the environment emerged. For the first time ever, the percentage of survey respondents who favored economic growth was higher than those who favored environmental protection (Gallup 2013). In 2011, this trend peaked with 54% of Americans saying economic growth should be prioritized over the environment (Gallup 2013). These responses are significant because, even during the 1980s when environmental protection was not a priority of the White House, polls still revealed that Americans ranked environmental protection above economic growth. Data from the Spring of 2018 indicates a shift since then in that more Americans prioritized the environment (57%) over economic growth (35%) (Gallup 2018). In early 2022, that gap narrowed with 53% prioritizing environmental protection as compared to 42% prioritizing economic growth (Gallup 2022). Other standard questions about environmental protection ask if the government is doing too much or too little regarding the environment. Since 2000, the percentage of Americans who think the environment is doing too much increased from 10 to 17% in 2012 and 18% in 2022 (Gallup 2022). This coincides with a fluctuation in the percentage of Americans who think the government is doing too little to 54% in 2022, down from 62% in 2018 and down from an all-time peak of 68% in 1992 (Gallup 2022). During the Trump administration, growing numbers of Americans said that the government was doing too little for the environment, but these figures have gone in the opposite directions since the emergence of the Covid-19 pandemic and the subsequent economic tumult. Finally, Americans remain pessimistic about the overall state of the environment; a majority of respondents (59%) told pollsters in March 2022 that they think the condition of the environment is getting worse, while 35% thought it is getting better and only six percent believed it is about the same (Gallup 2022).

These shifts in public opinion should be considered along with public sentiment about climate change, as opinions on this issue offer insights about other aspects of this policy area. Typically, when a new threat—environmental or otherwise—emerges on the national scene, we observe a period in which the public gains knowledge about the threat and comes to understand it better. With climate change, polling indicates that the public is more knowledgeable, yet increasingly convinced that the concern over climate change is exaggerated. Gallup has been asking for 30 years about Americans' knowledge and assessments of climate change. In 1992, only 11% of respondents said they understood the issue very well, with 42% saying they understood it fairly well, 44% saying they did not understand it very well or at all (Gallup 2022). By 2008, 80% of respondents said they understood climate change very well or fairly well and only 20% said they did not (Gallup 2022). We have seen some variation in Americans' stated knowledge of the issue, including declines in the number who say they understand it very or fairly well while around 20% continue to say they do not understand it (Gallup 2022). In 2006, 38% of Americans thought the seriousness of climate change was underestimated, 30% thought it was exaggerated, and 28% thought it was about correct. Then, in 2010, 48% of Americans thought its seriousness was exaggerated, and the remaining percentages were about evenly split between underestimates and generally correct. Those numbers have flipped again, and in 2022, 40% of Americans reported that the threat is underestimated while 38% said it is exaggerated. Other polls have tracked Americans' understanding of the causes of climate change—and whether or not it is even a problem. In the Spring of 2020, 60% of Americans reported that human activity mostly causes climate change and 24% said it is caused by natural phenomena (CBS News Poll 2020). The numbers of Americans who think climate change does not exist has been declining since 2018 when 13% of Americans do not think climate change is real; that figure in 2020 was five percent (CBS News Poll 2020). Although the science of climate change has become increasingly certain, additional studies point to the seriousness of the issue, and much of the rest of the world comprehends its magnitude, Americans are still divided over addressing the issue. In a Pew Research Center Study in January 2022, four in ten Americans say that climate change should be a top priority for the federal government (Schaeffer, 2022; see also Borick and Lachapelle 2022). This is just a snapshot of one particular environmental issue and how public opinion is far from predictable.

By way of summary of Americans' perceptions about the environment since the first Earth Day, several points are warranted. First, for the most part, Americans consistently say the environment needs to be protected and that more should be done (Dunlap 2002). However, it is easy to abstractly respond to a pollster and say more action is needed and that the environment should be protected. The more significant question is that of salience—or how prominent environmental concern is for the average American and whether that concern translates into political action. This is where things are more muddled. Support for environmental protection is largely contingent on the broader economic realities confronting Americans, as well as reaction to recent and significant environmental events such as major disasters (Daniels et al. 2012). Therefore, just because there is support for environmental concerns, it does not mean that these concerns drive government, as Americans and lawmakers have to prioritize their actions. For some voters, particularly younger voters, environmental issues can drive voting behavior, but that is not the case for many voters. And economic conditions frequently outweigh environmental concerns in voters' minds. In the 2020 election, two-thirds of covers said that climate change is a serious problem and Biden won seven in ten voters who said climate change was significant whereas Trump won three in ten (NBC News 2020). Public opinion about particular environmental issues is complicated. We touched on the complexities of opinions surrounding climate change as one example. Much of what we think about environmental issues has a lot to do with how we seek out and consume highly scientific and technical information as well.

ROLE OF SCIENCE IN PUBLIC DISCOURSE

The final section of this chapter investigates how Americans talk about and consume scientific and highly technical information. You might be wondering why a chapter focusing on the evolution of environmental policy concludes with a discussion of how science is treated in policy discourse. The answer is simple: scientific and technical knowledge drives complex policy discussions and actions, including in the environmental arena. Keep in mind that biologist Rachel Carson conveyed, in an easy-to-understand manner, the ill effects of pesticides on wildlife, and she did so in a way that helped precipitate the modern environmental movement. In today's public discourse, however, scientific information is met with disregard. And the examples of this disregard are evident in a range of policy areas from the Covid-19 pandemic to climate change (see Chapter 8 for more on valuation). While all scientific information should be evaluated critically, there is a difference between appropriate inquiry into it and outright rejection of the information it offers. For instance, unlike most of the rest of the world, there are sizable portions of Americans and their politicians that debate whether or not the planet's climate is experiencing fundamental change even though that is accepted as settled science. To understand some of the reasons why Americans think the way they do about the environment, we need to examine how Americans view scientific information and how its reception has changed over time.

As we delve into this topic, first consider the nature of science and how the scientific method works. We are taught in school the broad counters of the scientific method. First, scientists formulate a question and then they do research to generate a hypothesis, or an educated guess, as to a possible answer to that question. Next, scientists figure out a way to conduct a test to see if their hypotheses are supported or not. After the test, the data are analyzed and an answer is determined. This method is simple enough and its essence permeates so many aspects of our lives. However, as with most things, the scientific method is not that simple.

With the scientific method and its widespread veneration, we strive for rational, orderly studies of phenomena that we do not understand. The scientific method applies rationality and linearity to understanding something and enabling future researchers to build on the work of those in the past. At the conclusion of an experiment—and so frequently our minds go to laboratories full of individuals with beakers in hand and white labcoats—we expect a single, uniform answer. After all, that is what science is to us. We await the answers science gives us. However, what we desire from science is not always what we get, particularly when we couple science with politics.

Politics and science mix in many policy arenas, but particularly when we consider protection of our natural environment. President Obama's second EPA administrator, Gina McCarthy, pledged in her first speech to Congress, that the agency would be driven by science, particularly when it came to the controversial requirements under the Clean Power Plan to limit carbon pollution and combat climate change (Daley 2013). By contrast, President Trump's first EPA administrator Scott Pruitt was uncertain if science even supports the conclusion that the climate is changing (*The Guardian* 2017). Utilizing science is not quite so simple. Scientific knowledge provides us information, but we increasingly find that information is marred in debates—and even battles—over what that information actually tells us. Our simplistic notion of the scientific method and the results it provides gets caught up in debates about whether the science was done correctly or actually answers more questions than it produces. After all, one scientific study often gives us more questions than answers. There are arguments over whether appropriate scientific tests were employed or the "right" data were gathered in the "right" manner— all of which presumes there is one right way to study anything, and there simply is not. There are, indeed, plenty of widely accepted research protocols, but that does not imply universality. Moreover, as we learn more about the world around us and advance technologically, we figure out new ways to study phenomena. Just remember, in the Middle Ages, it was commonly thought that draining the blood of a patient with the help of leeches alleviated many ailments. Today, medical science cringes at the thought of this widely accepted notion. All of this discussion is not to undermine or de-legitimize the role and value of science; rather, it is simply important to remember that just because there are methods of studying something does not mean that someone will not find fault with how that study was done.

A few additional points about science that are paramount when we talk about how science intersects politics. Rarely, if ever, will scientists "prove" anything. In fact, proving something is anathema to most scientists. Instead, scientists work at ruling out a causal factor or some other explanatory variable and, rather, help us understand what might be a possible explanation. This always leaves a degree of uncertainty, and this is exactly where politics come in. And science takes time. The Covid-19 pandemic and research into masks, treatments, and vaccines took time to conduct and, as a result, sometimes scientific information and guidance evolves. This evolution does not signal that science was wrong per se, but rather additional evidence was gathered enabling better insights.

Politics are often discussed as a struggle over who gets what and, in that struggle, there are vested interests on all sides of whatever issue. As a result, supporters and opponents of a particular policy are going to leap on any uncertainty in the work of scientists—and there is always going to be uncertainty—and exploit it in the pursuit of their policy goals. Small disagreements among scientists over largely procedural issues end up being characterized in public discourse as tremendous dissension among scientists, all of which leave the public perplexed and wondering who to believe. This frustration among the public is hard to grapple with because our understanding of science is that scientific study will find us solutions to problems because, well, it generally has.

Think of all the wretched diseases that used to plague young people: mumps, measles, and even chicken pox. Through the hard and diligent work of scientists, most young people have no idea what any of those childhood diseases are like because we have vaccines for them. Parents today never experienced more debilitating diseases such as polio that their parents' generation faced because of advances in science. Parallel arguments to this one can be made in so many facets of life, from portable mp3 devices replacing CD players that replaced record players to automotive safety features such as air bags and all sorts of driver-assist technologies.

Scientists are often unfairly subjected to scrutiny because the public does not fully grasp the work of scientists and how they do what they do. In a Pew Research Center study, approximately two-thirds of Americans say that science has generally had a positive effect on society with 28% saying its effects are mixed (Spencer and Funk 2022). Confidence in science, however, seems to be retreating a bit and experiencing a growing partisan divide. In a 2021 Gallup Poll, 64% of Americans express confidence in science, compared to 70% in 1975 (Jones 2021). That confidence has grown among Democrats from 67 to 79% over the same time span while it has shrunk to 45% of Republicans in 2021 compared to 72% in 1975 (Jones 2021). When pollsters ask directly about the work of scientists on climate change, there is less support for the conclusions of scientists. These fluctuations in opinion should be noted and considered. Scientists have the scientific method, but that method does not reduce uncertainty, and the results scientists do provide us have to exist in a broader context that includes behavioral, social, cultural, and economic values. This is where science and politics intersect. On the one hand, just because we have the science, does not mean the government will adopt it and follow its recommendations. On the other hand, just because a law is passed and makes it through the political process does not mean it is based on the best available science and technical knowledge. Chapter 3 will pick up here and help us understand the messy roles that scientists and other policy stakeholders play in crafting and passing laws related to the environment.

Chapter Wrap-Up

This chapter has explored the American experience with environmental policy historically. Over time, we have seen the government progress from a minimal level of involvement to significant action. Public support for environmental action has driven much of our broad structure of environmental laws in the US, with much aid from the scientific advances of the twentieth century. However, the first part of the twenty-first century seems to indicate pretty significant changes to how Americans have traditionally approached environmental issues. Due in part to significant shifts in our nation's focus on global security and the economy, environmental concerns remain largely in the shadows of policy discussions and even in political campaigns. Major environmental legislation has not been passed in decades, whereas scientific knowledge continues to advance. However, how Americans consume science and view science is changing, in large part due to the increasing tendency to question the work of scientists and exploit the inherent nature of uncertainty that is endemic in science. Accordingly, we turn, in the next chapter, to looking at how policy gets made and how policy debates today are largely a function of our country's history with environmental policy, what Americans think about environmental issues, and their levels of salience.

Case Study: Water is Safe to Drink, Right?

After reading this chapter, it is easy to conclude that substantial progress has been made in the US addressing major environmental issues; therefore, it should be plausible that seemingly basic issues like clean drinking water should not be a problem anymore. However, the cleanliness of drinking water in the twenty-first century is still an issue in some American communities—just look at Flint, Michigan. A study published in the winter of 2018 in the *Proceedings of the National Academy of Sciences* documented that almost 21 million Americans relied on water from community water systems that violated basic standards in 2015 alone (Rice 2018). The study examines water systems in the US from 1982 through 2015 and found that as many as 45 million Americans—28% of the US population—were subject to systems that do not meet standards (Rice 2018). Just because a water system does not meet minimum standards, though, does not mean people will be sick; rather, this research demonstrates that regular access to safe and clean water is not just an issue in other parts of the world, it is a problem in the US. Flint is just one example.

In early 2016, the water crisis in Flint catapulted to national attention when then Governor Rick Snyder (Michigan) declared a state of emergency in Genesee County because of the lead in the water supply of Flint. Lead can cause a host of long-term health problems, many of which are irreversible, particularly in young children. A federal state of emergency came just two weeks later. Nevertheless, the problems began much earlier. Starting in the summer of 2012, the City of Flint began looking for ways to save money by changing the provider of water to its residents as Flint's finances—just like many other communities—were stretched thin. Flint had relied on water from the Detroit Water and Sewerage

Department (DWSD), but the city began to explore getting water from the Karegnondi Water Authority (KWD). By the spring of 2013, the decision was made to switch to the KWD, which would require building a pipeline. Therefore, in the interim, in 2014, Flint decides to get water from the Flint River, which had been the city's water source until the 1960s. The water drawn from the Flint River was not immediately treated because there was concern that the chemicals that would be used to treat the water might cause pipe corrosion.

It did not take long before residents started complaining about poor water quality. Complaints ranged from issues with the smell and color of the water and multiple boil advisories were subsequently issued. By October 2014, General Motors stopped using water from the Flint River because it was damaging its machines. In January 2015, Flint was found to be in violation of the Safe Drinking Water Act over levels of total trihalomethanes (TTHM), so the state decided to buy bottled water for its government employees. Flint is back in compliance by September 2015.

Concern about the quality of the water continued, compelling ongoing testing. By the end of 2015, exceptionally high levels of lead were found in the water. Researchers from Virginia Tech documented lead levels in one resident's home at 13,200 parts per billion, whereas 5,000 ppb is considered hazardous (Kennedy 2016). Additional research finds high levels of lead in children and lead advisories go into effect. The corrosion of the city's pipes is what allowed lead to leach into the water supply and sicken residents. By mid-October 2015, Flint switched back to DWSD—now known as the Great Lakes Water Authority.

The problems did not stop with the switch back to DWSD. There were several Legionnaires disease outbreaks, which is caused by bacteria in water inadequately treated. A court settlement was reached in March of 2017 authorizing $97 million to replace water pipes in Flint with the remaining costs being covered by the state of Michigan. The City of Flint started a program to check service lines for lead and replace them at no cost to residents. As of June 2021, the city replaced 10,041 lead pipes and checked service lines at 27,092 homes, but the work remains ongoing (City of Flint 2021).

The actions of local government officials have been investigated and a number of them were charged with crimes, including Governor Snyder and Michigan's former health director. In November of 2021, another settlement was reached that ordered $626 million to be paid to Flint residents who were exposed to lead in their drinking water, with $600 million being paid by the state of Michigan (Ly 2021). The terms of this settlement mainly focus on young victims (roughly 80% of the settlement) who were under the age of 18 years old during the water crisis (Ly 2021).

The takeaway from this case study is that even environmental issues that the nation seemingly addressed in legislation decades ago can still present problems. In the case of our drinking water, the pipes that carry water to us get old and reflect the construction practices of years gone by. In 2020, the average water pipeline reached 45 years old and some may be as old as 150 years (Parks-Ramage 2018). The bipartisan infrastructure bill passed in 2021 intends to target replacing and updating the old infrastructure in this country, including waterlines. Additionally, the effects of redlining and other practices that have segregated communities continue to have implications for the infrastructure of communities, including access to clean water. Environmental challenges are far more complicated than they might appear to be and the policy process—which we explore in the next chapter—can and does yield solutions. However, those solutions are only as effective as their implementation allows and may not solve every dimension of the problem.

Challenge Question for the Environmental Policy Classroom

Much of our environmental policy history is about using the land and extracting resources from it, and these actions have often necessitated moving people from their land. Define colonization. How does this definition apply to environmental policy history? What are the implications of its lasting legacy for environmental policy today?

SUGGESTED RESOURCES

Readings and Websites

Andrews, Richard L. *Managing the Environment, Managing Ourselves: A History of American Environmental Policy.* 3rd edition. New Haven, CT: Yale University Press, 2020.

Brinkley, Douglas. *The Wilderness Warrior: Theodore Roosevelt and the Crusade for America.* New York: Harper Perennial, 2010.

Carson, Rachel. *Silent Spring.* New York: Houghton Mifflin, 1962.

Layzer, Judith. *Open for Business: Conservatives' Opposition to Environmental Regulation.* Cambridge, MA: MIT Press, 2012.

Merchant, Carolyn. 2007. *American Environmental History: An Introduction.* New York: Columbia University Press.

Milazzo, Paul Charles. *Unlikely Environmentalists: Congress and Clean Water, 1945-1972.* Lawrence, Kans.: University Press of Kansas, 2016.

Scheberle, Denise L. *Industrial Disasters and Environmental Policy: Stories of Villains, Heroes, and the Rest of Us.* New York: Routledge, 2018.

Films or Video

An Inconvenient Truth. Directed by Davis Guggenheim. 2006. Lawrence Bender Productions, Participant Media. DVD.

An Inconvenient Sequel: Truth to Power. Directed by Jon Shenk and Bonni Cohen. 2017. Actual Films, Participant Media. DVD.

War on the EPA. PBS Frontline. 2017.

REFERENCES

Andrews, Richard L. *Managing the Environment, Managing Ourselves: A History of American Environmental Policy.* 3rd edition. New Haven, CT: Yale University Press, 2020.

Bagenstose, Kyle. "Biden Reverses Trump to Restore Environmental Law on Highways, Bridges, Other Projects." *USA Today.* April 19, 2022. https://www.usatoday.com/story/news/2022/04/19/biden-trump-climate-change-environmental-law/7366575001/.

Beeler, Carolyn. "Trump and the Environment, One Year into the Presidency." PRI's The World. January 19, 2018. https://www.pri.org/stories/2018-01-19/trump-and-environment-one-year-presidency.

Borick, Christopher and Erick Lachapelle. "Politics, Prices, and Proof: American Public Opinion on Environmental Policy." In *Environmental Policy: New Directions for the 21st Century.* 11th edition, edited by Norman J. Vig,

Michael E. Kraft, and Barry G. Rabe, 63–86. Thousand Oaks, CA: Sage/CQ Press, 2022

CBS News Poll. https://pollingreport.com/enviro.htm, 2020. Accessed May 6, 2022.

Chariton, Jordan, & LeDuff, Charlie. "Revealed: The Flint Water Poisoning Charges That Never Came to Light." *The Guardian*. January 17, 2022. https://www.theguardian.com/us-news/2022/jan/17/flint-water-poisoning-charges

Childress, Sarah. "We Found Dozens of Uncounted Deaths During the Flint Water Crisis. Here's How." *PBS: Frontline*. September 10, 2019. https://www.pbs.org/wgbh/pages/frontline/interactive/how-we-found-dozens-of-uncounted-deaths-during-flint-water-crisis/#:~:text=The%20Legionnaires%E2%80%99%20disease%20outbreak%20during%20the%20water%20crisis,strongly%20suggests%20the%20actual%20toll%20was%20much%20higher.

City of Flint. "Mayor Neeley Calls on all Flint Residents to Get Water Pipes Checked Now—Service Line Replacement Program Ending Soon". *City of Flint News*. June 25, 2021. https://www.cityofflint.com/2021/06/25/mayor-neeley-calls-on-all-flint-residents-to-get-water-pipes-checked-now-service-line-replacement-program-ending-soon/.

Daley, Beth. "EPA Chief Vows to Develop Carbon Rules Based on Science." *Boston Globe*. July 31, 2013. http://www.bostonglobe.com/.

Daniels, David P., Jon A. Krosnick, Michael P. Tichy, and Trevor Tompson. "Public Opinion on Environmental Policy in the US." In *The Oxford Handbook of US Environmental Policy*, edited by Sheldon Kamieniecki and Michael Kraft, 461–486. New York: Oxford University Press, 2012.

Dunlap, Riley E. "Public Opinion on the Environment in the Reagan Era." *Environment* 29, no. 6 (July–August 1987): 7–11, 32–37.

Dunlap, Riley E. "Trends in Public Opinion Toward Environmental Issues." *Society and Natural Resources* 4 (1991): 285–312.

Dunlap, Riley E. "An Enduring Concern." *Public Perspective* no. 10–14 (September–October 2002): n.p.

Domonoske, Camila. "States Sue the EPA to Protect Obama-Era Fuel Efficiency Standards." *National Public Radio*. May 1, 2018. https://www.npr.org/sections/thetwo-way/2018/05/01/607447344/states-sue-the-epa-to-protect-obama-era-fuel-efficiency-standards.

"Environment." Gallup Poll. Accessed July 15, 2013. http://www.gallup.com/poll/1615/Environment.aspx?version=print.

"Environment." Gallup Poll. Accessed May 30, 2018. http://www.pollingreport.com/enviro.htm.

"EPA Head Scott Pruitt Denise that Carbon Dioxide Causes Global Warming." *The Guardian*. March 9, 2017. https://www.theguardian.com/enviro nment/2017/mar/09/epa-scott-pruitt-carbon-dioxide-global-warming-cli mate-change.

Davenport, Coral. "Biden Restores California's Power to Set Stringent Tailpipe Rules." *The New York Times*. March 9, 2022. https://www.nytimes.com/ 2022/03/09/climate/biden-california-tailpipe-waiver.html.

Davenport, Coral and Lisa Friedman. "Lawmakers, Lobbyists and the Adminis tration Join Forces to Overhaul the Endangered Species Act." *The New York Times*. July 22, 2018. https://www.nytimes.com/2018/07/22/climate/end angered-species-act-trump-administration.html.

Friedman, Lisa. "Andrew Wheeler, New EPA Chief, Details His Energy Lobbying Past." *The New York Times*. August 1, 2018. https://www.nytimes.com/ 2018/08/01/climate/andrew-wheeler-epa-lobbying.html.

Funk, Cary. "Mixed Messages About Public Trust in Science." *Pew Research Center*. December 8, 2017. http://www.pewinternet.org/2017/12/08/ mixed-messages-about-public-trust-in-science/.

Gallup Poll. "Environment." 2022. https://news.gallup.com/poll/1615/enviro nment.aspx.

Intergovernmental Panel on Climate Change (IPCC). *Third Assessment Report*. 2001. Accessed June 19, 2013. http://www.grida.no/publications/other/ ipcc_tar/.

"Investigation of Climate Scientist at Penn State Complete." Office of the Vice President for Research at Penn State. Penn State. July 1, 2010. http://www. research.psu.edu/news/2010/michael-mann-decision.

Irfan, Umair. "The Mess That Biden's EPA Chief Michael Regan Will Inherit, Explained." *Vox*. March 11, 2021. https://www.vox.com/22266602/biden- epa-michael-regan-climate-change-environmental-protection-agency-trump.

Jones, Jeffrey M. "Democratic, Republican Confidence in Science Diverges." Gallup Poll. July 16, 2021. https://news.gallup.com/poll/352397/democr atic-republican-confidence-science-diverges.aspx.

Kaufman, Alexander C. "Scott Pruitt's First Year Set the EPA Back Anywhere from a Few Years to 3 Decades." *Huffington Post*. January 20, 2018. https://www.huffingtonpost.com/entry/pruitt-one-year_us_5a61 0a5ce4b074ce7a06beb4.

Kennedy, Merrit. "Lead-Laced Water in Flint: A Step-by-Step Look at the Makings of a Crisis." *National Public Radio*. April 20, 2016. https://www. npr.org/sections/thetwo-way/2016/04/20/465545378/lead-laced-water- in-flint-a-step-by-step-look-at-the-makings-of-a-crisis

Kingdon, John W. *Agendas, Alternatives and Public Policies*. Updated 2nd edition. New York: Longman, 2011.

Klyza, Christopher McGrory and David Sousa. *American Environmental Policy: Beyond Gridlock.* Updated and expanded edition. Cambridge: MIT Press, 2013.

Kormann, Carolyn. "In Andrew Wheeler, Trump Gets a Cannier EPA Chief." *The New Yorker.* July 11, 2018. https://www.newyorker.com/news/newsdesk/in-andrew-wheeler-trump-gets-a-cannier-epa-chief.

Kraft, Michael E. *Environmental Policy and Politics.* 5th edition. New York: Longman, 2011.

Layzer, Judith. *Open for Business: Conservatives' Opposition to Environmental Regulation.* Cambridge: MIT Press, 2012.

Lee, Stephen, Pat Rizzuto, Dean Scott, and Jennifer Hijazi. "EPA Would See Highest Funding Under Biden Budget Plan." *Bloomberg Law.* March 28, 2022. https://news.bloomberglaw.com/environment-and-energy/epa-would-see-highest-funding-level-ever-under-biden-budget-plan.

Lepore, Jill. "The Right Way to Remember Rachel Carson." *The New Yorker.* March 26, 2018. https://www.newyorker.com/magazine/2018/03/26/the-right-way-to-remember-rachel-carson.

Lewis, Michael. "The 5th Risk." *Vanity Fair* (September 2017): 192–197, 240–246.

Ly, Kaura. "Judge Gives Final Approval of $626 Million Settlement for People Affected by Flint Water Crisis." *CNN.* November 10, 2021. https://www.cnn.com/2021/11/10/us/flint-michigan-water-crisis-judge-approves-settlement/index.html

Mooney, Chris. "The Hockey Stick: The Most Controversial Chart in Science, Explained." *The Atlantic Monthly*, May 10, 2013. http://www.theatlantic.com/technology/archive/2013/05/the-hockey-stick-the-most-controversial-chart-in-science-explained/275753/.

Nash, Roderick. *American Environmentalism.* 3rd edition. New York: McGraw-Hill, 1990.

NBC News. "Highlights and Analysis from Election Day 2020." 2020. https://www.nbcnews.com/politics/2020-election/blog/election-day-2020-live-updates-n1245892/ncrd1246266#blogHeader.

Parks-Ramage, Jonathan. "These US Cities are Dealing with the Worst Drinking Water Problems Nationwide." *Vice.* February 5, 2018. https://impact.vice.com/en_us/article/wj4qvx/these-us-cities-are-dealing-with-the-worst-drinking-water-problems-nationwide.

Portney, Paul R. "Air Pollution Policy." In *Public Policies for Environmental Protection.* Washington, DC: Resources for the Future, 2000.

Quinnipiac University Poll. April 20–24, 2018. Available at http://www.pollingreport.com/trump_ad.htm.

Rabe, Barry. *Greenhouse Governance: Addressing Climate Change in America.* Washington, DC: The Brookings Institution, 2010.

Rice, Doyle. "Tens of Millions of Americans Exposed to Unsafe Drinking Water Each Year." *USA Today*. February 12, 2018. https://www.usatoday.com/story/news/health/2018/02/12/tens-millions-americans-exposed-unsafe-drinking-water-each-year/330516002/

Ringquist, Evan J. *Environmental Protection at the State Level: Politics and Progress in Controlling Pollution*. Armonk, NY: M. E. Sharpe, 1993.

Rosenbaum, Walter A. *Environmental Politics and Policy*. Washington, DC: CQ Press, 2011.

Roston, Eric and Christopher Flavelle. "Shrinking EPA Workforce Has Already Reached Reagan-Era Levels." *Bloomberg*. January 11, 2018. https://www.bloomberg.com/news/articles/2018-01-11/shrinking-epa-workforce-has-alre ady-reached-reagan-era-levels.

Saad, Lydia and Riley E. Dunlap. "Only One in Four Americans Are Anxious About the Environment." *Gallup Poll Monthly* no. 407 (April 2001): n.p.

Schaeffer, Katherine. "For Earth Day, Key Facts About Americans' Views of Climate Change and Renewable Energy." Pew Research Center. April 22, 2022. https://www.pewresearch.org/fact-tank/2022/04/22/for-earth-day-key-facts-about-americans-views-of-climate-change-and-renewable-energy/.

Shabecoff, Philip. "Reagan Order on Cost-Benefit Analysis Stirs Economic and Political Debate." *New York Times*. November 7, 1981. http://www.nytimes.com/.

Shabecoff, Philip. "Reagan and Environment: To Many, a Stalemate." *The New York Times*. January 2, 1989. http://www.nytimes.com/.

Shelbourne, Mallory. "Rick Perry Misunderstood Energy Secretary Job: Report." *The Hill*. January 18, 2017. http://thehill.com/policy/energy-environment/315005-rick-perry-misunderstood-energy-secretary-job-report.

Skowronek, Stephen, John A. Dearborn, and Desmond King. 2021. *Phantoms of a Beleaguered Republic: The Deep State and the Unitary Executive*. New York: Oxford University Press.

Spencer, Alison and Cary Funk. "When Americans Think About Science, What Do They Have in Mind?" Pew Research Center. March 25, 2022. https://www.pewresearch.org/fact-tank/2022/03/25/when-americans-think-about-science-what-do-they-have-in-mind/.

Stahl, Lesley. "President Trump on Christine Blasey Ford, His Relationships with Vladimir Putin and Kim Jong Un and More." *60 Minutes* Interview Transcript. October 15, 2018. https://www.cbsnews.com/news/donald-trump-interview-60-minutes-full-transcript-lesley-stahl-jamal-khashoggi-james-mattis-brett-kavanaugh-vladimir-putin-2018-10-14/

Sussman, Glen, Byron W. Daynes, and Jonathan P. West. *American Politics and the Environment*. New York: Longman, 2002.

Talbot, Margaret. "Scott Pruitt's Dirty Politics: How the Environmental Protection Agency Became the Fossil-Fuel Industry's Best Friend." *The New Yorker*.

April 2, 2018. https://www.newyorker.com/magazine/2018/04/02/scott-pruitts-dirty-politics?mbid=nl_Daily%20032618&CNDID=46231412&spM ailingID=13196148&spUserID=MTcwMDQ5OTAxNzk5S0&spJobID=136 2395989&spReportId=MTM2MjM5NTk4OQS2

Vaughn, Jacqueline. *Environmental Politics: Domestic and Global Dimensions.* 5th edition. New York: Thomas Wadsworth, 2007.

Vaughn, Jacqueline and Hanna J. Cortner. *George W. Bush's Health Forests: Reframing the Environmental Debate.* Boulder: University Press of Colorado, 2005.

"Washington Post-ABC News Poll." *Washington Post*, December 10–13, 2009. http://www.washingtonpost.com/wp-srv/politics/polls/postpoll_121 509.html.

Wong, Edward. "Trump Has Called Climate Change a Chinese Hoax. Beijing Says It Is Anything But." *The New York Times.* November 18, 2016. https://www.nytimes.com/2016/11/19/world/asia/china-trump-cli mate-change.html.

CHAPTER 3

The Messy Process of Making Environmental Policy

Introductory Story: The Stories of Two Mayors Tackling Climate Change

In the third decade of the twenty-first century, there is much debate among citizens and lawmakers as to what the government should do about myriad environmental challenges, and especially climate change. The Donald Trump administration demonstrated that, at the federal level, the government is very susceptible to dramatic shifts in approaches to environmental issues with changes in presidential administrations. In particular, the incremental progress that had been made under Barack Obama's presidency regarding climate change was reversed with Trump. Then, upon entering office, the Joseph Biden administration began to reprioritize climate change policy in the US. The influence of presidential administrations and the federal structure in the US help explain the difficulties of addressing climate change. Two examples—one at the state level and one at the local level—demonstrate these challenges.

Michigan Governor Gretchen Whitmer and Los Angeles Mayor Eric Garcetti are two actors who have taken the lead on establishing state and local level climate action. Whitmer is one of the twenty-five governors that formed the bipartisan coalition, the US Climate Alliance (US Climate Alliance 2019). This coalition creates coordinated state action that aligns with the goals of the Paris Climate Agreement and was developed after the

S. R. Rinfret and M. C. Pautz, *US Environmental Policy in Action*,
https://doi.org/10.1007/978-3-031-17503-9_3

US withdrew from the Paris Agreement during the Trump administration. The state of California is also a member of this coordinated effort. Mayor Garcetti co-founded Climate Mayors, another bipartisan effort of more than four-hundred seventy US mayors who are committed to local climate leadership and build political power to push for federal and global climate action (Climate Mayors 2020).

Both Whitmer and Garcetti released climate plans that set the target of carbon neutrality by 2050. The Michigan Healthy Climate Plan and the Sustainable City pLAn, also known as the Green New Deal, focus on generating clean energy jobs, protecting natural resources, safeguarding public health, and providing environmental justice to underserved communities (Office of Governor Gretchen Whitmer 2020; City of Los Angeles 2019). These plans take a multi-sectored approach to upholding the Paris Climate Agreement. Michigan has long been known as the auto industry capital of the US and the goal of carbon neutrality by 2050 signals a commitment and opportunity to shift the auto industry toward electric powered cars and create clean energy jobs. The City of LA has already pursued that path and leads the country with the highest number of electrical vehicles and commercial electric vehicle chargers. Garcetti plans to invest more in public transportation and kick-start innovative programs like the electric car-sharing program in underserved communities (City of Los Angeles 2019).

Governor Whitmer and Mayor Garcetti bring examples of the power of coordinated climate efforts at the varying levels of government. The federal system of government in the US provides opportunities and challenges, as we have already discussed throughout this textbook. In this example, a governor and a mayor were able to take actions on their own to pursue environmental priorities despite federal inaction. From one point of view, a federal system that enables diversity and action in policymaking is exciting as various efforts can be tried and states do not have to wait for the federal government to be in lockstep. But from a contrasting perspective, the federal system of government further complicates making environmental policy as one state out of 50 may be taking these actions (it is worth noting that other states and localities are pursuing their own efforts to combat climate change too). States and cities in a federal structure only have so much power as the federal government retains supremacy. As this chapter reveals, the messy process of environmental policymaking is often driven by the challenges of our federal system of government.

Thinking about all of the major environmental laws that we discussed in the last chapter about the history of environmental policy in the US may lead one easily to conclude that environmental laws are fairly simple to pass. Although this observation is logical, it is far from accurate. With today's hyper-partisanship in Washington, DC and elsewhere, we are acutely aware of the politics involved in policymaking, but that is only part of the story. Policymaking is often described as akin to sausage making—you never want to know what goes into the process; rather, you should just focus on the end result. Once you get those images out of your mind, we focus our attention to the messy process of making environmental policy. As you will discover, policymaking is messy and, in reflecting on the process, it is increasingly impressive that we have as many environmental laws as we do, and it is unsurprising that we see so many challenges surrounding environmental policymaking today.

Our examination of the policymaking process in this chapter reveals several themes: (1) the complexity of policymaking is exacerbated by the numerous steps in the process, (2) the nature of the process is unlikely to yield the perfect legislation or solution, and (3) the process ensures that what does become policy has survived an arduous (and imperfect) process that required consensus among lots of stakeholders. These themes echo in our discussions of what policy is, how policy is made, and that the broader the context that policy is made in, is wrought with competing factors. It would be easy to read this chapter and conclude that policymaking is a mess and nothing good could come of it. However, such a reading misses the point that the system was designed to be messy and if we start there, our study of policymaking will be much more fulfilling.

What Is Environmental Policy?

Frequently, the best place to start with a new concept is with a definition. However, before we can define environmental policy, we need to back up and consider what policy is more generally, as environmental policy is but one type. Countless definitions of public policy abound and we make mention of a few of them here. Sara Rinfret, Denise Scheberle, and Michelle Pautz (2023) define public policy as "a course of action adopted or created by the government in response to public problems" (20). Michael Kraft and Scott Furlong (2018) define public policy as what is done or not done about public problems (4). B. Guy Peters (2004) defines public policy as the sum of government activities whether acting directly or through agents that influences the lives of citizens (5–6). Finally, Thomas Birkland (2020) defines policy as "a statement by government—at whatever level, in whatever form—of what it intends to do about a public problem" (6). From just this handful of policy definitions, we can deduce several important attributes: policy is the action or inaction of government to a particular problem, and the government makes policy even if it is other actors (e.g., private contractors) who carry out the policy.

Public policy itself can take many forms. Policy may be statutes passed by Congress (or another legislative body at the state or local level of government); policy may be regulations written by an administrative agency (such as the Bureau of Land Management); policy may be the decision in a court (such as the Supreme Court's decision in the 1978 *Tennessee Valley Authority v. Hill* case that, because of the paper clip-sized snail darter fish, stopped a dam project that had already seen hundreds of millions of dollars spent); or policy may be a government agency's activities (such as Smokey the Bear's campaign to remind us that only we can prevent forest fires). It is important to understand that references to public policy can be any or all of the aforementioned manifestations of policy. The bulk of this chapter focuses on the actions of a legislative body—Congress—and the work of government agencies.

As you might surmise from the previous paragraphs, environmental policy is just one area of public policy that the government is called to address by its citizenry. More specifically, environmental policy is government action related to the natural environment. Under the rubric of environmental policy, we might encounter policies related to controlling or limiting pollution, addressing natural resources issues, such as forests and endangered species, or contending with energy and transportation concerns. In this text, we use the term "environmental policy" as a broad umbrella term to encompass all these areas of policy, although they are often found to be their own policy subfields.

THE CONTEXT OF POLICYMAKING

At this juncture, note that environmental policy, like any other policy arena, exists in a much broader context, and it is easy to dive deeply into it and forget that environmental policy unfolds alongside many other policy arenas, events, and circumstances. Put differently, environmental policy does not exist in isolation from other issues or concerns. To help examine the various factors that impact environmental policy, we consider four different categories of factors. First, current circumstances and realities, along with public opinion on issues, affect environmental policymaking. "Focusing events" is the term political scientists and policy scholars use to describe major events that galvanize attention on a particular issue such as a crisis or a disaster (Kingdon 2011, 94). For instance, in the spring of 2010, an environmental focusing event was the explosion and subsequent sinking of the drilling platform Deepwater Horizon in the Gulf of Mexico. However, focusing events may or may not result in major policy action, and this one did not. Other notable environmental focusing events that led to policy enactments include the 1989 Exxon Valdez oil spill disaster off the coast of Alaska, which resulted in the Oil Pollution Act of 1990, or the actions of the residents of Love Canal, New York in the late 1970s, which ultimately brought about the Superfund law. Focusing events are defined events, or a series of events, that garner the attention of citizens and lawmakers around a particular issue.

Also part of this category of factors that influences policymaking is the mood of the public and public opinion about issues. For example, as we saw in Chapter 2, public opinion and activism in the 1960s and 1970s helped spur the long list of environmental laws that were passed. In a country with a democratic tradition of government of the people, by the people, and for the people, the people ultimately have to want policy change and compel their lawmakers to enact it. The Deepwater Horizon incident surprised many environmental policy observers because it did not lead to significant legislation about the drilling of oil offshore. We can point to the mood of the public as a significant reason such policy was not made. Rightly or wrongly, at the time of the event, the public was mired with an economic downturn and believed low energy prices to be important for economic recovery; therefore, there was no public will to stop, or even slow, offshore drilling.

Finally, this example helps demonstrate another dimension of this factor that influences policymaking—consideration of what else might be going on. What are the other priorities that may compete with a particular policy? Just as you can only take so many classes during a semester, governmental policymakers (and the public, for that matter) can only take on so many policy issues at any given time; therefore, different issues and policies are always competing for time and attention. Moreover, when crises emerge, some policy issues get crowded out in the environmental realm. Continuing with the example of the Deepwater Horizon explosion and sinking, the public and its lawmakers were consumed with many other competing priorities in 2010, and changes to offshore drilling policies did not make it onto the government's agenda.

A second category of factors that influences environmental policy-making is economic considerations. As is the case in numerous facets of life, money matters. Often policymaking is contingent on the condition of the overall American economy, and even the global economy. Typically, when the economy is doing well, Americans are willing to consider quality-of-life issues such as the health and condition of the natural environment. When the economy is not doing well, Americans are usually more concerned with immediate financial considerations than environmental ones. In other words, if a policy might adversely impact the job market—or even just give the appearance of negatively influencing job prospects—many Americans will not support environmental policies for fear of further damaging a fragile economy (at least historically).

Related to the overall condition of the economy are concerns about the cost of a particular policy proposal. Nearly all policies come with a price tag and, in the creation and passage of policy, these costs become a significant factor. How policies might be paid for garner significant debate. Perhaps, other programs or policies will be cut to pay for the new environmental policy or, maybe, new revenues will have to be raised, and either scenario begets debate. New revenues in the environmental realm might include increases in fees for permits or grazing cattle, or utilization of tax changes to reward environmentally friendly technology at firms and punish those with older, more antiquated technology.

A third category of factors that impacts environmental policymaking has to do with politics. Political timing is essential in most facets of governmental action. In particular, proximity to elections matter. For instance, if the next congressional election is just around the corner and a member of Congress is from a district that is overwhelmingly supportive of a new environmental law, then it behooves her to support the legislation as she seeks re-election, and vice versa. Furthermore, many policy issues get tabled if the next election is upon lawmakers because they may not want to take a stand on a particular issue and would rather focus their time on campaigning. For instance, during Biden's first year in office, the White House advocated for a range of sweeping legislation that included actions related to climate change and energy. By early 2022 with the midterm elections in sight, Congress appears to be stalled on aspects the climate aspects of Biden's Build Back Better plan (Davenport and

Friedman 2022). However, if the election is a long way off, a lawmaker may act differently. Additionally, political calculations enter into play here. If a lawmaker is looking for support from a particular interest group or constituency, he might be more or less willing to support a particular policy if it aligns with his efforts to secure support (such as from the coal industry if his district's largest industry is coal mining). Finally, the actions and positions of the two major political parties influence which policies gain traction in government or go nowhere. Each political party chooses which issues it will emphasize and the positions that it endorses. Because of the role of parties in campaigns and also in how elected bodies function and are organized, if a party does not endorse action, then action is unlikely to happen.

A final category of factors that impacts environmental policymaking has to do with the broader culture and values in the US. The values Americans hold (such as liberty, equality, property rights, etc.) set the broad parameters for what is possible when it comes to policymaking. In other words, how the American populace feels on the whole about what the government should and should not do sets the tone for all governmental action. For example, an argument might be made that, in order to combat pollution from mobile sources (e.g., cars), everyone should drive a Toyota Prius or a plug-in electric car. Would such a policy ever stand a chance of passing Congress? Absolutely not! The reason for this is that Americans value a free market economy that emphasizes consumer choice. This may be an extreme example, but it demonstrates the broad values—not those values that are typically ascribed to particular political ideologies—that set the outer bounds for policymaking. It is important to point out, particularly as environmental issues are increasingly polarized politically, that the government is involved in environmental protection because the citizens want it to do so. In our form of government, and under the auspices of the social contract, government acts when it is directed to do so by the governed. Public opinion routinely demonstrates that the government has a role in environmental protection, but it is the extent of that role that is debated and vacillates over time (Dunlap 2002; Sussman et al. 2002, 58; Borick and Lachapelle 2022). An August 2021 NBC News Poll reported 14% of Americans said the government is doing enough to address climate change while 52% said it was not doing enough and 31% said it should not be involved (NBC News Poll 2021).

So far, through the lens of environmental policy, we have defined the major influences driving policymaking. It is easy to grow frustrated with elected lawmakers for the slow speed at which they pass policies (or do not pass them), but it is essential to remember that citizens demand much from their lawmakers across a variety of policy arenas, not just in the environmental realm. This is not to say that lawmakers could not strive to be more efficient and effective, but rather it is a reminder that policymaking is messy business in an often busy context. The next section of this chapter explains the policy process, and demonstrates that process is far more complicated in light of this context. This chapter focuses on exploring the process, and Chapters 4 and 5 investigate the role of all the actors in the policy process.

THE POLICY PROCESS

Now we look to demystifying that process after having established the context in which that process unfolds. We focus on the stages model to policymaking, which is the policy model that dominates the academic study of the public policy process. But first, a few comments about policy models are necessary. As in so many areas of study, models are sought in policy studies in an effort to derive some order and pattern to the policy process. It is hoped that this order might help provide some predictability to policymaking. In addition, policy models offer us a common vocabulary to talk about how policy is or is not made.

Although these attributes of policy models are beneficial, it should also be noted that policy models do not always fulfill our aspirations for them. For instance, there is far from one universally accepted policy model. We are going to spend the bulk of our time working through the stages model because it is the most detailed and commonly used policy model (cf. deLeon 1999; Nakamura 1987). However, this model and many others are far from predictive and do not always (or even generally) explain every policy that is enacted. The stages model assumes that the steps happen sequentially and in a linear fashion; again, as we will see, this may or may not describe policymaking in reality. You might be wondering why we are bringing up all of these issues with a model before we even discuss the model. The reason for these caveats is it is important to know from the outset that policymaking is difficult and it is, perhaps, a Sisyphean task to derive a policy model that explains it all. However, to understand this messy process, we must begin somewhere.

STAGES MODEL OF POLICYMAKING

The stages model to policymaking (sometimes also referred to as the text-book model or the stages heuristic model) continues to endure in policy studies and textbooks (cf. deLeon 1999; Nakamura 1987). The model articulates six steps to policymaking: (1) problem identification and definition, (2) agenda setting, (3) policy formulation, (4) policy legitimation, (5) policy implementation, and (6) policy evaluation (see Table 3.1).

Each of these six steps in the policymaking process comprises many dimensions, and each merits individual consideration.

Problem Identification and Definition

Before policy can be crafted, there has to be a problem. We often hear that the first step to solving a problem is articulating that problem, and the same is true in policymaking. This initial stage of the policy process requires that a problem be identified and defined. Although this step might seem obvious and clear, it is far more involved than initially indicated. First, consider how a problem is even acknowledged. All sorts of circumstances lead to the identification of a problem. In some instances, a singular event might focus citizens' and lawmakers' attention on a particular issue; an investigative journalist might call attention to a problem; scientists might publish a report indicating a major issue in need of a solution; or citizens might organize at the grassroots level and lobby for action to address an issue. Just because an issue is thought to be a problem by some people does not mean it is a problem to everyone. In addition, there may be a major problem, but few recognize the threat of the problem. For example, escalating carbon dioxide emissions have been an issue for decades, yet it has only been since the 1990s that there has been concerted discussion of how carbon dioxide is a greenhouse gas. We

Table 3.1 Steps of the policymaking process		
	1	Problem identification and definition
	2	Agenda setting
	3	Policy formulation
	4	Policy legitimation
	5	Policy implementation
	6	Policy evaluation

can only guess what environmental issues that are already present today are going to be major issues 30 years from now.

Complicating problem identification in environmental policy is the tension between individual and societal values and the health and protection of the environment. Americans value their individual freedoms, such as their right to choose the kind of car they drive, but collectively the nation might prefer to see fuel efficient and low emissions vehicles for the sake of the planet. Reconciling these competing values can be difficult in the best of circumstances and downright impossible in others.

At this juncture, let us consider an example of problem identification related to the environment: gas prices. What might spur the notice of citizens and lawmakers about high gas prices? Perhaps, a rapid jump in gas prices over a short period of time might focus attention. Or, maybe, an environmental disaster at an oil refinery might threaten to bring about a major spike in gas prices as the refinery (which produces significant quantities of gasoline) will be shutdown indefinitely. Or, maybe, consumer groups get together and advocate for action regarding gas prices because of the struggling economy. Just because gas prices are high might not be a sufficient impetus to get lawmakers thinking about policy action because their attention could be focused elsewhere.

Simply uncovering a problem is only part of this step; the second half of problem identification encompasses defining that problem. This might seem simple enough—in our example, gas prices are high—but it is not quite that simple. Why is something a problem? Who says it is a problem? What is the cause of the problem? Answers to these questions are vital in policy discussions because these answers drive the rest of the policymaking process. As you might imagine, defining a problem becomes political; even with issues that you might consider to be highly technical and belonging to the realm of experts and scientists, those definitions can become highly charged. Consider the current discussions about climate change. Nearly all scientists conclude that carbon dioxide emissions are increasing globally and that human activity is the cause of those emissions, which is raising average temperatures across the planet. However, naysayers maintain that the scientists are wrong and that carbon dioxide levels are cyclical and caused by nature (Mann 2012; Powell 2011). The politics of the issue—and the implications that politicians will face if they acknowledge the problem—are trumping the science of the issue.

Much of how you define problems has to do with your vantage point and assessment of the situation, along with society's take on the matter.

Put differently, problem definition is largely a social construction. Helen Ingram et al. (2007) point out that there is no single view of reality, as people understand and interpret reality differently. According to Deborah Stone (2002) "[p]roblem definition is a matter of representation because every description of a situation is a portrayal from only one of many points of view" (133). Accordingly, problem definitions are not correct or incorrect; rather, the definition is a function of the information, data, and sources used to understand that problem and the social context of that problem definition. Just as a college student's conception of a study session in college may include loud music and various beverages and the parents' view might not, the same is true in any policy arena, especially with regard to environmental issues.

A lot of the consternation over environmental issues has to do with how the various actors conceive of a problem. For some, saving a population of sea turtles might be a major issue that should command whatever resources are necessary, whereas, to others, saving sea turtles is great, but not at the expense of feeding the poor. Moreover, others may say that populations of sea turtles elsewhere will survive; therefore, we should not be too concerned with a few sea turtles in one geographic area. This example is rather stark and presents some false choices; nevertheless, it does demonstrate how different perceptions come into play when defining a problem. The social construction of issues is evident when we talk about saving polar bears—after all, society thinks they are cute and cuddly, as compared with saving a reptile or an insect. Society collectively places values on animals, and this value determination affects our problem identification and definition. How society comes to understand problems is a function of past policies, our institutions, culture, and the populations involved, according to Ingram et al. (2007, 3). These constructions of reality and value are particularly important when society is weighing which communities and which problems are worth time and resources to solve and which are not. As we will discuss in a subsequent chapter when we tackle environmental justice, some communities are seen by society as more worthy than others to help. And some communities are left to endure environmental disasters when others would not be. For example, the crisis over clean drinking water in Flint, Michigan that began in 2014 had a lot to do with the characteristics of the Flint community and how lawmakers and society felt about the ability of certain communities to endure environmental harm.

Let us return to our example of gas prices. Working from the recognition of high gas prices, how might you explain them? Why are gas prices high? Is it because there are not enough oil refineries to produce gasoline? Is it because we simply need more petroleum extraction than we currently have? Is it because our cars need more gas? Is it because more people have cars that are fuel inefficient? As you can see, answers to these questions go a long way in determining how the problem of high gas prices is conceptualized. If you think gas prices are high because there is not enough refining capacity or enough petroleum to refine into gasoline, then we have a supply issue. If you think gas prices are high because cars need to be more fuel efficient or people should drive less, then we have a demand issue. One's understanding of the problem will dramatically affect the rest of the policy process because an understanding of the problem coincides with possible solutions to it and how those solutions might receive adequate attention to facilitate action.

Agenda Setting

Step two in the policy process, after figuring out that there is a problem, is how to get the problem on the agenda of the government. Thomas Birkland (2020) defines the agenda as "the list of things that are being discussed and sometimes acted upon by an institution, the news media, or the public at large" (207). Simply having a problem defined may not be enough to compel it onto the radar of government. That problem has to become part of the government's agenda. "Agenda setting is the process by which problems and alternative solutions gain or lose public and elite attention, or the activities of various actors and groups that cause issues to gain greater attention or prevent them from gaining attention" (Birkland 2020, 210). Put differently, there are many identified public problems, but that does not mean that all those problems are being worked on by lawmakers or that solutions are being formulated. Only so many environmental issues, for instance, may find themselves scheduled on the calendars of lawmakers or the subject of committee hearings, or talked about in the public square. Accordingly, the obvious follow-up question is what does it take to get something on the government's agenda?

Getting a problem onto the agenda of government is difficult and unpredictable. Much of the progress from step one to step two in the policy process has to do with the actions of individuals and significant events, often referred to as focusing events. Let us take each factor in turn.

First, individuals and organized groups do much to galvanize the government's attention and action on public problems. For example, much is being made of the process of hydraulic fracturing to extract natural gas from the shale beneath the earth's surface. Some groups are opposed to the process because of environmental concerns and are actively lobbying lawmakers to slowdown or thwart permits allowing this process to occur. Many groups mobilized in the 1990s to protect specific types of animals such as whales and polar bears. In these circumstances, groups committed to a particular issue work to get lawmakers to act on the issue.

A second factor is the influence of focusing events. A focusing event is "a sudden event that can generate attention to public problems or issues, particularly, issues and problems that are actually or potentially harmful" (Birkland 2020, 224). Put more succinctly, a focusing event draws the public's attention to a problem (Kingdon 2011). The outbreak of COVID-19 and the pandemic is a clear example of a focusing event that reshaped the nation's agenda. Furthermore, there are examples of focusing events, as we mentioned earlier, in the environmental realm that led to passage of environmental policy such as the Exxon Valdez spill off the coast of Alaska that led to the 1990 Oil Pollution Act, and examples of events that did not result in major legislation such as the Deepwater Horizon incident in 2010.

A third factor in bringing public problems to the agenda of government is the activities of key individuals, sometimes referred to as policy entrepreneurs. These individuals—many of whom might hold key government positions such as a legislative director for a member of Congress or similar positions in interest groups—often do much to advance a particular policy issue by having the ability to access key decisionmakers. According to John Kingdon (2011), the defining characteristic of policy entrepreneurs "is their willingness to invest their resources... in the hope of a future return. That return might come to them in the form of policies" (122–123). In addition, researchers might put forth significant new work that demonstrates the emergence or discovery of a new problem or the increased severity of an existing problem. Such efforts can lead to an issue being propelled onto the government's agenda. A historical example is biologist Rachel Carson's publication of *Silent Spring* in 1962 that did much to raise alarm about the dangers of pesticides. Moreover, an elected official may fixate on a particular problem and do much to champion a policy solution for it. This individual's loud and persistent calls for action may galvanize support from fellow lawmakers.

Finally, the mood and focus of the general public might do much to catapult an issue onto the policymaking agenda. If enough members of the public get worked up over a particular issue and speak out about it, then the government may be inclined to appease its constituents and take action on that issue. Furthermore, if lawmakers are fixated on an issue, but the general public seems apathetic about it, there is a good chance that such a policy proposal might not gain the requisite traction in government to bring about policy change. President Biden's Build Back Better legislation contained many provisions related to climate change and sustainability and while there is a push for some members of Congress to pass those pieces of the legislation, there is not support from enough of Congress to take action (Davenport and Friedman 2022). And, Americans are relatively split on whether Biden should be doing more on climate change (Quinnipiac University Poll 2021). All of this equates to stalled legislative progress as there is simply not enough interest from the public or Congress.

Environmental issues continue to face a couple of significant challenges in jettisoning them onto the government's agenda. In particular, the complexity of many environmental issues often stands in the way of them making it through this stage of the policy process. Put differently, many environmental issues—such as the loss of species biodiversity—are so complex and so many factors contribute to the problem, it can be difficult for government to take up the issue because tackling it is anything but straightforward. Moreover, issues like biodiversity are difficult to reduce to political rhetoric or slogans. What is the catchphrase for ensuring adequate biodiversity? It is not as easy as "Save the whales!".

A related issue is the increasing political polarization surrounding environmental concerns. Much like marriage equality and abortion are litmus tests for a politician's political ideology, environmental concerns are more frequently becoming part of this calculus. Environmental issues are increasingly seen as issues important to liberals or progressives, even though that was not always the case. Finally, recalling the discussion in Chapter 2 about the role of science in public discourse, environmental issues frequently fail to get on the government's agenda as a result of how society thinks and consumes scientific information and the Covid-19 pandemic has only exacerbated the challenges of public consumption of scientific information.

As we have done throughout our discussion of the policy process thus far, let us bring back the example of gas prices. We have already detailed how problem identification and definition is important in this example; therefore, we will pick up where we left off and consider how high gas prices might make it onto the agenda of government. From our discussion of the factors that often compel a problem onto the agenda, one way that gas prices might make it onto the agenda is that different organized groups mobilize and protest what they believe to be arbitrary price hikes. Or a major fire at a refinery and the subsequent halting of gasoline production might be enough of a focusing event for lawmakers to fret over gas prices increasing. Or a new economic forecast might be released that projects gas prices will double in the next 12 months. Or a report from an organization such as the American Automobile Association (AAA) may indicate that only half the number of Americans took to the nation's roadways for the Fourth of July holiday because of high prices. Any of these scenarios might make gas prices a focus for policymakers. But it is essential to remember that just because prices may be high at the gas pump is not enough to get the issue on the agenda; other factors come into play.

Policy Formulation

After an issue is identified, defined, and put on the agenda of the government, policy formulation occurs. In terms of a definition, this is the stage of the policy process that comes when government is actively considering action on a particular issue and works to figure out what should be done, and also what should and should not be included as part of the policy solution. Birkland (2020) reminds us that this part of the process necessitates both technical analysis and politics. In other words, a technically devised and rational solution to a problem has to be balanced with political calculations to secure passage. This balance is why policies often get passed that may not be the best solution to a problem, as political expediency has to come into consideration at this stage. Furthermore, because of different conceptions of problem definition, the best solution is likely to be as elusive as a unicorn.

Before we can get into the various steps a government can and cannot take to solve a public problem, there are a number of policy design elements that Thomas Birkland (2020) articulates: goals, causes, tools, targets, and implementation that merit consideration. With government actively considering action on a particular problem, we first have to understand the goals or the intentions of that action. Is the intention to eliminate the problem altogether or simply make things better in the short term? Are efforts supposed to stop the problem from getting worse or make conditions better than what they are currently? Consider climate change as an example of something that policymakers might tackle. In evaluating climate change policy options, are the goals to stop it from happening? Or is the goal to slow the pace of climate change? Is the emphasis on diminishing the rates of carbon dioxide released into the atmosphere or is it to reduce the total levels of carbon dioxide in the atmosphere? Answers to these questions dictate which tools or actions the government may take to address a policy problem. Questions about goals, moreover, beget a discussion of competing goals. In American society, numerous goals are espoused, including liberty, security, and efficiency (Birkland 2020; see also Stone 2012). The conceptual implication is that these goals can all be achieved simultaneously, whereas, in reality, that is often not the case.

Consider liberty and efficiency. Perhaps, the most efficient way for government to limit the emissions of carbon dioxide is for the government to mandate that all Americans take public transportation or carpool to any destination. Maybe such a policy approach is, by far, the most scientific and rational solution to the problem, along with the most efficient. Think for a moment, is this a policy solution that is ever going to be considered? The answer is emphatically no. Why? Because we value personal freedoms in this country and believe that we should not be constrained in the manner in which we get from one place to another. We want choice. Therefore, in this example, tensions between liberty and efficiency are on full display.

Answering questions about the goals of a policy further necessitates a consideration of causation. Policymaking depends heavily on the causes of problems because, without understanding those causes, how can a solution be devised (cf. Stone 2012)? For instance, is the climate changing because of significant growth in carbon dioxide emissions due to human sources? If so, then the policy tools that might be employed will be directed at human behavior. If, by contrast, the cause of climate change is the simple cycle of the natural environment, then the array of policy tools before policymakers will be radically different. As Deborah Stone (2012) reminds us, however, causal stories often "have a political life independent of the evidence for them" (207). In other words, science and research may tell us one thing about causation, whereas political rhetoric—in an effort to reduce problems to their most simplistic language for political motives—might tell us another story. Accordingly, different political forces might come up with competing stories, thereby complicating policy formulation. Even if causes can be determined, those causes must be readily linked to the ability of the government to address the matter.

A third element of policy design that Birkland (2020) discusses is the target of a particular policy. More specifically, Birkland is referring to whose behavior and whose actions a policy is intended to affect, and how those populations are viewed by society. Different populations that may or may not be affected by a particular policy solution are likely to garner more support and interest from policymakers than others (Schneider and Ingram 1997). For instance, there are certain groups of people in society that policymakers are likely to defend and seek to help, almost regardless of political party affiliation; such groups include small business owners and members of the military. These groups are considered more advantaged in our society than, say, individuals we consider deviants such as criminals, and even the poor and those on welfare (Schneider and Ingram 1997, 102–145).

Think for a moment, how often do you hear politicians talk about protecting small business owners versus protecting those individuals collecting welfare? Have you ever stopped to think about why? The reason is that we, as a society, think of small business owners as the epitome of the American dream—pursuing an endeavor and giving it all they have—whereas we often collectively think of those on welfare as lazy and needing to take more responsibility in life. Of course, these are gross overgeneralizations and even inaccurate, but they are indicative of how we view different groups in society. The views of groups in society affect how policymakers approach any possible policy solution that may impact these groups. As we have seen in recent years, this is why aid to small business owners is easier and more politically palatable for politicians to support, whereas additional aid for those collecting unemployment benefits, is much harder to get behind and accomplish politically.

In the realm of environmental issues, efforts to curb the effects of climate change may, indeed, have adverse effects on the manufacturing sector in the US and may bring about additional costs to employers.[1] As a

---

[1] Such a claim, however, is contentious in the realm of environmental regulation as there are countless examples of where environmental goals do not jeopardize economic

result, policy action proceeds tepidly because of how we view the companies that create jobs. By contrast, some fringe environmental groups advocate eco-terrorism (see Chapter 5's case study for further discussion) such as torching vehicles that are not fuel efficient or burning ski resorts or neighborhoods that are perceived as flagrantly wasting resources and, as such, are not viewed nearly as positively in society, regardless of one's opinions about the points these organizations may be endeavoring to make.

The final element of policy design that has to be considered is how a policy is going to be implemented. Here, Birkland (2020) is referring to the practical aspects of policy design. Who is going to carry out the policy and how are they going to do it? These dimensions are critical because if policymakers are going to invest the time and energy in a policy solution, then they want to be sure that the policy has a good chance of succeeding in achieving its desired ends. Particular issues here refer to which government agency at which level of government (i.e., federal, state, or local) is going to be responsible for implementation. Moreover, is it the policymakers themselves who are going to write all the particular rules or is a government agency going to do that and might those affected by new rules be part of the rulemaking process (more on this subject in Chapter 7)? In deciding what to do about a particular problem, policymakers consider these important questions at this juncture of policy formulation. This discussion about implementation leads us into a conversation about the more tangible policy tools at the disposal of government.

When policymakers are actively working on a policy solution to a given problem, they have a lot of different options or tools for how to address the issue. Simply put, policy tools are the various methods at the disposal of policymakers to achieve their goal. Policymakers have a variety of ways of getting individuals or organizations to do things or stop from doing things. James Anderson (2002) discusses policy tools as "techniques of control" whereas Anne Schneider and Helen Ingram (1997) discuss tools as the aspects of policy "that cause agents or targets to do something they would not do otherwise with the intention of modifying behavior to solve public problems" (Schneider and Ingram 1997, 93). At this juncture, stop and think about all the different ways government achieves

---

goals, although society oftentimes views these aims as mutually exclusive. The use of this debate here is more for an example rather than an advocacy of one view over the other.

its goals; government collects money, gives out money, tells us only we can stop a forest fire, mandates safety features on cars, and ensures that the foods we eat have labels to tell us what is in them and their nutritional values. These are just a handful of many examples of the methods in government's policy toolbox.

To help us organize our discussion of policy tools, there are numerous typologies devised by policy scholars. Here, we look to B. Guy Peters's (2004) categorization scheme that includes six broad categories of policy tools: laws, services, money, taxes, other economic instruments, and suasion. Consider each of these categories in turn. Laws refer to the regulations that tell people and organizations what they can and cannot do. They tell us that you must be 21 to purchase and consume alcohol and they tell facilities that, if they are going to emit air pollution, they must have a permit to do so. Laws directly dictate particular behaviors. Services comprise another category of policy tools. These include the direct provision of goods and services by government. For example, the government provides postal service to Americans and provides weather information and forecasts through the Department of Commerce's National Oceanographic and Atmospheric Administration (NOAA) and the National Weather Service.

A third category of tools is money. The government conveys funds, often through grants for all sorts of projects, from academic research on the causes of problems and possible solutions to creating and maintaining government corporations such as the Federal Deposit and Insurance Corporation and Amtrak, ensuring our money in banks is secure and providing passenger rail service, respectively. Taxation is another category of policy tools. The government collects taxes to spend money on everything from national security and snow removal to research into new alternative energies. Furthermore, the government provides tax credits for using energy-efficient products in homes or buying hybrid vehicles. Other economic instruments are another category that includes loans and subsidies to achieve policy goals. A prime example is student loans. The government helps its citizens access higher education by providing loans to help pay for it. In addition, the government employs various subsidies to farmers and insurance programs for those individuals who live in areas highly likely to flood. Finally, the government uses various methods of suasion to solve public problems. These are less direct ways that the government aims to encourage or discourage particular behaviors. For instance, the campaign of Smokey the Bear to prevent forest fires is an example, just as there are public service announcements about the ill effects of drug use or warnings on tobacco products.

In light of our discussion of the elements of policy design, we begin to get a sense of what this stage of the policy process entails. With these considerations, policymakers in this part of the process figure out what to do about a problem and how it might be solved, or at least ameliorated. It is important to point out that this step of the process has a multitude of actors (which will be discussed more thoroughly in Chapters 4 and 5) that impact the design of a policy solution and articulate—often competing— views on a problem and its proposed policy's goals, causation, targets, and means of implementation. All of which compounds the difficulties of this stage.

As we have with the preceding discussion of each step in the policy process, let us return to our example of high gas prices. Policy formulation surrounding this issue stems from how the problem was defined and what compelled the issue onto the agenda. Presume that the issue has been defined in such a way that stipulates that high demand is the cause of high gas prices and that the latest consumer craze among cars is a vehicle that is chic and stylish, but gets eight miles per gallon because it is massive and easily transports ten people. What might some policy solutions be? An option might be to stop the sale of vehicles with fuel efficiency less than ten miles per gallon, but, as discussed previously, how would competing goals and values of society respond to such a proposition? Moreover, regulation might achieve this end, but would a campaign of suasion be more effective in getting consumers to want to buy vehicles that are more fuel-efficient? Another option might be to encourage more citizens to take part in public transportation and to carpool. Think about what kinds of incentive programs—perhaps, tax credits or programs such as discounted fares—might make this policy solution more approachable. Any policy solution advocated must then take heed of the political forces in play and consider how the politics of the time might advance or impede such efforts. And this takes us to the fourth stage of the policy process.

Policy Legitimation

After policy formulation comes the fourth stage of the process, policy legitimation. This is the part of the policy process with which you are likely most familiar. In a nutshell, this is how a bill becomes a law. Indeed, many of us may remember the classic segment "I'm Just a Bill" from

Schoolhouse Rock (and if you do not, find it on YouTube). More formally, policy legitimation is the stage of the policy process when a proposed policy becomes law. This might happen in Congress for federal policy-making, or it may occur in state legislatures, or maybe even at the local level in entities like a city council. For our purposes, we are largely focused at the federal level. Therefore, let us briefly review how a bill makes it through Congress to become law.

After a policy solution has been advocated and the language drafted in the form of a bill, or proposed law, it is introduced in one chamber of Congress, either the House of Representatives or the Senate. We often think that all bills must start in the House, but that is only true of bills that raise revenues. A member of Congress must introduce the bill to a particular chamber, but that does not mean that a member has to write the bill. In fact, many bills are written by congressional staffers, members of interest groups, or other individuals rather than by a member of Congress. This wide range of authors allows for greater diversity in the authorship of a bill and greater democratic access to the process of crafting policy solutions.

When the bill is introduced, it may be referred to a particular committee, or very likely, may not go beyond simple introduction to a chamber of Congress. The process of committee referral in each chamber varies and is beyond our scope here, but it is important to note that the committee a bill is referred to makes all the difference in a bill's chances for passage. Bills are sent to committees for closer examination and revisions. Which committee a bill gets referred to depends on politics—which leaders in the chamber are doing the referring and whether or not those leaders want the bill to survive committee review or not. To start with, there are a multitude of committees with competing jurisdictions; therefore, it is not as simple as referring anything related to the environment to one committee; moreover, within committees, there are subcommittees to contend with. Table 3.2 lists the 117th (January 2021–January 2023) Congress' Committees and Subcommittees that have a connection with environmental and natural resource issues.

The use of committees is well intentioned in terms of contending with the scale and scope of the work before Congress at any given time; however, this same structure designed to ease the workload can also encumber the process of lawmaking. Indeed, most bills never make it out of committee. Multiple committees may have jurisdiction over an issue, such as gas prices, and the committee chairpersons might fight over getting a bill referred to their committee. Or a bill could face multiple committee assignments.

Table 3.2 Congressional committees and subcommittees pertaining to environmental and natural resource issues in the 117th Congress

House
- Agriculture
  - Commodity Exchanges, Energy, and Credit
  - Conservation and Forestry
  - Nutrition, Oversight, and Department Operations
  - General Farm Commodities and Risk Management
  - Biotechnology, Horticulture, and Research
  - Livestock and Foreign Agriculture
- Appropriations
  - Agriculture, Rural Development, Food and Drug Administration, and Related Agencies
  - Commerce, Justice, Science, and Related Agencies
  - Energy and Water Development, and Related Agencies
  - Interior, Environment, and Related Agencies
  - Labor, Health and Human Services, Education, and Related Agencies
- Energy and Commerce
  - Energy
  - Environment and Climate Change
  - Health
  - Oversight and Investigations
- Natural Resources
  - Energy and Mineral Resources
  - National Parks, Forests, and Public Lands
  - Oversight and Investigations
  - Water, Oceans, and Wildlife
- Science, Space, and Technology
  - Energy
  - Environment
  - Research and Technology
- Transportation and Infrastructure
  - Coast Guard and Maritime Transportation
  - Highways and Transit
  - Railroads, Pipelines, and Hazardous Materials
  - Water Resources and Environment

Senate
- Agriculture, Nutrition, and Forestry
  - Commodities, Risk Management, and Trade
  - Conservation, Climate, Forestry, and Natural Resources
  - Food and Nutrition, Specialty Crops, Organics, and Research
  - Livestock, Dairy, Poultry, Local Food Systems, and Food Safety and Security
  - Rural Development and Energy
- Appropriations
  - Agriculture, Rural Development, Food and Drug Administration, and Related Agencies
  - Commerce, Justice, Science, and Related Agencies
  - Energy and Water Development
  - Interior, Environment, and Related Agencies
  - Transportation, Housing and Urban Development, and Related Agencies

(continued)

Table 3.2 (continued)

- Commerce, Science, and Transportation
  - Aviation Safety, Operations, and Innovation
  - Consumer Protection, Product Safety, and Data Security
  - Oceans, Fisheries, Climate Change, and Manufacturing
  - Surface Transportation, Maritime, Freight, and Ports
  - Tourism, Trade, and Export Promotion
- Energy and Natural Resources
  - Energy
  - National Parks
  - Public Lands, Forests, and Mining
  - Water and Power
- Environment and Public Works
  - Chemical Safety, Waste Management, Environmental Justice, and Regulatory Oversight
  - Clean Air, Climate, and Nuclear Safety
  - Fisheries, Wildlife, and Water
  - Transportation and Infrastructure

Sources Available from: http://www.house.gov/committees/ and https://www.senate.gov/committees/

After a bill makes it to committee, the committees and subcommittees begin studying the problem, the proposed bill, and alternative solutions. Hearings are often held in which experts are called to testify before the committee and revisions to the bill take place. If a bill has survived all these steps, it may then be subjected to a committee vote. If the committee votes in favor of the bill, it will be referred to the entire chamber for consideration. Then, a bill may be scheduled for a floor debate before the entire membership of the chamber and, perhaps, even a vote. Only if a bill successfully survives this entire process might the bill pass one chamber of Congress and, then, go on to the other chamber to repeat this entire process.

If a bill survives the same process in the other chamber, only then does the bill go on to the White House for the president to consider. However, Congress cannot send the president two different versions of a bill. Although the bills before each chamber might start off as the same bill, they frequently get different revisions in the two chambers; therefore, those differences have to be worked out in a conference committee before heading to the president. Then, the president can sign the bill or veto it. More conversation about the actors involved in this process, particularly at this stage, follows in Chapters 4 and 5.

Let us return to our example of high gas prices. Based on a problem definition that there is not enough gas so the price per gallon has dramatically risen, a policy solution might be to increase offshore drilling such that there will be more oil extracted that can be refined into gasoline. Perhaps, a member of the House drafts a bill in consultation with her staffers and with some input from the American Petroleum Institute to help dictate which areas should be more easily drilled. Now the Let's Get More Oil Bill has been drafted and introduced to the House. A fight invariably ensues over which committee the bill should be referred to. On the one hand, the bill's sponsor wants to see her bill go before the House Energy and Commerce committee because she sits on the committee and she knows her committee chairperson is like-minded in what should be done about reducing the burden of high gas prices for Americans. On the other hand, other members of the House want to see the bill referred to the Natural Resources committee because that committee may be inclined to take a careful look at the threat to marine life that may be impacted if another drilling rig offshore suffers a catastrophic event such as Deepwater Horizon did. This committee could potentially rewrite significant portions of the Let's Get More Oil Bill so the bill effectively becomes the Let's Get More Oil as Long as We Don't Hurt the Fish Bill. Without taking this example too much further, it is already evident how political this process might become, even without the Congress considering other issues and worrying about the broader context (as we discussed earlier in this chapter) of the legislative environment.

It is understandable to decry the speed at which Congress legislates; however, a couple of important points should be mentioned. First, our founders intentionally set up Congress to function slowly because they feared the possible outcomes if the legislative process was too easy or too quick. This slower, more deliberative process ensures that the bills that are passed are truly what the majority want—and what the people want.

Second, the issues before Congress are frequently complex—just recall our discussion of how we define problems. Therefore, it can be advantageous that Congress takes its time considering how a proposed bill might solve—or at least ameliorate—a public problem. Complicated problems take time to understand and figure out solutions and rushing action is likely to cause more problems.

Third, as a result of the lawmaking process, compromise and consensus building are a must. As a result, the law that eventually passes may be quite different—or at least contain some rather unexpected provisions—simply because of what needed doing to get the bill passed. Reviewing the process in which a bill becomes a law reminds us how involved and slow lawmaking often is, but remember this is just the fourth of six steps in the policymaking process. At times, it is easy to wonder how any policy gets passed.

Policy Implementation

The passage of a bill and its signing into law—complete with a presidential signing ceremony with lots of ceremonial pens at the White House or some other picturesque location—is often where our attention to policies stop. After all, creation of the policy is the cantankerous part of the process, where anything can happen. After a bill becomes law, how interesting can things be? The simple answer is they can be quite interesting. Policy implementation is the fifth step of the policy process and this step is frequently removed from the public spotlight as it is presumed to be merely carrying out a law. Birkland (2020) defines policy implementation as the "process by which policies enacted by government are put into effect by the relevant agencies" (343). This is where the rubber meets the road; however, it is not quite that simple.

It is commonly thought that "implementation should be easy" and people are "upset when expected events do not occur or turn out badly" (Pressman and Wildavsky 1973, xi–xvii). Implementation can easily go awry when we stop to think about the actual language of a law that Congress gives the multitude of government agencies to work with to implement. For example, the 1972 Clean Water Act discusses the aims of the law to ensure the nation's waterways are "swimmable" and "fishable." Pause for a moment and consider this language. How would you define swimmable? Is swimmable simply a body of water that is liquid, one that you can paddle around in that is not radioactive? Or do you prefer a water body that is free of debris floating in it? But what about the pollution you cannot see in the water? So, perhaps, you would rather swim in a water body that is crystal clear and seemingly untouched by humans? Clearly, there are many interpretations of this vague statutory language, and herein lies the challenge of policy implementation.

To make the nation's waterways swimmable and fishable, standards need to be determined along with what is an acceptable level of pollution and what is unacceptable. Here is where scientists and other experts step in to figure out these standards based on evidence and modeling. Accordingly, policy implementation brings together lots of people and lots of organizations, frequently all over the country, in an effort to figure out what policymakers actually meant by the language in a newly created piece of legislation and how lofty goals can be given concrete action steps. It would be much simpler if laws were clear and specific regarding what the elected leaders of the country wanted done and how they wanted it done. However, laws are far from clear. Think back to the process of how a bill becomes a law. There is a lot of political wrangling and there is much compromise to even get that vague statutory language in the first place. Furthermore, a lot of the details are left to experts in the field. For example, Congress saved many of the details associated with the Clean Water Act to be worked out by the US Environmental Protection Agency (EPA) because that is where the scientists are, not (necessarily) in the halls of Congress. Given the significance of this often-negated step of the policy process, Chapters 6 and 7 will devote far more detail to this part of the process and examine the actors involved in this step.

When we last discussed high gas prices, the Let's Get More Oil Bill was working its way through a maze of congressional committees. When our fictional bill was passed by Congress and signed by the president, it contained provisions to allow more drilling offshore in the US, but only in selected areas. It might make sense for those areas to be determined by study of the reserves of oil under the seabed, for example, but Congress decided that to appease its members and ensure those members of Congress who did not want more drilling could go back to their districts and say they stopped drilling in certain areas; thus, the bill contains a list of areas where drilling is permitted. Some of those areas include Lake Michigan, the Cuyahoga River in Cleveland, and the East River in New York City. Consider for a moment how these designations fit with what even the average person knows about offshore drilling. Can you picture huge drilling rigs in these areas? Is it even worth drilling in these areas? This is an extreme example, of course, but it conveys that the provisions in bills may or may not make the most scientific sense, much less commercial sense. To implement this bill, Congress delegated responsibility to the Department of the Interior—more specifically, to the US Geological Survey and the Bureau of Ocean Energy Management, Regulation, and Enforcement. These subunits of the Interior Department then have the onerous task of figuring where, in the specified waterways, drilling can commence, what the parameters for drilling in those areas must be, especially taking into consideration that those waterways are used for lots of other purposes, including transportation and recreation. It is increasingly evident that there are numerous challenges ahead for this Department in implementing the Let's Get More Oil Bill, and it will invariably take a good bit of time. Again, we will return to the challenges of implementation in subsequent chapters.

Policy Evaluation

We have finally made it to the last stage of the policymaking process: policy evaluation. Formally, policy evaluation is an "assessment of whether policies and programs are working well" (Kraft and Furlong 2018, 104). This description seems straightforward enough; evaluation is about figuring out if the policy is working or not. However, as we have seen in each of the steps of the process so far, the process is much more complicated than it appears. For starters, a simple determination of whether a policy is working is far from a decisive conclusion. Rarely, if ever, is the answer a yes or a no. The answer usually lies somewhere between those two conclusions. Moreover, this does not even consider the difficulty in getting to a conclusion. Let us unpack some of the challenges associated with policy evaluation and the varying motivations behind policy, keeping in mind that a more robust conversation about these issues will come later in Chapter 8.

First, to figure out if a policy is working, you need to have a definition of what constitutes working. This may seem simple enough, but think about the challenges policies are supposed to overcome—cleaning the air, protecting the water, and preventing contamination. What is clean air? Does that mean the air is clean enough that it is pure oxygen? Is it clean enough not to make people sick? Well, what is clean enough? The significance of this conversation is that, if we do not have a clear understanding of what the goal of a policy is, it is difficult to assess the effects of that policy.

This leads us to a second issue in policy evaluation—determining causality. One must measure that if there is an observed change such as cleaner air, is it the result of a particular policy or something else? Herein lies the difficulty associated with determining causation in the social sciences. Does X cause Y? Does the Clean Air Act lead to improved air quality? Ultimately, it is difficult to make such conclusions because there are too many factors that might be influencing outcomes. Consider the classic social science causation scenario: as the number of churches in a town increases, so does the number of bars. Does this mean that churches incite more bars? No, not at all. So what is going on here? As a town grows in size, there are usually more places of religious worship, as well as more of everything else, including bars. Air quality may improve for a multitude of reasons that may or may not be attributable to a particular policy.

Third, the effects of a policy may be diffuse and difficult to measure. In other words, a policy may actually be helping improve a particular condition or even having its intended effects, but there are a lot of other effects; therefore, it is difficult to attribute those positive effects to the policy. Returning to the Let's Get More Oil Law, let us say that drilling is occurring in the East River and maybe gas prices are falling, but they are only falling by 5 cents a gallon. The drilling may actually be having a more profound effect on gas prices, but geopolitical tensions in other parts of the world are driving up the cost of gas; therefore, the effects of the Let's Get More Oil Law are not demonstrating the true nature of its impact.

All of the aforementioned challenges of policy evaluation presume that the data needed to study if a policy is working are obtainable. Data acquisition issues plague policy evaluation. How do we measure improvements in public health, for example? Associated with challenges in gathering data is also the issue of resistance. Oftentimes, the data sought to figure out if a policy is working has to come from the people and the agencies responsible for implementing that policy. Sometimes, they are freely willing to provide whatever data they can and, at other times, they are not. At first glance, you might be taken aback by a resistance from these officials, but on closer consideration it makes sense. Government agencies are much maligned in society; therefore, the releasing of data is often construed in a way to make an agency look bad and full of lazy, incompetent bureaucrats who are wasting time and money. And maybe the data out of context could be weaponized against an agency. Given the resource challenges of government agencies, they may have difficulty even collecting or managing the data in the first place.

Our brief discussion of the challenges associated with policy evaluation enables us to see that this step is far from simple, and it is increasingly evident how some individuals may read the evaluation of a policy one way, whereas others may perceive it differently. Again, a more robust conversation about policy evaluation emerges in Chapter 8.

Policy Failure and Change

The outcome of policy evaluation may be that a policy is not working as intended or perhaps is creating problems that were not anticipated when the policy was created and implemented. These findings may lead to conclusions that the policy is a failure, or that policy must be changed. It is important to note that a policy can be labeled a failure for any number of reasons that may or may not be substantiated by systematic research and evidence through policy evaluation. It may instead be based on political ideology or even a lack of complete information. Just like problem definition can vary based on different understandings of an issue, policy failure can be a result of contrasting views on a policy and how the objectives of that policy were operationalized and assessed. Therefore, to one stakeholder a policy may have failed while to another stakeholder a policy might be successful.

The reasons that policies fail are as varied as the policies themselves. Thomas Birkland (2020) summarizes existing policy research into a handful of explanations, including:

(1) other policy alternatives may have been more or less successful;
(2) circumstances changed effecting the success or failure of the policy in question;
(3) political institutions may have impeded the implementation of the policy;
(4) there were implementation problems associated with the policy;
(5) the understanding of the cause of the public problem was flawed; and
(6) the expectations for the ability of the policy to solve the problem were simply too grandiose.

Naturally, these explanations are simplistic, but they illustrate that even well-designed policy can fail and objective assessments of well-crafted policy can also conclude failure. But even in failure, lessons can and should be learned. Just as doing poorly on a particular exam or paper should encourage reflection and study as to what went wrong (e.g. a thorough understanding of a topic was erroneously presumed), policy failure should result in learning and improvements in the future. The use of high occupancy vehicle (HOV) lanes could be argued to be an example of policy failure. These lanes were conceived as a way to provide cars with multiple people the advantage of their own dedicated highway lanes on particularly congested stretches of road. The intent with these lanes was threefold: (1) gasoline usage and emissions would decrease, (2) carpooling would increase, and (3) vehicle traffic would decrease. These goals have not been achieved, and according to some studies, the use of these lanes has actually decreased (Ganos 2011)! It is worth mentioning that different regions have had varying experiences with these lands, but widespread reductions in vehicle traffic, gasoline usage, and emissions have not been realized with this policy.

After policy evaluation, it might be determined that policies simply need to change, that they need to evolve. Policy change encompasses revisions to existing policies or other efforts to make them more successful. It is uncommon for policies to be undone or canceled due to the huge number of stakeholders that are involved in the creation and maintenance of those policies (more on these actors in subsequent chapters).

FLAWS OF THE STAGES MODEL AND ALTERNATIVE POLICY MODELS

Many pages have been spent discussing the process of policymaking in an effort to organize the seemingly chaotic nature of making policy. In addition, we have to look at different policy theories or policy models beyond the stages model to help us make sense of the messy nature of the process. At this juncture, we likely ended up someplace far different than you were expecting when we began our look at the policymaking process. As in many areas of study, you might have imagined the process would be nice, neat, and easy to understand. After only this brief review of the process, you are likely to conclude that policymaking is messy and, seemingly, without much order. Now we are going to add to that frustration. The policy process that we have detailed is arguably the most common model for policymaking, but it is far from perfect; therefore, we need to consider the flaws associated with this model (cf. deLeon 1999).

The six-step policymaking process we have just covered is often referred to as the textbook approach or the stages model. These labels come from the model's ease of understanding and its, seemingly, orderly progression. However, these descriptors are also indicative of the model's flaws. First, this model assumes that policymaking happens in an orderly or linear way. Step one happens before step three, for example. The reality is, this may or may not be the case depending on the particular policy issue. For example, a policy solution may already be developing when a crisis happens, catapulting the issue onto the national agenda. Often in a crisis, there are already ideas or options to solve or even prevent that crisis in the first place that have been discussed prior. For example, prior to the Exxon Valdez oil spill, there were already recommendations and policy options about mandating double-hulls for oil tanker ships. Policy solutions are always being crafted, regardless of whether or not a problem is clearly identified and defined.

Second, the stages model does not take into account external forces that may impact policymaking at any step along the way. As we discussed earlier, policymaking does not happen in a vacuum—other forces and factors are likely to impact the success of a particular policy option—but where are those forces accounted for in this model? The simple answer is they are not beyond a consideration of how a policy idea comes to the agenda of government. The stages model isolates a particular policy issue so the broader policymaking context is neglected.

Third, little about this model is predictable. Just because agenda setting is occurring, this does not mean that the policy will move to policy formulation, and this model provides no indication of how long a policy may stay in one part of the process. Therefore, this model has little to no predictive capabilities. The stages model does not help us understand how long any of the stages of the model will take.

If there are so many flaws associated with it, you are probably wondering why we spent pages explaining this model to you? To begin, when we broach the subject of policymaking in the US, we have to start somewhere, and this model provides us with a good, concrete overview for individuals new to the policy process. In addition, this model affords us the ability to talk about key aspects of policymaking and gives us relevant vocabulary to build our understanding of the process.

Accordingly, this discussion demonstrates that there is not one clear model to follow when it comes to policymaking, and that is acceptable. In fact, that is part of what keeps the study of policymaking interesting. Numerous other policy models exist and are discussed in policy studies, but none more so than the stages model. The stages model, although far from perfect, achieves our introductory goals: first, it provides us some basics of policymaking and gives us a language to talk about the dimensions of the process and, second, it helps us understand the messy and unpredictable nature of the process.

In response to some of the shortcomings of the stages model, other policy models endeavor to represent more accurately the policymaking process. It is worth mentioning a couple of those models, particularly as they respond to the issues we have identified in the stages model. John Kingdon (2011), after studying policymaking in the health and transportation sectors, articulated the Multiple Streams Framework (MSF). This approach to policymaking demonstrates that it is not necessarily a neat, linear process and much happens simultaneously. There are three "streams" of activity that exist alongside one another: the politics stream, the problem stream, and the policy stream. Only when these three streams come together does policymaking happen.

While Kingdon's MSF responds to critiques of the stages model being too linear as compared with reality, the Advocacy Coalition Framework (ACF), developed by Paul Sabatier and Hank Jenkins-Smith (1993), strives to contend with complicated policy matters and accounting for the array of actors at multiple levels of government and the public sector who exert influence on the policy process in different ways and at different times of the process. The ACF also takes into account the external factors that might affect policymaking as well. Yet another policymaking theory is Punctuated Equilibrium that looks to explain policymaking in periods of relative stability, or "equilibria," and policymaking in times of instability, or "punctuations." Frank Baumgartner and Bryan Jones (1993) seek to explain how policy is often made incrementally but, on occasion, can be made dramatically during times of crises. These three models of policymaking—in addition to many other policy theories—endeavor to represent policymaking in the real world and overcome the shortcomings of the stages model. In the end, though, all of the models are imperfect, yet they do help advance our understanding of the messy nature of policymaking in the US.

ATTRIBUTES OF THE POLICYMAKING SYSTEM

The final section of this chapter discusses various attributes of the policymaking system that complicate the work of policymakers and challenge observers and students of the policymaking process. Some of these attributes are structural and products of our constitutional system while other attributes are a result of the evolution of our system and the nature of politics today.

Power Distribution and Fragmentation

From our founding as a nation, Americans have never liked to see power consolidated in any one aspect of government as we have always been skeptical of too much power in one place. As a result, we have a federalist organizational scheme to our government which contributes to the fragmentation inherent in our policymaking system. Also contributing to the distribution and fragmentation of power is our system of checks and balances. Federalism, fragmentation, and checks and balances have significant effects on the policymaking process in any policy arena and especially environmental policy.

The federal system of government employed in the US is a critical structural element of our government. Federalism is a system of government in which there is a national level of government with various subnational governmental units. Several other countries besides the US employ this sort of system, including Germany and India, but it is far from a common system. Here, we have a national government (often referred to as the federal government), we have 50 state governments, and we have more than 89,000 local units of government (based on the last Census Bureau Census of Governments), which include counties, towns, and school districts (US Census Bureau 2012).[2] Simply put, a federal system of government has a lot of different governmental units that have to be coordinated and may have to work collaboratively to accomplish the work of government. The effects of this factor are particularly apparent in environmental policy when you think about the fact that most major environmental laws were passed at the national level and then contain provisions for the involvement of the US EPA along with the relevant state agencies. For instance, consider the Clean Air Act. Congress passed this law, as discussed in the last chapter, then dictated to the US EPA to figure out the specifics, and then told the 50 states to implement the law. Part of the provisions of this law, along with many others, is that the federal government establishes the minimum standards or requirements for states to enforce. States can—and sometimes do—go beyond those requirements. Indeed, California is again taking the lead in the nation—with the Biden restoring legal authority to the state that had been rescinded under the Trump administration—by enacting new

---

[2] In case you are curious, Illinois has the most local government units, coming in at almost 7,000 units and Hawaii has the fewest with 21 (US Census 2012).

pollution limits on the tailpipes of buses, vans, tractor trailers, and other heavy-duty delivery vehicles, and these limits reflect the first changes in such standards since 2001 (Davenport 2022). And we saw with the chapter's opening story about the mayors who are trying to address climate change at the local level. These structural realities tie into fragmentation.

Several structural factors in the American government and society serve to influence how policy is made. First among these factors is the notion of checks and balances. In an effort to ensure that the three branches of government—the legislative, the executive, and the judicial—would stay in balance with one another, the founders put forth a variety of ways in which one branch of government can exercise control over the other branches. James Madison, in *Federalist 51*, spoke of a need to ensure that ambition must counteract ambition. Thus, these checks thwart the ability of one branch to dominate another. For instance, Congress checks executive power by approving the appointments a president makes to executive agencies and by overriding a presidential veto. The Congress checks judicial power by confirming federal judicial appointments, making the laws that may be considered by the courts, and being a key part of the process to amending the Constitution. The executive branch can veto laws passed by the Congress and is responsible for implementing the laws the legislature passes. In addition, the executive branch selects the members of the federal courts (with Senate confirmation). The courts are responsible for determining the constitutionality of laws made and the actions of the executive branch. These checks serve to complicate the policy process in that their considerations of the other branches of government and their probable actions could slow or stymie action. For example, much political wrangling over a piece of environmental legislation may come about because of what the White House may or may not do in response to a particular law, or Congress may decide that with the threat of a presidential veto, the already tepid support for a piece of environmental policy is not worth the trouble.

Fragmentation encompasses the separation of powers among the branches of government. In a way, our discussion of checks and balances and federalism feed into this additional influence on policymaking. In our system of government, three branches of government (and not just at the national level) play a role in policymaking. The legislative branch makes laws, the executive implements and enforces them, and the judicial interprets them. And this power distribution is mimicked at the state level too.

There are lots of government entities around the country, and, in addition to those units, there are many non-profit organizations that work with government entities or even on behalf of government to accomplish environmental policy goals. Accordingly, there are thousands and thousands of organizations working on environmental issues. Sometimes these organizations and their people work well and in coordination with others, but sometimes the work can be in tension with the efforts of others.

As a nation, we contend with fragmentation because of our federal system of government and our fears over too much power being consolidated within one branch of government or one entity, so we inevitably end up with lots of different governmental entities all involved in the same thing, including environmental issues. Fragmentation is not just the number of governmental units, and non-profits, either; it also includes the mechanisms within organizations for dealing with environmental issues. For instance, many different congressional committees, as we saw earlier, are involved in environmental issues, so there can be overlapping jurisdiction and guidance. Decentralization in the public sector ends up complicating matters.

The resulting fragmentation can have upsides and it can have downsides. On the one hand, fragmentation ensures that there are many people and organizations who can put their time and resources into achieving goals and networks to enable effective implementation. Fragmentation also fosters lots of opportunities for all sorts of people and interests to impact the policymaking process and to provide input about a potential government action. After all, in a democracy, access is vital. On the other hand, fragmentation results in many instances where policy efforts are duplicated; the process invariably becomes slower, and there are many more people and agencies that have to be coordinated to accomplish a particular task.

Politics, the Public, and Systemic Tendencies

In addition to how power is allocated in our system, we also have to consider some other, less structural dimensions, including the role of the public, our reactive tendencies, and the propensity for incrementalism.

As we discussed in the last chapter and will discuss in subsequent chapters, the role of the public is instrumental in taking policy action. Recall that in a democratic governmental system, government operates at the behest of the people who consent to be governed. The people express through public opinion polls, through electing (and re-electing) particular politicians, and through participating in governmental processes what they do and do not want to happen. Public opinion is also critical in the agenda setting and policy formulation stages of the policymaking process. And while the public does not shy away from expressing its preferences, the public generally does not want to see changes happen too rapidly.

Incrementalism is the idea that government does not generally engage in massive, abrupt change. Instead, government takes small steps—incremental steps—and steadily pursues goals. The notion of incrementalism originates from Charles Lindblom in the late 1950s. Although rational decisionmaking[3] is sought after, Lindblom argued that the realities of decisionmaking in the public sphere do not lend themselves to a methodical, careful consideration of every option for as long as is needed. Instead, public decisionmakers endeavor to make decisions and pursue courses of action in the most rational manner feasible, but the broader political environment stymies efforts at rational decisionmaking; therefore, we end up "muddling through" (Lindblom 1959). Stated differently, incrementalism and the idea of "muddling through" is the notion that governmental action is slow and rarely dramatic or drastic because making decisions methodically and with all the time in the world to consider possible alternatives is not the environment government finds itself in. As a result, the decisions that government does make are usually incremental changes to the existing structures, and change happens over time. Sweeping changes in government are generally rare and this is true in the context of environmental policy.

Along these lines, our government generally behaves in a reactionary manner rather than a proactive one. Our government is set up to respond to identified problems and deal with matters only after they become an issue. Rarely do you see the government taking action to solve a problem that has not yet presented itself as a problem. Therefore, it may seem that government cannot anticipate problems and address issues before they happen; this is because our government is not set up to be proactive, in fact, a proactive government would largely be anathema to our broad ideals of the role of government.

---

[3] Again, rational decision making refers to methodical, orderly decision making that carefully considers every option and its likely consequences.

Finally, as articulated by James Madison in *Federalist 10*, we have a pluralist tradition in the US. Pluralism is the notion that competition among different groups ensures that no single group will dominate government because there will be so many different groups competing with each other. To accomplish anything in government, some of these competing groups will have to work together. It is important to keep these different attributes in mind as they are an important component of the broader context in which policymaking occurs in the US. These aspects of our system, along with a deeper understanding of the policymaking process, might leave you pessimistic about the ability of our government to address environmental challenges. While such a conclusion can be accurate in some instances, action can and does occur. It is also important to note that non-legislative pathways (such as agency or state and local action) are pursued and the multitude of actors involved in this policy arena ensure that these topics are not ignored.

Chapter Wrap-Up

The focus of this chapter has been the process of how policy is made, and more specifically, the six steps of the process: (1) problem identification and definition, (2) agenda setting, (3) policy formulation, (4) policy legitimation, (5) policy implementation, and (6) policy evaluation. Although this process appears to be simple and logical, we discovered that the process is far from simple. Moreover, our look at this process might leave us amazed that any policy makes it through the process to become law and achieve its goals. Although the policy model helps us understand the messy process, we found that the model is far from a perfect depiction of the process; nevertheless, the model helps us organize conversation around policymaking and provides us a much-needed vocabulary to study and discuss policy.

Much of the messiness of the process has to do with structural and societal influences in policymaking. And this messiness reflects the complexity of these policy issues and the reality that rarely, if ever, is there a "perfect" solution to the problem. As a result, it is easy to view the process as debilitating and painfully slow. However, this process ensures that the policies that are passed have ample time for consideration by our elected leaders and multiple points at which the public can influence the process—conditions that are essential in a democracy. The speed of policymaking also reflects the consensus that is required. Our system of government relies on consensus, but achieving it can be slow and have implications for policy implementation.

The next two chapters will more fully investigate the individuals involved in the policy process, but, here, we can already identify numerous career paths that you can pursue related to the making of public policy. More specifically, possible career paths include working with an elected government official, in an environmental agency, for a group that lobbies for environmental policy, or in a research institution that studies environmental issues.

Case Study: Single-Use Plastics

For the case study in this chapter, we focus on the worldwide problem of single-use plastics. These plastics products are intended to be used once and then discarded, including shopping bags, food packaging, water bottles, and utensils. Creating these plastics is resource intensive and disposing of them is problematic as they degrade slowly and breakdown into smaller microplastics that contaminate soil and water (Chen et al. 2021). This is a problem that is global in scale as these products that make our lives more convenient also harm the environment by finding their way to landfills, oceans, storm drains, and the rest of our environment. Even if you cannot see the plastic waste, odds are that the microplastics that are left behind from the waste are nearby (cf. Abbing 2019).

Members of the United Nations have expressed interest in an agreement to reduce plastic waste, much like the Paris Climate Agreement. In the US, the use of plastic is unregulated at the federal level; however, a number of states and localities have adopted their own regulations (Kim et al. 2021). These regulations vary from taxing plastic bags, banning the use of single-use plastic, and incentivizing reusable bags (Kim et al. 2021). With the Covid-19 pandemic, the use of single-use plastics dramatically increased. Surprisingly, plastics regulation does draw bipartisan interest and several bills have been introduced to Congress that drew support from both parties (Kim et al. 2021). Because of the scope of this issue, there have been challenges to determining the most effective way to regulate plastic use.

To help us better understand the stages model to policymaking, we apply the six steps of the process to single-use plastic policy in the state of Hawaii.

Problem identification and definition: Single-use plastics are causing environmental problems globally because of their tendency to end up in oceans, rivers, and soils. In the US, the Hawaiian Islands have seen the most direct impacts of plastic pollution in the Pacific Ocean, along the shorelines, and threatening their wildlife. With this issue so close to home, many people in this state agree that single-use plastics are a pressing issue that needs to be phased out to prevent further pollution (Russo 2019). Economic interests are concerned that increased plastic bans will drive up the cost of operations and consumer cost (Russo 2019). Hawaii relies heavily on imports and is already an expensive place to live (Russo 2019). Part of the problem is determining the most effective ways to regulate plastics while protecting Hawaiians from high economic burden.

Agenda setting: Plastic pollution policy in Hawaii was not difficult to get on the agenda because it is such a visual problem that impacts the health of the environment, wildlife, people, and economy. Hawaii has a goal of carbon neutrality by 2045 and importing plastic that creates pollution significantly goes against this (State of Hawaii 2019). In addition, legislators identified the cleanup of plastic debris as one of the highest costs to taxpayers (State of Hawaii 2019).

Policy formulation: In 2015, Hawaii became the first state to ban plastic bags at grocery stores. Since then, varying levels of government have introduced bills to expand the 2015 legislation for broader impact. In 2019, the state legislature attempted to pass an extensive policy that would have prohibited the purchasing and disbursement of different types of plastic, but the only portion of the policy that passed was to establish a "plastic source reduction working group" that would develop a plan to remove single-use plastic packaging from Hawaii's waste stream by June 2022. Following this decision, the City and County of Honolulu, which covers the most populated island of Oahu home to 70% of Hawaiian residents, introduced what was commonly known as Bill 40 or the Disposable Food Ware Ordinance (City and County of Honolulu

2022). The original form of the bill was amended to address environmentalists' and food industry concerns (Russo 2019). The final version prohibited all food vendors, businesses, and city authorized providers from disbursing polystyrene foam food ware, disposable plastic food and service ware, and plastic straws (Honolulu City Council 2019). There are a few exemptions throughout the bill to account for challenges and necessities required by certain populations.

Policy legitimation: The Honolulu City Council passed Bill 40 with the proposed amendments. The Environmental Services Department was in charge of enforcement of these policies and violators could be fined (Honolulu City Council 2019). To transition to these new requirements, they outlined phases of implementation to allow time for businesses to adjust.

Policy implementation: The Director of Environmental Services was tasked with developing the implementation, administration, and enforcement of Bill 40 (Honolulu City Council 2019). Phase 1 of the plan went into effect in April 2021, after a delay from the pandemic, and started by banning food vendors from providing disposable plastics and city facilities from providing foam food ware. The second phase began in January 2022 and applied to disposable plastics with all food vendors and businesses.

Policy evaluation: Since the second phase of this policy just went into effect as we write this book, it is challenging to evaluate if Bill 40 is working as intended. For the City and County of Honolulu, measuring the operational costs for businesses and costs to the consumer will be an indicator of sustainability of the policy.

Challenge Question for the Environmental Policy Classroom

The policy process is complex and slow and one of the benefits of these attributes is the ability for people to engage in the process; however, ability to access and influence the process is not equal. How might different communities and stakeholders be stymied in their efforts to help shape agendas, help craft policy solutions, and help pass policies? What characteristics of particular communities and stakeholders might advance or hinder their access? What could be done to improve access of all communities and stakeholders to the policymaking process?

SUGGESTED RESOURCES

Readings and Websites

Abbing, Michiel Roscam. *Plastic Soup: An Atlas of Ocean Pollution*. Washington, DC: Island Press, 2019.

Birkland, Thomas A. *An Introduction to the Policy Process: Theories, Concepts, and Models of Public Policy Making*. 5th edition. New York: Routledge, 2020.

Gibbs, Lois Marie. *Love Canal and the Birth of the Environmental Health Movement*. Washington, DC: Island Press, 2010.

Kingdon, John W. *Agendas, Alternatives and Public Policies*. 2nd edition. New York: Longman, 2011.

Rinfret, Sara R., Denise Scheberle, and Michelle C. Pautz. *Public Policy: A Concise Introduction*. 2nd edition. Thousand Oaks, CA: Sage/CQ Press, 2022.

Schneider, Anne L. and Helen Ingram. *Policy Design for Democracy*. Lawrence: University Press of Kansas, 1997.

Stone, Deborah. *Policy Paradox: The Art of Political Decision Making*. 3rd edition. New York: W. W. Norton & Company, 2012.

Films or Videos

Schoolhouse Rock: America Rock. 1973. American Broadcasting Company. DVD.
War on the EPA. 2017. PBS Frontline. DVD.

REFERENCES

Abbing, Michiel Roscam. *Plastic Soup: An Atlas of Ocean Pollution*. Washington, DC: Island Press, 2019.

Anderson, James E. *Public Policymaking*. 5th edition. Boston, MA: Houghton Mifflin, 2002.

Baumgartner, Frank R. and Bryan D. Jones. *Agendas and Instability in American Politics*. Chicago, IL: University of Chicago Press, 1993.

Birkland, Thomas A. *An Introduction to the Policy Process: Theories, Concepts, and Models of Public Policy Making*. 5th edition. New York: Routledge, 2020.

Borick, Christopher and Erick Lachapelle. "Politics, Prices, and Proof: American Public Opinion on Environmental Policy." In *Environmental Policy: New Directions for the Twenty-First Century*, edited by Norman J. Vig, Michael E. Kraft, and Barry G. Rabe, 63–84. Thousand Oaks, CA: Sage/CQ Press, 2022.

Chen, Y., A.K. Awasthi, F. Wei, Q. Tan, and J. Li. Single-Use Plastics: Production, Usage, Disposal, and Adverse Impacts. *Science of the Total Environment* 752 (2021). https://doi.org/10.1016/j.scitotenv.2020.141772.

City of Los Angeles. *Mayor Garcetti Launched Los Angeles' Green New Deal.* 2019. https://www.lamayor.org/sustainability.

Climate Mayors. *Demonstrating Leadership on Climate Change Through Meaningful Actions in Our Communities.* 2020. https://climatemayors.org.

Davenport, Coral. "California Returns as Climate Leader, with Help from the White House." *New York Times.* February 15, 2002. https://www.nytimes.com/2022/02/15/climate/california-waiver-emissions.html?referringSource=articleShare.

Davenport, Coral and Lisa Friedman. "'Build Back Better' Hit a Wall, but Climate Action Could Move Forward." *New York Times.* January 20, 2022. https://www.nytimes.com/2022/01/20/climate/build-back-better-climate-change.html.

deLeon, Peter. "The Stages Approach to the Policy Process: What Has It Done? Where Is It Going?" In *Theories of the Policy Process*, edited by Paul A. Sabatier. Boulder, CO: Westview Press, 1999.

Dillon, Liam. "California to Rely on 100% Clean Electricity by 2045 Under Bill Signed by Gov. Jerry Brown." *Los Angeles Times.* September 10. Available at http://www.latimes.com/politics/la-pol-ca-renewable-energy-law-signed-20180910-story.html.

Dunlap, Riley E. "An Enduring Concern." *Public Perspective*, no. 10–14 (September/October 2002): n.p.

Eggers, Dave. "Jerry Brown Is Too Busy with Climate Change to Worry About His Legacy." *Vanity Fair.* July 7, 2017. Available at https://www.vanityfair.com/news/2017/07/jerry-brown-climate-change.

Ganos, Todd. "Diamond Lanes: Another Failed Energy/Environmental Policy." *Forbes.* 2011. https://www.forbes.com/sites/toddganos/2011/07/18/diamond-lanes-another-failed-energy-environmental-policy/#7b1e731744c4.

Honolulu City Council. *Bill 40: Relating to Plastic.* 2019. https://www.honolulu.gov/rep/site/env/envref/envref_docs/Bill_40_Ordinance_19-030.pdf.

Ingram, Helen, Anne L. Schneider, and Peter deLeon. "Social Construction and Policy Design." In *In Theories of the Policy Process*, edited by Paul A. Sabatier, 93–128. Cambridge, MA: Westview Press, 2007.

Jones, Van. "Green-Collar Jobs: Energy Bill Includes Christmas Present for Nation's Job Seekers." *Huffington Post.* December 21, 2007. http://www.huffingtonpost.com/.

Kim, C., T. Ross, and K. Rohde. *Regulating Plastic Bags.* The Regulatory Review. December 18, 2021. https://www.theregreview.org/2021/12/18/saturday-seminar-regulating-plastic-bags/.

Kingdon, John W. *Agendas, Alternatives and Public Policies.* 2nd edition. New York: Longman, 2011.

Kraft, Michael E. and Scott R. Furlong. *Public Policy: Politics, Analysis and Alternatives.* 6th edition. Washington, DC: CQ Press, 2018.

Lindblom, Charles E. "The Science of 'Muddling Through.'" *Public Administration Review* 19, no. 2 (Spring 1959): 79–88.

Lowenthal, A.S. *H.R.5845—Break Free From Plastic Pollution Act of 2020.* Congress. February 11, 2020. https://www.congress.gov/bill/116th-congress/house-bill/5845.

Mann, Michael E. *The Hockey Stick and the Climate Wars: Dispatches From the Front Lines.* New York: Columbia University Press, 2012.

Nakamura, Robert T. "The Textbook Policy Process and Implementation Research." *Policy Studies Review* 7, no. 1 (Autumn 1987): 142–154.

NBC News Poll. 2021. Available at https://pollingreport.com/enviro.htm. Accessed 11 February 2022.

The Office of Governor Gretchen Whitmer. *Governor Whitmer Announces Bold Action to Protect Public Health and Create Clean Energy Jobs by Making Michigan Carbon-Neutral by 2050.* September 23, 2020. https://www.michigan.gov/whitmer/0,9309,7-387-90499-540289--,00.html.

Peters, B. Guy. *American Public Policy: Promise and Performance.* Washington, DC: CQ Press, 2004.

Powell, James Lawrence. *The Inquisition of Climate Science.* New York: Columbia University Press, 2011.

Pressman, J. L. and Aaron Wildavsky. *Implementation: How Great Expectations in Washington are Dashed in Oakland; Or, Why It's Amazing That Federal Programs Work at All.* Oakland: University of California Press, 1973.

Quinnipiac University Poll. Environment. November 11–15, 2021. Accessed 18 February 2022. https://pollingreport.com/biden_adm.htm.

Rinfret, Sara R., Denise Scheberle, and Michelle C. Pautz. *Public Policy: A Concise Introduction.* 2nd edition. Thousand Oaks, Calif.: Sage/CQ Press, 2023.

Russo, Carla H. "Hawaii's Most Populated Island Passes Sweeping Single-Use Plastic Ban." *Huff Post.* December 8, 2019. Accessed April 19, 2022. https://www.huffpost.com/entry/hawaii-strict-plastic-ban_n_5de95c48e4b0d50f32b0a655

Sabatier, Paul A. and Hank C. Jenkins-Smith. *Policy Change and Learning: An Advocacy Coalition Approach.* New York: Routledge, 1993.

Schneider, Anne L. and Helen Ingram. *Policy Design for Democracy.* Lawrence: University Press of Kansas, 1997.

State of Hawaii. *SB 522: A Bill for an Act Relating to Plastic.* 2019. https://www.capitol.hawaii.gov/session2019/bills/SB522_CD1_.htm.

Stone, Deborah. *Policy Paradox: The Art of Political Decision Making.* Revised edition. New York: W. W. Norton & Company, 2002.

———. *Policy Paradox: The Art of Political Decision Making.* 3rd edition. New York: W. W. Norton & Company, 2012.

Sussman, Glen, Byron W. Daynes, and Jonathan P. West. *American Politics and the Environment.* New York: Longman, 2002.

Udall, T.S. *3944—A Bill to Amend the Solid Waste Disposal Act.* Congress. June 11, 2020. https://www.congress.gov/bill/116th-congress/senate-bill/3944

US Census Bureau. "Census Bureau Reports There Are 89,004 Local Governments in the US." US Census Bureau. 2012. https://www.census.gov/newsroom/releases/archives/governments/cb12-161.html.

US Climate Alliance. *United States Climate Alliance FAQ.* May 6, 2019. https://www.usclimatealliance.org/alliance-principles.

US Congress. "Resource Conservation and Recovery Act." US Environmental Protection Agency. Update/modified/accessed date 2013. http://www.epa.gov/agriculture/lrca.html.

US EPA. "Superfund: National Priorities List." 2018. Available at https://www.epa.gov/superfund/superfund-national-priorities-list-npl. Accessed 27 April 2018.

Whitaker, Bill. "The Governor Who's Castigating the President on Climate Change." CBS News. December 10, 2017. Available at https://www.cbsnews.com/news/the-governor-whos-castigating-the-president-on-climate-change/.

WWF, the Ellen MacArthur Foundation and BCG. *The Business Case for a UN Treaty on Plastic Pollution.* 2020. https://f.hubspotusercontent20.net/hubfs/4783129/Plastics/UN%20treaty%20plastic%20poll%20report%20a4_single_pages_v15-web-prerelease-3mb.pdf.

CHAPTER 4

Official Actors in the Policy Process

Introductory Story: Gina McCarthy, The First White House National Climate Change Advisor

The US—along with the rest of the planet—has experienced severe weather fluctuations due to climate change.. These weather patterns have caused colder and warmer days, resulting in melting polar ice caps, rising sea levels, and increasing summer forest fires in the western US. There has also been growing concern over the human health impacts of climate change due to air pollution, wildfire smoke, and extreme weather events (CDC 2021). To address such concerns, President Biden opened the Office of Climate Change and Health Equity in 2021. He selected Gina McCarthy to serve as the first-ever White House National Climate Change Advisor (Friedman 2021) due to her interdisciplinary background and expertise in public health and policy.

Gina McCarthy grew up in a working-class family in Boston, Massachusetts, obtaining undergraduate and graduate degrees in social anthropology, environmental health engineering, planning, and policy. Her training across the social and natural sciences shaped her commitment to public health and protecting the environment. To date, she has built a career advocating for as the environmental advisor for five Massachusetts governors and was the President and CEO of the Natural Resource Defense Council (Davenport 2021). She also served as President Obama's

---

S. R. Rinfret and M. C. Pautz, *US Environmental Policy in Action*, https://doi.org/10.1007/978-3-031-17503-9_4

Assistant Administrator of the EPA's Office of Air and Radiation and then later appointed as the 13th Administrator of the EPA (EPA 2021). In her EPA roles, she helped to create the Clean Power Plan Rule, which drafted regulations to reduce carbon pollution from power plants and expand the capacity for clean energy (EPA 2017).

As Biden's first-ever National Climate Change Advisor, McCarthy was able to set the tone for this newly created office to lead the nation in reducing carbon emissions. Most importantly, the following chapter outlines how individuals like McCarthy serve an instrumental role in using their expertise to work with institutional actors to make environmental policy in the US.

The Official Actors

This chapter explains how official actors within our three branches of the federal government (Congress, the President, and the US Supreme Court) impact US environmental policymaking. The US Constitution states in Article I that Congress is the lawmaking body, in Article II the President serves as the executive, and in Article III the courts resolve legal disputes. Although the official actors (elected officials, the president, and federal judges and Supreme Court justices) are important to our understanding of how environmental policy is made, we often forget about the significant amount of work the bureaucracy undertakes. Put differently, this chapter demonstrates that the bureaucracy also needs to be included in discussions about environmental policymaking because career civil servants, like Gina McCarthy, who work for the bureaucracy, are tasked by Congress with implementation of the major environmental laws. Accordingly, the intent of this chapter is to understand how the official, institutional policy actors play an essential role in US environmental policymaking.

We begin the chapter with an overview of how Congress has shifted from creating environmental legislation to gridlock. Second, we examine presidential State of the Union addresses from Presidents Nixon through Biden to determine their impact on environmental policy. Then, we shift our focus to the federal bureaucracy by defining it and exploring how agencies, such as the United States Environmental Protection Agency (USEPA) and the United States Fish and Wildlife Service (USFWS), affect environmental policy. Lastly, we conclude the chapter with a discussion about the federal courts in the US, with a particular focus on the US Supreme Court and the impact of some 2022 rulings.

In this chapter, a few themes will emerge. First, institutional actors in the US will continue to shape environmental policymaking well into the future; however, the role of those institutional actors varies. For instance, there are growing concerns that Congress is so entrenched in political debates that legislative action might never occur, and it is too early to tell if the 2022 elections could help to address environmental problems from public pressures for change. We also note that gridlock is not new and it will continue to ebb and flow. We argue that we must pay attention to how policies can be made within the US bureaucracy, as a result. Second, we contend that presidential State of the Union addresses serve as a guidepost for a president's platform to inform Congress on policy priorities for the environment. Specifically, in Article II, Section 3 of the US Constitution, the President must inform Congress "from time to time" information about the state of our union. The chapter concludes by questioning the US Supreme Court's role in determining the outcome of court cases defined by science.

Congress: The Making of Policy

In US Government and Politics 101 courses, we are taught how a bill becomes a law, with many professors remarking that it is complicated. To briefly review the process (see also the discussion in Chapter 3), a member of Congress sponsors a bill, and then, a bill is introduced and assigned to a committee. Within a committee, members of Congress (US House or US Senate) analyze the bill and make revisions. The committee decides whether to approve or reject the bill. If approved, the bill is debated on the floor of the House of Representatives or the US Senate. Then, the bill is voted on. If agreed upon by the majority of both the House of Representatives and the US Senate, it is sent to the president's desk to be considered and signed into law.

The aforementioned description of how a bill becomes a law, however, does not truly capture the messy nature of policymaking. According to Rosenbaum (2013), "Congress is still largely an institution of fragmented powers and divided geographical loyalties" (87). We do not intend to rehash the linear *Schoolhouse Rocks* version of the stages of lawmaking because this is not how it generally occurs. Instead, we need to remember that environmental legislation is often crisis inspired and reactionary, not proactive (Rosenbaum 2019). Michael Kraft (2017) articulates six elements that explain this congressional gridlock: (1) divergent policy perspectives of political parties; (2) separation of powers; (3) difficulties of environmental issues; (4) deficient public support; (5) role of interest groups; and (6) lack of political leadership. We briefly explain each in turn.

The divergence, or political polarization, between the dominant political parties, Republicans and Democrats, has grown over time. According to Kraft (2011), "On average they have differed nearly 25 points on a 100-point scale, and the differences grew wider during the 1980s and 1990s" (129). This growing polarization between the two parties exists in the environmental policy arena because politicians have strong viewpoints when it comes to issues such as climate change because these seemingly discrete environmental issues reach far beyond the environmental arena to include farm subsidies and even thornier questions about taxation of carbon (c.f. Rabe 2010).

The realities of constitutionally mandated separation of powers further complicate matters. For example, when politicians are confronted with issues of species protection or toxic chemicals, members of both parties of Congress and the president all have to agree on a policy. For example, it has not been since 2009 when the House of Representatives secured the necessary 219 votes out of 435 needed for climate change legislation, but the US Senate did not adopt the legislation (Rabe 2010). The lack of acceptance for climate change policy can be explained by Kraft's sixth criterion—political leadership. The Speaker of the House and Senate majority leader, regardless of what party they are from, must forge consensus between members of their own party and the opposition party. If this is not achievable, then the creation of legislation will fail.

Inextricably linked to political leadership is the support of various public interest groups. Since elected officials want to get re-elected, it can be difficult for them to justify policy decisions to protect the environment that may increase costs for their constituents when domestic issues (e.g., the economy and healthcare) are a pressing concern for the American public. In addition, linked to a congressional member's re-election quest is the financial support of interest groups. Although Congress supported the environment during the 1970s, its attention has shifted elsewhere, namely, to today's economy, social unrest, and a global pandemic. This is not to say that Congress will not shift back to environmental legislation.

Therefore, we continue our conversation about the complexities of environmental policy with a relic of the not too distant past with our chapter's case study about climate change. We focus on one of the most essential stages of lawmaking in the US—the congressional committee.

Case Study: Understanding the Wonky Role of the Select Committee

Before jumping into our case study, it is important to begin with the historical context of congressional committees. Congress has used the committee system to structure its operations since the beginning of the Republic (Aldrich and Rohde 2009). Typically, congressional legislation travels through the common process where a member of Congress introduces a bill, it is referred to a committee, the committee reports out a bill, the bill goes up for a vote in both houses of Congress, and is signed by the president (Lipinski 2009). However, few bills ever make it out of committee, let alone are passed by Congress. This is due, in part, to the power of committee chairs, historically, in determining what bills are reported out of committee (Aldrich and Rohde 2009). Committee chairpersons are typically selected through a seniority system, with little incentive to act upon party leadership policy goals (Aldrich and Rohde 2009). Furthermore, Lipinski (2009) notes that some committees may be more enthusiastic about a particular piece of legislation than others; therefore, the committee in which the legislation is referred may determine whether the legislation becomes law.

After 1975, committee chairpersons from both parties began to see their power erode due to changes that stripped power from chairs and generally shifted it toward party leadership (Aldrich and Rohde 2009; Evans and Grandy 2009). Party leaders have, since, exerted greater power over the committee system by influencing the language of bills in committee, bypassing committees altogether, controlling the floor agenda, and, often, more unorthodox lawmaking (Aldrich and Rohde 2009; Sinclair 2007). *Although our case may seem dated, it serves a purpose. This case illustrates as a key moment in our environmental policy history—it is the last time Congress considered climate policy.*

Throughout 2006, Speaker of the House, Nancy Pelosi (D-CA), created the select committee on Energy Independence and Global Warming to find a solution to address climate change and coordinate the actions of several committees to produce legislation on this issue (Lipinski 2009; Smallen 2007). Here, we evaluate the role of this select committee and its relevance in the legislative process. During the 110th Congress, Speaker Pelosi selected Representative Edward Markey (D-Massachusetts), a strong advocate for the environment as chair of the select committee on Energy Independence and Global Warming. She also appointed the remaining eight Democratic members, whereas former Republican Minority Leader John Boehner (R-Ohio) appointed the six Republican members (Cleaver 2007; Kriz 2007b; Pelosi 2007). Representative Markey and Chief Counsel David Moulton suggested that the premise of the committee was to provide the best political climate in the House of Representatives to produce climate change legislation (Kriz 2007a, b).

Representative Markey argued that the goal of the committee was to promote the need for a bill on climate change and advocate for its passage in the 110th Congress (Kriz 2007a). The committee held 50 hearings investigating issues driving climate change; the first hearing held by the committee was entitled *Geopolitical Implications of Rising Oil Dependence and Global Warming* (Select Committee 2007). Representative Markey called the inaugural hearing to illustrate the connection between energy consumption and climate change and to illustrate the need for swift action (Select Committee 2007). This hearing, along with others such as the *Dangerous Global Warming*, *Green Collar Jobs*, and *Voluntary Carbon Offsets*, represented the first congressional hearings ever held discussing these issues specifically (Select Committee 2008; Sensenbrenner 2009).

During the term, the House passed two major pieces of energy legislation that dealt with both energy dependence and climate change. The legislation included the Energy Independence and Security Act (EISA) of 2007 and the Energy Improvement and Extension Act (EIEA) of 2008 as a part of the Emergency Economic Stabilization Act of 2008 (Select Committee 2008).

First, the EISA contained several main provisions, including an increased fuel economy standard, a renewable fuel standard, energy-efficient appliance standards, a green jobs training program, and accelerated research and development for renewable energy. The development of this bill took the better part of a year, with President George W. Bush signing it into law in December 2007. Prior to its passage in the Senate and confirmation in the House, the select committee held hearings discussing several aspects of the final bill. These included hearings regarding the development of a green jobs program, the economic impacts of high energy prices, the future of biofuels, pathways to higher energy efficiency standards, and the overall impacts of climate change on the economy (Select Committee 2009). The final version of the EISA included policy proposals that in some way addressed many of the points brought up in these hearings, with legislative language addressing the new corporate average fuel economy (CAFE) standard for cars and trucks, renewable fuel standards, and green job training programs (Select Committee 2009).

Throughout the next year, House leadership worked on developing another piece of legislation to deal with a host of issues that ultimately were not a part of the final EISA. This included developing a response to the need for increased investments in renewable energy technologies, hybrid vehicles, smart grid technology, and biofuels. Again, the Select Committee held hearings regarding virtually all of these policy topics throughout the 110th Congress (Select Committee 2009). Ultimately, within H.R. 1424, the Emergency Economic Stabilization Act of 2008, Congress included the language of the previous Energy Improvement and Extension Act (H.R. 1424–110th Congress 2008). This act incorporated an extensive set of tax credits to increase the development and implementation of renewable electricity, carbon capture and sequestration research, biofuel production, and smart grid investments (Select Committee 2008; H.R. 6049–110th Congress 2008).

Finally, by the end of the 110th Congress, the select committee produced a report that illustrated the efforts of the committee and the 110th Congress to develop legislation to address the policy area of energy and climate change. Within this report, the committee included a set of recommendations for the following congressional session to pick up where this committee had left off. The committee recommended that the next Congress enact a cap and invest program for greenhouse gases (GHGs), boost efficiency of the power sector and residential buildings, expand renewable energy development, foster green job development, and transform the US transportation system (Select Committee 2008).

After Democratic majorities took control of both the legislative and executive branches of government, it appeared that the time was ripe for the development of a national response to climate change under the 111th Congress (Klyza and Sousa 2008). This is, in part, affirmed by the vote of the Democratic Caucus to remove Representative John Dingell (D-Michigan) as the chair of the Energy and Commerce Committee, in favor of Representative Henry Waxman (D-California). Waxman suggested that he would move more aggressively to produce a host of legislation, including comprehensive climate change legislation (Broder 2007). Moreover, Speaker Pelosi reauthorized the Select Committee to continue its work during the 111th Congress to produce feasible energy and climate change legislation (Sensenbrenner 2009).

Due to the severity of the economic recession inherited by the 111th Congress, both chambers moved quickly to spur economic growth and to avoid a catastrophic economic failure. Within the American Recovery and Reinvestment Act (also referred to as the Stimulus or Recovery Act) legislation, Congress included more than $80 billion to promote clean energy and energy efficiency, with investments directed toward weatherization and retrofitting of residential homes and federal buildings, energy efficiency and renewable energy research, renewable energy loan guarantees, state and local energy efficiency, smart grid development, smart appliances, and public transit improvements (Brost 2009). However, the stimulus bill did not address the primary recommendation from the Select Committee that encouraged Congress to develop a cap-and-trade program for carbon emissions (Select Committee 2008). As such, during the 111th Congress, the select committee began to focus its hearings toward the negative effects of climate change and the measures in which the US can mitigate these impacts

(Select Committee 2010). Many of these hearings revolved around a discussion that the science behind climate change was valuable, and that the technologies available should be used to address the issues driving climate change, illustrating the need for a cap-and-trade approach (Select Committee 2010).

As a result, the House passed the landmark legislation H.R. 2454: American Clean Energy and Security Act of 2009 that introduced a cap-and-trade program to reduce carbon dioxide and other GHG emissions. After the passage of this momentous legislation, a companion bill was never brought for a vote in the Senate due to partisan disagreement (Rabe 2010). Nevertheless, the select committee continued to hold hearings discussing the importance of energy security, renewable energy development, and climate change throughout the remainder of the 111th Congress (Select Committee 2010). However, after the Republican victories in the 2010 elections, the new majority dissolved the select committee and it now remains a moment in history or the one attempt by members of Congress to address climate policy (Steinhauer 2010).

With the absence of the select committee focused on climate policy in the 112th, 113th, 114th, and 115th Congress, the overall number of hearings discussing climate change as a national policy issue precipitously dropped, thereby reducing the number of viable policy proposals. More notably, under the Trump presidency, climate policy was not a top priority. Despite the lack of federal climate policy, this did not prevent California from adopting their own statewide cap and trade in 2013 to lower its emissions levels. Additionally, it remains to be scene how the 2022 elections will impact the important role committees will play in negotiating the future of cliamte policy.

As we conclude our discussion of Congress, we would be remiss not to mention a few other facets of this key institution. The presumption is for Congress to be representative of its people. As a result, we ask our readers to investigate the demographic makeup of the 117th Congress. The concern is if a variety of backgrounds are not present in Congress, it could continue gridlock, not seeing new solutions for environmental policy.

THE PRESIDENT, THE ENVIRONMENT, AND SETTING THE AGENDA

Our understanding of the congressional role in environmental policy-making is important; however, we cannot overlook the powerful presence of the president. As the nation's chief executive, the president impacts environmental policymaking in a variety of ways. Starting with constitutionally expressed or enumerated powers, the president can propose or veto legislation, propose policy priorities to Congress, issue executive orders, and appoint federal judges and heads of agencies. These powers can affect environmental policy.

Appointment powers, for example, allow a president to shape an agency's actions by selecting its leadership. Although the US Senate must confirm these appointments, the president is influential and generally gets his chosen leaders. In Chapter 6, we discuss President Biden's presidential appointee to oversee the US EPA, Michael Regan. Additionally, presidents also shape the makeup of federal courts and most notably, the US Supreme Court. Again, the president nominates justices and the US Senate confirms such appointments. President Trump significantly changed the direction of the US Supreme Court with the selection of three justices. President Biden was able to nominate the first-ever Black woman to the US Supreme Court, Justice Kentaji Brown. The Trump-appointed justices to the Supreme Court have far-reaching policy implications for environmental policy, which we discuss later on in this chapter.

The president also has inherent or implied powers which they can infer power from the Constitution. This means that these powers are not explicitly stated, but are powers that the president has assumed over time. For instance, the president cannot declare war—Congress does—yet, Congress has not declared war since World War II. Therefore, "[i]n practice, presidential ability to capitalize on the presidency's political resources for environmental purposes has varied greatly. One explanation for this variability is the many ways in which circumstances can alter the political climate surrounding the White House—events such as economic recessions, changing congressional majorities, and the changes in the political 'seasons'" (Rosenbaum 2019, 82).

Dennis Soden's (1999) *The Environmental Presidency* develops the administrative presidency model to document that a president can impact environmental policy through their role as commander-in-chief (head of the military), chief diplomat (negotiations with other countries), chief executive (oversight of federal agencies), legislative leader (policy suggestions to Congress), and party leader (head of his party). For example, as commander-in-chief, the president can order the national guard to implement public policies, such as Presidents Kennedy and Johnson did during the desegregation of the South.

As the chief diplomat, a president can enter into discussions with countries abroad about climate change, just as President Biden did at the COP26 Summit in Glasgow, Scotland. As the legislative leader, the president can set the policymaking agenda, promoting to Congress and the American people his policy initiatives. For instance, President Obama in June 2013 addressed the nation with regard to climate change, stating, "The question is not whether we need to act. The question is whether we will have the courage to act before it's too late" (Graves 2013). By way of comparison, President Trump significantly rollbacked environmental regulations, focusing his efforts on opening oil and gas leases on federal lands. We argue that presidential approaches are significant because many large-scale pieces of environmental legislation have not been updated since the 1970s.

We focus our attention on presidential speeches, State of the Union addresses from Presidents Nixon through Biden to document how US presidents set the policymaking agenda for the environment. State of the Union addresses are important indicators of a president's environmental stances or preferences. For instance, Mathew Moen (1988) notes, "scholars long have understood that the clearest expression of an administration's priorities may be found in the president's annual State of the Union message" (775). Moreover, as Vig (2019) suggests, "the 'bully pulpit" can be used to rally public support behind these proposals, especially during the president's first year in office" (311). It is important to look past the rhetoric to determine if presidential speeches add up to a strong environmental record.

THE PRESIDENCY AND THE ENVIRONMENT

We often forget that the largest amount of environmental policy made in the US was enacted by a Republican President, Richard Nixon. Accordingly, the question becomes what role a president plays in promoting or shaping environmental policy. To address this question, we review environmental statements made at the beginning of their terms during

State of the Union addresses for each president, from Nixon through Biden. These statements are compared with each president's overall environmental record (i.e., legislation). The goal is to determine if an Environmental President has ever existed, and if so, who deserves the title.

Richard Nixon (1969–1974)

> The great question of the seventies is, shall we surrender to our surroundings, or shall we make our peace with nature and begin to make reparations for the damage we have done to our air, to our land, and to our water?
>
> (Nixon 1970)

President Nixon certainly used the most forceful language to promote environmental policy during his first State of the Union address, making it a cornerstone of his legislative agenda. In fact, Nixon (1970) called for "the most comprehensive and costly program in this field in America's history." Outside of promoting plans to clean up the air, Nixon also called for the development of wastewater treatment plants nationwide, new funding for parks, preserving open space, and for improvements in automotive fuel efficiency.

Despite the costs, Nixon argued that his environmental policies would actually help the economy by not abandoning growth but redirecting it. He suggested that "For example we should turn toward ending congestion and eliminating smog the same reservoir of inventive genius that created them in the first place" (Nixon 1970). He then called on Americans to "make some minimal demands on themselves" to leave the environment "a little cleaner, a little better, a little more pleasant for [themselves] and those around [them]" (Nixon 1970).

Riding the wave of his success, Nixon used the State of the Union address in his short-lived second term to promote a new energy policy for the US. He set the goal of being energy independent by 1980, arguing that the "US will not be dependent on any other country for the energy we need" (Nixon 1974). He proposed new funding for energy research and development and increased funding for mass transit to help achieve this goal. However, he was unable to push these policies through Congress because he later resigned amid the Watergate scandal.

Gerald Ford (1974–1977)

We depend on others for essential energy.

(Ford 1975)

President Ford built upon President Nixon's arguments to direct a new energy policy program for the US. However, his policies were far more focused on the exploration of fossil fuels and deregulation for the coal industry under the Clean Air Act (CAA) because he wanted the economy to improve. In fact, he argued that "voluntary conservation continues to be essential" in his first State of the Union address.

Much of his focus was on exploiting existing resources, especially oil, both on and offshore, calling for drilling at Elk Hills Naval Petroleum Reserve in California. Moreover, he promoted increased coal mining, submitting amendments for the CAA to "allow greater coal use without sacrificing clean air goals" (Ford 1975). In addition, he vetoed strip mining legislation passed by Congress because it was too stringent on coal. His vision for the future included "200 major nuclear power plants; 250 major new coal mines; 150 major coal-fired power plants; 30 major new [oil] refineries; 20 major new synthetic fuel plants; the drilling of many thousands of new oil wells; the insulation of 18 million homes; and the manufacturing and the sale of millions of new automobiles, trucks, and buses that use much less fuel" (Ford 1975).

Ultimately, Ford did see the opening of Elk Hills to drilling, and Congress did pass amendments to the CAA, but not until after President Ford left office. He was unsuccessful in implementing the majority of his energy program and, in particular, his energy tax due to lack of congressional support.

Jimmy Carter (1977–1981)

Almost 5 years after the oil embargo dramatized the problem for us all, we still do not have a national energy program.

(Carter 1977)

President Carter used the State of the Union address to emphasize energy priorities. He suggested that it was time for the US to develop a national energy program to "use more of those fuels which are plentiful and more permanent" (Carter 1978). Carter was a major proponent of incorporating cleaner alternative energies such as solar and wind into the US energy mix. These priorities culminated with his effort to install a solar water-heating system on top of the White House (it was then removed by President Reagan, but President Obama had it re-installed in August 2013 and they remain today).

Legislatively, he oversaw the passage of the National Energy Act of 1978, which provided new tax incentives for renewable energy development, and required utilities to purchase this energy when it came online. Thus, President Carter was successful in pushing national energy policy forward. However, he was largely unsuccessful in achieving his other environmental initiatives, which did not even make it into his speech.

Ronald Reagan (1981–1989)

Now, we have no intention of dismantling the regulatory agencies, especially those necessary to protect environment and assure the public health and safety.

(Reagan 1981)

President Reagan paid lip service to protecting the environment in his first State of the Union address; however, his record speaks to the exact opposite. More specifically, much of the environmental regulation and the agencies responsible for that regulation were subject to substantial budget and staffing cuts to achieve his objective of smaller government. He did openly suggest in his first address that he wanted to repeal the Department of Energy's synthetic fuel program, which illustrates just one of the many efforts of the Reagan administration to walk back efforts to move toward promoting cleaner burning fuels and stronger environmental policies. Many of the gains made by Carter with regard to energy policy were undone, unfunded, or ignored by the Reagan administration.

However, by Reagan's second term, he was somewhat humbled by the backlash from the American public to his environmental rollback efforts. In his first address to Congress after becoming re-elected in 1984, he called for the "reauthorization and expanded funding for the Superfund program to continue cleaning up hazardous waste sites which threaten human health and the environment" (Reagan 1985). He did oversee the efforts of Congress to reauthorize this law in 1986; however, he attempted to veto efforts to amend and strengthen the Clean Water Act (CWA).

George H. W. Bush (1989–1993)

If we're to protect our future, we need a new attitude about the environment.

(H. W. Bush 1989)

President George H. W. Bush distanced himself from his predecessor's environmental record and used his first address to the nation as a platform to outline his environmental agenda. President Bush argued for a new and stronger CAA. In addition, he called for a program to reduce sulfur dioxide emissions, which cause acid rain, and advocated for more funding for national parks. Moreover, he placed a strong emphasis on enforcing laws against toxic waste dumping and he proposed doubling the government's efforts to clean up existing sites, arguing that America needs to "clean up the old mess that's left behind" (Bush 1989).

President Bush, however, took his own approach to pushing for new environmental policy by suggesting that the US needed to "respect the environment." In effect, this messaging indicates that economic development can occur as long as it takes the environment into account. In this fashion, he opened the door for further energy development, particularly in the Arctic National Wildlife Refuge (ANWR), arguing that it can and should be done, but in a way that respects the environment.

President Bush was quite successful in implementing his environmental agenda, particularly by steering the passage of the 1990 Clean Air Act Amendments, which provided regulation of more than 100 chemicals, and a cap-and-trade program to reduce sulfur dioxide emissions. He nearly achieved his directive to drill in the ANWR, but that effectively died after the Exxon Valdez Oil spill in 1989. Despite this setback, he did sign into law the Energy Policy Act of 1992, which promoted more energy development of both traditional fossil fuels and clean energy sources.

Bill Clinton (1993–2001)

> I recommend that we adopt a Btu tax on the heat content of energy as
> the best way to provide us with revenue to lower the deficit because it
> also combats pollution, promotes energy efficiency, promotes the indepen-
> dence, economically, of this country as well as helping to reduce the debt
> … and it is environmentally responsible
>
> (Clinton 1993)

President Clinton used his first State of the Union to call for a new
direction for the US, focusing on the economy, healthcare reform, and
reducing the debt. In this speech, Clinton showcased his top environmental policy proposal—a tax on energy sources based on the sources'
heat content in order to achieve deficit reductions. However, much like
most of the initiatives in Clinton's first term, this policy fell flat after the
1996 Republican takeover of the House of Representatives. As a result,
Clinton's efforts to achieve new environmental policy in his first term
were lackluster. However, he did manage to oversee the passage of the
Safe Drinking Water Act Amendments of 1996 that set new goals for
drinking water and methods to achieve those goals.

In comparison, Clinton's address in 1997 called for a much stronger
role for environmental policy for his second term. Clinton used this
speech to highlight the fact that his administration had already cleaned
up 250 toxic waste sites, with a goal to clean up 500 more. In order to
achieve this goal, he called for Congress to approve his proposal to "make
big polluters live by a simple rule: if you pollute our environment, you
should pay to clean it up." Moreover, Clinton argued for the revitalization
of America's rivers, suggesting his River Heritage program would prove
"once again that we can grow the economy as we protect the environment" (Clinton 1997). Finally, Clinton used this speech to highlight his
global initiatives and, in particular, his efforts to reduce GHG emissions
at the international level through the Kyoto Protocol.

President Clinton's speech was far more focused on promoting environmental protection but, again, Clinton's legislative initiatives largely
failed. His effort to make polluters pay, in effect reauthorizing the Superfund program, died in Congress. In addition, he never brought up
for ratification in the Senate the Kyoto Protocol on Climate Change,
requiring mandatory GHG emission cuts because it would have certainly
failed. Thus, despite Clinton's rhetoric shift, his success rate remained

low, especially for his major initiatives. However, one important or essential aspect of Clinton's administration was the work of his Vice President, Al Gore, who was, and still is, an ardent supporter of combatting climate change.

George W. Bush (2001–2009)

Excellent schools, quality health care, a secure retirement, a cleaner environment, a stronger defense, these are all important needs, and we fund them.

(G. W. Bush 2001)

In his first term address, President George W. Bush called for accelerated cleanup of toxic waste sites, full funding for the Land and Water Conservation Fund, and more funding for the upkeep of national parks. The cornerstone of his environmental and energy goals revolved around his call for a renewed push on energy policy, suggesting that "we can produce more energy at home while protecting our environment" through promoting "alternative energy sources and conservation" (Bush 2001).

Despite President Bush's commitments to the environment as noted in his speech, his policy record follows a similar track to that of President Reagan. Ultimately, the taskforce he created to develop the new energy program, headed by Vice President Dick Cheney, was focused almost exclusively on fossil fuel energy. Because of the backlash he received from Congress and the public regarding the secrecy of the proceedings and the lack of significant alternative energy components, Bush was unable to get his energy policy enacted in his first term.

After his second inauguration, President Bush again promoted the need for a new national energy policy. However, in this speech, he focused on the national security concerns of imported energy, urging "Congress to pass legislation that makes America more secure and less dependent on foreign energy" (Bush 2005). More specifically, Bush promoted the plan developed by Vice President Cheney in his first term, suggesting that his plan "encourages conservation, alternative sources, a modernized electricity grid, and more production here at home" (Bush 2005). In addition, he used this speech to promote his Clear Skies initiative that would "cut power plant pollution and improve the health of our citizens" (Bush 2005).

President Bush was successful regarding energy policy because Congress passed the Energy Policy Act of 2005. However, Bush's Clear Skies initiative was disregarded, with some observers suggesting the term Clear Skies was exactly the opposite of what would occur if the policy was enacted (the idea was to reduce power plant emissions, namely sulfur dioxide).

Barack Obama (2009–2017)

But to truly transform our economy, protect our security, and save our planet from the ravages of climate change, we need to ultimately make clean, renewable energy the profitable kind of energy.

(Obama 2009)

President Barack Obama, suggested "our survival depends on finding new sources of energy," has, perhaps, been the most vocal proponent of clean energy sources since President Carter (Obama 2009). Similar to Clinton, Obama argued that investing in energy would spur economic growth while also reducing the deficit. Moreover, Obama touted the passage of the American Recovery and Reinvestment Act (ARRA) of 2009, which provided funding for this energy research as well as funding for "constructing wind turbines and solar panels... [that] will double this nation's supply of renewable energy in the next three years" (Obama 2009). Moreover, Obama argued for a new market-based cap-and-trade program to reduce carbon pollution to drive "the production of more renewable energy in America" (Obama 2009). Finally, to meet this new demand for renewable energy, he called for investments of "fifteen billion dollars a year to develop technologies like wind power and solar power, advanced biofuels, clean coal, and more fuel-efficient cars and trucks built right here in America" (Obama 2009).

Obama's push for ARRA did have the intended effect of doubling renewable energy production in the US. In addition, the bill included funding for research and development for renewable energy, and he was successful in increasing renewable energy investment, although this success waned after the Republican takeover of the House in 2010. The most notable failure in Obama's presidency was his call for a cap-and-trade program for carbon emissions. Although it passed the Democrat-controlled House, it failed in the Senate.

After Obama's second inauguration, he renewed his call for action to reduce the effects of climate change, noting GHG emissions had slightly decreased, but "we must do more to combat climate change" (Obama 2013). Again, he called for a cap-and-trade program from Congress. He suggested, "We can make meaningful progress on this issue while driving strong economic growth" (Obama 2013). However, in this State of the Union address, he suggested that if Congress did not act on climate change, he would do so by issuing executive orders and using the EPA to create rules based upon existing legislation. As noted in Chapter 2, Obama kept this promise and instructed the EPA to promulgate a rule on GHG emissions from coal burning power plants, as noted previously under the direction of Gina McCarthy. This rule was not finalized by the end of his term and, therefore, targeted by President Trump's rollback efforts.

Donald J. Trump (2016–2021)

We have ended the war on American energy, and we have ended the war on beautiful clean coal. We are now very proudly an exporter of energy to the world.

(Trump 2018)

To the casual observer, President Trump's approaches to the environment are similar to that of his Republican colleague, Senator Ron Johnson. In his first few years in office, he touted efforts to undo climate policy efforts from the Obama administration. For example, he withdrew the US from the Paris Climate Accord, approved the permit to construct the controversial Keystone XL Pipeline, rolled back greenhouse gas emissions regulations, and opened the Arctic National Wildlife Refuge area for oil and gas drilling. Unlike many other world leaders, Trump suggests climate change is a hoax or simply, a con job by the scientific experts (Biesecker 2016)

President Trump's approach to environmental policy was in direct contrast to public opinion. In 2018, Pew Research Center reported that 67% of Americans believed that the US is not doing enough to reduce the impacts of climate change (Funk 2018). Typically, presidents promote public policy reflective of the populace. This was not been the case for President Trump. Instead, during his presidency, he rolled back more than 100 environmental regulations (Gushenko 2018).

Joseph Biden (2021–)

> The climate crisis is not our fight alone, either. It's a global fight. The US accounts, as all of you know, for less than 15% of carbon emissions. The rest of the world accounts for 85%. That's why I kept my commitment to rejoin the Paris Climate Agreement on my first day in office.
>
> (Biden 2021)

President Biden began his presidency with significant goals to address global climate change. In April 2021, he convened the "Leaders' Summit on the Climate," with heads of government agencies, international business organizations, and indigenous communities to tackle the climate crisis. The goal of this meeting was to find cross-sector strategies to cut greenhouse gas emissions by 50–52% at 2005 levels. In addition, he signed into law the Inflation Reduction Act. Climate policy, investment in renewable energy, and combatting environmental injustices are at the forefront of this legislation. As we write this text, it remains to be seen how large of an impact this legislation will have on environmental policy more broadly.

This brief review of some of the language used to tackle environmental concerns by presidents in their State of the Union addresses and then comparing it with their environmental initiatives provides an indication of where presidents stand regarding their commitment to the environment. With this examination, we can better define if any president truly is the environmental president.

IMPLICATIONS OF PRESIDENTIAL STATE OF THE UNION ADDRESSES

To evaluate if any president is a standout environmental leader, we examine some additional factors. First, each president attempts to justify environmental actions with regard to the economy. President Nixon (1970) argued that environmental policy would drive the economy; Presidents Clinton (1997) and Obama (2013) used similar arguments.

President George H. Bush (1989) suggested that the economy could grow, while also "respecting the environment." Finally, President George W. Bush (2005) used a less forceful argument, but did suggest that the economy required new affordable and environmentally responsible energy sources (i.e., exploration of oil and gas resources on public lands in the West).

Another prominent method used by presidents to promote their environmental goals is through a moral argument. Nixon (1970) was the first to do this, suggesting "those who make massive demands on society... need to make some minimal demands on themselves." President George H. Bush (1989) promoted his environmental initiatives as a necessary effort to "care for our future." Similarly, Clinton (1997) argued that his environmental policies were necessary "so that our children grow up next to parks, not poison." Obama (2013) used similar arguments, commenting on the need to implement his environmental policies "for the sake of our children and our future."

Several presidents have used a national security argument to promote environmental and energy goals. Presidents Nixon (1974), Ford (1975), and Carter (1978) all argued for a new energy program to reduce the impact of foreign sources of fuel, with Nixon indicating, "our growing dependence upon foreign sources has been adding to our vulnerability for years and years." President George H. Bush (1989) argued more succinctly that "our national security depends on it" and his policy would make America "more secure." And, Obama (2013) touted initiatives that have reduced oil imports to levels not seen in the past 20 years.

Presidents have used the State of the Union address to highlight emerging environmental issues and methods to solve them. Climate change has become an increasingly debated topic, and recent Democratic Presidents Clinton, Obama, and Biden made [combatting, not combating] combating climate change an important component of their legislative agendas. Clinton (1997) argued that the US should take a leadership position to meet challenges to the global environment. Obama suggested that embracing climate change policy could spur economic growth (Obama 2009, 2013). President Biden, early in his presidential tenure stated before world leaders in November 2021, "Will we seize the enormous opportunity before us? Or will we condemn future generations to suffer?" (Remarks by President Biden 2021). However, Clinton was unsuccessful in his legislative efforts and it remains to be seen what accomplishments President Biden will achieve. How future presidents frame this policy issue and other emerging concerns may help explain whether they achieve legislative success. Ultimately, both Presidents Nixon and George H. Bush had the strongest environmental records based upon initiatives proposed and subsequently carried out.

However, Ford's imported oil tax, Carter's support of renewable energy (i.e., solar panels on the White House), Clinton's Btu tax, and Obama's carbon cap-and-trade program could have had significant impacts on improving the condition of the environment, putting each of them on the same level as Nixon and George H. Bush, if such legislation had been successful in Congress. In this regard, with Nixon's Watergate scandal, it would seem that President George H. Bush may have been a more viable candidate than Clinton to assume the title of environmental president.

George H. Bush and Nixon, however, had something that Obama and Clinton did not, and that is a public consensus for the need to act on environmental issues. In the 1970s, public opinion was so much in favor of environmental policy that Nixon suggested that "restoring nature to its natural state is a cause beyond party and beyond factions. It has become a common cause of all the people of this country." Thus, many of the environmental policies advocated by Nixon were supported by both political parties, making their passage easier. President George H. Bush's policies found a similarly warm reception in Congress. This reception has dramatically changed since the Clinton administration. Environmental protection has become a highly partisan issue, with the poster child being climate change policy, and disregard for scientific evidence by many members of Congress, such as Senator Ron Johnson (R-WI). Moreover, the US has had a divided government during much of the past 25 years, making environmental policy increasingly difficult to produce. Finally, the American public has not been as vocal about environmental protection as it has been in the past; indeed, public opinion polls show that citizens are more concerned with the economy and other policy issues rather than the environment (see Chapters 2 and 3).

During the 2008 presidential campaign, however, one topic for discussion was climate change policy. As a result, former Senator John McCain and then-Senator Obama made climate change policy an important component of their election campaign platforms. However, with the onset of the Great Recession, this support waned and so too was the will of policymakers to act. Public opinion may be the most important component in determining presidential priorities and the best measure to determine presidential priorities, provided they can break through the legislative gridlock in this policy area.

Although presidents assert their legislative priorities in their State of the Union addresses, Presidents Obama, Trump, and Biden opted for the use of the administrative state. If presidents can no longer be successful in pushing environmental agendas through Congress, presidents can use their role as the chief executive to bypass congressional gridlock and use existing environmental laws to make policy in the federal bureaucracy (c.f. Klyza and Sousa 2013). Obama, Trump, and Biden are not the first presidents to take this approach. President Biden most recently issued an Executive Order stating that racial equity and serving marginalized communities are a priority. His goal is to diversify the workforce and offering more opportunities for individuals to use their expertise to shape policy like the environment. As our discussions of Congress and the presidency indicate, environmental policymaking is not an easy endeavor. We now turn to an important, yet overshadowed, piece of the environmental policymaking puzzle–the US bureaucracy.

THE ENVIRONMENTAL BUREAUCRACY

The argument consistently made throughout this book is that understanding the bureaucracy is essential for observers of American environmental policy. Chapter 2 provided a list of environmental policies created within the last several decades, and we cannot help but notice that not much is happening legislatively (c.f. Klyza and Sousa 2013). However, if we examine the *Federal Register* (website/portal—www.federalregister.gov for federal bureaucratic policymaking, which will be discussed further in Chapter 6), a great deal is happening as policymaking is occurring within the federal bureaucracy. The bureaucracy plays a significant role in environmental policy for the future. In Chapter 6, we will focus on how rulemaking is particularly important for environmental policy, but the focus in this section is on defining the bureaucracy and providing examples of what environmental agencies do.

We begin our discussion with perceptions and assumptions about the bureaucracy and its bureaucrats. For some, when we think about the bureaucracy, we think of red tape and inefficiency. When we think of a bureaucrat, what comes to mind is a lazy, incompetent, career civil servant. However, we argue otherwise. As Anthony Downs' *Inside Bureaucracy* (1964) reminds us:

It is ironic that the bureaucracy is still primarily a term of scorn, even though bureaus are among the most important institutions in every nation in the world. Not only do bureaus provide employment for a very significant fraction of the world's population, but also they make critical decisions which shape the economic, political, social, and even moral lives of nearly everyone on earth. (130)

The bureaucracy and a bureaucrat's role in society are much more than the common stereotypes.

There are a variety of ways scholars have defined "bureaucracy." According to William Niskanen (1971), "the original use of the term, I understand, referred to cloth covering the desk (bureau) of eighteenth-century French officials" (23). More recently, the bureaucracy, as defined by James Q. Wilson (1991), is "a complex and varied phenomenon, not a simple category or political epithet" (10). Armies, schools, and prisons, as Wilson (1991) notes, are all bureaucracies. Moreover, the seminal approach to define the bureaucracy originates from the work of Max Weber (1947). For Weber, the bureaucracy is synonymous for defining all large organizations. However, the underlying idea is that the bureaucracy was created by Congress to translate vague congressional statues and to implement the policies. It is the people within the bureaucracy, the bureaucrats, or civil servants—police officers, teachers, or environmental inspectors—who carry out legislation on a daily basis (Niskanen 1971). More succinctly, "The term bureaucrat will sometimes be used in the more general sense to define any full-time employee of a bureau" (23). Thus, the question becomes why Congress would delegate its power to allow bureaucrats to carry out public policy?

Delegation of Authority

As Table 4.1 suggests, there are a variety of federal agencies in the US created by Congress to carry out environmental policy. Each of the agencies listed in Table 4.1 receives its authority from Congress, which is known as delegation of authority—when Congress provides policymaking power to the executive branch (i.e., the bureaucracy or federal agencies). We discuss this in greater detail in Chapter 6, but a few details are worth noting here.

Table 4.1 Sample list of federal environmental agencies

- Bureau of Land Management (BLM)
- National Park Service (NPS)
- US Fish & Wildlife Service (USFWS)
- Environmental Protection Agency (EPA)
- US Geologic Service (USGS)
- Bureau of Safety & Environmental Enforcement (BSEE)
- Bureau of Ocean Energy Management (BSEE)
- Office of Surface Mining Reclamation & Enforcement (OSMRE)
- US Forest Service (USFS)

Delegation occurs because programs are necessary and no one (meaning Congress or the president) is willing to set specific guidelines. Congress may prefer delegation for a number of reasons. First, the bureaucracy has more expertise in these policy areas and more flexibility to make changes if necessary. Take the CAA for instance; with the 1990 amendments, the EPA had to carryout more than 300 rules to meet the requirements set forth by Congress. Second, Morris Fiorina (1981) argues that Congress delegates its authority in order to "shift the responsibility" of decisionmaking to the agencies; this way Congress can avoid the controversy and criticism associated with such policies by leaving open the possibility of blaming the bureaucracy.

One of the overriding questions about this delegation of authority is the role of accountability. Members of Congress are held accountable through elections by the people but members of the federal bureaucracy, or those individuals who work for an agency, are not elected, so accountability is less obvious and direct. Civil servants are selected for their positions based upon their expertise and hired through a merit process. For instance, a biologist may be hired by the US Forest Service to oversee forest management in the Coconino National Forest in Flagstaff, Arizona. Although expertise is important to carryout congressional statutes, members of elected institutions can influence agency policy and limit discretion through a variety of oversight techniques by Congress and the President. As Sara Rinfret and Scott Furlong (2012) note, "This dual political oversight demonstrates the interesting situation of an agency having multiple principals or, in other words, needing to respond to two different 'bosses.' On the one hand, Congress provides statutory and budget authority to the agencies; on the other hand, the president is the head of the executive branch and ultimately sits at the top of the bureaucratic hierarchy" (374).

To demonstrate the far-reaching impact that the federal bureaucracy has on environmental policymaking, we offer a brief examination of two environmental agencies—the EPA and USFWS. We focus on the EPA and the USFWS for a couple of reasons. First, the EPA is the largest environmental agency in the US and one of the oldest environmental protection agencies in the world. More specifically, the focus of the EPA is to protect "human health and the environment." In turn, we also offer an analysis of the USFWS—an agency designed to protect and restore our nation's plants and animals. This protection is done through the Endangered Species Act of 1973 (ESA), which is legislation crafted to protect species, and something that many countries do not have.

One of the Oldest Environmental Agencies in the World

The creation of the EPA dates back to the so-called environmental decade when people became more concerned with the nation's deteriorating air, water, and land resources. According to Dunlap and Mertig (1992), "In the terminology of public opinion analysts, environmental protection had become a consensual issue by 1970, as surveys found a majority of the public expressing pro-environmental opinions and typically only a small minority expressing anti-environment opinions" (93). With growing public sentiment for environmental protection, the US embarked on a dramatic outpouring of federal legislation to protect the environment, from the National Environmental Policy Act of 1969 to the Resource Conservation and Recovery Act of 1976 (see Chapter 2).

On December 2, 1970, President Nixon issued an Executive Order (an order by the president that carries the same weight as a congressional statute) to create the Environmental Protection Agency. With one pen stroke, the EPA became an agency with 5,000 employees from a variety of existing organizations: the National Air Pollution Control Administration; the Public Health Service Bureaus of solid waste, water hygiene, radiological hygiene, and pesticide research; the Federal Water Quality Administration; pesticide regulation for the Department of Agriculture; pesticide research programs from the Department of Interior; and radiation regulation from the Atomic Energy Commission. The EPA converted several agencies into one, creating an amalgam of existing programs and cultures without an overall mission or framework (Andrews 2006).

To transform the internal structure of the EPA, the first administrator, William Ruckelshaus, used an aggressive managerial approach. The creation of ten regional offices helped to enforce and carry out massive 1970s federal environmental initiatives—the CAA, CWA, Federal Environmental Pesticides and Control Act, Safe Drinking Water Act, Toxic Substances Control Act, Resource Conservation and Recovery Act, and the Comprehensive Environmental Response, Compensation, and Liability Act (CERCLA or the Superfund Act). But most important, as Jack Lewis (1985) stated, "The EPA has developed into the most competent agency in the federal government, and morale is still very high among our extremely talented and dedicated staff" (npn).

The EPA is dominated by its top-down bureaucratic organizational structure, with its sole purpose being environmental protection (Andrews 2020). More specifically, the organizational structure of the EPA contains an administrator who is appointed by the president and confirmed by the Senate. The headquarters are located in Washington, DC, and ten regional offices are located around the country. The primary duties of EPA offices are to regulate and protect air quality, water quality, hazardous waste, chemicals (i.e., pesticides), and, sometimes, the transportation of equipment.

Protecting Species for the Future

The origin of the USFWS dates back to the early nineteenth century when it was tasked with overseeing the nation's fish and wildlife supplies, respectively. The Commission of Fish and Fisheries studied the supply of coastal and lake fisheries, which later become the Bureau of Fisheries in the Department of Commerce. In 1905, the Bureau of Biological Survey in the Department of Agriculture was established, with the stated mission of studying birds and mammals in the US (Loomis 1993).

By 1939, as Richard Andrews (2020) notes, one of Franklin Roosevelt's New Deal policies was to consolidate these two agencies (the Bureau of Fisheries and the Bureau of Biological Survey) under one umbrella within the Department of Interior; this consolidation created the USFWS. According to Bird Loomis (1993), the primary responsibilities of USFWS are to manage migratory birds, develop hunting regulations, acquire/protect habitats, and enforce international treaties that protect migratory birds. To provide financial support for the agency, the first administrator of USFWS, Jay "Ding" Darling, used monies from the Duck Stamp Act of 1934 and the Pittman–Robertson Act of 1937 (licensing fees from hunting and taxes on sporting goods or ammunition) to create a funding source outside the annual federal budget. Beyond finding monetary support, a few of the USFWS' first acts included the establishment of a River Basin Study to prevent damage to fish and wildlife from water projects and improving the management of migratory waterfowl hunting. Then, in 1956, the Fish and Wildlife Act created two new bureaus: the Bureau of Commercial Fisheries and the Bureau of Sports Fisheries and Wildlife. The Bureau of Fisheries, in turn, became the National Marine Fisheries Service in 1970 and transferred its jurisdiction to the Department of Commerce (Andrews 2006).

The broadest sources of statutory authority for the USFWS are the Fish and Wildlife Act of 1956, the National Environmental Policy Act (NEPA) of 1969, and the Endangered Species Act of 1973. The Fish and Wildlife Act of 1956 is important because, as Loomis (1993) stated, "Under this act, the agency is instructed to take steps required for the protection, conservation, and advancement of fish and wildlife resources" (60). Then, in 1969, NEPA served as a formal vehicle for USFWS to analyze the impact of projects on all types of fish and wildlife through environmental assessments.

The other key directive for USFWS came in 1973 with the passage of the ESA to protect endangered or threatened plants and animals. Under the ESA, USFWS, along with the Department of Commerce, is responsible for carrying out this law through rulemaking processes. The language of the ESA directs USFWS to use only the best scientific data to list a species, develop a recovery plan, and designate critical habitats once a species goes through the rulemaking process and is listed as endangered or threatened. Thus, the sole mission of USFWS is to work with others to conserve, protect, and enhance fish, wildlife, plants and their habitats for the continuing benefit of the American people.

By way of comparison, the organizational structure is somewhat similar to that of the EPA. The director's office and the major program areas are located in Washington, DC. In addition to deputy staff, the USFWS has regional offices across the US too. Again, this is helpful in carrying out national policies such as the ESA and managing our nation's wildlife refuges.

In order to protect our nation's wildlife, air, and water, both agencies offer a wide range of expertise varying from science to policy. This is not a small task, and without these agencies, species such as the Salt Creek

Tiger Beetle in Nebraska would no longer exist, nor would some of the nation's Great Lakes be swimmable or drinkable.

Environmental Bureaucracies

In summary, the bureaucracy plays a definitive role in implementing environmental policy in the US. First, the bureaucracy was created to implement public policy in the US because members of Congress do not have the time or expertise to carry out the laws they pass. Thus, environmental agencies, including the EPA and the USFWS, fulfill an essential role in ensuring that landmark legislation such as the CAA or the ESA is carried out and implemented. This section on the bureaucracy provides a basic understanding about the federal bureaucracy so that we can explore the processes of bureaucratic decisionmaking in Chapter 6 and the role of the states in environmental protection in Chapter 7.

THE NINE—THE FINAL DECIDERS

Even if a policy is passed by Congress, promoted by the president, and implemented by the bureaucracy, we have not reached the end of the story. The Supreme Court can enter into decisionmaking and change the course of how environmental policy is implemented. We conclude this chapter explaining how the US Supreme Court has affected US environmental policy in the twenty-first century.

When we think about the US Supreme Court and its impact on environmental policy in the US, we frequently turn to *Chevron, USA v. Natural Resource Defense Council* (1984) or *Massachusetts v. Environmental Protection Agency* (2007). In the 2007 landmark decision, the Supreme Court ruled that carbon dioxide could be regulated by the EPA under the CAA. The Supreme Court noted that the EPA had to determine if carbon dioxide emissions were, indeed, a threat to human health and the environment, and if so, the agency needed to write regulations to curb these emissions under the CAA. In 2009, the EPA, for the first time, promulgated a rule (more in Chapter 6 about this process) to address GHG emissions. However, in June 2022, the US Supreme Court has determined in *West Virginia v. EPA* that the EPA cannot regulate carbon emissions in the 1970 Clean Air Act because Congress did not specifically authorize the EPA to do so. In this decision, the court applied the nondelegation doctrine which states the agencies, such as the EPA, cannot update and write new regulations unless Congress explicitly delegates them the authority. Although the implications of this case are still being investigated at the time of the writing, this decision appears to be a major curtailment of EPA's ability to protect the environment.

Nonetheless, it is important we consider the broader role that the US court system plays in environmental policy. To begin with a basic understanding of the US court system, we turn to Fig. 4.1. As Fig. 4.1 indicates, we have a dual court system in the US. For instance, there are three types of law in the US: public, criminal, and civil. Public law often deals with constitutional and administrative questions related to government actions. Criminal law regulates the conduct of individuals and civil law deals with disputes between individuals or organizations. Moreover, there are differences between federal and state courts. For instance, the entry point for all federal criminal cases (such as robbing a bank) or civil cases (disputes between states or individuals, such as divorce) is the US district court. If convicted at the US district court level, the accused have the right to appeal your case. If the appeal is heard, this would take place at the US Court of Appeals (13 total, 11 geographically located, and two specialty circuits for bankruptcy and patents). If again convicted, cases can be appealed to the US Supreme Court. However, keep in mind that, on average, the US Supreme Court hears about 70–80 cases per year, representing approximately 1–5% of all cases appealed to the court.

The state process is somewhat similar, with the entry point being the state trial court for civil, criminal, and public cases. If convicted, individuals can appeal their cases and, if granted, be heard at the state appellate level. The state supreme court, or the court of last resort, is where individuals can appeal cases from the state appellate level. In order for a state case to make it to the US Supreme Court (federal), the case must have reached the state court of last resort and ask a constitutional question (Ginsberg et al. 2013).

For our purposes here, we focus on the federal court system, and, specifically, how the US Supreme Court affects environmental decisions. The US Supreme Court includes nine justices who are appointed by the president and confirmed by the Senate. The justices can serve for life, providing "good behavior." The common assumption is that a Supreme Court justice decides a case from either the so-called perspective of activist or one who advocates constraint. More specifically, an activist justice views the law or the Constitution as a living document, with an interpretation that changes over time. In contrast, a justice who embraces judicial

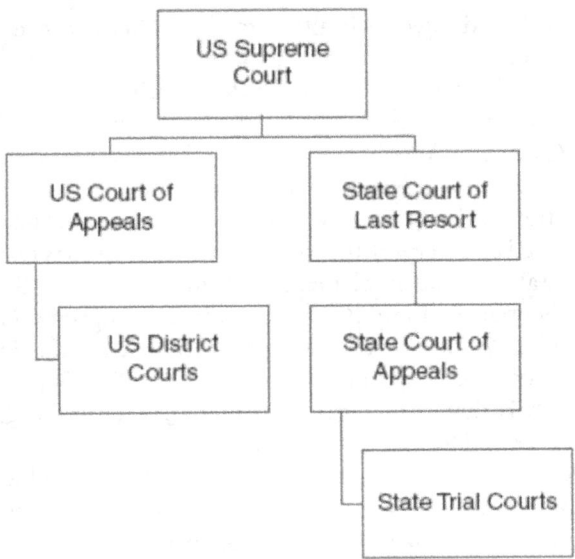

Fig. 4.1 US court system

constraint values the way in which the Constitution was written in 1787, and tries to stick to the original language and meaning of the framers (Ginsberg et al. 2013). In particular, one will be able to determine if a specific justice is pro- or anti-environment in using an activist or constraint approach. For instance, justices who use an activist approach can rule in favor of environmental protection, whereas judicial constraint could be viewed as anti-environmental.

Recognizing that these different interpretations of the Constitution are important, Rosemary O'Leary (2013) and Kimberly Smith (2022) explain a few ways the courts can shape environmental policy. For example, the courts determine who has the right to sue. If standing to sue is established, the second way that the courts can shape policy is by determining the ripeness of a case, or in other words, if a case is ready for review. Put differently, standing to sue means in order to file a lawsuit in court the individual must have to be directly affected by the legal dispute you are suing about. For instance, if the company that you work for caused health defects because of a chemical it was using, you could sue your employer because you suffered adverse health effects, whereas someone who was not affected directly could not sue.

Furthermore, the courts may have more of a direct impact on environmental policy when asked to consider how legislation drafted decades ago (e.g., 1970 Clean Air Act) has an impact on current conditions (Smith 2022). If a company decides to sue the government because the business believes that the CAA placed unwarranted economic burdens, then, the court would need to interpret the intent of the law. Courts can also supervise how federal agencies implement environmental laws (Smith 2022). We saw this happen in June 2022 when the US Supreme Court determined the US EPA cannot regulate greenhouse gas emissions because Congress did not give them the authority in the 1970 Clean Air Act.

One concern is that many environmental laws require a great deal of scientific expertise. The backgrounds of many Supreme Court justices originate from previous experiences as lawyers or lower-level judges rather than expertise in the natural sciences such as climatology or hydrology. The question becomes whether the legal backgrounds of justices are adequate to decipher highly technical scientific information. For example, in 2009, the Court had to determine if the US Navy's high-powered sonar off the California coast was endangering dolphins and whales (Savage 2008). Another example is the 2018 Supreme Court decision *Weyerhauser Company the United States Fish and Wildlife Service*. As we examine in Chapters 6 and 9, the USFWS has the authority to designate critical habitat for species. In this case, the court noted that the USFWS was using too broad of an interpretation of critical habitat for the endangered dusky gopher frog (Smith 2022). Arguably, the technical knowledge of the justices is important to recognize because, "A more recent study predicts that the courts will become an increasingly important pathway for revising policies since Congress has been legislatively gridlocked since 1990" (O'Leary 2013, 153). Table 4.2 examines seven recent cases that deal with environmental issues, allowing the reader to decide if an individual with a legal background has the best judgment to determine the outcome of scientifically driven environmental cases.

Courts and Environmental Policy

To understand the role that the Supreme Court has played in environmental issues during the last decade, we have put together a brief list of environmental cases for review (see Table 4.2). The seven cases represent

Table 4.2 Sample of US Supreme Court Environmental cases from 2000 to 2020

Year	Case	Decision
2000	*Palazzolo v. Rhode Island*	5 (Rehnquist, O'Connor, Scalia, Kennedy, Thomas)-4 (Stevens, Souter, Ginsburg, Breyer)
2003	*Alaska Department of Environmental Conservation v. EPA*	5 (Stevens, O'Connor, Souter, Ginsberg, Breyer)-4 (Rehnquist, Scalia, Kennedy, Thomas)
2006	*Environmental Defense v. Duke Energy Corp*	9 (Roberts, Stevens, Souter, Scalia, Kennedy, Thomas, Ginsburg, Breyer, Alito)-0
2009	*Burlington Northern v. United States*	8 (Roberts, Stevens, Scalia, Kennedy, Souter, Thomas, Breyer, Alito)-1 (Ginsburg)
2013	*American Trucking Associations v. City of Los Angeles*	9 (Roberts, Scalia, Kennedy, Thomas, Ginsburg, Breyer, Alito, Sotomayr, Kagan)-0
2015	*Michigan v. EPA*	5 (Scalia, Roberts, Kenney, Thomas, Alito) (Ginsburg, Breyer, Sotomayor, Kagan)-4
2020	*County of Maui v. Hawaii Wildlife Fund*	6 (Breyer, Roberts Ginsburg, Sotomayr, Kagan, Kavanaugh) -1 (Alito)

a 15-year time span. The goal is to understand the cases, the actors, and the decisions made by the court. We argue that having a better understanding of how Supreme Court justices determine environmental cases over time provides a benchmark for how future cases will be decided or if an environmental background is, indeed, needed.

Our first case for consideration, *Palazzolo v. Rhode Island,* resulted in a 5–4 decision by the US Supreme Court. The facts of the case surround a waterfront property in Rhode Island owned by Anthony Palazzolo. This parcel of land was brought into question by the Rhode Island Resources Management Council's Coastal Resources Management Program because Palazzolo's property is considered a salt marsh. Palazzolo tried to develop this land, which is restricted due to its salt marsh designation; thus, he argued that Rhode Island's wetlands regulations were a violation of the Fifth Amendment's takings clause because he was deprived compensation. In the 5–4 decision, the court ruled that Palazzolo was allowed to challenge the state's wetland regulations under the Fifth Amendment.

The second case, *Alaska Department of Environmental Conservation v. EPA*, examines the "best available technology" clause within the Clean Air Act. Simply put, under the CAA, federal and state agencies are required to implement the law. In this case, state agencies try to prevent air pollution by requiring that companies use the best technology available to limit pollution. However, in 1998, a mining company in Alaska, Teck Cominco Alaska, requested from the Alaska Department of Environmental Conservation (ADEC) a permit to build an additional generator at one of its mining facilities. The US EPA stated that the ADEC did not issue a permit with the best available technology in mind. Thus, the ADEC responded that the US EPA did not have the right to interfere with its decisionmaking when issuing permits. In a 5–4 decision, the Supreme Court determined that the US EPA does have the authority to tell the ADEC what constitutes best available technology.

Our third, fourth, fifth, and six cases for consideration, *Environmental Defense v. Duke Energy Corp, Burlington Northern v. United States*, and *American Trucking Associations v. City of Los Angeles*, represent more decisive decisions by the court. *Environmental Defense v. Duke Energy Corp* centers on the definition of the CAA's Prevention of Significant Deterioration Program (PSD), in which the US EPA requires that power companies must apply for permits to modify emissions increases. In this case, the Environmental Defense Fund, along with other environmental groups and the US EPA, sued Duke Energy Corporation because it did not obtain PSD permits for 29 improvements for power plants. The Duke Energy Corporation argument was that the EPA modification process was unclear; thus, they did not need to comply. Nevertheless, the Supreme Court ruled otherwise in a unanimous decision, noting that EPA requirements needed to be followed.

In *Burlington Northern v. United States*, there was one dissention in the court, Justice Ruth Bader Ginsburg, but this is explainable. In this case, the EPA and California's Department of Toxic Substances Control (DTSC) sued responsible parties (Burlington Northern Railroad, Santa Fe Railway, and Shell Oil Company) for the cleanup of contaminated land. However, the US Court of Appeals noted that the companies were only responsible for a portion of the cleanup due to statutory language specified within CERCLA. The major issue at hand is who is the arranger for the contamination of the site in question. The Court argued that the companies did not intend or arrange for their products to be disposed of in an improper fashion. Justice Ginsburg dissented from her colleagues because she argued that Shell Oil should qualify as the arranger of the contaminated site.

Our fifth case, also a unanimous decision by the Court, centers on *American Trucking Associations v. City of Los Angeles*. The focus in this case is the expansion of cargo terminals in the port of Los Angeles. The driving concern was that this expansion would increase air pollution and, as a result, the Board of Harbor Commissioners Clean Air Action Plan, reduce emissions in the port area, focusing on drayage trucks. The American Trucking Association (ATA) sued the City of Los Angeles for this plan. In the end, the court unanimously decided that a city government cannot limit federally licensed motor carriers from a port.

The sixth case for consideration, *Michigan v. EPA*, resulted in a 5–4 decision. The Clean Air Act is the focus here and costs for electric utility steam generating units (EGUs). Simply put, in writing the majority opinion, Scalia argued that the EPA must examine costs when determining a regulation and, in this case, power plants. This determination should be made prior to the EPA's decision that a regulation is appropriate and necessary.

In our seventh and final case review, *County of Maui v. Hawaii Wildlife Fund* addressed concerns surrounding the Clean Water Act (CWA). The issue in the case examined whether effluent from a sewage treatment plant that is injected into groundwater wells but ultimately migrates into navigable waters (in County of Maui, the Pacific Ocean) constitutes a "discharge" of pollutants requiring a permit from federal or state authorities under the CWA (Frank 2020). According to Frank (2020), "The environmental organization bringing the suit contended that a permit is always required under such circumstances to avoid a major circumvention of CWA regulatory jurisdiction. The County of Maui (supported by the Trump administration), on the other hand, argued that the intervening injection of treated sewage effluent into groundwater aquifers necessarily and fully removes such discharges from CWA permit jurisdiction" (npn). Some argue this was a significant case, upholding decisionmaking authority for agencies.

Although many of these cases did not make national news like *Massachusetts v. EPA*, our purpose is to demonstrate that environmental cases are far-reaching, often dealing with highly technical information. We must continue to evaluate how the justices make their decisions from the perspectives of judicial activism or constraint. The 2000 and 2003 cases each had four dissenters. In comparing the two cases, Justices

William Rehnquist, Antonin Scalia, Clarence Thomas, and Anthony Kennedy agreed with the person or organization bringing suit against environmental perspectives, applying a strict constructionist approach. In comparison, Souter, Breyer, and Ginsburg were known for their activist perspective, viewing the Constitution as a living document. However, Stevens and O'Connor varied in their approaches in the 2000 and 2003 decisions, indicating that the approach used depended on the case.

We need to recognize that the composition of the US Supreme Court has changed drastically in the last 20 years. Under the Trump administration, three new justices were appointed—Neil Gorsuch (2017), Brett Kavanaugh (2017), and Amy Coney Barrett (2020)—tilting the court's balance. With the retirement of Justice Breyer in 2022, President Biden had the opportunity to appoint a new justice, Kentaji Jackson Brown. Some speculate that the changing landscape of the court does have significant future of environmental policy, especially with decisions made in June 2022 such as *West Virginia v. EPA* (Howe 2021). According to Epps (2021), "The supreme court, with its life-tenured justices second-guessing the work of the political branches, is only one feature of a system that makes bold governmental action difficult" (npn). In short, the courts do play a role in environmental policymaking—after all, they do have the final say. Therefore, it is important to take the time to pay attention to the cases reviewed by the Court, why they are decided, and whether justices do have the expertise to understand highly technical cases.

CHAPTER WRAP-UP

This Chapter offers a tour of the institutional actors—Congress, the President, the bureaucracy, and the Courts—that shape environmental policy in the US. When it comes to Congress and environmental policy, not much has changed since the 1990s in terms of reauthorizing the major laws of the 1970s. For some, this is alarming, but explainable, because of gridlock.

Although scholars spend a significant amount of time deciphering the presidential impact on environmental policy, we contend that it is often rhetoric. In examining brief excerpts from State of the Union addresses from Presidents Nixon through Biden, the conclusion can be made that presidents can make statements in their inaugural addresses to Congress, but legislative action still remains stalled. However, as we have learned, Presidents such as Nixon and George H. Bush were successful in turning words into action and others like Clinton, Obama, and Biden use the administrative state as an alternative pathway.

In our examination of the bureaucracy, or the fourth branch of government, we argue that understanding it is essential to understand the future of environmental policy. In this section of the chapter, we offer a snapshot of the mission and structure of two environmental agencies, the EPA and the USFWS. Expertise is important in both of these agencies in order to effectively carry out congressional law. In our final section of the chapter, our discussion about the US Supreme Court offers a brief review of cases over the course of 20 years. This examination of cases explains the actors involved, how justices make decisions, and whether the court has the background to determine the outcomes of highly technical environmental cases. Expertise matters and we should be paying attention because June 2022 hallmarks a significant change in direction and will impact environmental policy in the future.

As students of public policy, we can participate and inform institutional policymaking (e.g., protests, registering to vote, internships, submitting public comments), which we cover throughout this book. We also close with encouragement to examine how institutional actors engage us in their decisionmaking. Specifically, who has the power to decide and do these decisions promote the well-being of groups that do not have a seat at the table.

Challenge Question for the Environmental Policy Classroom

Review President Biden's Executive Order of Diversity, Equity, and Inclusion for the federal workforce: https://www.whitehouse.gov/briefing-room/presidential-actions/2021/06/25/executive-order-on-diversity-equity-inclusion-and-accessibility-in-the-federal-workforce/. Upon review, how will his approach to Diversity, Equity, and Inclusion (DEI) impact the future of environmental policymaking?

SUGGESTED RESOURCES

Readings and Websites

Durant, Robert and Daniel Fiorino. *Environmental Governance Reconsidered.* MIT Press.

Graham, Ottis. 2015. *Presidents and American Environment.* University of Kansas Press.

Huffington Post. 2013. Retrieved from: http://www.huffingtonpost.com/2013/02/17/forward-on-climate-rally_n_2702575.html.

Lipsky, Michael. 1983. *Street Level Bureaucracy: Dilemmas of the Individual in Public Service.* Russell Sage Foundation Publications.

Films or Videos

Netflix. Don't Look Up. 2021.

PBS. Frontline. Climate Change: Ade on the Frontline. Retrieved from: https://www.wpbstv.org/climate-change-ade-on-the-frontline-preview/.

PBS. Frontline. Climate of Doubt. 2012. Retrieved from: http://www.pbs.org/wgbh/pages/frontline/climate-of-doubt/.

PBS. Decoding the Weather Machine. 2018. Retrieved from: www.pbs.org/wnet/peril-and-promise/2018/04/watch-now-decoding-weather-machine/.

REFERENCES

Alaska Department of Environmental Conservation v. EPA.

Aldrich, John H. and David W. Rohde. "Congressional Committees in a Continuing Partisan Era." In *Congress Reconsidered*, edited by Lawerence C. Dodd and Bruce I Oppenheimer. 9th edition, 337–360. Washington, DC: Sage Publication, 2009.

American Trucking Associations v. City of Los Angeles.

Andrews, Richard N. L. *Managing the Environment, Managing Ourselves: A History of American Environmental Policy.* 2nd edition. New Haven, CT: Yale University Press, 2006.

Biesecker, Michael. 2016. Retrieved from: https://apnews.com/9f61f5a9f8b242bc8eb12a9b36449b54.

Boxer, Barbara. *Boxer Op-Ed: Creating Jobs and Putting America Back in Control of Our Energy Future.* 2009. Retrieved from: http://www.boxer.senate.gov/en/press/opeds/100709.cfm.

Brost, K. *Summary: American Recovery and Reinvestment Conference Agreement* [Press Release]. February 13, 2009. Retrieved from Committee on

Appropriations website: http://democrats.appropriations.house.gov/images/stories/pdf/PressSummary02-13-09.pdf.

Burlington Northern v. United States.

Bush, George, W. "Address Before a Joint Session of the Congress on Administration Goals." In *Speech.* Washington, DC: The American Presidency Project. February 27, 2001. http://www.presidency.ucsb.edu/ws/index.php?pid=29643.

———. "Address Before a Joint Session of the Congress on the State of the Union." In *Speech.* Washington, DC: The American Presidency Project. February 2, 2005. http://www.presidency.ucsb.edu/ws/index.php?pid=58746.

Bush, Herbert Walker. "Address on Administration Goals Before a Joint Session of Congress." In *Speech.* Washington, DC: The American Presidency Project. February 9, 1989. http://www.presidency.ucsb.edu/ws/index.php?pid=16660.

Carter, Jimmy. "The State of the Union Address Delivered Before a Joint Session of The Congress." In *Speech.* Washington, DC: The American Presidency. 1978. http://www.presidency.ucsb.edu/ws/index.php?pid=30856.

CBS Los Angeles. *Wildfires Spark Debate on Climate Change Among Calif. Politicians.* 2013. Retrieved from: http://losangeles.cbslocal.com/2013/08/08/sen-boxer-severe-fireseason-in-southland-evidence-of-climate-change/.

CDC. "Climate Effects on Health." March 2, 2021. https://www.cdc.gov/climateandhealth/effects/default.htm.

Cleaver, E. *Press Release: Speaker Pelosi Announces the Appointment of Congressman Cleaver to New Select Committee On Global Warming.* March 9, 2007. Retrieved from House of Representative website at: http://www.house.gov/list/press/mo05_cleaver/SelectCommitteeEstablishment.html.

Clinton, William J. "Address Before a Joint Session of Congress on Goals." In *Speech.* Washington, DC: The American Presidency Project. February 17, 1993. http://www.presidency.ucsb.edu/ws/index.php?pid=47232.

———. "Address Before a Joint Session of the Congress on the State of the Union." In *Speech.* Washington, DC: The American Presidency Project. February 4, 1997. http://www.presidency.ucsb.edu/ws/index.php?pid=53358.

CNN Politics. 2009. "Obama Signs Sweeping Public Land Reform Legislation." Accessed February 10, 2014. http://www.cnn.com/2009/POLITICS/03/30/obama.lands.bill.

Cochrane, Emily. "Senate Passes $1 Trillion Infrastructure Bill, Handing Biden a Bipartisan Win." *New York Times.* August 10, 2021. https://www.nytimes.com/2021/08/10/us/politics/infrastructure-bill-passes.html.

Cohen, R. Power Surge. In *National Journal* (20–25) (2007). Retrieved from Academic Search Complete.

Cox, Raymond, Susan Buck, and Betty Morgan. *Public Administration Theory and Practice*. London: Longman-Pearson, 2011.

Davenport, Coral. "Biden Is Pushing a Climate Agenda, Gina McCarthy Has To Make It Stick." *New York Times*. April 20, 2021. https://www.nytimes.com/2021/04/20/climate/gina-mccarthy-climate.html?searchResultPosition=4.

Davenport, Coral and Lisa Friedman. "Bipartisan Infrastructure Deal Omits Big Climate Measures." *New York Times*. November 6, 2021. https://www.nytimes.com/2021/06/24/climate/biden-climate-infrastructure.html?searchResultPosition=15.

Downs, Anthony. *Inside Bureaucracy*. Long Grove, IL: Waveland Press, 1964.

Eco Talks Archives. "Senator Barbara Boxer Gives a Damn." Accessed January 21, 2014. http://blogsofbainbridge.typepad.com/ecotalkblog/2007/04/senator_barbara.html.

Environmental Defense v. Duke Energy Corp.

EPA. "FACT SHEET: Overview of the Clean Power Plan." May 9, 2017. https://archive.epa.gov/epa/cleanpowerplan/fact-sheet-overview-clean-power-plan.html.

———. "EPA's Administrators." September 16, 2021. https://www.epa.gov/history/epas-administrators.

Epps, Daniel. "How the US Supreme Court Could be a Threat to Climate Change." November 3, 2021. https://www.theguardian.com/commentisfree/2021/nov/03/how-the-us-supreme-court-could-be-a-threat-to-climate-action-in-the-us.

Evans, C. Lawrence and Claire E. Grandy. "The Whip Systems of Congress." In *Congress Reconsidered*, edited by B. I. Oppenheimer, and L. C. Dodd. 9th edition, 189–215. Washington, DC: CQ Press, 2009.

Ford, Gerald. "Address Before a Joint Session of the Congress Reporting on the State of the Union." Washington, DC: The American Presidency Project. January 15, 1975. http://www.presidency.ucsb.edu/ws/index.php?pid=4938.

Fiorina, Morris P. *Retrospective voting in American national elections*. Yale University Press, 1981.

Frank, Richard. "The US Supreme Court's Most Important 2020 Environmental Law Decisions." December 29, 2020. https://legal-planet.org/2020/12/29/the-u-s-supreme-courts-most-important-2020-environmental-law-decisions/.

Friedman, Lisa. "Biden Opens New Federal Office for Climate Change, Health and Equity." *New York Times*. November 2, 2021. https://www.nytimes.com/2021/08/30/climate/biden-climate-change-health-equity.html?searchResultPosition=1.

Funk. Accessed October 19, 2018. http://www.pewinternet.org/2018/05/14/majorities-see-government-efforts-to-protect-the-environment-as-insuffici
ent/.
Ginsberg, B., Theodore J. Lowi, Margaret Weir, and Caroline Tolbert. *We the People: An Introduction to American Politics*. New York, NY: W. W. Norton and Company, 2013.
Graves, Lucia. "Obama Climate Change Policy." *Huffington Post*. 2013. Accessed January 21, 2014. http://www.huffingtonpost.com/2013/06/25/obama-cli
mate-change-2013_n_3497151.html.
Gushenko. Accessed October 19, 2018. https://news.nationalgeographic.com/2017/03/how-trump-is-changing-science-environment/?user.testname=
none.
Hagan, Lisa. "House Democrats Overcome Major Hurdles, Pass Infrastructure Bill in Big Win for Biden." *US News*. November 6, 2021. https://www.usn
ews.com/news/politics/articles/2021-11-06/house-democrats-overcome-major-hurdles-pass-infrastructure-bill-in-big-win-for-biden.
Howe, Amy. "Justices Agree to Review EPA's Authority to Regulate Greenhouse Gas Emissions." October 29, 2021. https://www.scotusblog.com/2021/10/justices-agree-to-review-epas-authority-to-regulate-greenhouse-gases/.
H.R. 3684. "Infrastructure Investment and Jobs Act." Congress.gov. November 15, 2021. https://www.congress.gov/bill/117th-congress/house-bill/3684.
IPCC Press Release. Accessed October 18, 2018. http://www.ipcc.ch/pdf/ses
sion48/pr_181008_P48_spm_en.pdf.
Joselow, Maxine. "Biden Says Democrats Can Pass 'Big Chunks' of Build Back Better, Including Climate." *Washington Post*. January 20, 2022. https://www.washingtonpost.com/politics/2022/01/20/biden-says-democrats-can-pass-big-chunks-build-back-better-including-climate/.
Klyza and Sousa. 2008.https://www.amazon.com/American-Environmental-Policy-Gridlock-Comparative/dp/0262525046/ref=sr_1_1?crid=1ZKKI2FGQ
EMCF&keywords=klyza+and+sousa&qid=166840080&sprefix=klyza+and+sousa%2Caps%2C131&sr=8-1
Klyza, Christopher McGrory, and David Sousa. *American Environmental Policy 1990–2012: Beyond the Gridlock*. Cambridge: The MIT Press, 2013.
Kraft, Michael E. *Environmental Policy and Politics*. 5th edition. New York: Longman, 2011.
Kraft. 2017.https://www.amazon.com/Environmental-Policy-Politics-Michae
lKraft/dp/1138218790/ref=sr_1_fkmr2_2?crid=22MRVS933UTT&key
words=mike+kraft+environmental+policy&qid=1668399919&sprefix=mike+kraft+environmental+policy%2Caps%2C136&sr=8-2-fkmr2
Kriz, M. "On the Hot Seat." *National Journal* 43–44 (May 19, 2007a). Retrieved from Academic Search Complete.

————. "House Select Energy Independence and Global Warming Committee." *National Journal* 96 (June 23, 2007b). Retrieved from Academic Search Complete.

League of Conservation Voters. *Barbara Boxer, National Environmental Scorecard.* 2012. Retrieved from: http://scorecard.lcv.org/moc/barbara-boxer.

Lewis, Jack. "The Birth of the EPA." 1985. Accessed 23 June 2008. Available at: http://www.epa.gov/history/topics/epa/15c.htm.

Lipinski, D. "Navigating Congressional Policy Processes: The Inside Perspective on How Laws Are Made." In *Congress Reconsidered,* edited by Lawerence C. Dodd and Bruce I Oppenheimer. 9th edition, 217–240. Washington, DC: Sage Publication, 2009.

Loomis, John. *Integrated Public Lands Management.* New York: Columbia University Press, 1993.

Mayhew, David. *Congress: The Electoral Connection.* New Haven: Yale University Press, 2004.

Meek, Chanda. "Evaluating the Effect of Federal Agency Culture, Structure and History on Institutional Performance." Paper presented at the International PhD School for Studies of Arctic Societies, Fairbanks, Alaska, 2006.

Moen, Mathew. "The Political Agenda or Ronald Regan: A Content Analysis of State of the Union Addresses." *Presidential Studies Quarterly* 18, no. 4 (1988): 775–785.

National Women's Political Caucus. *Barbara Boxer.* 2013. Retrieved from: http://www.nwpc.org/barbaraboxer.

Nixon, Richard. "Annual Message to the Congress on the State of the Union." In *Speech.* Washington, DC: The American Presidency Project. January 22, 1970. http://www.presidency.ucsb.edu/ws/index.php?pid=2921.

————. "Address on the State of the Union Delivered Before a Joint Session of the Congress." In *Speech.* Washington, DC: The American Presidency Project. January 30, 1974. http://www.presidency.ucsb.edu/ws/index.php?pid=4327.

Niskanen, William. *Bureaucracy and Representative Government.* London: Aldine Transaction, 1971.

Obama, Barack. "Address Before a Joint Session of the Congress." In *Speech.* Washington, DC: The American Presidency Project. February 24, 2009. http://www.presidency.ucsb.edu/ws/index.php?pid=85753.

————. "Address Before a Joint Session of Congress on the State of the Union." In *Speech.* Washington, DC: The American Presidency Project. February 12, 2013. http://www.presidency.ucsb.edu/ws/index.php?pid=102826.

O'Leary, Rosemary. "Environmental Policy in the Courts." In *Environmental Policy: New Directions for the 21st Century,* edited by Norman J. Vig and Michael E. Kraft, 135–137. Washington, DC: CQ Press, 2013.

Osborne, David and Ted Gaebler. *Reinventing Government*. New York: Basic Books, 1999.

Palazzolo v. Rhode Island.

Pelosi, N. "Pelosi Announces Members of Select Committee on Energy Independence and Global Warming." In *FDCH Press Releases*. 2007. Retrieved from Newspaper Source Plus.

Rabe, B. (ed.). *Greenhouse Governance: Addressing Climate Change in America* (pp. 1–20). Washington, DC: The Brookings Institution, 2010.

Reagan, Ronald. "Address Before a Joint Session of the Congress on the Program for Economic Recovery." In *Speech*. Washington, DC: The American Presidency Project. February 18, 1981. http://www.presidency.ucsb.edu/ws/index.php?pid=43425.

———. "Address Before a Joint Session of the Congress on the State of the Union." In *Speech*. Washington, DC: The American Presidency Project. February 6, 1985. http://www.presidency.ucsb.edu/ws/index.php?pid=38069.

Remarks by President Biden. "Remarks by President Biden at the COP26 Leaders Statement." November 1, 2021. https://www.whitehouse.gov/briefing-room/speeches-remarks/2021/11/01/remarks-by-president-biden-at-the-cop26-leaders-statement/.

Rinfret, Sara R. and Scott Furlong. "Defining Environmental Rulemaking." In *Oxford Handbook of U.S. Environmental Policy*, edited by Michael E. Kraft and Sheldon Kamieniecki, 372–383. New York: Oxford University Press, 2012.

Rosenbaum, Walter A. 2013.https://www.amazon.com/Environmental-Politics-Policy-Walter-Rosenbaum/dp/1544325045

Rosenbaum, Walter A. *Environmental Politics and Policy*. 9th edition. Washington, DC: CQ Press, 2019.

Sandall, Clayton and Jennifer Duck. *Al Gore Brings Global Warming Crusade to Congress*. 2007. Retrieved from: http://abcnews.go.com/Politics/story?id=2970093&page=1.

Savage, David. 2008. Retrieved from: http://www.latimes.com/news/nationworld/lana-scotus24–2008jun24,0,3345943.story.

Select Committee on Energy Independence and Global Warming. *Geopolitical Implications of Rising Oil Dependence and Global Warming*. April 18, 2007. Retrieved from Select Committee website at: http://globalwarming.house.gov/files/HRG/FullTranscripts/110-1_2007-04-18.pdf.

———. *110th Congress Final Staff Report*. November 21, 2008. Retrieved from Select Committee website at: http://globalwarming.house.gov/pubs/archives_110?id=0059#main_content.

———. *Hearings from the House and Senate (including the Select Committee) Regarding Energy Independence and Global Warming*. 2009. Retrieved from

Select Committee website at: http://globalwarming.house.gov/files/WEB/ EIGWHearings/110_EIGW_hearings.pdf.

———. *Select committee Hearing Testimony*. 2010. Retrieved from Select Committee website at: http://globalwarming.house.gov/pubs/testimony.

Sensenbrenner, J. "Sensenbrenner Looks Forward to Extending Congressional Record on Energy Security and Climate Change." In *FDCH Press Releases*. December 8, 2000. Retrieved from Newspaper Source Plus.

———. "Sensenbrenner Reappointed as Select Committee Ranking Republican." In *FDCH Press Releases*. January 15, 2009. Retrieved from Newspaper Source Plus.

Sinclair, Barbara. *Unorthodox Lawmaking: New Legislative Processes in the U.S. Congress*. Washington, DC: CQ Press, 2007.

Smallen, J. "Pelosi Creates Global-Warming Panel." In *National Journal* 47. January 20, 2007. Retrieved from Academic Search Complete.

Smith, Kimberly. "Environmental Policy in the Court." In *Environmental Policy: New Directions for the Twenty-First Century*. 11th edition. Written by Michael Kraft, Norman Vig, and Barry Rabe. 2022.

Soden, Dennis. *The Environmental Presidency*. Albany, NY: SUNY Press, 1999.

Spinelli, Dan. "Landmark Children's Lawsuit hits Roadblock." Accessed November 11, 2018. https://grist.org/article/landmark-childrens-climate-lawsuit-hits-new-roadblock/.

Steinhauer, J. "Republicans Killing Climate Committee." In *New York Times* 26. December 2, 2010. Retrieved from Academic Search Complete at: www.ebs cohost.com.

Sunlight Foundation. 2014. "Only Four Percent of Bills Become Law." *Huffington Post*. Accessed January 21 2014. http://www.huffingtonpost.com/wires/2009/08/25/the-vast-majority-of-bill_ws_268630.html.

Sussman, Glen, Byron W. Daynes, and Jonathan P. West. *American Politics and the Environment*. New York: Longman, 2001.

The White House. Fact Sheet: Historic Bipartisan Infrastructure Deal. 2021. https://www.whitehouse.gov/briefing-room/statements-releases/2021/07/28/fact-sheet-historic-bipartisan-infrastructure-deal/.

Vaughn, Jacqueline. *Environmental Politics: Domestic and Global Dimensions*. 5th edition. New York: Thomson Wadsworth, 2007.

Vig, Norman and Michael E. Kraft. *Environmental Policy in the 1980s: Reagan's New Agenda*. Washington, DC: CQ Press, 1984.

Vig, Norman J. "Presidential Powers and Environmental Policy." In *Environmental Policy: New Directions for the 21st Century*, edited by Norman J. Vig and Michael E. Kraft. Washington, DC: CQ Press, 2013.

Vig, Norman and Michael E. Kraft. *Environmental Policy: New Directions for the 21st Century*. Washington, DC: CQ Press, 2013.

Weber, Max. *Capitalism, Bureaucracy, and Religion*. New York: Routledge, 1947.

Wilson, James Q. *Bureaucracy: What Government Agencies Do and Why They Do It*. New York: Basic Books, 1991.

CHAPTER 5

Unofficial Actors in the Policy Process

Introductory Story: "Detox the Box"
We consume products in our everyday lives. As consumers, we might not consider the broader effects that products have on the environment and our own health. Founded in 1995, Women's Voices for the Earth (WVE) was created to reduce toxic exposure for people who menstruate. Detox the Box is just one of WVE's campaigns to reduce toxic chemicals in period care products. In their *Chem Fatale Report*,[1] WVE found, to name a few (Scranton 2013):

- Period care products are a $3 billion-dollar industry in US.
- Tampons include hazardous materials, including chlorine bleach from the processes to maintain the bright white color.
- Pads contain unknown fragrance chemicals, which can cause allergic rashes.
- Menstruation wipes can use hazardous ingredients such as iodopropynyl butylcarbamate where exposure can lead to cancer or endocrine disruption.

The chemicals used in period care products are often unregulated by the Food and Drug Administration (FDA) because they are classified as cosmetics (Scranton 2013). More specifically, products such as tampons and pads are categorized as medical devices and therefore, do not have

---

© The Author(s), under exclusive license to Springer Nature Switzerland AG 2023
S. R. Rinfret and M. C. Pautz, *US Environmental Policy in Action*,
https://doi.org/10.1007/978-3-031-17503-9_5

to disclose the ingredients. Accordingly, WVE has used their scientific research to inform conversations at the federal level and lobbied members of Congress and companies for the passage of the Safe Cosmetics and Personal Care Products Act (2013), which was assigned to a subcommittee and tabled in the summer of 2013 (Schakowsky 2013).

Measures have been taken at the state level to pass laws that require disclosure of all ingredients on the label of menstrual products. In the 2019–2020 legislative session in New York, the first bill in the nation passed that requires all menstrual products sold in New York State to contain a printed list of all the ingredients including percentages of each ingredient (Persaud 2019). Other states have attempted to follow New York's example, but not all of these laws are created equally. For instance, California passed a similar disclosure bill that falls short by not requiring all allergens and fragrances to be reported on the label (WVE 2020).

Due to their small budget, WVE adapted its approaches to engender discussion through social media (e.g., Twitter hashtags, YouTube videos) to educate the public about the intricacies of menstrual products. On one of their YouTube videos, for example, they attempt to educate and caution people who menstruate about the drawbacks of using period care products. This approach is intended to create visibility online for offline action. WVE has also seen success with the use of online petitions and protests at major period care producing company headquarters (Abrams 2015). Procter & Gamble and Kimberly-Clark, the corporations that own Always, Tampax, and Kotex period care products, started to release the ingredients in some of their products in response to the pressure from WVE and advocates for transparent menstrual product labels (Abrams 2015).

Although you might see a disconnect between WVE and the environment, consider that the products we consume end up in the landfill (see Chapter 1); harmful toxins can and are found in our food, as described in Chapter 10; and all of this suggests a broader connection between our consumerism behaviors and our impact on the environment. In the following pages, we demonstrate how the WVE is just one example of an unofficial policy actor, attempting to invoke policy change. Such efforts can and do find resistance. As we show in this chapter, groups challenge each other in the public policymaking arena to influence the actions of official policy actors and have even been classified as eco-terrorists.

---

[1] https://www.womensvoices.org/feminine-care-products/detox-the-box/.

In contrast to the last chapter, this one turns to understanding organizations such as WVE who are unofficial actors within environmental policy. Unofficial actors are those individuals and organizations—a political party or interest groups—that try to influence the actions of official actors (Congress, the president, the courts, and the bureaucracy) and the outcomes of elections. Accordingly, we review the different types of unofficial actors. First, we discuss political parties and interest groups because both try to influence the decisionmaking of government. "Political parties and interest groups serve as linkage institutions tying citizens to their representatives in government. Political parties control the institutional arrangement of the government, [and] interest groups mobilize in a variety of ways to influence the behavior of politicians who control the apparatus of government" (Sussman et al. 2001, 88). More specifically, to truly understand how organized interests exert their influence, we offer two examples. The first example considers how interest groups try to influence the US Congress in its role overseeing oil subsidies. The second example examines how interest groups try to influence the bureaucracy.

The second section of this chapter focuses on how unofficial actors use the media to mobilize public opinion. Interest groups try to use traditional media (television advertising), and increasingly social media (Facebook, Twitter), to reach the public regarding environmental issues. Specifically, groups use a variety of approaches to garner media attention to make their voice heard. The final section of the chapter provides a peculiar case study that unpacks the story of Daniel McGowan, who was involved with the environmental organization Earth Liberation Front (ELF) and convicted for conspiracy and arson. The point of this chapter is to demonstrate the myriad of actors outside government who affect the decisions of official policy actors, informing environmental policy.

Upon completion of this chapter, several themes will materialize. The first area for consideration is influence—how unofficial actors try to use different strategies to impact official policy decisions. The second theme of the chapter pushes us to consider which tactics are more effective, such as writing a policy report like Chem Fatale, or eco-terrorism. We want the reader to consider if the efforts used by unofficial actors are enough to breakthrough congressional gridlock.

UNOFFICIAL POLICY ACTORS

Unofficial policy actors are those individuals and organizations who try to shape policy outcomes. Although the media is considered an unofficial policy actor as an introduction, we focus on defining two unofficial actors: political parties and interest groups. The purpose of a political party is to represent the policy preferences of the American people and put forward candidates to win elections. In comparison, the goal of an interest group is to influence the actions of official policy actors to gain favorable outcomes for their particular group. The following discussion provides a brief overview of the role of political parties in environmental policy, before turning to interest groups.

POLITICAL PARTIES

In the United States, elections are dominated by a two-party system, meaning that two political parties vie for winning elections at the local, state, and federal level. Historically, the two parties that have maintained a strong presence are the Republicans and Democrats. As Amy Below (2012) notes, "Republican ideology argues for individual liberty as opposed to government interference. Its preference for small government coincides with a pro-business, free-market attitude and thus an aversion to government control" (527). In comparison, "Democratic ideology is more commonly associated with liberalism and an acceptance of government involvement in the political, economic, and social lives of people" (Below 2012, 527). These perspectives affect who the American people believe is the best candidate to protect the environment.

To distinguish how a party affects the electoral decisions of the populace, a party has a platform. This platform is used to inform citizens about the party's perspectives or attitudes about a particular topic. For instance, in the 2020 presidential election, the Democratic Party was identified as pro-environment and the Republican Party as anti-environment, which, as we noted in Chapter 2, was not always the case.

The environment is not necessarily *the* focal point of US elections due to conversations focused on the economy, high gas prices, a global pandemic, or women's reproductive rights. According to Below, "The majority of political discussions around the environment are among specialists rather than among the general electorate" (531). More specifically, environmental issues have become low salience—meaning they are not a pressing issue for many Americans. As a result, national parties do not make environmental issues their primary target during campaigns. Instead, candidates running for office focus on issues like jobs or health-care—topics that resonate with voters within their districts and help to get them elected. For instance, in the 2020 election between Donald J. Trump and Joseph Biden, efforts centered around government response to the Covid-19 pandemic and ways to improve the economy. The public's attention was on the pandemic and both candidates targeted this in different ways.

INTEREST GROUPS

Interest groups, which are organized groups of individuals who fight for a cause, are another type of unofficial actor. When we think about environmental policy, interest groups are usually broken down into business and environmental organizations. These groups are far-reaching, from protecting whales in the Pacific Ocean to coal miners' rights in West Virginia, for example. Robert Duffy (2003) argues, "Today there are perhaps tens of thousands of organized interests active in environmental and natural resource policymaking across all levels of government" (506). Thus, interest groups invest their time and resources to impact policies in the US.

More specifically, interest groups are "[i]ndividuals who organize to influence the government's programs and policies" (Ginsberg et al. 2013, 435). There are several types of interest groups in the US, ranging from businesses and professional associations to public interest and ideological interest groups. As we examine a few of these types to provide a broader overview, keep in mind that this list (see Table 5.1) is not exhaustive. The goal for the remainder of the chapter is to evaluate how business and environmental groups try to affect US environmental policy.

As Table 5.1 indicates, there are three broad ways we can categorize interest groups in the US. For instance, a *business interest group* wants to protect economic interests and includes groups such as chambers of commerce or the American Farm Bureau Federation, which represents farm and ranching individuals in the US. In turn, *professional interest groups* include organizations such as the American Bar Association (which represents lawyers), the American Medical Association (which includes medical professionals such as physicians), and the American Political

Table 5.1   Understanding interest groups

Type of interest group	Purpose or goal	Examples
Business Interest Group	To promote economic interests	Chamber of Commerce, American Farm Bureau Federation, American Coal Council
Professional Interest Group	To represent the interest of a professional field or expertise	American Bar Association, American Medical Association, American Political Science Association, Association of Energy Engineers
Public Interest Group	To promote the protection of a particular issue	Sierra Club, Greenpeace, Natural Resources Defense Council, National Audubon Society
Ideological Interest Group	To address extreme political currents	Christian Coalition, National Organization for Women, National Association for the Advancement of Colored People

Science Association (which is largely an academic organization for those individuals researching in the field of political science).

In addition to these basic descriptions, business and professional interest groups do play a role in environmental policymaking. The US Chamber of Commerce and the American Farm Bureau Federation, for example, have been pivotal in questioning whether or not the EPA has the authority to regulate greenhouse gas (GHG) emissions under the Clean Air Act (CAA). In particular, these groups have sued the EPA, maintaining that Congress never intended the EPA to regulate GHG emissions; thus, the EPA does not have the authority to move forward with such regulations (US Chamber of Commerce 2013).

Public interest groups include those organizations that advocate for causes such as consumer or environmental protection. One of the oldest and largest environmental interest groups in the US is the Sierra Club, founded in 1892, whose mission is "to explore, enjoy, and protect the wild places of the earth; to practice and promote the responsible use of the earth's ecosystems and resources; to educate and enlist humanity to protect and restore the quality of the natural and human environment;

and to use all lawful means to carry out these objectives." One of the major issues that the Sierra Club is currently working on is to focus on renewable sources of energy beyond coal burning power plants.

The final type of interest group, *ideological groups*, promotes broader political perspectives and government ideologies. For instance, individuals from a more conservative, religious perspective might be attracted to the Christian Coalition (CC). The purpose of the Christian Coalition is to use faith-based initiatives to use religion to impact policy outcomes. When it comes to environmental issues, the CC believes that the exploration of drilling should increase domestically in order to lessen the reliance by the US to use foreign sources of fuel.

Beyond the descriptions of the aforementioned types of interest groups, each group does advocate for specific causes. Recall that the Sierra Club advocates for the US to move beyond coal, focusing on renewable sources of energy. US Chamber of Commerce is fighting the EPA's efforts to regulate GHGs under the CAA. Further, we offer additional examples of how specific groups, such as the National Audubon Society, Greenpeace, the National Wetlands Association, and Americans for Balanced Energy Choices approach environmental issues.

BIRDSONGS, PETRELS, AND WHALES

The goal of an interest group is to promote a particular cause by garnering public support, which, in turn, can pressure lawmakers to act in a particular way. We consider examples from the National Audubon Society and Greenpeace. The National Audubon Society, which focuses on the conservation of birds and wildlife, revamped its approach to activism during the global pandemic through the For the Birds: The Birdsong Project. This project is led by famous composer, Randall Poster, whose goal was to compile original compositions inspired by birdsong. Famous songwriters across the globe submitted their work during stay at home orders with 172 new pieces of music. The assumption is that if the National Audubon Society's 600,000 members purchase the birdsong music, this money would be used to lobby Congress to protect the habitat of birds being effected by our changing climate letters to Congress, and their voices could make a difference (McGlashen 2022). The question becomes whether these efforts are sufficient to convince members of Congress to do something to save these imperiled birds.

By way of comparison, some environmental organizations, such as Greenpeace, do not necessarily believe conventional fundraising campaigns make an impact. Instead, environmental activism, in their opinion, should use unconventional efforts (e.g., Diane Wilson poured syrup on her head as a proxy for arguments against oil during a congressional hearing). Greenpeace tries to be the "leading independent campaigning organization that uses peaceful protest and creative communication to expose global environmental problems and to promote solutions that are essential to a green and peaceful future" (Greenpeace 2013). The Rainbow Warrior is a ship used by Greenpeace to travel the ocean and challenge those they oppose. For instance, in their campaign to protect whales, Greenpeace used the Rainbow Warrior ship to board a Russian oil rig to protect the species. Although this may have halted the oil rig's production for the day, it did not stop extraction altogether; rather, Greenpeace used this approach to demonstrate a global message that oceanic oil extraction hinders the migration patterns of whales (Greenpeace 2013).

Our first two examples were about environmental organizations, but business groups are also effective in impacting policymaking and public perceptions about the environment. Business groups, more broadly, are successful in running public relations campaigns to support their endeavors, or what some might classify as greenwashing—the idea is that a company will spend money on advertising, claiming that it is working on green technology or providing a green product, but this is only a small fraction of what the company does overall (Vaughn 2007). As Glenn Sussman et al. (2001) note, "The National Wetlands Coalition is not concerned with protecting the nation's wetlands but rather is committed to reducing the burden of wetlands regulations on real estate from oil and gas interests" (114). In 2020, the company SC Johnson produced a new Windex that claimed to be made from 100% recycled ocean plastic. The marketing of the product misled consumers to believe the plastic was retrieved directly from the ocean when it was actually made from plastic banks in Indonesia, the Philippines, and Haiti. SC Johnson is also known for advertising Windex as non-toxic, but there are legal disputes that it is harmful to humans and the environment. The corporation's effort to appeal to the public by showing they are environmentally conscious is another attempt for businesses to serve their own best interests.

In short, there are several different types of interest groups, and each impacts environmental policy through a variety of approaches. These groups are composed of American people, and their tactics attempt to encourage lawmakers to act on behalf of their group.

The Adventures of a Lobbyist

Most Americans belong to many interest groups without even thinking about it (such as parent–teacher associations, the American Automobile Association, etc.). Typically, there is an annual membership fee to be a member of an interest group. The idea is that, by becoming a "dues paying member" of an interest group, you receive benefits. These benefits could include a monthly newsletter that keeps citizens informed about issues to discounts on nature hikes or a cute stuffed animal. However, one of the most notable benefits is that this organization will fight for causes that you believe in. This often occurs through lobbying members of Congress. Each of the aforementioned types of interest groups generally uses membership dues to employ lobbyists.

Lobbyists often have degrees in political science or law and may have even been a congressional staffer or even a member of Congress. A lobbyist uses the power of persuasion when meeting with members of Congress. As Nick Naylor, a tobacco lobbyist in the film *Thank You for Smoking*, notes, "I get paid for talking." The goal of a lobbyist is to persuade members of Congress by presenting research and evidence that supports his or her cause in the hope that Congress will pass legislation in the group's favor. For instance, a lobbyist from the Sierra Club may urge members of Congress to support legislation to curb emissions that cause climate change. In turn, a business interest group, such as the American Petroleum Institute, might counter the Sierra Club's lobbying efforts with its own lobbyist, arguing that legislation to curb climate change in the US could be devastating for the economy. As a result, these lobbyists compete with each other to persuade members of Congress.

REBRANDING

A professional career in lobbying can carry a negative stereotype due to historical cases of corruption or money laundering scandals. A former lobbyist, Jack Abramoff, was recently convicted of illegally providing gifts to members of Congress in exchange for votes on pieces of legislation.

The Lobbying Disclosure Act of 1995 (2 U.S.C.§ 1601) is supposed to prevent illegal activity such as this and requires every lobbyist in the US to register with the US House of Representatives.

Because of the negative perceptions about the profession, Clines (2013) argues that the term "lobbying" needs rebranding. The traditional view is that lobbyists meet with members of Congress to impact the outcome of legislation. Instead, the contemporary lobbyist has transcended into other venues, such as political strategy and campaign fundraising. The idea, based upon a survey conducted by the American League of Lobbyists (an organized group to represent lobbyists in the United States), suggests a new name for lobbyists: government relations professionals (Clines 2013). It still remains to be seen if the name change matters, but lobbyists continue to have an impact on the outcome of public policy in the US.

Many interest groups have their own Political Action Committee (PAC). The purpose of an interest group's PAC is to influence electoral politics through candidate selection and election outcomes. A PAC provides financial support to a candidate running for office. As of 2022, there are more than 7,000 PACs in the US that contribute to federal-level elections (i.e., running for the US Congress; Center for Responsive Politics 2022). The idea is that these members will then support legislation if elected into office.

The natural concern becomes that interest groups, through their various activities, can exert too much power into the policymaking process. "The framers of the U.S. Constitution feared the power that could be wielded by organized interests. Yet they believed that interest groups thrived because of liberty–the freedom that all Americans enjoy to organize and to express their views" (Ginsberg et al. 2013, 435). Nevertheless, the idea is that if one group of organized interests forms to address a particular issue, another group will form to challenge. Therefore, competing groups balance one another when competing for access to influence congressional decisionmaking. To make this point clearer, we turn to an example of how interest groups do try to influence congressional policymaking.

Influence

Interest group influence on national policy has been a closely watched and well-documented phenomenon by scholars. Some argue that only a few, the *political elite*, have the power to influence policymaking in a democratic society (c.f. Mills 1956). However, David Truman (1951) and Robert Dahl (1961) contend that all people in the US have equal power to influence decisionmaking because we live in a pluralistic society. However, Mancur Olson (1965) and Charles Lindblom (1977) criticize the pluralist framework, asserting that business-oriented groups possessed a significant advantage due to their greater access to resources.

Examining how much interest groups influence policy is still up for debate, yet, it is abundantly clear that they at least try to do so (Baumgartner and Leech 2001; Baumgartner et al. 2009; Kingdon 2003; Lowi 1972). This is especially evident within the environmental arena, and we use the example of energy tax policy, and, more specifically, fossil fuel subsidies, to provide some insight into how interest groups can influence congressional policy. After our investigation of how interest groups try to influence congressional policymaking, we then note that students of public policy and environmental policy cannot forget that interest group influence also occurs within the bureaucratic realm.

OIL OR CLEAN ENERGY?

Energy tax policy in the US for much of the twentieth century has favored oil and gas development, as economic growth is championed (Sherlock 2010). More specifically, the intangible drilling costs (IDCs) tax credit introduced in 1916 and the depletion tax credit introduced in 1926 are two of the longest standing fossil fuel subsidies. More specifically, the IDC tax credit allows developers to fully deduct expenses that may be incurred at a well site during the first year, as opposed to paying taxes on its depreciated value over time. In comparison, the depletion credit allows developers to deduct a fixed percentage from their tax bill, as opposed to a percentage based upon price, as they extract more of the resource from the well. Although these subsidies were reduced in the 1970s and again in the 1980s, on balance, these and other energy tax provisions continued to favor fossil fuels over the emerging clean energy industry for more than a century. However, the American Recovery and Reinvestment Act of 2009

(ARRA), clean energy surpassed oil and gas in terms of total tax incentives (Sherlock 2010).

Nevertheless, fossil fuel subsidies continue to amount to nearly $20.5 billion in government spending every year (Bertrand 2021). As a result, since the 1970s policymakers discussed reforming the energy tax code. In 2021, President Biden passed an Executive Order called *Tackling the Climate Crisis at Home and Abroad* which called for the elimination of fossil fuel subsidies in the federal budget (Bertrand 2021). To meet this goal, 13 fossil fuel tax preferences were repealed (Bertrand 2021).

Biden's Executive Order reflects public opinion regarding the growing concern over climate change. The Yale Project on Climate Change and Communication conducted a survey in December of 2020, finding 59% of Americans are alarmed or concerned about climate change, with a substantial increase in the alarmed category over the past five years. This study also found that 66% of registered voters believe developing clean energy should be a high priority for the government, 72% support transitioning the U.S. economy from fossil fuels to clean energy by 2050, 55% support increasing federal subsidies for renewable energy, and 49% support decreasing subsidies for the fossil fuel industry.

Despite the public's support for clean energy sources over fossil fuels, Congress has struggled to create comprehensive policy. Although President Biden's Executive Order will alter the tax code, this method can be easily overturned by the next president. To better understand the pressures Congress faces to maintain the status quo of fossil fuels, we examine interest group influence through an evaluation of congressional lobbying expenditures to provide one potential explanation.

The Center for Responsive Politics (CFRP) documents interest group campaign and lobbying expenditures on an annual basis. In 2021, the top five oil industry lobbyists included Koch Industries, Royal Dutch Shell, Occidental Petroleum, Exxon Mobil, and Chevron Corporation that spent a combined total of $39 million (CFRP 2021d). In addition, the top five natural gas industry lobbyists included the OAO Gazprom, Cheniere Energy, Enbridge Inc., American Gas Association, and Williams Companies, which spent a combined total over $8 million to lobby members of Congress (CFRP 2021c).

In comparison, the top five alternative energy lobbyists include the American Clean Power Association, Solar Energy Industries Association, Poet LLC, Growth Energy, and National Biodiesel Board all of which spent a combined total of $8.5 million (CFRP 2021a). Finally, the top environmental lobbying firms include the Nature Conservancy, ClearPath Foundation, Breakthrough Energy, Americans for Carbon Dividends, and Natural Resources Defense Council spent just over $7 million collectively (CFRP 2021b). While the alternative energy and environmental lobbying interest groups have increased their spending in response to the ignited interest in climate change mitigation in recent years, it still does not come close to that of oil and gas.

Clearly, the fossil fuel interests have a resource advantage over that of the clean energy supporters, with just the top ten players in the oil and gas industry spending more than three times the amount of money on lobbying for their interests than their counterparts. In addition, it is unlikely that the environmental and alternative energy lobbyists are focusing all of their resources trying to repeal oil and gas subsidies alone, making the spending disparity even larger. More specifically, research organizations, like the Center for Responsive Politics, enable members of the public to track the involvement of interest groups in national policy. As this example shows, regardless of the extent of a given interest group's resources, groups spend a lot of money trying to impact policymakers' decisions.

It is not just within the halls of Congress that interest groups are influential, however. Groups are increasingly involved across the stages of the rulemaking process (Kerwin and Furlong 2011). Unfortunately, assessing influence within the regulatory or bureaucratic realm is difficult to track because most of the interactions between agencies and interest groups occur off the record and out of the public eye (Cook and Rinfret 2013). Therefore, although scholars have a better understanding of what interest groups do at the congressional level, as noted in the aforementioned example, it is far less certain how they impact administrative rulemaking, which is of growing importance in the environmental arena (Klyza and Sousa 2013). As a result, we offer a brief overview in the next section of how interest groups can and are influential during agency policymaking.

Agencymakers

Chapter 4 explained that the bureaucracy plays a major role in environmental policymaking because agencies translate vague congressional law into policy. Interest group involvement with the bureaucracy and Congress varies. One way that interest groups can influence the bureaucracy is by working with Congress (Baumgartner and Leech 1998;

McCubbins et al. 1987). This occurs when Congress pressures agency personnel to favor interest groups during policy implementation. The issue of climate change is an example of how congressional members, such as Representative Edward Markey (D-Michigan), sided with environmental groups to exert pressure for policy change utilizing rulemaking processes instead of through congressional legislation. For example, Representative Markey agreed with the Sierra Club that the US needed to regulate climate change-causing agents such as carbon dioxide. Due to congressional gridlock on climate change, Representative Markey worked with the EPA on ways to move forward with the regulation of carbon dioxide under the Clean Air Act (Morris 2009). Representative Markey bypassed the gridlock by using the EPA and its regulatory processes to enact policy change. In 2022, the Supreme Court's West *Virginia v. EPA* found that the EPA does not have the authority to regulated greenhouse gas emissions under the Clean Air Act of 1970.

Our second example illustrates ways organized interests have tried to influence agency policymaking, known as rulemaking. Rulemaking is the process by which every federal agency—such as the National Park Service (NPS) or the EPA—writes, a rule based upon congressional legislation. As previously discussed, Congress creates laws that are vague; therefore, agencies have to make sense of this vague language to carry out the law's implementation. Rules offer clearer specifications for the implementation of a law passed by Congress. For instance, Congress created the Endangered Species Act of 1973 in which agencies, including the US Fish and Wildlife Service (USFWS), must ensure the protection of species from becoming endangered or extinct. In order to interpret the law, agencies, such as the USFWS, must first propose a rule in the *Federal Register*.

This announcement of draft rules asks for the public to submit comments about the proposed rules. Usually, comments range from someone angry about a given rule to a scientist who provides technical expertise about the pros and cons of the rule. Often, agencies receive thousands of comments, which is a concern because generally only one or two staff members examine the comments. However, one approach that agencies use when examining public comments is a computer software program, Discover Text, which detects for duplicative comments. However, submitting public comments to an agency is not like lobbying your member of Congress. The agency is seeking substantive comments about the rule. Thus, submitting public comments is one way for organized interests or the general public to influence agency decisionmaking

(Magat et al. 1986; Golden 1998; West 2004; Chapter 6 explores this area of research in much greater detail).

Ultimately, there are a variety of pathways—congressional and bureaucratic—for interest groups to influence environmental policymaking in the US, and this chapter presented two ways in which this can occur. Agenda setting is often achieved through acts of lobbying, but another important piece of the puzzle for unofficial policy actors is how best to use the media to persuade not only members of Congress or the bureaucracy, but also the American public. Accordingly, we turn to how the media can set or lessen the agenda for particular interest groups to influence environmental policymaking.

The Media and Interest Groups

There are several useful functions of the media that are utilized by interest groups to set the policymaking agenda. We focus our attention in this final section of the chapter on: how different types of media are utilized by a group, who controls media coverage, and how social media applications (apps) are changing the contemporary landscape for driving political participation for environmental issues.

First, in the US, there are three ways to classify the different types of media—*broadcast*, *print*, and *the Internet*. Put simply, broadcast media includes radio and television, print encompasses newspapers and magazines, and the Internet is an online resource that incorporates cyber versions of the more traditional media sources. Interest groups use all types of the media to market their message to the public, trying to garner support for their stances on particular issues. Nevertheless, the usage of these types of media has varied throughout history (Ginsberg et al. 2013).

Historically, print (notably, newspapers) has been one of the dominant sources for groups to convey to the public that they should support or be against a certain issue. Benjamin Franklin, for example, used the *Pennsylvania Gazette* to try to persuade politicians to address water pollution in Philadelphia (Sussman et al. 2001). Although this example is from a prominent official policy actor, it helped to lead the way for environmental interests to gain traction in garnering public support for pollution prevention. For instance, print media has been able to use images such as the Cuyahoga River on fire in the 1960s or the satellite images of the ozone depletion in the Earth's atmosphere to demonstrate the need for action. However, using print media as a way to attract the public's support for groups has become more difficult in the twenty-first century, as we will see in our further discussion.

Traditionally, it was common for the political elite (elected officials) to rely upon print media to examine information about a particular issue (Ginsberg et al. 2013); however, a shift in the 1960s to television became a popular approach for groups to promote environmental protection to entice the American public. After all, this is about the time television became a prominent fixture in the majority of American households. With less Americans paying for a monthly subscription to cable TV, social media has become an outlet for influence. Republican members of Congress such as Steve Daines (R-MT) use Twitter to blame the rising gas prices on President Biden, calling on increased production of domestic sources of fuel.

Due to the lack of financial resources for advertisements, many environmental organizations alternatively use the popular site YouTube to reach a broader audience or TikTok. In particular, the Natural Resources Defense Council (NRDC) gained thousands of viewers with its "Great Plastic Purge" YouTube clip, explaining that major companies that produce plastic need to curb their practices because of the detrimental impacts that plastic has on nearby oceans (NRDC 2013). The TikTok influencer Taylor Bright is using the social media platform to raise awareness about the impact the fashion industry, specifically denim, has on the environment. Although interest groups use these sources or approaches, the question is: what effect do these have?

WHO GETS AIR TIME?

In addition to the types of media in the US, we also need to consider that coverage plays a large role in shaping Americans' perceptions about the environment. After all, "News coverage of the environment has a significant impact on public opinion, policymaking, and whether we, as a society, expand and deepen our stewardship ethic" (Miller and Pollak 2012, 3). Journalists—those individuals who report stories to an audience—play an important role in news coverage because these are the people who are interpreting or framing the story to the public. Framing is a powerful mechanism, as Christen and Huberty (2007) argue, because it shapes a person's preferences regarding policy priorities. Headlines of news stories such as "Artic Drilling Would Set Bad Precedent" or "Bush:

Cut Trees to Save Forests" impact an individual's perspective on an issue (Christen and Huberty 2007).

Moreover, framing has added to an overarching argument that environmental activism is anti-jobs or anti-worker (Guber and Bosso 2013). This particular argument can be expanded through the analysis of how climate change is framed in US environmental organizations such as the Sierra Club, National Wildlife Federation, and the National Audubon Society, all of which argued that climate change is the result of human activities, and legislation needs to pass to further prevent further warming of the Earth. In 2021, the United Nations International Panel on Climate Change released a report "Code Red for Humanity" stating that human-induced climate change has reached an irreversible point where urgent, dramatic action is needed (UN News). Even with the overwhelming evidence, the counter-perspective from business lobbyists has been strong in creating an atmosphere in which many Americans believe that climate change is not the result of humans. The climate-deniers, including Senator Ted Cruz, maintain that climate change is a ploy by environmental groups to create legislation that would inhibit the US economy. Therefore, framing of either side of the climate change debate is playing out in advertisement.

Closely linked to framing and shaping someone's perception about a topic is the role of priming. When a journalist or president uses images (e.g., photos, videos, or Tweets), priming occurs. For instance, think about the images of seagulls and other ocean life covered in oil after the Exxon Valdez oil spill, or in the 1960s when the Cuyahoga River in Cleveland, Ohio, caught fire. These images stick in the minds of the American public, and groups use them to support their causes. Social media is another form of framing—consider how former President Donald Trump used Twitter to communicate with Americans. Images or statements on Twitter can be re-tweeted by millions of followers. GIFs, memes, or videos are also used in Instagram, Snapchat, or TikTok, impacting Americans' perceptions about environmental issues. However, these issues only garner the public's attention for a short period of time.

One explanation for lack of coverage is that many environmental problems are inherently difficult for journalists to cover because they do not understand the science or data. Moreover, if a person cannot visualize the problem or results, covering environmental problems becomes problematic. For example, take smog in the 1970s; the sea of smog covering many of our US cities drove action because people could see that it was a problem. However, carbon monoxide, one of the leading drivers of climate change, is not visibly apparent to the public in the same way as dirty skies. Thus, if we cannot see something happening in front of our own eyes, it is hard to press for change.

Second, inextricably linked to media coverage is also understanding who owns many of the news outlets in the US. For instance, CNN is owned by AT&T, and Fox News is owned by Rupert Murdoch. The idea here is that these individuals also affect the portrayal or coverage of a story. After all, the media's goal is to make money; therefore, the question becomes how covering environmental stories lends itself to making money. According to a study conducted by the *Pew Project for Excellence in Journalism*, only 1.2% of news headlines in the US focus on the environment. Media Matters found "between January 1, 2011 and June 26, 2012, prominent newspapers and television news from major networks and cable stations mentioned reality TV stars the Kardashians a combined 2,133 times while ocean acidification was only mentioned 45 times in the same period" (Environmental Coverage 2013, 3). Even more startling is evidence found by Alexandria Miller and Lucia Bolles about the drop in environmental coverage from 2019 to 2020. Specifically, they found during the peak of the Covid-19 pandemic, coverage of environmental issues in the *New York Times* and *Wall Street Journal* dropped 78%.

In the 1950s, the *Christian Science Monitor* published an article written by Robert Cohen (1957) that questioned whether humans were changing the climate. However, media coverage of climate change was sparse throughout the 1960s and 1970s, not returning to the front pages until 1988 when James Hansen, a government scientist, testified in the US Congress that he was 99% certain that warming temperatures were due to the burning of fossil fuels. His statements fueled a great deal of public interest, but the US media then began to scrutinize science. This is partly because of the efforts spearheaded by former Senator James Inhofe (R-OK) who argued that climate change is a hoax. Moreover, Michael Crichton's fictional *State of Fear* challenged the conclusion that climate change is caused by humans. However, he was invited by President George W. Bush to discuss climate policy (Boykoff and Ravi Rajan 2007). In examining several major newspapers (*The Los Angeles Times, The New York Times, The Wall Street Journal, The Washington Post, & USA Today*) over a 10-year period, 2009–2018, there were 32,006 articles relating to climate change (Sklair and Boykoff, 2019). Coverage has increased and often aligns with events that draw National attention such as the Paris Climate Accord and UN Climate Talks (Sklair and Boykoff 2019).

There are other news sources that continue to investigate environmental issues such as Columbia Law School's Sabin Center for Climate Change Law, *The Huffington Post*, and the state of Washington's *The Daily Herald* (Environmental Coverage 2013). Moreover, we are seeing a growing trend of providing information to viewers through alternative sources of media. This is often referred to as the "alternative movement" where retired experts from agencies such as the National Park Service or Environmental Protection Agency have created AltNPS or AltEPA for followers on Twitter to receive information. Arguably, this was out of resistance to President Trump's rollback of the Obama administration's environmental policies and formulated alternative websites (e.g., silencing science tracker) to provide information. With the Biden administration's response to environmental policy, these movements' necessity is not as prevalent and many activists are turning to social media to engender action.

ALTERNATIVE MEDIA

Clickivism or Activism

Due to the lack of attention and coverage by the mainstream media, interest groups are becoming more creative in using technological advancements for their benefit. For those individuals wanting quick information, blogs, TikTok, or Twitter might be a way to go. This allows individuals to like or share information about specific causes with the friends or family or create a hashtag movement to promote information (e.g., #DetoxtheBox video). The Environmentalblog.org covers a variety of aspects of green living in order for readers to get involved in the community. One blog entry—"6 Powerful Tips to Save Energy and the Environment around your House" (June 26, 2018)—explains simple household tips on ways to reduce energy consumption. Although this example might not be from specific, organized interests' groups, they highlight how individuals consume environmental information. This information could lead to action (e.g., protesting, pressuring lawmakers to act).

There is concern that the online–offline environmental engagement is not quite like sinking a boat in the Gulf of Mexico or participating in a sit-in on Capitol Hill. Quite simply have we become clickivists or activists? A study in 2019 showed that online activism through petitions or retweeting does not displace physical environmental engagement and actually draws new audiences into the movement (Boykoff 2020). For example, the popular video game, Fortnite, has a "ClimateFortnite" channel where players can find climate researchers within the game to talk to and learn more about climate change (Boykoff 2020). Not all of the public follows traditional news sources and so this avenue offers scientists a new way to reach people.

In short, when news coverage dissipates across mainstream media, different types of technology are being used to engage individuals to address environmental issues. Social media is just one mechanism to promote action.

CHAPTER WRAP-UP

Unofficial policy actors do matter in the environmental policymaking arena. Political parties help shape the viewpoints of the electorate, but have not played as large of a role in recent history. Alternatively, this chapter describes that there are a sufficient number of interest groups in the US for anyone to become involved, whatever the issue of the day. Nevertheless, for the purposes of environmental policy, interest groups are usually delineated as either environmental organizations or business organizations.

One of the most effective ways a group can exert influence is through lobbying. Lobbying, as we suggest in this chapter, usually occurs when a lobbyist from an organization tries to influence a member of Congress. However, due to congressional gridlock, we argue that more attention should be paid to how interest groups influence bureaucratic decision-making or rulemaking. In our description of how individuals or groups can submit comments on agency rules, the general argument is that business groups dominate the submission of public comments.

In our last section of the chapter, we observe that the media's waning coverage of environmental issues might cause concern; however, we note that there are additional social networking venues in which organizations are trying to engender a new wave of environmental interest.

Unofficial policy actors are just one piece of the larger puzzle that helps us to understand and investigate environmental policymaking. The mechanisms in which organized interests attempt to influence decisionmaking are not easy, but, in terms of environmental protection, we need to be mindful of tracing who gets what, when, and how. One environmental expert reminds us, "Industry and environmental groups can lobby all they want, but we have to keep the environment safe." The question becomes what measures individuals or groups are willing to take to protect or to fight for the environment? Creating an alternative website for information may be one outlet, but we end this chapter with the case of Daniel McGowan and the Earth Liberation Front. His actions to protect the environment were classified as too extreme or eco-terrorism.

Case Study: Environmentalist or Terrorist? Daniel McGowan and the Earth Liberation Front

In 2007, Daniel McGowan was convicted of arson, labeled an eco-terrorist, and given a terrorist enhancement sentence (Cascadia 2007). This meant he was sentenced to 7 years in federal prison and spent most of his time in a Communicating Management Unit (CMU), which, following the 9/11 attacks, is a special federal prison designed specifically for terrorists (McGowan 2013). How McGowan met this fate highlights two pressing debates with regard to environmental policy and activism: how environmentalists should achieve their priorities and whether actions associated with those priorities can be labeled terrorism.

McGowan's story dates back to events in 1997 in Eugene, Oregon. At the time, 11 environmental activists attempted to protect 40 large trees in downtown Eugene from being removed for a new parking lot (Mercado 2013). The activists climbed the trees, and the police used pepper spray to remove the activists; one activist endured a dozen canisters of pepper spray before giving in (Mercado 2013). The activists failed in their attempt, and the trees were removed. In response to the nonviolent protests, McGowan said "what's the point why bother, it's not getting us anywhere... I like a lot of people I knew at the time experienced a massive loss of faith that systemic change could happen through the system regulating itself or reforming itself" (McGowan 2011). Therefore, McGowan decided to take a different approach and joined an environmental organization called the ELF, which focused on inflicting property damage on those who harm the environment (Harden 2006).

That same year, McGowan started his violent activism by protesting against a Brooklyn, New York Macy's for selling furs by breaking windows and spray-painting ALF, or Animal Liberation Front (a sister organization of ELF), on the building (Cascadia 2007). In 2000, McGowan participated in the Black Bloc protest in Seattle. After his protests in Seattle, McGowan became an important member of the ELF "Family." He traveled to the Midwest and participated in an ELF attack on a US Forest Service's Biotechnology Facility in Rhinelander, Wisconsin, which was developing genetically modified timber products.

Subsequently, McGowan returned to the West Coast where he participated in his two most notorious acts of arson against Superior Lumber and the Jefferson Poplar Farm (Cascadia 2007). McGowan noted that Superior Lumber was targeted because it was a timber company and Jefferson Poplar Farm because ELF suspected that the facility was growing genetically modified trees (McGowan 2011).

However, when McGowan found out that the Jefferson Poplar Farm was not growing genetically modified trees, he began to rethink his work with ELF. McGowan commented that, at the time, "I thought it was effective [when] you're in the thick of it, it's hard to look at all the consequences and the real repercussions of that. Did this action push them in a better direction? Did it scare them? Did it help the movement in any capacity?... There are a lot of questions but I don't think at the time I was asking those questions too much" (McGowan 2011). Upon reflection, McGowan concluded that "this is futile, there has to be better ways of addressing what's going on in the world than just burning things down" (McGowan 2011).

As a result, McGowan returned to New York City in 2002 and continued his advocacy work, but, this time, through conventional means. In New York, he worked on a number of causes including rainforest preservation, national forest protection, and biodiversity (Support for Daniel McGowan 2013). In 2005, he entered a graduate program at the Tri-State College of Acupuncture, with interests in providing medical care for those who cannot afford it (Support for Daniel McGowan 2013). However, the law caught up to him, and he was arrested in 2005 as a part of the Federal Bureau of Investigation's Operation Backfire in which 11 members of ELF were indicted (Harden 2006).

Then, US Attorney General Alberto Gonzales praised the arrests, arguing "today's indictment proves that we will not tolerate any group that terrorizes the American people, no matter its intentions or objectives" (Harden 2006). McGowan was released from prison in December 2012 (Woodhouse 2012). However, he was briefly jailed again in April 2013 for allegedly violating his terms of release when he published an article in *The Huffington Post* that was critical of the government (McGowan 2013). However, he was released shortly thereafter, when his lawyers found that the regulation allowing this arrest was found unconstitutional (Sledge 2013). Post-release, McGowan attempted to file a class action lawsuit for his first amendment rights (free speech) for being violated while in prison. This case was unsuccessful.

McGowan's story raises an important question—what type of approaches impact policy outcomes? Is it the unconventional approaches of McGowan, or is it donation campaigns to members of Congress? Further, if you use unconventional approaches, should these mechanisms be classified as eco-terrorism? McGowan is highly critical of the use of the term "eco-terrorist" in relation to his actions because he argues that it is a buzzword or: "a boogeyman word. It's, like, whoever I really disagree with is a terrorist" (McGowan 2011). Lauren Regan (2007), a member of his legal team, agreed, arguing that labeling McGowan and the other plaintiffs as terrorists was a mistake because these individuals were "charged with property crimes that didn't cause any harm to human life." However, Assistant US Attorney Stephen Peifer (2011) argued that the terrorist label was justified because "terrorist acts, under the definition of the law, can vary all over the board. There's no requirement for purposes of terrorism that you physically endanger another person's life." The Federal Bureau of Investigation also defines eco-terrorism as "the use or threatened use of violence of a criminal nature against innocent victims or property by an environmentally-oriented, subnational group for environmental-political reasons, or aimed at an audience beyond the target, often of a symbolic nature" (Jarboe 2002). Although McGowan's actions led to no physical human harm, under the law, he was labeled a terrorist and sent to prison (Stewart 2011).

Since McGowan was convicted of terrorism, the definition of eco-terrorism has expanded to include "setting mink free at fur farms, campaigns to financially bankrupt animal testing firms and protests in front of the homes of some of those firms' executives" (Eilperin 2012). Nevertheless, it remains to be seen if this is the end of the movement toward violent environmental activism, or if it is simply dormant, waiting for the next generation of McGowans.

Challenge Question for the Environmental Policy Classroom

Use https://www.followthemoney.org/ and click on your home state. What type of group donated the most money to an elected official. Now, research this organization, what is their mission. Does the mission of their organization promote issues keeping current structures in power or providing access to decisionmaking for a wide variety of individuals?

SUGGESTED RESOURCES

Readings and Websites

Braun, Ashley. "Facebook App Translates Online Efforts into Real-World Environmental Change." Grist, 2013. http://grist.org/article/2009–05–12-facebook-efforts-real-change/.

Discover Text. Collaborative Text Analytics Solution. June 14, 2014. http://www.discover-text.com/.

"Is Using Social Media Bad for the Environment?" October 15, 2018. https://www.vice.com/en_uk/article/d3wa7a/is-using-social-media-bad-for-the-environment

Sledge, Matt. "I Got Snatched." Huffington Post. Accessed January 22, 2014. http://www.huffingtonpost.com/2013/09/12/daniel-mcgowan-prison_n_3860426.html.

Wilson, Diane. Diary of an Eco-outlaw: An Unreasonable Woman Breaks the Law for Mother Earth. White River Junction, VT: Chelsea Green Publishing, 2011.

———. *An Unreasonable Woman: A True Story of Shrimpers, Politicos, Polluters, and the Fight for Seadrift, Texas*. White River Junction, VT: Chelsea Green Publishing, 2005.

Films or Video

If a Tree Falls: A Story of the Earth Liberation Front. Directed by Marshall Curry, 2012. Independent Television Service, Corporation for Public Broadcasting. DVD.
Thank You for Smoking. Directed by Jason Reitman. 2005. Fox Searchlight. DVD.
Miss Sloane. Directed by Jonathan Perera, 2016.

REFERENCES

Abrams, Rachel. "Under Pressure, Feminine Product Makers Disclose Ingredients." *New York Times*. October 26, 2015. https://www.nytimes.com/2015/10/27/business/under-pressure-feminine-product-makers-disclose-ing redients.html?_r=1.
About Us: National Audubon Society. Accessed June 13, 2013. http://www.aud ubon.org/about-us.
Baumgartner, Frank and Beth Leech. *Basic Interests: The Importance of Groups in Politics in Political Science*. Princeton, NJ: Princeton University Press, 1998.
———. "Interest Niches and Policy Bandwagons: Patterns of Interest Group Involvement in National Politics." *The Journal of Politics* 63, no. 4 (2001): 1191–1213.
Baumgartner, Frank R., Jeffrey M. Berry, Marie Hojnacki, David C. Kimball, and Beth Leech. *Lobbying and Policy Change: Who Wins, Who Loses, and Why*. Chicago: University of Chicago Press, 2009.
Below, Amy. "Parties, Campaigns, and Elections: Their Influence on Environmental Politics and Policymaking." In *Oxford Handbook of US Environmental Policy*, edited by Michael E. Kraft and Sheldon Kamiencki, 525–553. New York: Oxford University Press, 2012.
Bertrand, Savannah. *Fact Sheet: Proposals to Reduce Fossil Fuel Subsidies*. Environmental and Energy Study Institute. 2021. https://www.eesi.org/files/Fac tSheet_Fossil_Fuel_Subsidies_2021.pdf#:~:text=Proposals%20to%20Reduce%20Fossil%20Fuel%20Subsidies%20%282021%29%20July,subsidies.1%20When%20externalities%20such%20as%20health%2C%20environmental%2C%20and.
Boykoff, Maxwell. "Digital Cultures and Climate Change: 'Here and Now'." January 2020. http://sciencepolicy.colorado.edu/admin/publication_files/2020.01.pdf

Boykoff, Maxwell and S. Ravi Rajan. "US Library of Medicine." March 2007. http://www.ncbi.nlm.nih.gov/pmc/articles/PMC1808044/.

Cascadia, Gumby. "Daniel McGowan's Sentencing Report." Portland Independent Media Center, June 4, 2007. http://portland.indymedia.org/en/2007/06/360572.shtml.

Center for Responsive Politics (CFRP). *Alternative Energy Production & Services: Lobbying*. 2021a. Accessed February 4, 2022. https://www.opensecrets.org/industries/lobbying.php?ind=E1500.

Center for Responsive Politics. (2022) https://www.influencewatch.org/nonprofit/center-for-responsive-politics/

———. *Environment: Lobbying*. 2021b. Accessed February 4, 2022. https://www.opensecrets.org/industries/lobbying.php?cycle=2012&ind=Q11.

———. *Natural Gas Pipelines: Lobbying*. 2021c. Accessed February 4, 2022. https://www.opensecrets.org/industries/lobbying.php?ind=E1140.

———. *Oil & Gas: Lobbying*. 2021d. Accessed February 4, 2022. https://www.opensecrets.org/industries/lobbying.php?cycle=2022&ind=E01.

Christen, Cindy T., and Kelli E. Huberty. "Media Reach, Media Influence? The Effects of Local, National and Internet News on Public Opinion Inferences." *Journalism & Mass Communication Quarterly* 84, no. 2 (2007): 315–334.

Clines, Francis X. "Lobbyist Look for Euphemism." *New York Times*. September 21, 2013. http://www.nytimes.com/.

Cook, Jeffrey and Sara R. Rinfret. "A Revised Look: EPA Rulemaking Processes." *Journal of Environmental Studies and Sciences* 3, no. 3 (2013): 279–289.

Cohen, Robert C. "Are Men Changing Earth's Weather?" *Christian Science Monitor* 4 (December 1957): 13.

Dahl, Robert A. *Who Governs? Democracy and Power in an American City*. New Haven, CT: Yale University Press, 1961.

Duffy, Robert J. *The Green Agenda in American Politics: New Strategies for the Twenty-First Century*. Lawrence: University Press of Kansas, 2003.

Eilperin, Juliet. "As Eco-Terrorism Wanes, Governments Still Target Activist Groups Seen as Threat." *Washington Post*. August 8, 2012. http://articles.washingtonpost.com/.

Environmental Coverage. (2013). https://www.mediamatters.org/new-york-times/study-kardashians-get-40-times-more-news-coverage-ocean-acidification

Friends of Natural Gas. August 2, 2013. http://www.friendsofnaturalgasny.com/.

Ginsberg, Benjamin, Theodore J. Lowi, Margaret Weir, and Caroline J. Tolbert. *We the People: An Introduction to American Politics*. New York: W. W. Norton & Company, 2013.

Greenpeace. "About Us." August 23, 2013. http://www.greenpeace.org/usa/en/.

Golden, Marissa Martino. "Interest Groups in the Rule-Making Process: Who Participates? Whose Voices Get Heard?" *Journal of Public Administration Research and Theory* 8, no. 2 (1998): 245–270.

Guber, Deborah Lynn and Christopher J. Bosso. "High Hopes and Bitter Disappointment." In *Environmental Policy: New Directions for the 21st Century*, edited by Michael E. Kraft and Norman J. Vig, 525–553. Washington, DC: CQ Press, 2013.

Harden, Blaine. "11 Indicted in 'Eco-Terrorism' Case." *Washington Post*. 2006. Accessed August 8, 2013. http://www.washingtonpost.com/.

Jarboe, James F. "Testimony Before the House Resources Committee, Subcommittee on Forests and Forest Health." Federal Bureau of Investigation. 2002. http://www.fbi.gov/news/testimony/the-threat-of-eco-terrorism.

Kerwin, Cornelious M. and Furlong, Scott R. *Rulemaking: How Government Agencies Write Law and Make Policy*. Washington, DC: CQ Press, 2011.

Kingdon, John W. *Agendas, Alternatives and Public Policies*. 2nd edition. New York: Longman, 2003.

Klyza, Christopher McGrory and David Sousa. *American Environmental Policy, 1990–2006: Beyond Gridlock*. Cambridge: MIT Press, 2013.

Lindblom, Charles. *Politics and Markets*. New York: Basic Books, 1977.

Lowi, Theodore. "Four Systems of Policy, Politics and Choice." *Public Administration Review* 32, no. 4 (1972): 298–310.

Magat, Wesley, Alan Krupnick, and Winston Harrington. *Rules in the Making: A Statistical of Regulatory Agency Behavior*. Washington, DC: Resources for the Future Press, 1986.

McCubbins, Matthew D., Roger G. Noll, and Barry R. Weingast. "Administrative Procedures as Instruments of Political Control." *Journal of Law, Economics, and Organization* 3 (1987): 243–277.

McGlashen, Andy. https://www.audubon.org/news/some-musics-biggest-names-create-trove-new-tunes-help-birds. Accessed May 18, 2022.

McGowan, Daniel. *If a Tree Falls: A Story of the Earth Liberation Front*. Directed by Marshall Curry and Sam Cullman. Oscilloscope Pictures, 2011. DVD.

———. "Court Documents Prove I Was Sent to Communication Management Units (CMU) for My Political Speech." *Huffington Post*. August 8, 2013. http://www.huffingtonpost.com/.

Mercado, Jeffrey. "In Defense of Trees." *Envision Environmental Journalism*. August 7, 2013. http://envision.uoregon.edu/archives/1697.

Miller, Tyler and Todd Pollak. Environmental Coverage in Mainstream News: We Need. More. 2012. Accessed July 13, 2014. http://greeningthemedia.org/wp-content/uploads/Environmental-Coverage-in-the-Mainstream-News.pdf.

Miller, Alexandria and Lucia Bolles. Available from: https://digitalcommons.usm.maine.edu/thinking-matters-symposium/2021/poster-sessions/30/.

Mills, C. W. *The Power Elite*. London: Oxford University Press, 1956.

Morris, David. 2009. Accessed August 26, 2014. http://grist.org/article/2009-10-05-new-roposed-climate-change-bill-in-washington-is-simpler-and-mor/

Natural Resources Defense Council (NRDC). Accessed February 13, 2013. http://www.nrdc.org/globalwarming/.

NBC News/Wall Street Journal. *Study #11091. Wall Street Journal.* 2011. Accessed August 23, 2013. http://online.wsj.com/article/SB1000142405 2748704005404576176981643217882.html.

Olson, Mancur. *The Logic of Collective Action: Public Goods and the Theory of Groups.* Cambridge, MA: Harvard University Press, 1965.

Peifer, Stephen. In *If a Tree Falls: A Story of the Earth Liberation Front.* Directed by Marshall Curry and Sam Cullman. City of Production: Oscilloscope Pictures, 2011. DVD.

Persaud, Roxanne. *Senate Bill S2387.* The New York State Senate. January 24, 2019. https://www.nysenate.gov/legislation/bills/2019/s2387/ame ndment/original.

Regan, Lauren. Interview by Amy Goodman and Juan Gonzalez. *Democracy Now a Daily Independent Global News House with Amy Goodman & Juan Gonzalez.* 2007. Accessed August 9, 2013. http://www.democracynow.org/2007/6/11/exclusive_facing_seven_years_in_jail.

Schakowsky, Janice. *H.R. 1385—Safe Cosmetics and Personal Care Products Act of 2013.* Congress. July 8, 2013. https://www.congress.gov/bill/113th-con gress/house-bill/1385.

Scranton, Alexandra. 2013. Accessed October 15, 2018. https://www.womens voices.org/wp-content/uploads/2013/11/Chem-Fatale-Report.pdf.

Sherlock, Molly F. "Energy Tax Policy: Historical Perspectives on and Current Status of Energy Tax Expenditures." 2010. Accessed August 23, 2013. http://www.national-aglawcenter.org/assets/crs/R41227.pdf.

Sklair, L., and M. Boykoff. Mass Media Representations of Anthromes. *Encyclopedia of the World's Biomes* (2019): 407–414. https://www.sciencedirect.com/science/article/pii/B9780124095489121219?via%3Dihub.

Sledge, Matt. "Daniel McGowan Released After Lawyers Confirm He Was Jailed for HuffPost Blog." *Huffington Post.* August 8, 2013. http://www.huffingto npost.com/.

Stewart, Christopher S. "Little Gitmo." *New York Magazine.* 2011. Accessed August 8, 2013. http://nymag.com/news/features/yassin-aref-2011-7/.

"Support for Daniel McGowan." Accessed 9, 2013. http://www.supportdaniel.org/whois/bio.php.

Sussman, Glen, Byron W. Daynes, and Jonathan P. West. *American Politics and the Environment.* New York: Longman, 2001.

The Guardian. "Prop 37: Food Companies Spend $45 Million to Defeat California GM Bill." Accessed August 9, 2013. http://www.theguardian.com/environment/2012/nov/05/prop-37-food-gm-bill.

Truman, David. *The Governmental Process.* New York: Alfred A. Knopf, 1951.

UN News. IPCC Report: 'Code Red' for Human Driven Global Heating, Warns UN Chief. United Nations. 2021. Accessed February 6, 2022. https://news.un.org/en/story/2021/08/1097362.

US Chamber of Commerce, American Farm Bureau Federation, and the State of Alaska v. Environmental Protection Agency (EPA). Accessed February 12, 2013. http://www.chamberlitigation.com/us-chamber-commerce-american-farm-bureau-federation-and-state-alaska-v-environmental-protection-agen.

US EPA. "The Toxics Release Inventory: A National Perspective." *A Report on the First Year of Data Collected Under Section 313 of the Emergency Planning and Community Right-to-Know Act of 1986.* Washington, DC: GPO, 1987.

Vaughn, Jacqueline. *Environmental Politics: Domestic and Global Dimensions.* 5th edition. New York: Thomas Wadsworth, 2007.

Vig, Norman and Michael E. Kraft. *Environmental Policy: A New Direction for the 21st Century.* 5th edition. Washington, DC: CQ Press, 2013.

West, William. "Formal Procedures, Informal Procedures, Accountability, and Responsiveness in Bureaucratic Policymaking. An Institutional Policy Analysis." *Public Administration Review* 46, no. 2 (2004): 66–80.

WVE. WVE's Statement on the Passing of California's AB 1989. September 30, 2020. https://www.womensvoices.org/2020/09/30/statement-passing-of-ab1989-period-product-ingredient-disclosure-bill/.

Woodhouse, Leighton. "Earth Liberation Front Activist Released After 7 Years in 'Little Guantanamo.'" *Huffington Post.* 2012. Accessed August 8, 2013. http://www.huffing-tonpost.com/.leighton-woodhouse/earth lib eration-front ac_b_2295064.html.

Yale Project on Climate Change and Communication. *Politics & Global Warming.* 2020. https://climatecommunication.yale.edu/wp-content/upl oads/2021/01/politics-global-warming-december-2020b.pdf

(YLN) Young Lobbyist Network. Accessed August 28, 2013. http://www.alldc.org/youngleaders/index.cfm.

CHAPTER 6

Translating Vague Statutes into Rules and Regulations

Introductory Story: An Environmental Justice Political Appointee, the US Environmental Protection Agency, and Rulemaking
If you were walking down the street one afternoon and a news reporter asked for your candid thoughts on environmental rulemaking, you would probably respond with a blank stare or you might say the act of rulemaking included a bureaucrat sitting behind a computer all day, filling out forms. As you will learn in this chapter, rulemaking is an essential component to a thorough understanding of how environmental policy works. While this aspect of the policymaking processes is not normally covered in your American government textbook, that might change due to lessons learned from EPA administrator, Michael Regan.

Rulemaking comprises the agency process of translating congressional legislation into specific, actionable rules. Rule-writers, or regulatory analysts, within agencies like the EPA are charged with this task. There is far more to the process than simply having a bureaucrat sit behind a computer, filling out forms. How an agency constructs a rule, what policy options it selects to carry out that rule, and the methods used to invite stakeholder input are all components of the rule-writing process, which make it particularly complicated. These complexities can lead to disgruntled members of regulated facilities or interest groups who might find

© The Author(s), under exclusive license to Springer Nature
Switzerland AG 2023
S. R. Rinfret and M. C. Pautz, *US Environmental Policy in Action*,
https://doi.org/10.1007/978-3-031-17503-9_6

it challenging to implement new procedures such as meeting emissions standards under the Clean Air Act.

Yet, what happens when the head of the EPA becomes an individual that has spent an entire career fighting to prevent environmental injustices often caused by the pollution of a regulated community. In March of 2021, President Biden nominated Michael Regan as the 16th Administrator of the EPA (EPA 2021). Administrator Regan is the first Black man to lead the agency. Regan brings with him a strong background in environmental negotiation, experience in rulemaking, and intersectionality.

Prior to becoming the EPA Administrator, Regan served as the Secretary of the North Carolina Department of Environmental Quality where he developed and implemented the plans for the state's response to climate change and transition to a clean energy economy (EPA 2021). While in this position he led the largest coal ash cleanup in US history and spearheaded negotiations for the toxic waste cleanup of the Cape Fear River (EPA 2021). In this position, he also established the state's first Environmental Justice and Equity Advisory board (EPA 2021). Previously, he also held positions as the Associate Vice President of US Climate and Energy, the Southeast Regional Director of the Environmental Defense Fund, and a National Program Manager for the EPA, all of which built his career in preparation for the Administrator role (EPA 2021).

In November of 2021, Administrator Regan started his new role with a "Journey to Justice Tour" (Regan et al. 2021). On this trip, Regan visited low-income, communities who have suffered from environmental injustices. Upon returning from the tour, Regan released a set of specific actions the EPA would adopt to respond to the concerns witnessed in Mississippi, Louisiana, and Texas, with additional agency-wide actions announcements (EPA 2022). Under Regan's leadership, the EPA will focus on rulemaking and actions that are grounded in the best available science, equity, and justice. In addition, Regan is attempting to rebuild the agency and reinstate regulations that the Trump administration rolled back (Regan et al. 2021). As noted in Chapter 5, the EPA administrator can affect policy implementation in addition to the president. In particular, the EPA administrator can help to shape the agency's federal regulatory process—rulemaking. The following pages uncover the importance of environmental rulemaking and our understanding of its stages.

The Office of Budget and Management (OMB) suggests federal regulations provide up to 218 billion dollars in benefits for the US (Longley 2021). Undoubtedly, this is significant benefit; therefore, we should pay attention to how an agency writes rules. Remember, many of the environmental laws of the 1970s are still used today by government agencies to implement policy. However, translating vague environmental statutes (legislation) into environmental rules and regulations is not an easy task, as Fiorino's story suggests. This chapter is unusual because it offers a perspective of environmental policy that other textbooks do not—the role of administrative rulemaking, what it entails, and how interest groups attempt to influence the process.

The goal of this chapter is to explain what happens after Congress passes a law through the lens of administrative rulemaking. Within environmental policymaking, rulemaking is the way policy creation happens beyond congressional gridlock (Klyza and Sousa 2013). Agencies such as the National Park Service (NPS) or the US Fish and Wildlife Service (USFWS) create environmental rules that range from protecting the habitat of the polar bear to determining the amount of snowmobiles allowed each winter in Yellowstone National Park.

Accordingly, this chapter starts with an explanation of how agency employees have the authority to make rules, which are laws. Then, we explain the stages of rulemaking and how particular groups try to influence rulemaking. After our discussion of the stages of rulemaking, our chapter case study puts the rulemaking process into practice through the lens of Corporate Average Fuel Economy (CAFE) standards rule and the impact of political appointees. Our chapter concludes with a comparison between federal and state rulemaking processes. We cannot forget that states are making important decisionmakers in how we implement environmental policy on a daily basis. Most importantly, we argue throughout this chapter that the work of a rule-writer is ever changing and provides a significant opportunity to shape the direction of environmental policy.

Upon completion of this chapter, a few themes become apparent. We have noted repeatedly throughout this text environmental rulemaking matters because it is where environmental policy is translated into concrete action. Federal and state rule-writers across the US have a significant amount of discretion to interpret federal and state legislation to create rules that affect the future of the environment. However, most people have never heard of the *Federal Register*. We demonstrate the *Federal Register* is an important tool in a democracy for individuals to participate in policymaking.

WHY WOULD CONGRESS DELEGATE ITS AUTHORITY?

The bureaucracy, or the fourth branch of government, is not described in the US Constitution, but it has a lot of power to make rules. Because of the significant amount of time it takes to carry out or implement congressional legislation, Congress delegates its authority to agencies for a variety of reasons. Put succinctly, the process by which Congress shifts responsibilities to the bureaucracy is more commonly known as the delegation of authority. There are a variety of reasons why members of Congress choose to delegate their power. One reason why members of Congress delegate is because of their lack of time and expertise. To implement public policy, Congress delegates its authority to the experts in the bureaucracy because of technical expertise required to understand the details of a given law. In addition, the time—months, if not years—required to promulgate (or write) a rule is beyond the time any member of Congress has to devote to one specific issue. For example, the CAFE standards program was established by Congress as a method to reduce oil consumption from vehicles in response to the 1973 Oil Embargo. After passing the Energy Policy and Conservation Act (EPCA) of 1975 (42 U.S.C. §6201), Congress directed the National Highway Traffic and Safety Administration (NHTSA) to establish higher fuel economy standards for cars and light trucks. Congress delegated its authority because the NHTSA is composed of trained experts in the technical aspects of fuel economy standards.

The second and, arguably, most important reason why Congress delegates its authority is what Morris Fiorina (1982) argues is a "shift the responsibility" rationale. Congress can avoid the controversy and criticism associated with policies it created by shifting the responsibility to an agency. For example, a member of Congress can use the agency and its rulemaking process as a scapegoat. Although some may scratch their heads and question the constitutionality of Congress' actions of shifting its responsibility to unelected members of the bureaucracy to make decisions about the law, it becomes clearer with the Supreme Court's interpretation.

The Supreme Court's interpretation of "Legislative power vested in Congress of the US" (Article I, Section I, US Constitution) changed with the shifts in the makeup of the Court, and with the passage of the Administrative Procedure Act (which will be discussed later), and a variety of laws enacted in the 1960s and 1970s (Rinfret and Furlong 2013). In several cases, the Supreme Court has upheld a broader interpretation of delegation authority and has allowed Congress to provide significant policymaking power to executive agencies (see *Industrial Union Department, AFL-CIO v. American Petroleum Institute* (1980), *American Textile Manufacturers Institute v. Donovan* (1981), and *Whitman v. American Trucking Associations* ([2001]). However, it remains to be seen the impact *West Virginia v. EPA* (2022) has on Congress' ability to delegate lawmaking authority to administrative agencies.

Typically, agencies have a significant amount of discretion. However, before exploring some of the ways agency decisions are checked by other branches of government, we must first expand our understanding of delegation with a discussion of discretion. As the aforementioned CAFE standards example suggests, when the Energy Policy Act (EPCA) of 1975 mandated a CAFE standard of 27.5 miles per gallon for cars and a 20.7 miles per gallon (mpg) standard for light trucks, the NHTSA was given discretion (or the authority) to set standards for Model Year (MY) 1978 vehicles. Thus, since the NHTSA was delegated authority by Congress, it had the discretion to determine how these standards were implemented and were most recently revised by the Biden administration in March 2022 to 49 mpg for passenger cars and light trucks in model year 2026.

Mechanisms of Accountability

Agency discretion is limited by several accountability mechanisms—Congress and the president have different means to check the bureaucracy's work. As Sara Rinfret and Scott Furlong (2013) note:

> This relationship between elected leaders and the bureaucratic agencies is described by the principal-agent model, which refers to the ongoing relationship between the political principal and the bureaucratic agent and how each tries to achieve its sometimes inconsistent goals (see Kerwin and Furlong 2011). Gary Bryner (1987) characterizes the tools that political principals use as falling into three categories: administrative procedures, economic and scientific decision rules, and political oversight. (375)

There are a number of ways to check the power of the bureaucracy to make decisions, which we explore next.

Congressional and Presidential Oversight: Congress and the President can exercise oversight to ensure the accountability of agency actions. Congress can write legislation stating what limits an agency has in writing a rule and can even change the course of previous actions of an agency. Consider our example on the NHTSA and CAFE standards. During the 1990s, there was significant debate regarding whether the CAFE standards were effective; automobile manufacturers contended that Americans demanded bigger vehicles and higher efficiency standards would not accommodate this demand. To an extent, manufacturers were correct because as sport utility vehicles (SUVs) became popular in the 1990s, public relations campaigns by the industry to thwart CAFE standard increases were successful (Plungis 2000). In fact, for much of the 1990s, Congress made it impossible to increase the CAFE standards. From 1995 to 1999, Congress attached an amendment to an appropriations bill to stop the NHTSA from studying the need for increased standards (McCutcheon 2001). Moreover, from 1997 to 2001, Congress instituted a freeze on the CAFE standards for light trucks (Lorenzetti 2005). However, as oil prices continued to climb during the early 2000s, industry began to lose momentum and the NHTSA was then again able to slowly increase fuel economy standards for light trucks (Lorenzetti 2005). This example shows that, although an agency such as NHTSA has been created to carry out CAFE standards, there are limits set by Congress.

Moreover, agencies need monetary resources to carry out policy. Congress authorizes agency budgets and how much money can be spent on particular programs. Specifically, the Appropriations Committees in the House of Representatives and the Senate distribute available funds among all federal agencies. If Congress does not like a specific program or agency, money can be cut from an agency or redirected. Congress can also approve the presidential nomination of a political appointee to set policy directives favorable to that of their own.

Another oversight function Congress can use is a "hammer." A hammer is a provision in a piece of legislation that states if an agency fails to finalize a rule by a certain date, then Congress will force action. Often, the regulated community does not appreciate hammers. This is because, if the EPA is supposed to create a rule by a certain date and if it does not, Congress could state within the legislation that certain chemicals used by the regulated community are then banned from use until the EPA can finalize the rule. Therefore, it is up to the agency to examine a particular product by the deadline and, if it does not, it could impact the business that produces it.

A final example of congressional oversight can be classified as either police patrol or fire alarms. The police patrol approach is the notion that Congress examines every rule or action taken by an agency that is seen as costly and inefficient. The other approach is the fire alarm, in which Congress conducts oversight hearings of problem areas to ensure the processes that agencies use are effective (Kerwin and Furlong 2018). Nevertheless, there are a variety of ways that Congress can check the bureaucracy and the actions it takes.

Congressional forms of oversight are important, but presidents also perform oversight functions. These mechanisms include appointments, executive orders, and even reorganization. The president has the authority to appoint an individual to oversee an agency. These appointments have to be confirmed by the US Senate, but presidential appointments can and do impact the direction of an agency. For instance, President Biden's EPA administrator Michael Regan set an agenda focused on climate change and environmental justice, counter to the previous administrator's agenda of regulatory rollbacks.

Another form of presidential oversight of the federal bureaucracy is the use of executive orders. Executive orders are mandates by the president that carry the same weight as a law passed by Congress. In 2009, President Obama issued Executive Order 13514, which instructed all federal agencies to set sustainability goals. More specifically, within 90 days of the issuance of the order, each agency had to create and submit a 2020 greenhouse gas pollution reduction target, explaining how its agency would become more environmentally friendly (Council on Environmental Quality 2014). President Trump's Executive Order 13783 stressed that the US will become energy independent by opening federal lands to oil and gas leasing (see Chapter 9), which President Biden quickly rolled back once elected to office. In 2021, President Biden signed Executive Order 14008 titled "Tackling the Climate Crisis at Home and Abroad" which outlined a holistic approach to mitigating the impacts of climate change in the US and abroad.

The last example of presidential oversight is the authority of the president to reorganize the federal bureaucracy. This rarely occurs, but it is a way for a president to combine agencies to either reward or punish them or perhaps focus on a particular issue. One recent example of presidential reorganization was in 2011 after the Deepwater Horizon oil spill. One of the primary agencies responsible for overseeing this offshore drilling was the Minerals Management Service (MMS); however, due to its poor industrial oversight of offshore drilling procedures, the Obama administration created two new agencies (the Bureau of Safety and Environmental Enforcement and the Bureau of Ocean, Energy Management, Regulation and Enforcement) to reorganize the efforts of MMS. In 2018, President Trump announced plans to reorganize the Department of Interior to consolidate agencies and programs deemed redundant or unnecessary, another attempt to reduce the size of government. However, President Biden used an executive order to revoke Trump's regulatory rollback efforts (White House 2021).

Although there are concerns that the bureaucracy runs amuck when making public policy, Congress and the president have a number of ways to oversee its processes. More importantly, we need to remember that Congress delegates its authority for a variety of reasons, namely, to shift its responsibility to those who have more time and expertise. The notion of delegating congressional power might seem questionable; however, oversight mechanisms are in place to ensure that unelected officials do not abuse their power. We turn to one of the most essential duties of the federal bureaucracy—rulemaking, or as the title of the chapter describes, how members of the bureaucracy turn vague congressional statutes into law.

RULES IN THE MAKING

Rulemaking is the process used by government employees to translate vague congressional statues into law. The administrative rulemaking process includes many stages and access points for both stakeholders and the public to participate. This section begins with a brief historical overview of the Administrative Procedures Act (APA) and how this act helps define the stages of the rulemaking process (also referred to as the promulgation process). Then, we discuss how groups try to influence different stages of this process.

The Administrative Procedures Act

From 1933 to 1945, there was significant growth in the size of the federal government in order to implement President Franklin D. Roosevelt's New Deal policies and programs to help bring the nation out of the economic depression and to address the nation's war efforts. With this growth came the creation of a multitude of federal agencies such as the

Civilian Conservation Corps (CCC). In response, the APA was adopted in 1946 as an oversight and accountability tool for the rapidly expanding government under the New Deal.

The APA requires agencies to follow administrative rulemaking guidelines to ensure that government entities carry out congressional statutes in a uniform, prescribed manner. According to the APA, a rule "means the whole or part of an agency statement of general or particular applicability and future effect designed to implement, interpret, or prescribe law or policy." A rule created by an agency then carries the same legal force as a law. Administrative rulemaking is comprised of various stages by which an agency creates and implements a rule. The description of the rulemaking stages, in the following, demonstrates that the APA requirement of public participation during the notice and comment portion of the rulemaking processes allows for significant public involvement.

There are many forms of administrative rulemaking: formal, informal, negotiated, and hybrid. Formal rulemaking demands official hearings that resemble the proceedings of a courtroom. Informal rulemaking, also known as "notice and comment," requires that agencies encourage the public to participate in the process by submitting comments once a draft or final rule is published in the *Federal Register*. Over the last decade, the *Federal Register* has become available online (https://www.federa lregister.gov/) and a resource for the public to search when an agency publishes a rule and to provide feedback. An additional resource for the public is also Regulations.gov, which describes to the public, by agency, the rulemaking actions that agencies are taking. Negotiated rulemaking (sometimes informally referred to as "reg neg," as noted in the introduction of this chapter) occurs when agency officials organize and participate in negotiations with stakeholders to develop a rule. Hybrid rulemaking, in comparison, happens relatively infrequently and involves agencies using aspects of both informal and formal processes (Cooper 2007). With a working understanding of rulemaking and different approaches, we focus on notice and comment rulemaking because it is the most common process.

DIFFERENT THAN CONGRESSIONAL LAWMAKING

Figure 6.1 illustrates the common stages of the process for formal or notice and comment rulemaking. Typically, these stages occur across 11 detailed stages; however, for the purposes of brevity, we have condensed our explanation into three stages.

Fig. 6.1 Stages of rulemaking

Stage 1: Rule development is the first stage and it includes an agency's efforts to gather technical, scientific, and economic information regarding why a rule is necessary, as well as how a rule should be developed. For example, the EPA creates rules associated with the CAA. Therefore, at this stage, EPA agency personnel often work with stakeholders from a variety of perspectives (e.g., public health, environmental, and industry) to produce a draft rule. However, the way in which the agency and stakeholders discuss information at this stage is via informal communication and is not subject to legal restrictions from the APA, but is simply a way for agencies to collect information (Rinfret and Furlong 2013). Even though this might seem alarming, the rule development stage is also a way for an agency to uncover any issues that might arise regarding controversial rules. For instance, the USFWS designation of critical habitats for the polar bear in parts of Alaska created a great deal of concern—notably, about issues surrounding land preservation and oil production—from a variety of industry and environmental groups.

As a result, there are other approaches that an agency can use during the rule development phase, which can range from an Advanced Notice of Proposed.

Rulemaking (ANPRM), Notice of Intent (NOI), or outreach meetings. The ANPRM and NOI are published in the *Federal Register* (more details will be provided in our explanation of stage 2) and the agency can solicit comments about particular ideas (e.g., certain sections of land to be set aside for the polar bear's habitat). Furthermore, an agency can offer stakeholder outreach sessions by inviting groups to meet with an agency to discuss topics pertaining to a particular rule.

As the agency finalizes information within the first stage, agencies must also conduct economic and scientific analyses (Kerwin and Furlong 2018). President Reagan issued Executive Order 12291 that required agencies to conduct regulatory impact analyses showing that the potential costs to society would outweigh the benefits when moving forward with a rule, and the Office of Management and Budget (OMB) oversees this process. Then, in 1993, President Clinton replaced Reagan's Executive Order 12291 with Executive Order 12866, which continues the use of cost-benefit analysis and encourages agencies to conduct risk assessments or performance-based standards (see Chapter 8 for more details). Executive Order 12866 delegated that the Office of Information and Regulatory Affairs (OIRA, which is within OMB) to coordinate rulemakings to encourage these aforementioned priorities. After OIRA signs off on a draft rule, an agency is then able to move into the next phase of the process.

Shapiro (2006) argues that these added layers of the rulemaking process create "paralysis analysis." Put differently, this means that the additional analysis that an agency is required to conduct can inhibit its efforts to move forward quickly. However, extensive analysis could also lead to a better outcome. For example, consider the rule surrounding a "dangerous dust," also known as silica, which are tiny stone particles produced when a worker blasts material such as sandstone, brick, or concrete (Verchick 2013). The Occupational Safety and Health Administration (OSHA) wants to create a new rule that would lessen the amount of silica that a person could inhale on the job. The idea is that this would save a great number of lives, but it took OSHA more than 9 years to propose this rule. In the time it took to write this rule, 1,400 lives could have been saved (Verchick 2013). Nevertheless, during stage 1 of the process, an agency conducts a great deal of research in order to move forward.

Stage 2: The second stage, notice and comment, is where the agency publishes a Notice of Proposed Rulemaking (NPRM) in the *Federal Register*, which is a daily publication of all federal rules. This required stage in the process ensures that an agency provides notice and a way for the public to participate in the process. When an agency publishes an NPRM, it typically grants the public 30 to 60 days to submit a public comment about the rule.

Before 2002, if a person or group wanted to submit a public comment to the *Federal Register*, it had to be mailed. Then, if someone wanted to read the public comments submitted by others, this information needed to be requested from either the *Federal Register* or the agency issuing the rule. This might be a difficult endeavor as, across all federal agencies in the US, approximately 8,000 rules are proposed each year (Kerwin and Furlong 2011). However, within the last decade, agencies are required to allow the public to electronically submit comments on Regulations.gov. This online resource has provided a timelier way of following a rule's development. In 2021, Regulations.gov made our lives even easier by updating their search engine where one can search by agency and rule, to increase the speed and relevancy of results to users. With nearly 10 million documents on Regulations.gov, the search engine now divides results into 3 categories: Dockets, Documents, and Comments, to make it easier for the public to sort through information. The public can still subscribe for notifications about agency regulations and now, when documents are added, modified, or withdrawn, subscribers are notified. In addition, the commenting process has been streamlined across the agencies to create a standardized comment form that asks the same information for all comments.

Stage 3: When the comment period ends, the agency moves to stage 3, the final publication stage, and examines the comments to determine the language of the final rule. Once a rule is final, it is published in the *Federal Register*. However, during this final phase, the agency must sometimes prepare for litigation in the form of petitions for reconsideration of a rule from stakeholder groups. For instance, several meat industry organizations sued the US Department of Agriculture over the country-of-origin labeling rule (COOL). The argument made by these manufacturers was that this particular rule places an undue burden on their respective companies to place an origin label on each meat and poultry package, which ultimately increases prices for the consumer (Supermarket News 2013). Then, in 2015, the World Trade Organization (WTO) stated the COOL requirements disadvantaged beef and pork products coming from outside the US and violated trade agreements signed by the US As a result, the WTO would allow Mexico and Canada to impose retaliatory tariffs on US products. In 2016, a final ruling of COOL passed which removed muscle cut beef and pork, and ground beef and pork from the labeling requirements.

Now that we have a basic understanding of the process used by all federal agencies to create a rule and why Congress delegates its authority, it is helpful to contextualize this process with a more thorough example—one that may even help to explain why it would take an agency 9 years to write a rule.

Case Study: Stalled: Achieving the Unthinkable, Raising the CAFE Standards
In order to truly understand how contemporary environmental policy is made, we turn back to the example of the CAFE standards program administered by the National Highway Traffic Safety Administration (NHTSA). This case contains has a rich history, illustrating how a rule transitions through the stages of the process, interest group participation, and post-rulemaking activities. From 2010 to 2021, the NHTSA rule also reveals how presidential administrations can effect outcomes.

Stage 1: In May of 2010, President Obama issued a Presidential Memorandum. This memorandum noted that the NHTSA and the EPA should conduct a rulemaking setting standards from MY 2017 to MY 2025. This encouraged the participation with stakeholder groups and California (Obama 2010). The NHTSA and the EPA conducted stakeholder outreach meetings with manufacturers, labor unions, and environmental groups to gather information regarding emerging technologies to improve fuel economy and capabilities to commercialize these and other existing technologies (NHTSA 2010). The agencies, in conjunction with the California Air Resources Board (CARB), produced a Technical Assessment Report (TAR) that compiled this information into one document.

The EPA and NHTSA published an NOI in the *Federal Register* in September 2010. The NOI outlined the agencies' findings from TAR and provided a listing of potential stringency levels for the new standards. The agencies used this document to set the rulemaking timetable, with a proposed rule planned for September 30, 2011, and a final rule published by July 31, 2012 (EPA and NHTSA 2010a). The agencies offered a 30-day comment period on this document and the two agencies received comments from 30 organizations and 100,000 people.

The agencies produced a supplementary NOI in November that outlined responses to comments from the first NOI. It was noted that there was significant support from commenters to set a 6-percent annual reduction in GHG emissions, resulting in a 60-mpg standard by 2025. However, industry commenters were concerned about the costs associated with technologies that would be required to implement this standard.

During the course of the next six months, the agencies continued to negotiate with automobile manufacturers, which included three weeks of intensive negotiations between the agencies, CARB, members of the Executive Office of the President, and manufacturers. After these negotiations, the agency submitted another supplementary NOI in July 2011. However, the agencies had secured Letters of Commitment from 13 major car companies, representing almost 90% of the market, including Ford, GM, Toyota, Honda, and Chrysler (NHTSA 2011).

This supplementary NOI was, however, significantly different from the first two because the agencies took a strong position promoting a five percent annual reduction in GHG emissions level, which would result in a 54.5 mpg CAFE standard. In addition, the agency included several new incentives and methods to achieve these standards, including a new incentive multiplier for electric vehicles and plug-in hybrids, an incentive credit for game-changing technology on full-size trucks, and credits for air conditioner efficiency improvements, among others. Finally, the agencies also included a midterm review requirement to assess the ability of manufacturers to achieve the standards from MY 2022 to MY 2025. With the publication of this supplementary NOI, President Obama gave a speech promoting the policy, suggesting that it would save consumers nearly $2 trillion in fuel costs, and reduce oil consumption by 2.2 million barrels per day (Obama 2011).

Stages 2 and 3: The agency reviewed the comments on this NOI and published a Notice of Proposed Rulemaking (NPRM) in the *Federal Register* in December 2011 (EPA and NHTSA 2011). The agency held three public hearings—one each in Detroit,

Philadelphia, and San Francisco. The agencies received 300,000 comments from the general public, with 400 additional comments from the three public hearings, and 140 comments from various organizations (EPA and NHTSA 2012).

After reviewing the comments, the agencies published the final rule in the *Federal Register* in October 2012. In this rule, the agencies made many minor changes that focused on definitions and minor analytical adjustments. In terms of substance, the agencies did clarify that a future rulemaking after the midterm review would determine the mandatory requirements for the MY 2022 to MY 2025. Furthermore, the agencies modified market penetration requirements for some existing incentives (EPA and NHTSA 2012). Nevertheless, the major tenants of the rulemaking remained unchanged from the NPRM to the final rule. What once was impossible—getting not just some vehicle manufacturers, but nearly 90% of them to accept CAFE standard increases—became a reality.

Some question the auto industry's acceptance of this rulemaking. A likely explanation is because the Obama administration granted California the Clean Air Act waiver. If the federal government did not act, California might have. Therefore, the manufacturers would have had an incentive to see the federal government produce a rule as opposed to producing two types of cars to comply with different standards.

Post-Rulemaking Activity: Rulemaking is one plausible pathway around congressional gridlock. It allows an agency to use existing policy (CAA in this case) to create rules. As this chapter discusses, there are checks on an agency's ability to make policy. Presidents can issue executive orders and their appointments drive policy directives. The successes of the revised CAFÉ standards were short-lived and the Trump administration on August 2018 announced that the EPA and NHTSA would abandon long-term fuel economy standards for passenger cars and light trucks. The Trump administration plan was to freeze standards at the 2021 levels, not to pursue the goal of 54 miles per gallon by 2025, and revoke California's Clean Air Act waiver. This resulted in California and 16 other states suing the EPA (Roberts 2018). However, by 2021, President Biden finalized the national greenhouse gas emission standards for 2023–2026 rolling back the Trump administration's approach and re-instated California's waiver to the Clean Air Act (EPA 2021; NHTSA & DOT 2021).

Inevitably, this case provides an interesting look into how agencies produce policy through rulemaking. As noted, administrative rulemaking is structured by the APA, which requires a notice of a proposed rulemaking and a public comment period. However, as this case illustrates, there is so much more to the process than meets the eye.

INFLUENCE: WHERE IT OCCURS

As our case study indicates, influence can and does occur in rulemaking processes. Yet, at what stage in the process of rulemaking can a group be influential? For instance, being involved during the pre-proposal phase enables groups to speak with agency rule-writers about potential language or provide important information that the agency may not have due to lack of resources or expertise. For instance, one rule-writer was writing the language of proposed critical habitat for the Holmgren Milkvetch (a type of plant in parts of Arizona and Utah) for the USFWS but did not necessarily have the appropriate background to write such a rule, so reaching out to others in the scientific community was necessary (Rinfret 2011a). Remember that neither is participating in this stage of the process required by the APA, nor does the APA require that an agency discloses this information. However, submitting a public comment via the *Federal Register* can also be influential, again providing important information to the agency that it might not have considered. Next, we examine influence during the stages of the rulemaking process.

Behind the Scenes: As our case illustrated, stakeholders are heavily involved during the first stage of rulemaking (rule development/pre-proposal phase; see West 2009; Hoefer and Ferguson 2007; Naughton et al. 2009; Rinfret 2011a; Rinfret 2011b; Rinfret and Furlong 2013; Yackee 2012; Cook and Rinfret 2013). For example, interest groups can use their resources (i.e., studies or reports) to give agency decisionmakers advice during the pre-proposal stage in exchange for gaining a better idea of what actions an agency is considering taking (Hoefer and Ferguson

2007). Moreover, Sara Rinfret (2011a) even suggests that these groups are working behind the scenes because they are exchanging information with an agency via ex parte communication, or off the record. Put differently, the APA does not require the agency to provide information about the exchanges going on during this stage.

But, what if your organization is not part of the groups that are asked by the agency to help with rule development processes? Susan Webb Yackee (2012) tried to quantify this stage by examining pre-rule classification of the Unified Agenda. The Unified Agenda is a semiannual publication listed in the *Federal Register* that describes all the actions that any federal agency has taken on a given rule. Here you are able to search the Unified Agenda by the stage in the process.

Another approach to determine who is involved is to ask the agency for a list of participants and, then, talk with these individuals to confirm. The presumption is that influence can indeed occur at this stage. However, we also suggest that these findings are alarming because only certain groups are invited to the table to participate during the first stage of the process, shutting others out. Thus, we encourage additional research surrounding this stage of the process.

Put it on the Record: Another approach used by scholars is to examine the comments submitted during the publication of an NPRM to determine influence. For example, one argument is that business groups dominate the phase in which participants can submit comments to an agency with regard to a particular rule (see Fritschler 1989; Golden 1998; Kerwin and Furlong 2011; Magat et al. 1986; West 2004). In examining the EPA's regulatory standards for water pollution, Wesley Magat (1986) concluded that industry interest groups participated far more often than any other group in agency rulemaking. The reason for industry's heavy participation is because of the implications for its individual businesses if regulations would increase.

More alarming about this stage is the use of "bots" by outside global actors to influence US decisionmaking. A 2018 Wall Street Journal investigation disclosed that for the Federal Communication Commission's net neutrality rule thousands of fraudulent public comments. These comments were from fake accounts, attempting to influence the outcome of the final rule (Grimaldi and Overberg 2018).

Regardless of the stage, it is apparent that groups are involved often throughout the process to impact agency decisionmaking. Moreover, it is important for students to realize that interest groups are not only involved in congressional decisionmaking, but also agency decisionmaking. Do note, however, that the purpose of the aforementioned discussion is to provide clarity in the way in which stakeholders or interest groups try to approach a member of Congress is much different than an agency rule-writer.

Expanding Our Understanding of Environmental Rulemaking

We have only skimmed the surface with just a few examples of how agency decisionmaking is shaping the future of environmental policy. To expand the breadth of how far-reaching rulemaking is, we end this chapter with additional examples for consideration. We use examples from the EPA, New York, and the Department of Energy (DOE) to stress why rulemaking will continue to be important for decades to come in the environmental arena.

Reg Neg or Reg Neg Lite?

The EPA has employed different approaches to create environmental rules in order to bring a variety of groups (e.g., environmental organizations and industry groups) to the table to discuss a particular rulemaking. As noted, throughout the 1980s and 1990s, the EPA used reg neg. Remember, reg neg is a voluntary approach adopted by agencies such as the EPA to develop the terms of a rule prior to publishing an NPRM in the *Federal Register*. During reg neg, with a formal mediator presiding over the conversations with a variety of groups, an agency convenes negotiations to achieve consensus (Harter 1982). Over time, the use of reg neg decreased because it could be a time-intensive process, thereby increasing costs for an agency (Harter 1982; Susskind and McMahon 1985)—thus, the decline of its use (Harter 1982; Kerwin and Langbein 2000).

This is not to say that rulemaking innovation is dead, however. The EPA has sought alternatives, trying to salvage some of ideas of reg neg (Kerwin and Furlong 2011). In 2007, the Council for Excellence in Government stated that the Office of Transportation and Air Quality (OTAQ), a division within the EPA, was using a new method—shuttle diplomacy—to create rules. Basically, shuttle diplomacy is a way for an agency to bring groups together informally to discuss a rule—it is not a formal process with an official mediator such as reg neg, but a way for groups to explain their perspectives on a given rulemaking (Rinfret and Cook 2013).

States Matter

Federal rulemaking processes are important, but state rulemaking also matters. Recall in Chapter 3, we discuss how our system of governance is driven by federalism. After all, we have seen many policy arenas where states arrive at quite different policies, such as climate change, same-sex marriage, or marijuana use when there is a lack of federal policy available. As a result, we see a policy patchwork throughout the country (Rinfret et al. 2018). This often allows for trial and error at the state level before a major policy is adopted at the federal level. Federalism endures because it offers a useful way to bring state governments together to achieve larger goals, while at the same time offering many points of access into the policy process.

Because hydraulic fracturing or fracking is one of the top environmental issues of the twenty-first century, we use it as an example to touch upon state rulemaking and its importance. With fracking, states find themselves overseeing this policy area because the 2005 Energy Policy Act's so-called Halliburton Loophole exempted fracking oversight from the US EPA (42 U.S.C. §15801). In 2016, the EPA conducted a study on hydraulic fracturing to assess the impact it has on drinking water and found that certain activities can impact water resources (EPA 2016). Congress, since 2017, has attempted to provide a law for guidance—the Fracturing Responsibility and Awareness Chemicals Act (a.k.a FracAct), but the bill has continually died after introduction. However, in March of 2021, it was reintroduced to the House, and approval is still pending as this book is published.

Consider New York as an example. Rulemaking must follow the State Administrative Procedure Act (SAPA) and the process unfolds over three stages. The process begins with an internal agency review to determine if rulemaking is the best or most appropriate action to address a particular problem. At this stage, agency staff often will reach out to stakeholder groups to receive input on the issue. Stage 2 of the process unfolds when the agency submits a formal proposed rulemaking in the *New York State Register*. After the agency publishes the notice of proposed rulemaking, the public comment period begins. The agency has 180 days to review and respond to public comments, as well as to determine what action to take on a rule. Stage 3 of the rulemaking process begins when the agency provides a complete text of the rule to notify the Governor, the President of the Senate, the Speaker of the Assembly, and the Administrative Regulations Reviews Commission (within the New York State Senate) that a rule is being finalized. Therefore, at this stage, the filing of the final terms of the rule is published in the *New York State Register* (Rinfret et al. 2014).

Thus, states use their own form of rulemaking processes to implement state law (Rinfret et al. 2014). State rulemaking is of additional importance when there is a lack of federal policy. For instance, due to the lack of federal policy for fracking, it is up to states to use rulemaking processes to come up with their own policies. In their examination of fracking rules in Colorado, New York, and Ohio, Rinfret et al. (2014) found that states are offering unique frameworks to solve the fracking debate. However, the question still remains whether the federal government will adopt one of these approaches on a national scale. We do know that states have taken steps, using rulemaking to provide policy when there is a lack of federal law. New York, Vermont, Washington, and Maryland have decided to ban fracking within their states altogether due to public health concerns (e.g., contamination of water due to extraction processes).

The Social Cost of Carbon

Although state rulemaking processes are important, we offer another example, about the DOE's approach to making our household microwaves more energy efficient. There was something notably different about the DOE's rulemaking to improve the energy efficiency of microwave ovens: the agency changed the Social Cost of Carbon (SCC) metric to determine the benefits of reducing greenhouse gases.

As Jeffrey Cook and Sara Rinfret (2013b) note, "The SCC was first developed in 2010 by a task force of twelve US agencies including the Environmental Protection Agency (EPA), DOE, and the National Economic Council, among others. These agencies developed the SCC metric to standardize how federal agencies quantify the benefits of reduced carbon pollution." This new approach to rulemaking engendered a great deal of discussion, and possibly outright controversy, because when the DOE was creating the microwave oven rule, the agency reported a new social cost of carbon, $36 per ton, versus the previous value of $22 per ton. Critics suggested that this change in cost favored environmental interests. However, as Cook and Rinfret (2013b) concluded, "In its microwave oven rule, the DOE argued that the 2013 White House Economic Report called for agencies to revise the SCC in order to reflect new scientific information on the impacts of climate change on the environment and public health. Thus, the agency argued that it was only following necessary procedures when it updated the SCC to reflect new information."

In 2022, the carbon cost sparked by the microwave oven might seem odd, but it demonstrates another way rulemaking can be used as a policy tool to decrease greenhouse gas emissions. As Renee Cho notes, "For example, say new regulations for appliances are being proposed that are expected to cost $40 million, and cut carbon emissions by 1 million tons at a SCC rate of $51 per ton. Because the benefits would be worth $51 million, $11 million more than the cost, the policy would be justified. A lower SCC would result in the costs of the proposed regulation outweighing its benefits" (npn).

Chapter Wrap-Up

This chapter documents the stages of the federal rulemaking process, and how groups, court cases, and changing presidential administrations can shape this process. The CAFÉ rule offers insight into understanding how groups vying for access shape agency policy. Arguably, being involved early and often in rulemaking is important, but most Americans do not vote, let alone understand the intricacies of the *Federal Register*. Thus, increasing our knowledge about rulemaking is essential.

Beyond process and influence, there are a variety of future pathways for rulemaking—particularly at the state level. More specifically, there is a lack of research at the state level, and it is important to expand our understanding when there is limited federal direction on tackling issues such as fracking. Furthermore, in order for us to be informed participants about regulatory affairs, receiving a weekly email from the University of Pennsylvania's Regulatory Review may spark your interests to become more involved in regulatory affairs.

Our discussion about rulemaking provides a nice transition into our next chapter on implementing environmental policy, which focuses on what occurs after a rule becomes law. It is up to individuals such as environmental inspectors to ensure that the rules written are carried out. To this end, we offer an important lesson from Neil Kerwin and Scott Furlong (2011).

> We must convince those with little or no direct stake in the outcome of rulemaking that they too should be concerned with the result. This is a very tough sell when people are able to keep up with only a fraction of the issues that profoundly affect their daily lives and become involved in only a few of them. In a nation where so many fail to vote, is it reasonable to expect an outpouring of interest in rulemaking from average citizens with comparatively little to win or lose? Perhaps not, but lowering our expectations is a dangerous choice. (293)

Challenge Question for the Environmental Policy Classroom

Regulations.gov is the primary mechanisms for individuals to monitor and participate in the federal rulemaking process. Visit Regulations.gov—in what ways does (or does not) this website offer inclusive options to participate?

SUGGESTED RESOURCES

Readings and Websites

Deadly Dust. YouTube. Accessed June 13, 2014. http://www.youtube.com/watch?v=eXsGJ1C4Xcw.

Federal Register. Accessed June 13, 2014. https://www.federalregister.gov/.

Journey to Justice. Accessed April 17, 2022. https://www.epa.gov/environmentaljustice/journey-justice.

Penn Program on Regulation: Regulatory Review. Accessed April 17, 2022. https://www.theregreview.org/.

Regulations.gov: The Voice of Federal Decision-Making. Accessed October 19, 2018. http://www.regulations.gov/#!home.

Unified Agenda. Accessed October 19, 2018. http://www.reginfo.gov/public/do/eAgendaMain.

Films or Videos

If a Tree Falls: A Story of the Earth Liberation Front. Directed by Marshall Curry. 2012. Independent Television Service, Corporation for Public Broadcasting. DVD.

Food, Inc. Director Robert Kenner. 2009. Magnolia Home Entertainment. DVD.

The Cove. Directed Louie Psihoyos. 2009. Lions Gate. DVD.

REFERENCES

Bryner, Gary. *Bureaucratic Discretion: Law and Policy in Federal Regulatory Agencies.* New York: Pergamon Press, 1987.

Cho, Renee. "Social Cost of Carbon: What Is It, and Why Do We Need to Calculate It?" Accessed June 12, 2022. columbia.edu.

Cook, Jeffrey J. and Sara R. Rinfret. "The EPA Regulates GHG Emissions: Is Anyone Paying Attention?" *Review of Policy Research* 30, no. 3 (2013a): 263–280.

———. "Adjusting the Social Cost of Carbon: A Commonsense Revision." University of Pennsylvania Law School's Regulatory Blog. August 20, 2013b. www.regblog.org/2013/08/20-cook-rinfret-scc.htm.

Cooper, Phillip. *Public Law and Public Administration.* Belmont, CA: Thomson Wadsworth, 2007.

Council for Excellence in Government. "Working with Stakeholders: The Nonroad Diesel Rule." Washington, DC: GPO, 2007.

Council on Environmental Quality. "Federal Leadership in Environmental Energy and Economic Performance—Executive Order 13514." Accessed January 27, 2014. http://www.whitehouse.gov/administration/eop/ceq/sustainability.

EPA. "EPA's Study of Hydraulic Fracturing and Its Potential Impact on Drinking Water Resources". 2016. https://cfpub.epa.gov/ncea/hfstudy/recordisplay.cfm?deid=332990.

———. "EPA Administrator: Michael Regan." 2021a. https://www.epa.gov/aboutepa/epa-administrator.

———. "Notice of Reconsideration of a Previous Withdrawal of a Waiver for California's Advanced Clean Car Program (Light-Duty Vehicle Greenhouse Gas Emission Standards and Zero Emission Vehicle Requirements)". 2021b. https://www.epa.gov/regulations-emissions-vehicles-and-engines/notice-reconsideration-previous-withdrawal-waiver.

———. "Regulations for Greenhouse Gas Emissions from Passenger Cars and Trucks". 2021c. https://www.epa.gov/regulations-emissions-vehicles-and-engines/regulations-greenhouse-gas-emissions-passenger-cars-and.

———. "Journey to Justice." 2022. https://www.epa.gov/environmentalju stice/journey-justice.

EPA and NHTSA. "2017 and Later Model Year Light-Duty Vehicle GHG Emissions and CAFE Standards: Notice of Intent." *Federal Register*. 2010a.

———. "2017 and Later Model Year Light-Duty Vehicle GHG Emissions and CAFE Standards: Supplemental Notice of Intent." *Federal Register*. 2010b.

"EPA and NHTSA 2017–2025 Model Year Light-Duty Vehicle GHG Emissions and CAFE Standards: Supplemental Notice of Intent." *Federal Register*. 2011.

"EPA and NHTSA 2012. 2017 and Later Model Year Light-Duty Vehicle Greenhouse Gas Emissions and Corporate Average Fuel Economy Standards; Final Rule." *Federal Register (77)199 (62623–63200)*. Washington, DC: GPO, 2012.

Fiorina, Morris. "Legislative Choice of Regulatory Forms: Legal Process or Administrative Process." *Public Choice* 39 (1982): 33–66.

Fritschler, Lee A. *Smoking and Politics*. Upper Saddle River, NJ: Prentice Hall, 1989.

Golden, Marissa Martino. "Interest Groups in the Rule-Making Process: Who Participates? Whose Voices Get Heard?" *Journal of Public Administration Research and Theory* 8, no. 2 (1998): 245–270.

Jamves V. Grimaldi and Paul Overberg. 2018. https://www.wsj.com/articles/ millions-of-people-post-comments-on-federal-regulations-many-are-fake-151 3099188.

Harter, Phil. "Negotiating Regulations: A Cure for Malaise." *Georgetown Law Journal* 71 (1982): 1–116.

Hoefer, R. and K. Ferguson. "Controlling the Levers of Power: How Advocacy Organizations Affect the Regulation Writing Process." *Journal of Sociology and Social Welfare* 34, no. 2 (2007): 83–108.

Keneally, Meghan and Stephanie Ebbs. 2018. https://abcnews.go.com/Politics/ timeline-scott-pruitts-bumpy-time-epa/story?id=56394470.

Kerwin, Cornelius and Laura Langbein. "Regulatory Negotiation: Claims, Counter Claims, and Empirical Evidence." *Journal of Public Administration Research and Theory* 10 (2000): 599–632.

Kerwin, Cornelius and Scott R. Furlong. *Rulemaking: How Government Agencies Write Law and Make Policy*. Washington, DC: Island Press, 2011.

Kerwin and Furlong. (2018). https://www.amazon.com/Rulemaking-Govern ment-Agencies-Write-Policy/dp/1483352811

Klyza, Christopher McGrory and David Sousa. *American Environmental Policy, 1990–2006: Beyond Gridlock*. Cambridge: MIT Press, 2013.

Longley, Robert. 2021. Accessed June 12, 2022. https://www.thoughtco.com/ costs-and-benefits-of-government-regulations-4068946.

Lorenzetti, Maureen. "Revised CAFE Standards Gaining Wider Support." 2005. Accessed January 3, 2014. http://www.cqweekly.com.

Lubbers, Jeffrey. "Achieving Policymaking Consensus: The (unfortunate) Waning of Negotiated Rulemaking." *South Texas Law Review* (1996): 987–1017.

Magat, W., A. Krupnick, and W. Harrington. *Rules in the Making: A Statistical Analysis of Regulatory Agency Behavior.* Washington, DC: Resources for the Future Press, 1986.

McCutcheon, Chuck. "Bush Urged to Shift Emphasis to Fuel Efficiency Standards." *CQ Weekly.* 2001. Accessed January 3, 2014. http://www.cqweekly.com.

Naughton, Keith, Celeste Schmid, Susan Webb Yackee, and Xueyong Zhan. "Understanding Commenter Influence During Rule Development." *Journal of Policy Analysis and Management* 28, no. 2 (2009): 258–277.

NHTSA. *NHTSA and EPA to Propose Greenhouse Gas and Fuel Efficiency Standards for Medium- and Heavy-Duty Trucks; Begin Process for Further Light-Duty Standards: Fact Sheet.* 2010. Accessed August 7, 2013. http://www.nhtsa.gov/fuel-economy.

———. *Letters of Commitment from Stakeholders Supporting the MYs 2017–2025 Rulemaking Process.* 2011. Accessed August 7, 2013. http://www.nhtsa.gov/Laws+&+Regulations/CAFE+-+Fuel+Economy/Letters+of+Commitment+from+Stakeholders+Supporting+the+MYs+2017-2025+Rulemaking+Process.

NHTSA & DOT. "Corporate Average Fuel Economy (CAFÉ) Preemption." *Federal Register.* 2021.

Obama, Barack. *Presidential Memorandum Regarding Fuel Efficiency Standards.* 2010. Accessed August 7, 2013. http://www.whitehouse.gov/the-press-office/presidential-memorandum-regarding-fuel-efficiency-standards.

———. "Remarks by the President on Fuel Efficiency Standards." 2011. Accessed August 7, 2013. http://www.whitehouse.gov/the-press-office/2011/07/29/remarks-president-fuel-efficiency-standards.

Plungis, Jeff. "GOP Again Blocks Changes in Fuel Efficiency Standard." *CQ Weekly.* 2000. Accessed January 3, 2014. http://www.cqweekly.com.

Regan, Michael and Richard Newell. "Policy Leadership Series with EPA Administrator Michael Regan." Resources for the Future. 2021. https://www.rff.org/events/pls/epa-administrator-michael-regan/.

Rinfret, Sara R. "Behind the Shadows: Interest Groups and the U.S. Fish and Wildlife Service." *Human Dimensions of Wildlife: An International Journal* 16, no. 1 (2011a): 1–14.

———. "Frames of Influence: U.S. Environmental Rulemaking Case Studies." *Review of Policy Research* 28, no. 3 (2011b): 231–246.

Rinfret, Sara R. and Jeffrey J. Cook. "Environmental Policy Can Happen: Shuttle Diplomacy and the Reality of Reg Neg Lite." *Environmental Policy and Governance* 24, no. 2 (2013): 122–133.

Rinfret, Sara R. and Scott Furlong. "Defining Environmental Rulemaking." In *Oxford Handbook of U.S. Environmental Policy*, edited by Michael E. Kraft and Sheldon Kamieniecki, 372–394. New York: Oxford University Press, 2013.

Rinfret, Sara R., Jeffrey J. Cook, and Michelle C. Pautz. "Understanding State Rulemaking Processes: Developing Fracking Rules in Colorado, New York, and Ohio." *Review of Policy Research* 31, no. 2 (2014): 88–104.

Roberts, David. 2018. https://www.vox.com/energy-and-environment/2018/5/3/17314000/trump-epa-cars-trucks-fuel-economy-cafe-standards.

Shapiro, Stuart. "Political and Regulatory Policy Analysis." Rutgers University. 2006. Accessed January 27, 2014. http://policy.rutgers.edu/faculty/shapiro/regulation%20article.pdf.

State Administrative Procedure Act (SAPA). New York. Accessed January 3, 2014. http://www.dos.ny.gov/info/rulemakingmanual.html.

Supermarket News. "Industry Groups Sue USDA over COOL Rule." Accessed January 4, 2013. http://supermarketnews.com/laws-amp-regulations/industry-groups-sueusda-over-final-cool-rule.

Susskind, Lawrence and Gerard McMahon. "The Theory and Practice of Negotiated Rulemaking." *Yale Journal on Regulation* 3 (1985): 133–165.

U.S. Department of the Interior. "Unified Interior Regional Boundaries." 2018. Accessed February 10, 2022. https://www.doi.gov/employees/reorg/unified-regional-boundaries#:~:text=The%20reorganization%20of%20DOI%20from%2049%20regions%20across,partners%20-%20became%20final%20on%20August%2022%2C%202018.

Verchick, Robert. "Dangerous Dust and Deadly Delay: OSHA's Proposed Silica Rule." University of Pennsylvania Reg Blog. 2013. Accessed January 3, 2014. http://www.regblog.org/2013/11/26-verchick-silica.html.

West, William. "Formal Procedures, Informal Procedures, Accountability, and Responsiveness in Bureaucratic Policymaking: An Institutional Policy Analysis." *Public Administration Review* 46, no. 2 (2004): 66–80.

———. "Inside the Black Box: The Development of Proposed Rules and the Limits of Procedural Controls." *Administration and Society* 41, no. 5 (2009): 576–599.

White House. "Executive Order on Revocation of Certain Executive Orders Concerning Federal Regulation." 2021. https://www.whitehouse.gov/briefing-room/presidential-actions/2021/01/20/executive-order-revocation-of-certain-executive-orders-concerning-federal-regulation/.

Yackee, Susan W. "The Politics of Ex Parte Lobbying: Pre-proposal Agenda Building and Blocking During Agency Rulemaking." *Journal of Public Administration Research and Theory* 22 (2012): 373–393.

CHAPTER 7

Implementing Environmental Policy and Regulations: Where the Rubber Meets the Road

Introductory Story: Dodging Tomatoes and Being an Oreo Cookie as a Hazardous Waste Inspector

Given the widely held negative perceptions about government bureaucrats, you might cringe at the outset of a story about a government regulator at a state environmental agency. Despite the disdain afforded most government regulators, Brandon's story is worth telling. We should note first, however, that given the negative attitudes about regulators and the polarization of our politics, we have opted to keep Brandon's identity confidential (both his name and his state environmental agency). Nevertheless, Brandon's experiences encapsulate those of many of his colleagues across the 50 states and the District of Columbia.

Brandon has worked for a state environmental protection agency for more than two decades and he has spent the bulk of that time working in hazardous waste. He began his career as a Resource Conservation and Recovery Act (RCRA) inspector and, over time, became a supervisor for RCRA inspectors. His primary job duties include ensuring that facilities in his assigned geographic region are properly permitted and that they comply with applicable state and federal law regarding the treatment, storage, and disposal of hazardous wastes. He and his colleagues spend a good deal of time—although they generally wish it was more time—out in the field checking on facilities such as landfills to see environmental

S. R. Rinfret and M. C. Pautz, *US Environmental Policy in Action*, https://doi.org/10.1007/978-3-031-17503-9_7

regulation in action. For the most part, Brandon finds he has a good working relationship with the regulated community he oversees, and he thinks these positive interactions are vital to ensuring compliance. Brandon describes his work as being the cream in an Oreo cookie—he is caught in the middle between industry and citizens and helps hold it all together. Moreover, he believes it takes everyone to ensure adequate protection of the environment.

Although Brandon would rather think of Oreos, he has also come face to face—literally—with tomatoes. Part of Brandon's role with the RCRA is participating in public hearings when operating permits, which allow facilities to deal with hazardous wastes, are being issued. One of Brandon's assigned facilities sought a modification to its permit so it could accept another type of hazardous waste, and part of the process for amending a permit (as we will discuss further in this chapter) typically involves a public hearing to facilitate discussion with the public about any concerns it might have with the facility modifying its operations. Brandon showed up at the public hearing to represent his agency and explain that the facility had appropriately requested approval to take a different type of waste and had properly filed a permit modification and, upon review, his agency found the modifications were within the parameters of the hazardous waste regulations in the state. This particular facility, however, did not have the best relationship with its neighbors—especially a number of citizens whose homes share the same road with the facility.

By the number of people at the meeting, Brandon quickly got a sense that things might get heated. Many residents who disliked the facility and its operations were irate that the government would allow the facility to take more types of wastes, but these residents did not understand that the regulations from the RCRA mostly provide processes for dealing with waste and, as long as processes are followed, the facility can take on more. However, instead of taking their frustrations out on the policymakers who created the RCRA decades ago or state legislators who could make modifications to relevant state laws and procedures, Brandon bore the brunt of their frustrations in the form of flying fruit. Tomatoes were thrown at Brandon during the course of the public hearing. Fortunately, Brandon has quick reflexes—all those years of outdoor activities gave him that—so he managed to dodge most of the tomatoes. Brandon still laughs about the story today as he retells it because, to him, it clearly demonstrates his role in environmental protection as the cream of an Oreo cookie. Government regulators are stuck between industry and citizens, and that is where they should be in his estimation. After all, he and his fellow regulators are the ones who *do* environmental policy—not the activists, not the industry representatives, and not the politicians in Washington, DC, and state capitals. Therefore, these front-line regulators are the Oreo cream that holds the cookie together.

The "doing" of environmental policy is, arguably, the most crucial component of governmental efforts regarding environmental protection, and it is often neglected by politicians, activists, and even academics. In Chapter 6, we began our exploration of how policy language gets translated into practice, and this chapter continues in a similar fashion by focusing on the implementation of policy, notably through the work of those on the front-lines. As you might guess at this point, policy implementation is difficult, and the way policies are carried out may not be at all that you expected. Recall from Chapter 3 that policy implementation is the "process by which policies enacted by government are put into effect by the relevant agencies" (Birkland 2016, 332). This is where the rubber meets the road; yet, it is not quite that simple. In many ways, policy implementation is replete with all the challenges of creating policy in the first place.

Implementation is challenging because it encompasses the "interaction between the setting of goals and actions geared to achieving them" (Pressman and Wildavsky 1984, 341). Think for a moment about your own goals for the semester. Perhaps, you want to earn "all A's" this term to give a boost to your overall GPA, but you know you have a tough science class, and while you want an A, you are expecting a B. Those are your goals. Now, how will you implement these goals? You have been down this path before in other semesters. How did your goals match up with the end result? Presumably, you have had a few of those moments where you recalled your overly optimistic goals and how they may not have aligned with the results at the end of the semester. This analogy helps us understand the implementation of environmental policy.

If policy implementation is so important, it is natural to wonder why such a crucial topic is frequently overlooked in environmental policy discussions and even textbooks. There are many reasons for this neglect. First, policy implementation is often not as riveting to observers as the politics and the wrangling associated with passing laws. After all, stories of political deals and intrigue—such as the veto of the Clean Water Act and congressional action to override the veto—tend to be more exciting than the process of translating the Clean Water Act (CAA) into concrete action. Furthermore, passing laws usually happens in a much narrower time horizon, whereas the process of implementation unfolds over many years. Media coverage of implementation is much harder and would require lots of detailed explanations that may not be suited to the rapid pace of the news these days. Finally, as Jeffrey Pressman and Aaron Wildavsky (1984) discuss, it is presumed that "implementation should be easy" (340). As we have come to understand in this text—and particularly through Chapter 2—as time progresses, fewer and fewer major laws are passed by Congress; however, this does not mean that environmental policy is not happening. In light of congressional gridlock, Christopher McGrory Klyza and David Sousa (2008, 2013), remind us that environmental policy is increasingly happening through the work of government agencies—or put differently, in the stage of policy implementation.

This chapter explores the often-neglected area of policy implementation by beginning with a discussion of the process associated with implementation and picking up where Chapter 6 concluded. We will focus on command and control regulations as they are the foundation of the regulatory approach of American environmental policy. Then, we will investigate how command and control regulations are employed and endeavor to assess whether they work. Afterward, the specifics of this regulatory tool will be outlined, before we turn our attention to the day-to-day realities of implementing and monitoring environmental regulations. Finally, we will consider the actors involved in implementation—actors just like Brandon. A case study about an industrial wastewater processor is presented, which demonstrates some of the many complexities associated with implementing environmental regulations. The chapter concludes by discussing factors that affect implementation and what the future might look like for the future of the dominant environmental policy tool, command, and control regulations.

As we proceed, several themes emerge as we focus on implementing environmental policy. First, it is important—if not, arguably, more important—to pay attention to policy implementation rather than just policy formulation in the environmental context. Just because a piece of legislation makes it through Congress or a state legislature does not mean it is going to be implemented as prescribed, nor does it mean it will achieve its goals. After all, it is a lot easier to devise goals than it is to achieve them. Second, as the nation works toward protecting the environment, implementing environmental policy, which continues to be heavily dependent on command and control regulations, requires the coordination of many individuals who are rarely, if ever, considered. Understanding their jobs—and contemplating if they embody the role of the Oreo, as Brandon describes—is essential to understanding how environmental protection works in the US, and how it sometimes does not. Third, although command and control regulations have been the foundation for achieving environmental goals and their use is unlikely to go away, the evolving nature of environmental challenges coupled with partisanship and polarization require other paths to protect the nation's environment.

OVERVIEW OF ENVIRONMENTAL POLICY IMPLEMENTATION

From our discussion of the policy process (refer to Chapter 3), we know that implementation comes after a policy has passed both chambers of Congress and has been approved by the president. It is worth reiterating that lawmakers have many types of policy tools at their disposal in environmental policy, including taxes, subsidies, financial incentives, or even suasion campaigns, such as Smokey the Bear in US Forest Service commercials. When most of our major environmental laws were passed decades ago, however, the focus was on stopping and cleaning up pollution and it was thought that command and control regulations would be the most effective policy tool to utilize. The previous chapter (Chapter 6) expanded our understanding of the policy process by detailing how vague environmental statutes get translated from laudable goals such as "clean water" to language that is actionable: so that clean water, as a goal, becomes many components such as total maximum daily load permits and classifications of the nation's waterways. These actions are usually taken by government agencies such as the Environmental Protection Agency (EPA) or the Department of Energy, because policymakers leave the specifics to the agencies, and their rule-writers, that are delegated authority. This chapter picks up by focusing on how those rules get translated into action and various government agencies ensure that those rules are monitored for compliance. We begin, though, with an overview of this dominant policy tool.

Command and Control Regulations

Although command and control regulations are employed in a range of policy areas beyond the environmental realm, this type of regulation is, frequently, the first tool that comes to mind when we think about environmental issues. Indeed, efforts at protecting the environment usually conjure images of telling a firm to stop doing something, like releasing pollutants into a nearby river. Of the more than 15,000 pages of federal environmental regulations that govern the more than 40,000 stationary air sources, 90,000 facilities that discharge effluent into waterways, the more than 425,000 hazardous waste facilities, and the 173,000 drinking water systems, the majority of those regulations can be characterized as "command and control" (Fiorino 2006, 1, 83; Kraft et al. 2011, 3).

As the name might suggest, command and control regulations direct individuals and/or organizations to comply with particular standards, achieve predetermined controls, and/or employ particular processes and technologies (e.g., emission limits or a particular type of pollution control equipment to be employed). These regulations are established by government officials, or rule-writers, through the rulemaking process.

> Under command and control, government agencies develop a set of rules or standards. These determine technologies to be used or avoided; amounts of pollutants that can be emitted from a particular waste pipe, smokestack, or factor; and/or the amounts or kinds of resources that may be extracted from a common pool such as a fishery or a forest. These agencies issue commands in the form of regulations and permits to control the behavior of private firms, other government agencies, and/ or individuals. (Dietz and Stern 2002, 3)

Stated differently, command and control regulations are often the go-to policy tool for protecting the environment because they set specific limits on pollutants, such as nitrous oxides, that may be released from a facility, or they mandate the particular type of pollution abatement technology that another facility must use.

With this explanation of command and control regulations, the next obvious question is: do they work? Generally speaking, this form of regulation in the environmental arena works and produces results (c.f. Press and Mazmanian 2013; Davies and Mazurek 1997). According to data from the US EPA in 2021, the emissions from the major air pollutants regulated by the Clean Air Act have decreased from 1970 to 2016.

Concentrations of the following air pollutants have dropped significantly since 1990: carbon monoxide is down 73%, nitrogen dioxide is down 61%, sulfur dioxide is down 91%, and particular matter is down from 26 to 41% (depending upon what size)—all while the economy grew, the population climbed, vehicle travel increased, and energy consumption rose (US EPA 2021). Additionally, there has been a virtual elimination of some harmful pollutants (such as polychlorinated biphenyls (PCBs) and mercury), and there have been significant reductions in emissions and concentrations of common water pollutants (Fiorino 2006, 66). The nation's waterways have also benefited from the Clean Water Act as of the more than 3.5 million miles of waterways about around 600,000 miles continue to be assessed as "impaired" (US EPA National Water Quality Inventory: Report to Congress 2017). The traditional approach to environmental regulation has unquestionably led to improvements in the condition of the environment, but ongoing work undoubtedly remains.

Indeed, the US' regulatory structure boasts expertise, comprises an impressive legal framework that numerous other countries endeavor to replicate, and has built an intimidating set of institutions tasked with environmental protection. However, this regulatory approach has been less effective in some areas, including pollution from non-point sources, the amount of waste generated domestically, emissions of carbon dioxide and other greenhouse gases (GHGs), and the volume of toxic wastes accumulating in the environment, including microplastics.

These accomplishments and ongoing challenges naturally give rise to questions about costs and other burdens this approach to environmental regulation has imposed. As you might imagine, arriving at those cost estimates can be difficult given the variation in how estimates are derived and what factors comprise the statistics. Therefore, let us consider a variety of figures. According to the most recently available figures from the White House Office of Management and Budget (OMB), the cost of environmental regulations from 2005 to 2015 about $47 billion (in 2014 dollars) while the benefits amounted to $427 billion (OMB 2016). And each year, about one percent of all federal government spending is on environmental programs—this is far less than spending for housing, transportation, education, and much less than entitlement programs, including Medicare, social security, and unemployment benefits. In 2019, approximately $30 billion of federal spending was allocated for the totality of conservation and management of natural resources and other environmental programs across all federal government agencies (Center on

Budget and Policy Priorities 2020). In 2020, US EPA's operating budget, however, was only slightly higher than it was in 1980 despite having many additional responsibilities (Kraft and Vig 2022, 20).

It can be difficult to truly grasp these dollar figures, much less make assessments as to whether the costs outweigh the benefits of environmental regulation. Much of this challenge lies in the difficulty in reducing intangibles, like clean air, into monetary terms. Suffice it to say, to date, command, and control regulations have generated improvements in the condition of the natural environment and have brought with them costs borne by government, industry, and citizens alike.

Developing and Implementing Command and Control Regulations

Command and control regulations are not, typically, the statutory language Congress enacts; rather, the process of creating these regulations is simply started by the passage of legislation. Chapter 6 detailed this process at a macro level, as part of the focus on federal rulemaking. Here, we continue those conversations as it concerns promulgating command and control regulations. The process comprises several stages of setting and enforcing command and control regulations: (1) goal setting, (2) criteria determination, (3) standard setting, and (4) enforcement of the standards (see Table 7.1).

The first stage in establishing command control regulation is the process of setting goals. For example, in the Clean Water Act (CWA) of 1972, one of the law's goals includes eliminating high amounts of toxic pollutants to make the nation's water "swimmable," "fishable," and "navigable." Without being specific, Congress (or another legislative body, like a state general assembly) often establishes broad goals that a law is designed to achieve. In the lead up to the CWA, Congress pursued a national standard of "swimmable" because there was no way it would be implemented the same way everywhere, thereby allowing for regional variation, which was important to getting the bill passed (Milazzo 2006,

Table 7.1 Stages of command and control regulation

- Goal Setting
- Criteria Determination
- Standard Setting
- Enforcement of Standards

201). Numerous political and institutional reasons explain the level of generality in legislation. Elected lawmakers recognize that the expertise for setting specific rules falls to the civil servants in the federal government agencies who have the wherewithal to turn broad goals into actionable steps. Moreover, for reasons of consensus building and political expediency, legislators focus on articulating goals and employing politically palatable language to articulate those goals. At this stage, broad goals are defined and weighed against myriad social and economic considerations. These considerations often explain why statutory language may be unclear, confusing, or even contradictory. Once lawmakers, as the people's representatives, come to agreement about those goals, they then delegate authority to various administrative agencies (see Chapter 4 for more detail about the work of administrative agencies).

Next, criteria must be determined during the second stage. For instance, what is meant by "clean water" or "clean air?" Such goal language is laudable, but its meaning is elusive. With the delegation of authority, Congress acknowledges it does not have the technical prowess or the political capacity to determine which pollutants are most harmful to waterways and to establish what the limits on releases of those pollutants should be. Congress leaves those determinations to agencies such as the US EPA. Establishing criteria can be difficult because extensive research and data collection are needed on pollutants and their effects, and much of that information may not be readily available and may take a lot of time. With these data and research, agencies start putting specifics around lofty goals of clean air and clean water. The connections between the ill effects of pollution are considered during this stage of the process, along with their relationship to public health and other ecological risk assessments. These determinations are still quite general in nature, but they are far more specific than statutory language.

After determining the criteria, agencies move into the third stage of command and control regulations: setting standards. After the criteria have determined the broad aims of the regulations, standards are established to describe the specific means of achieving those broad aims. For example, to reduce the presence of 189 hazardous air pollutants (HAPs) identified by the CAA, the standards determine how much a facility may be allowed to emit of HAPs, depending on the facility's size and industry type. These are the standards that polluting facilities must comply with and that environmental inspectors assess compliance against during inspections. These standards reflect determinations about the level of pollution that is acceptable when weighed against health and other ecological considerations, as well as risk assessments such as the maximum level of a pollutant that is allowed to be discharged in a wastewater stream, or the standards may establish a particular type of technology or a process that must be employed to mitigate the adverse effects of an operation on the environment.

The final stage of command and control regulations has to do with enforcement. This is the part where facilities that are subjected to these regulations are monitored to see if they are complying with applicable regulations. Environmental inspectors conduct inspections as part of this stage which can include the review of required reports with logs of emissions data and other such compliance-monitoring activities. It is up to these inspectors, or environmental regulators, to assess compliance with the established standards. To determine compliance, these inspectors routinely visit facilities—generally, through unannounced inspections— that generate pollution, and gauge their compliance with applicable standards. If a regulator finds a facility out of compliance with a particular standard, the regulator will begin the enforcement process to see that the facility returns to compliance and that the nation's environmental goals are being met. More on this part of the process comes later in this chapter.

Fundamental Assumptions of Command and Control Regulation

We have broadly outlined the process of establishing command and control regulations. At this juncture, let us pause and consider a few fundamental attributes of this kind of regulation. First, these regulations are top–down, or created by the government. Government dictates these rules, and everyone must comply or else face enforcement proceedings. Although we learned in our discussion of rulemaking in the last chapter that various stakeholders are often part of the process of crafting these regulations, the burden still rests on the government to determine the regulations. As a result, the rules come not from those individuals at facilities that generate pollution, but from the civil servants in governmental agencies.

A second important assumption—and one related to the first—is that these regulations presume that government is in the position to know best. Put differently, it is assumed that government has all the information from the best science and technology about what the appropriate standards are and what are the best technologies to mandate. Devising these regulations requires extensive research and modeling about potential effects of one environmental harm or another; therefore, the government must be the one who has all this information in order to craft the best regulations. This reality, coupled with the challenge for devising the regulations, puts a significant burden on government. And it is worth noting that regulated industries may be well-positioned to know how to reduce the environmental impacts of their operations.

Third, these regulations employ a "one-size-fits-all" approach to compliance. All organizations are subject to these regulations, with little differentiation for size and scope of a facility's operations.[1] Therefore, a local dry cleaner has to deal with the same kinds of requirements regarding the use of various chemicals in the dry cleaning process that a huge chain of dry cleaners has to contend with; that large chain, presumably, has a few people whose jobs are devoted to compliance with environmental regulations, whereas the local, single storefront operation has to manage compliance by itself with its smaller staff. This is not to say that there are not some considerations for different kinds of facilities, but generally speaking, the regulations apply across the board.

Fourth, compliance with these regulations is pursued through a deterrence strategy. A deterrence strategy means that facilities must comply or else they face the consequences set forth by government (these consequences include a range of enforcement options including court-ordered compliance). The presumption of this regulatory approach is that those organizations subjected to regulation have no wish to comply with the rules and would rather pollute the environment. This may have been a more accurate statement decades ago when the environmental regulatory state was being crafted, and this may even still be true for a handful of nefarious operations that could care less about the environment; however, such a sweeping statement is not true for the majority of regulated facilities today (c.f. Hoffman 2001; Pautz and Rinfret 2013). Just as deterrence may be an effective strategy for a parent, other strategies may also prove equally, if not more, effective as well. Sometimes, incentives and other similar tools might encourage good environmental stewardship rather than just a looming threat of getting in trouble with government regulators.

---

[1] This statement merits qualification: Facilities that are in the same industry and are operating at similar levels have the same standards to meet. Small businesses are often subject to altered regulations.

A final and related point about these regulations is that there is little incentive for firms to improve their environmental performance if they are meeting established standards. For example, if a facility is environmentally conscientious and is abiding by all the applicable environmental regulations and producing ten units of pollution annually, where is the incentive for it to work at reducing that impact? There is little about command and control regulations that encourage the firm to strive to generate only nine units of pollution the following year. This is not to say that the firm would not do that on its own for a host of reasons, but there may be little regulatory benefit for the firm that might have to purchase new technologies or equipment to reduce its environmental impact. It is worth noting that the purpose of this type of regulations is to limit behavior or pollution not prevent it in the first place.

COMMAND AND CONTROL REGULATIONS IN ACTION

After the overview of command and control regulations and a review of some of their fundamental assumptions, consider how these regulations work on a day-to-day basis. It is important to point out that this consideration of the front-lines is often missing in discussions of environmental policy, and this is unsettling because we have to understand how these regulations work in practice to fully comprehend how environmental policy operates today and how it might in the future. Instrumental to the daily implementation of these regulations are the actors involved and the permitting and compliance monitoring components of these regulations.

Regulatory Structure

Command and control regulations require a variety of regulators at the federal, state, and, sometimes, even the local level. Typically, federal regulators (notably those with the US EPA) are tasked with promulgating regulations, as detailed in Chapter 6, through rulemaking processes. States can impose additional requirements beyond federal ones, but they are not required to do so. Some states choose to impose more stringent regulations, such as California with its air quality laws.

After the regulations have been promulgated, much of the work is delegated to the states for implementation, and typically, state environmental protection agencies assume primary responsibility for the implementation of these laws. Table 7.2 lists the state environmental protection agencies.

Table 7.2 State environmental protection agencies

Alabama Department of Environmental Management
Alaska Department of Environmental Conservation
Arizona Department of Environmental Quality
Arkansas Department of Energy and Environment
California Environmental Protection Agency
Colorado Department of Public Health and Environment
Connecticut Department of Energy and Environmental Protection
Delaware Department of Natural Resources and Environmental Control
Florida Department of Environmental Protection
Georgia Department of Natural Resources
Hawaii State Department of Health
Idaho Department of Environmental Quality
Illinois Environmental Protection Agency
Indiana Department of Environmental Management
Iowa Department of Natural Resources
Kansas Department of Health and Environment
Kentucky Department for Environmental Protection
Louisiana Department of Environmental Quality
Maine Department of Environmental Protection
Maryland Department of the Environment
Massachusetts Department of Environmental Protection
Michigan Department of Environmental, Great Lakes, and Energy
Minnesota Pollution Control Agency
Mississippi Department of Environmental Quality
Missouri Department of Natural Resources
Montana Department of Environmental Quality
Nebraska Department of Environmental and Energy
Nevada Department of Conservation and Natural Resources
New Hampshire Department of Environmental Services
New Jersey Department of Environmental Protection
New Mexico Environment Department
New York Department of Environmental Conservation
North Carolina Department of Environmental Quality
North Dakota Department of Environmental Quality
Ohio Environmental Protection Agency
Oklahoma Department of Environmental Quality
Oregon Department of Environmental Quality

(continued)

Table 7.2   (continued)

Alabama Department of Environmental Management
Pennsylvania Department of Environmental Protection
Rhode Island Department of Environmental Management
South Carolina Department of Health and Environmental Control
South Dakota Department of Environment and Natural Resources
Tennessee Department of Environment and Conservation
Texas Commission on Environmental Quality
Vermont Department of Environmental Conservation
Virginia Department of Environmental Quality
Washington Department of Ecology
West Virginia Department of Environmental Protection
Wisconsin Department of Natural Resources
Wyoming Department of Environmental Quality

This delegation of authority to the state level is a function of our federal structure of government. The agencies listed in Table 7.2 are, for the most part, delegated the responsibility of taking federal environmental laws and regulations and implementing them within their state. The majority of states typically issue the environmental permits and complete most of the environmental enforcement actions rather than the federal government. However, there are some cases in which the federal government has not granted such authority. For example, two states, Massachusetts and New Hampshire, have not been granted program authority to administer the National Pollutant Discharge Elimination System (NPDES) permits under the Clean Water Act (US EPA 2021). Notwithstanding these few exceptions, the states have a tremendous role in implementing environmental policy "as they operate more than 90% of all federal environmental programs that can be delegated" (Rabe 2022, 37). These agencies fund this work through a combination of money from their state and from the federal government. In a typical year, states receive anywhere between 20 and 33% of their total spending on environmental and natural resources efforts from the federal government through grants (Rabe 2022, 48). This means that states increasingly have to fund their work to implement federal environmental programs, along with their own agency's initiatives, and they are doing so in an era where state budgets and staffing levels are also being cut. It is the states and their front-line regulators that are primarily tasked with overseeing implementation of environmental regulations nationwide. The federal government's regulators can and do oversee these programs, but it is the state regulators who are on the front-lines of ensuring environmental protection.[2] In practical terms, states permit and monitor facilities throughout their state for compliance with environmental regulations and may have their federal counterparts check in and oversee these efforts from time to time. The following section explores these activities and examines both sides of regulatory interaction: the regulator and the members of the regulated community.

Permitting and Compliance Monitoring

Carrying out environmental regulations requires permitting and monitoring. When a firm (or regulated company) is beginning its operation and constructing a new facility (or when it is making major modifications to its existing facility and/or operations), it is required to apply for a permit to operate and generate pollution. As previously discussed, the federal government's regulations set forth the minimum environmental standards, such as the amount of discharge or the kind of process or technologies to use in the firm's operations. States may choose to go above and beyond these requirements and have additional obligations. A firm would comply with the requirements and complete the application process which varies state to state. These permit applications can be fairly brief or constitute hundreds of pages of technical information and descriptions of a facility's operation. A front-line regulator then reviews the permit application, seeks any additional information or clarification, and ensures that all conditions are met. In some cases, a public hearing is held to seek input from citizens. Finally, a permit is issued to the facility to begin operations. It is important to note that, if a facility undergoes major modifications or renovations to its facility or changes its production process, it typically has to apply for a permit modification—just like in our introductory story. Permits are issued for a fixed period of time, and then a renewal process occurs. This is not unlike the processes many of us are familiar with regarding driver's licenses.

---

[2] The relationship between federal environmental regulators and state regulators can be complex; Denise Scheberle (2004) offers a thorough and much needed analysis of the dynamics of these federal/state interactions.

The permit to operate outlines various conditions that a firm must meet. These conditions are stipulated by the command and control regulations discussed earlier. They typically include an array of monitoring data that must be collected and reviewed, and frequently incorporate the use of particular pollution control equipment and production process requirements. To guarantee that the requisite monitoring is done and other requirements complied with, firms are subjected to compliance inspections from their regulatory counterparts: regulators.

Inspection Process

Inspections vary greatly in their frequency, length, and involvement of key actors. They can be brief or they can last for days, depending on why a facility is regulated and the size of the facility and its operations. These inspections are typically done by a single regulator (or inspector). A regulator begins the inspection process by arriving at a facility, generally unannounced. Regulators conduct the vast majority of their inspections unannounced so they can observe the facility operating normally, rather than when the facility is prepared for a regulator's visit.[3] A brief meeting usually occurs between the regulator and facility contact, reviewing the facility's compliance history and any pertinent issues or concerns. Afterward, the physical site inspection commences in which the regulators review the production process, walks the operations floor, see product being made, and record their findings while talking with the facility contact.

Regulators examine pollution abatement technologies and monitoring equipment. They also review various paperwork and data that must be maintained on site. The most frequent activity that regulators report is explaining regulations to members of the regulated community (Pautz and Rinfret 2013, 24). Generally, at the conclusion of the physical inspection there is a debriefing between the regulator and the facility contact to go over anything significant and to give the facility a preliminary assessment of the facility's compliance status. During this meeting any

---

[3] There are, of course, exceptions to the general policy of unannounced inspections. Facilities with extensive security measures in place frequently require advanced notice of an inspection. For example, many US Department of Defense facilities require security clearances to be on site, so inspectors have little choice but to notify the facility in advance of their arrival.

additional reports, monitoring data, or questions are addressed. After the closing meeting is conducted, the regulator returns to their office to begin their formal write-up of the inspection and to discuss with their supervisor any issues.

Inspections occur with varying frequency and level of scrutiny. For example, small firms, such as a printing operation may only discharge a small amount of air pollutants, so they are would find themselves being inspected every three to five years. By contrast, a large power generation might expect annual inspections since they are a major source of pollution. Inspections may not always be a physical site inspection either. In some cases, the review of monitoring logs and other paperwork may constitute the inspection.

Noncompliance During Inspections

After a physical site inspection or a paperwork inspection, if a regulator finds a problem, there are multiple avenues to resolve the issue. These avenues vary state to state, as each agency has its own policies and procedures. Most regulators aim to facilitate the resolution of the issue as quickly and painlessly as possible and without utilizing formal mechanisms (c.f. Pautz and Rinfret 2013). It is important to note that decisions about how to resolve issues that arise during inspections (or during any other point in compliance monitoring) do not occur in isolation; in other words, inspectors and their superiors make these decisions in a broader organizational and even political context. Here, we chart some of the paths toward resolution and then will explore this broader context.

A regulator can informally have the firm address the issue on site and, hopefully, resolve the issue then and there. For instance, if, during the inspection, improperly labeled chemical containers are found, a regulator is likely to point out the issue—and permit violation—to the facility. Ideally, the facility representative ensures the problem is remedied immediately by getting labels corrected. If the matter was resolved as soon as it was pointed out, the regulator might only note the issue in their inspection write-up, rather than pursue any formal means of corrective action. If, however, the facility representative is not cooperative and the labeling is not addressed, then a regulator begins the process of correcting a violation. If the matter cannot be resolved immediately, then a regulator may issue a Request for Corrective Action (RCA).[4] Although an RCA is a formal document that becomes part of a facility's file, as long as the issue is resolved within the timeframe specified by the regulator (e.g., 30 days), there are no significant ramifications for the facility. The regulator will follow up with the facility in the timeframe established to ensure the issue has been corrected and that will, typically, be the end of the matter.

If the regulator, guided by their agency's policies and processes, determines the violation is severe, an RCA may not be appropriate or severe enough given the violation. Violations run the gamut from a container of solvent-soaked rags that is left uncovered on a production floor to printing inks with volatile organic compound (VOC) emissions beyond permitted levels to the improper dumping of chemicals. After consultation with the regulator's supervisor, a formal warning letter may be drafted and issued to the facility.[5]

If the formal warning letter is not sufficient to compel compliance, the state will pursue a formal Notice of Violation (NOV). NOVs are, typically, the next step in the enforcement process and, as might be expected, facility representatives do not relish receipt of a NOV. Issuance of a NOV, typically, involves not only the regulator and his/her supervisor, but also representatives from either an attorney housed within the agency or with the states's attorneys general office. Beyond this step, in a typical enforcement proceeding; state attorneys get involved because the environmental agency is unable to get a recalcitrant facility to come back into compliance. In some instances, civil suits or even criminal suits are pursued. Although criminal charges are not commonly pursued in environmental cases, there are some notable exceptions. Donald Blankenship, CEO of Massey Energy Company, was sentenced to one year in prison and fined $250,000 following a conviction for conspiracy to violate federal mine safety standards. The violations were part of the investigation into the 2010 explosion of the Upper Big Branch mine explosion in West Virginia that killed 29 miners (Blinder 2016). With the introduction of attorneys, regulators play a less prominent role in pursuing compliance.

---

[4] Again, these are general statements about enforcement proceedings because each state has its own guidelines and procedures surrounding enforcement actions. Frequently, the best place to learn about a state's enforcement policies and procedures is through the agency's website.

[5] Warning letters may also be used more readily with facilities that have a history of compliance issues.

Major findings of noncompliance often elicit the involvement of federal regulators as well. Recall that while state environmental agencies are likely the entities that uncover the noncompliance, major problems usually trigger a collaborative approach to rectify the situation from both state and federal regulators. After all, the federal government typically has the ultimate authority as they have delegated authority to the states to implement federal statutes and regulations.

Findings of noncompliance are not typically viewed positively as they indicate that environmental standards are not being met, and there is a significant chance that harm is being done to the environment. That said, how regulators and their agencies respond to those findings can vary for a host of reasons, from organizational reasons, such as staffing challenges that reduce frequencies of inspections and organizational emphases on particular industrial sectors, to political reasons, such as the priorities of a governor or president. The Trump administration, for example, opted not to pursue enforcement actions at similar rates from previous administrations of both political parties (Lipton and Ivory 2017). Investigative reporting from *The New York Times* and other media outlets concluded that significant decreases in enforcement efforts defined the early years of the US EPA under the Trump administration, which aligned with EPA Administrator Scott Pruitt's orders to back off enforcement of environmental laws per the request of oil and gas industry executives (Lipton and Ivory 2017). By contrast, the early years of the Biden administration signaled a tougher stance on enforcement. In one notable example, the administration issued a rare order to shut down a refinery in the US Virgin Islands over violations of the Clean Air Act (Hijazi 2021).

The intermingling of federal and state roles in permitting and monitoring compliance with environmental regulations helps us glimpse the multitude of actors who are involved in environmental protection. Of particular interest are the populations of actors whose day-to-day job is environmental compliance—the front-line regulators and their counterparts at the firms subject to environmental regulations.

Front-Line Regulators

Front-line regulators work for state environmental agencies and they permit, inspect, and, generally, oversee the environmental activities of facilities in the state. They have an array of responsibilities, which keeps their jobs anything but dull because they are the ones who most frequently and consistently are the bridge between environmental policy-makers and the regulated community. In many instances, these individuals have backgrounds in the natural sciences and/or engineering and are often at the base of their agencies' organizational pyramid. Accordingly, their work constitutes what Michael Lipsky (1980) and others define as street-level bureaucrats or front-line workers because they interact daily with the public, and their actions constitute the implementation of environmental policy (c.f. Maynard-Moody and Musheno 2003; Riccucci 2005). As Stephen Fineman (1998) summarizes, "like other street-level bureaucrats environmental inspectors deal with people who may not voluntarily desire their services and who experience some ambiguity in exercising appropriate control" (953). To explore the work and impact of regulators, we begin with their organizational context.

Mirroring the organization of the US EPA (discussed in Chapter 4) most state environmental agencies are structured around the major environmental issues, or environmental "media," and their corresponding statutes.[6] For instance, the 1970 Clean Air Act and its subsequent amendments have compelled federal and state environmental agencies to establish divisions or bureaus dedicated to implementing and enforcing the mandates of clean air legislation. The same holds for water and waste (although most waste programs are segregated into solid waste and hazardous waste) and there are frequently delineations in water programs between drinking water and other facets of water laws. Accordingly, environmental regulators specialize in air, water (sometimes delineated between drinking water and groundwater), solid, or hazardous waste.

These media-specific delineations may create problems for both the enforcement of environmental laws and for the facilities themselves (c.f. US EPA Office of Inspector General 2006; US Government Accountability Office 2003; Pautz and Rinfret 2013; Rabe 2002). Because

---

[6] It is worth noting that states vary in their organizational responses to environmental protection. Some states have multiple agencies that are responsible for environmental concerns (e.g., a Department of Environmental Quality and a Department of Natural Resources), whereas other states have one comprehensive agency. The majority of states that participated in our study have multiple agencies and a few (e.g., Wisconsin and New York) have a single comprehensive agency. Within these state agencies, there is a range of organizational schemes that have implications for the implementation and enforcement of environmental regulations. See Hopper (2020) for a thorough review of these organizational approaches.

regulators focus on a specific environmental media, they learn the intricacies of the environmental laws surrounding their appointed media, and may not be as conversant in the regulations regarding other media. This specialization can be problematic because, for example, modifying a production process at a regulated facility to improve air quality may adversely impact water quality.

As is the case with other front-line workers, environmental regulators contend with competing agency goals (c.f. Lipsky 1980; Maynard-Moody and Musheno 2003; Riccucci 2005). The stated goals of most environmental agencies include the protection of human health and the environment without impeding development. For instance, the US EPA's mission statement is "to protect human health and the environment" (US EPA 2022). However, beyond that statement, the US EPA also specifies that "[e]nvironmental stewardship is integral to US policies concerning natural resources, human health, economic growth, energy, transportation, agriculture, industry, and international trade, and these factors are similarly considered in establishing environmental policy" (US EPA 2022). Therefore, while protecting health and the natural environment is the goal of the agency, the agency also stipulates that economic growth and related factors are a consideration in its work. Although these objectives can work in concert with one another, they can be in tension with each other. For instance, additional requirements on facilities might lessen their environmental impact, but they may require the installation of pollution abatement technology, which could be a substantial investment up front before any environmental impact can be realized.

At the state level, for example, new governors—through their appointees—can alter the direction of state environmental agencies, as we have seen in recent years, presenting even more challenges for regulators, who often serve in their capacity as regulators under numerous administrations. For example, Glenn Youngkin (R) took office in early 2022 as Governor of the Commonwealth of Virginia and nominated Andrew Wheeler as Secretary of Natural Resources. Wheeler previously served as head of the US EPA under the Trump administration and would have represented a significant departure from the previous priorities of the agency. However, the Virginia Senate voted down Wheeler's nomination.

Within this organizational structure, the day-to-day tasks of regulators are quite similar, although they work in different environmental media. Given the term regulator, one may rightly assume that a regulator engages in "routine inspections and check visits," but there are many other aspects of a regulator's job duties (Hutter 1997, 107). In the course of any workday, a regulator may or may not be in the office, but rarely does a day go by in which a regulator does not deal directly with a regulated facility.

Generally, regulators spend their time in the office preparing to be out of the office and visiting facilities. In the field is where pollution control happens (Hawkins 1984, 47). However, regulators spend, on average, more than 70% of their time in the office, much to their dismay (Pautz and Rinfret 2013, 22). Being in the field brings with it a variety of experiences. A regulator is responsible for anywhere from a handful of facilities to hundreds of facilities. The number depends upon the types of facilities she oversees and how they are regulated; for example, are the facilities major sources, as defined by US EPA, or are they facilities that are shutdown, but have ongoing monitoring? The number of facilities a regulator is responsible for varies considerably, depending on the nature of the regulation. One study reports that the typical workload for a regulator is 50 facilities, with water and waste regulators generally responsible for more facilities than their regulatory counterparts in air (Pautz and Rinfret 2013, 23).

To prepare for a visit to assess compliance, a regulator begins by reviewing a facility's permit, compliance history, and other documents related to a facility's operation. Keep in mind that regulators are often responsible for a host of facilities with various operations, which can prove challenging for regulators. For example, an air regulator could be responsible for nearly 200 facilities that range from a cigarette producing plant to several printing operations, from a power plant to a plastic injection molding facility. Needless to say, keeping up with such diverse facility operations can prove taxing for a regulator, but this is simply part of the job.

The requirements and frequency of physical site inspections vary depending on many different factors. The size of a facility's operation and the reasons it is regulated determine how often a regulator must visit the facility and how involved the inspection is while the regulator is there. For example, minor sources of air pollution, such as a dry cleaner, only require physical site inspections once every 3 to 5 years. The same is true for facilities that have boilers—such as older school buildings. However, large facilities, such as power-generating stations, may see their regulators quarterly. The frequency and extent of the physical site inspections are determined by the conditions of a facility's permit, which may vary state to state, as discussed earlier in the chapter.

Physical site inspections are not the only type of inspections. Many inspections are conducted based on paperwork and other reports that a facility submits to the agency, as required by permit conditions and other regulations. Regulators have to keep up with voluminous reports such as stack testing reports, opacity readings, and other data provided by pollution abatement technology and various other monitors. Verifying the reports and then reviewing them for any problems can be time consuming, particularly when some reports are hundreds of pages each and submitted quarterly.

Misperceptions About Regulators

This discussion of regulators may seem rather unsatisfying because it does not substantiate a lot of perceptions about this group of actors. For starters, environmental regulators cannot shutdown facilities regardless of environmental harms—that is something that courts may do only in extreme, rare cases.[7] Moreover, as subsequent discussion will demonstrate, the interactions between regulators and members of the regulated community are generally productive and cooperative, defying images conveyed to us from seemingly innocuous sources (such as movies) that the regulator and the regulated cannot get along (c.f. Pautz and Rinfret 2013). Indeed, the confrontational interaction portrayed in the original *Ghostbusters* film from 1984 where the EPA inspector, Walter Peck, wants to shut down the Ghostbusters' valiant efforts at ridding the world of meddlesome supernatural beings is far from the norm; however, these are the images that can dominate our perceptions about regulators. Moreover, perceptions about environmental regulators may stem from other types of government regulators, such as workplace safety inspectors or even police officers—as both sets of actors have more authority to act with immediate ramifications, such as forcing a facility to stop operations. Environmental regulators do not have this kind of authority. Additionally, in thinking about regulators and our perceptions, considerations of the

---

[7] It is often thought that environmental regulators can act like Occupational Safety and Health Administration (OSHA) inspectors, who do retain some powers—again in extreme circumstances—to shut down a facility if violations are found. This not the case with environmental inspectors.

role of gender and race/ethnicity are also warranted as the attitudes and expectations brought to these interactions will affect them (c.f. Rinfret 2021).

MEMBERS OF THE REGULATED COMMUNITY

Regulators cannot implement environmental policy without the regulated community; both parties need one another. The term regulated community is used to describe the individuals at regulated facilities who interact with the regulators in an effort to comply with environmental regulations. Employed by an array of organizations—from pharmaceutical companies and water-treatment facilities to dry cleaners and quarries—members of the regulated community are responsible for dealing with environmental matters on a routine basis. In large, well-established facilities, these individuals are often full-time environmental managers who may have an entire staff devoted to achieving compliance with environmental regulations, and they are likely well trained in environmental engineering, science, or related fields. At the other end of the spectrum are facility personnel who are responsible for environmental matters as just one of many job duties. These individuals may not have extensive backgrounds in environmental matters and might even be the small business owners who shoulder the responsibility for everything the business does. Accordingly, it is difficult to succinctly characterize this diverse group. Generally speaking, these members of the regulated community are committed to their jobs and their companies and are not intentionally out to harm the environment. Violations of environmental regulations are frequently the result of ignorance or confusion over requirements rather than malicious attempts to endanger the environment (c.f. Pautz 2009; Pautz and Rinfret 2013).

Despite the importance of these actors, little is known about them or their interactions with regulators. Eugene Bardach and Robert Kagan (1982/2002) simply talk, with little elaboration, about the "good apples" and the "bad apples" that environmental regulators encounter. They do conclude, however, that most of the time regulators encounter "good apples," but the experiences with the "bad apples" tend to sour the experiences for everyone involved. Keith Hawkins (1984) focuses somewhat more on the people with whom inspectors interact, but only insofar as to assert four categories of "images of polluters:" socially responsible, unfortunate, careless, and malicious (110–113). According to Hawkins, most of the time, inspectors encounter facility personnel who are socially responsible and are endeavoring to comply with regulations as a matter of principle. Bridget Hutter (1997) builds on existing literature (notably Bardach and Kagan's good and bad apples) by arguing that there are finer distinctions among facilities: poor, reasonable, fairly good, responsible, very good, and exemplary. It is evident from this discussion of the regulated community that misperceptions can, and do, persist about this group of actors.

Misperceptions of the Regulated Community

With the stories of rampant pollution and nefarious companies that are out to harm the environment in the name of profit, it is easy to presume that the regulated community is a malicious group of individuals representing industries that could care less about the environment. From tales of Hooker Chemical Company in Love Canal, New York to Exxon and the Valdez spill to the BP disaster in the Gulf of Mexico, it might seem that these incidents are representative of the regulated community. Indeed, film is no stranger to such depictions in movies like *A Civil Action* or *Erin Brockovich*. However, these portraits of industry are simplistic and, although there are some companies that intentionally harm the environment and defy environmental regulations, they are far from the majority. Indeed, research into the regulated community portrays a far different picture than common perceptions or Hollywood might have us believe. Most members of the regulated community recognize that environmental regulations are important and being good stewards of the environment is good for business (c.f. Coglianese and Nash 2001; Hoffman 2001; Kamieniecki 2006).

The persistence of the misperceptions of both regulators and the regulated community can be attributed, in part, to the prevailing narratives about good and bad. Regulation of any kind is rarely popular, yet it prevails because the people want government to protect something or do something. And in such scenarios, there are "good guys" and "bad guys." Depending on your political perspective, the actors that are good and the actors who are bad may vary. But, as we have seen already, reality is never quite that simple. You should be getting a sense from this chapter (and, indeed, the entire text) that environmental protection requires the collaboration and diligence of many groups of people that may seem adversarial on the surface but have to work together to achieve common goals.

REGULATORY INTERACTIONS

Beginning three decades ago, Ian Ayers and John Braithwaite (1992) helped shift the conversation about regulations and their implementation with their notion of "responsive regulation." Their seminal work, *Responsive Regulation,* helped change the conversation about regulatory enforcement and advance the notion that regulatory encounters are not all the same and often vary—and this is not a bad thing. While such conclusions may seem logical today, the notion that regulatory interactions would be anything other than an authority figure (e.g., the regulator) telling someone (e.g., the regulated community) what to do in a tense situation, was commonplace, since it was thought that only through force, or the threat of force, that compliance would be achieved. We have come to understand that these interactions between regulators and the regulated community are far more complex (c.f. Van de Walle and Raaphorst 2019). However, perceptions that these interactions are confrontational are still ever-present beyond practitioner and academic circles.

The significance of these regulatory encounters is significant in environmental regulation as it is during these encounters and repeated interactions that the actual work of environmental protection happens. At the most basic level, regulators and members of the regulated community are tasked with implementing environmental regulations and ensuring compliance with them, and neither party can do this alone. Individuals at regulated facilities routinely depend on regulators to help interpret regulations and give guidance on new methods for achieving compliance, and regulators rely on the facilities for environmental impact reports and education about the industry, operations of the facility, and the latest technologies and best practices. This interdependence leads Keith Hawkins (1984) to call this relationship "symbiotic" (45). Ultimately, a "substantial amount" of a regulator's time is "spent creating and preserving good relations" with members of the regulated community (Hawkins 1984, 42; see also Pautz and Rinfret 2013). Bridget Hutter (1997) also notes that inspectors and facility personnel "often build up quite a close working relationship" (167).

Exploring the interactions of regulators and members of the regulated community helps us better understand the day-to-day realities of implementing environmental regulations. Typically, the study of these interactions centers on the regulatory style a particular regulator may use, and we can think of these styles as forming the ends of an enforcement spectrum. On one side of the spectrum, a regulator may opt for a compliance-oriented (c.f. Hawkins 1984; Reiss 1984) or accommodative approach (c.f. Hutter 1989, 1988; Richardson et al. 1983) in which securing compliance with regulations is sought through cooperative or more conciliatory means. In contrast to this approach, the deterrence (c.f. Reiss 1984) or sanctioning approach (c.f. Hawkins 1984) emphasizes coercion or other more punitive means of achieving compliance. Table 7.3 highlights these different regulatory approaches.

Instead of regulators adopting one of the two approaches in their work implementing environmental regulation, research has demonstrated that regulators employ both approaches in varying combinations, depending on the circumstances, settings, and policy arenas (c.f. Braithwaite et al. 1987; Gormley 1998; Hutter 1989, 1988; May and Burby 1998; May and Winter 2000; Pautz and Rinfret 2013; Scholz and Feng 1986). The different regulatory approaches are determined by a host of factors at the individual, agency, and societal levels (c.f. Gormley 1997; Hutter 1989).

This focus on a regulator's enforcement approach provides does not offer insight into the behavior of the regulated community. Historically, regulatory action (or inaction) was generally explained by individuals pursuing their own self-interests, notably under the rubric of capture theory (c.f. Peltzman 1976; Stigler 1971). The interests of the regulatory community are diverse, and their actions may be guided by a plethora of motives, including monetary considerations, job retention or future

Table 7.3 Regulatory enforcement approaches	*Formal, rule-oriented*	*Flexible, results-oriented*
	Enforcement Approach	*Enforcement Approach*
	• Focuses on rules	• Understands the perspective of the regulated community
	• Emphasis on consistency, regardless of circumstances	• Gives the regulated community the benefit of the doubt
	• Tough enforcement	• Uses persuasion instead of threats
	• Deterrence as motivation for compliance	• Is flexible as appropriate
	• Adversarial posture	• Cooperative

employment aspirations (the "revolving door" effect), self-gratification, or the desire for tranquility between entities (c.f. Gormley 1997; Laffont and Tirole 1991; Levine and Forrence 1990). In contrast to the self-interest perspective, the public interest theory of regulation posits that the ultimate goal of compliance is some measure of public good and, therefore, regulatory actors act to benefit citizens and/or the environment (c.f. Joskow and Noll 1981; Viscusi et al. 2005).

More recent research focuses on the factors that compel firms to comply with regulations (c.f. Simpson and Rorie 2011; Kagan et al. 2003; Prakash 2000). As Peter May (2005) summarizes, the motivations for compliance with regulations generally fit into one of three categories: (1) deterrence or fear of consequences for being found out of compliance, (2) a sense of civic duty and responsibility to comply, and (3) social motivation or pressure to achieve compliance.

These insights are undoubtedly useful; however, they focus on the regulatory actors in isolation and are unable to describe how regulators and the regulated community interact with each other. Eugene Bardach and Robert Kagan (1982/2002) were among the first to explore interactions between actors, but their focus was largely on the nature of the regulations and the approaches the regulators took (e.g., deterrent or accommodative) more than four decades ago. Their acknowledgment of interactions is more of a digression rather than a focused study, and there is little else to draw on regarding these interactions. Nevertheless, in a variety of settings, from banking and securities to construction and pharmaceuticals, it has been shown that interdependence develops between the regulators and the regulated community (c.f. Braithwaite 1984; Hawthorne 2005; May and Wood 2003). In particular, this interdependence breeds strong ties between the regulator and the regulated community (McCaffrey et al. 2007). And some research has shown that environmental regulators do note the collaborative nature of their work and the need to employ varying combinations of both regulatory enforcement approaches depending on the situation and the regulated firm (Pautz and Rinfret 2013). Moreover, with repeated interactions, expectations develop and the relationships between the parties grow, sometimes, into mutual cooperation.

Indeed, some researchers have concluded that cooperation can increase regulatory effectiveness for a host of reasons, including conflict reduction, improved communication, and an increased willingness of parties to work together to achieve a common goal (c.f. Bardach and Kagan 1982/2002;

Potoski and Prakash 2004; Scholz 1991). While more research in this area is undoubtedly needed, it is increasingly clear that cooperation and even trust among regulatory actors can lead to improved regulatory outcomes (c.f. Pautz and Wamsley 2012).

There are two takeaways from this section. First, by considering the interactions of the two parties largely responsible for the day-to-day work of environmental regulation, we understand what environmental protection looks like on the front-lines. And second, we recognize that perceptions of these regulatory interactions may be simplistic and perhaps even wrought with confrontational attitudes, rather than the often collaborative nature of those interactions in reality.

CHALLENGES OF IMPLEMENTING COMMAND AND CONTROL REGULATIONS

After unpacking the nature of regulatory interactions, which are at the core of implementing command and control regulations, it is evident that there are a number of challenges associated with implementing these regulations, including: (1) politics and competing priorities, (2) federalism, (3) resource constraints, (4) administrative structures and discretion, and (5) concerns of regulatory capture.

Politics and Competing Priorities

As we have seen, environmental policy is both highly technical and highly political. Therefore, political pressures and priorities have a tremendous effect on this policy area, just as they do in many others. Elected leaders set the agenda for legislation and the work of government agencies, so if a president or governor wants to achieve particular objectives, then she will advance those efforts. For example, a governor who wants to rekindle industry in his state may encourage a state environmental agency to deprioritize rigorous inspections to give industry the space to innovate and reinvest in their operations. Or a newly elected president may champion efforts to curb the harmful effects of climate change and direct the US EPA to focus all its activities on achieving those goals. For instance, President Joe Biden did just this and early in his administration announced four key priorities, including combatting climate change. Time will tell what success his administration may have in this regard. The point is the priorities established via political processes and our elected politicians can dramatically impact the work of environmental regulations. It is also worth noting that the priorities may be at odds with others, thereby confusing or complicating implementation.

Along these lines, there are less tangible but equally significant factors including the goals and policy objectives of the nation. Recall that the US EPA's mission statement is "to protect human health and the environment" (US EPA 2022). On the most basic level, there are inherent tensions in such a statement because humans are ultimately responsible for many kinds of environmental damage. Furthermore, environmental concerns are just one of countless areas of focus for the government, and all of those different issues vie for the nation's attention. Quite simply, not all these priorities can be focused on simultaneously and, sometimes, certain priorities—for example, economic recovery or fighting terrorism—crowd out others.

Federalism

Competing priorities and the agendas of politicians can complicate implementation, and that is often exacerbated by the federal structure of government in the US.. Most environmental regulations, as we discussed earlier, are promulgated at the federal level and then delegated to states and, sometimes, even local governments for implementation. The rationale for such an approach is as old as the US and its desire to keep government close to the people; nevertheless, such a structure can compound difficulties in implementation because multiple organizations have to coordinate among themselves the implementation of environmental protections. Multiple, overlapping agencies become involved in carrying out the same regulations, leading to coordination challenges. As we have discussed elsewhere, during the Trump administration, the US EPA scaled back its efforts related to mitigating the effects of climate change but this did not stopped state, and in some cases local, governments from advancing programs and initiatives to combat climate change in their jurisdiction. This represents a significant shift in that in the mid-twentieth century, the federal government was at the forefront on environmental protection efforts while states had to be coaxed along whereas more recently, the state and local governments are leading the way (where they have power to) while the federal government is resistant. Indeed, California is among the most proactive governments in the world endeavoring to address climate change (Rabe 2022, 44). But while California is making great strides, many states lag behind, including Ohio and West Virginia. These differing approaches can add to the challenges for the regulated community in trying to abide by an even more complex regulatory thicket. In other instances, regional collaborations have arisen, including the Regional Greenhouse Gas Initiative (RGGI), which is the first cap-and-trade program to reduce carbon dioxide emissions from the power generation sector. The RGGI currently includes states in the northeast and the RGGI has set a cap on carbon dioxide emissions from power plants in the region.

Resource Constraints

It takes a lot of resources—both in terms of sheer dollars from government and industry as well as in people and expertise—to implement environmental regulations. At the federal level, those resources are generally under the control of Congress and the White House, as the EPA's budget and personnel have seen periods of significant growth and contraction (see Table 7.4). Trends in agency budgets and personnel help us understand the overall prioritization of the agency's work and reflect the political priorities of elected officials. For instance, in the first budget year the Trump administration could influence, the White House requested a budget of $5.677 billion dollars, representing about a 30% cut from one year to the next (ECOS 2017). Cuts this dramatic were not ultimately implemented as Congress rejected such a move. The EPA's enacted budget remained over eight billion dollars during the Trump administration. In the opening months of the Biden administration, the White House requested a significant increase in the agency's budget—over eleven billion dollars—to support administration priorities and to bring on board more than 1,000 full-time employees to accomplish those priorities (ECOS 2021; EPA 2022).

It is important, moreover, to note that the federal government provides much in the way of grants and other resources to state and local agencies; therefore, if the federal government is contracting spending, then, those effects are going to be felt at the subnational level as well. Moreover, state and local governments experience periods of government expansion and contraction.

Table 7.4 US EPA's budget and workforce

Federal fiscal year	Enacted budget	Workforce
FY 2021	$9,237,153,000	14,297
FY 2020	$9,057,401,000	14,172
FY 2019	$8,849,488,000	14,172
FY 2018	$8,824,488,000	14,172
FY 2017	$8,058,488,000	15,408
FY 2016	$8,139,887,000	14,779
FY 2015	$8,139,887,000	14,725
FY 2014	$8,200,000,000	15,408
FY 2013	$7,901,104,000	15,913
FY 2012	$8,449,385,000	17,106
FY 2011	$8,682,117,000	17,359
FY 2010	$10,297,864,000	17,278
FY 2009	$7,643,674,000	17,049
FY 2008	$7,472,324,000	16,916
FY 2007	$7,725,130,000	17,072
FY 2006	$7,617,416,000	17,355
FY 2005	$8,023,483,000	17,495
FY 2004	$8,365,420,000	17,611
FY 2003	$8,078,703,000	17,741
FY 2002	$8,078,813,000	17,590
FY 2001	$7,832,211,000	17,558
FY 2000	$7,562,811,000	17,726
FY 1999	$7,590,352,000	18,110
FY 1998	$7,363,046,000	17,739
FY 1997	$6,799,393,000	17,152
FY 1996	$6,522,953,000	17,082
FY 1995	$7,248,412,000	17,508
FY 1994	$6,578,927,000	17,106
FY 1993	$6,861,199,000	17,280
FY 1992	$6,668,853,000	17,010
FY 1991	$6,094,287,000	16,415
FY 1990	$5,461,808,000	16,318
FY 1989	$5,155,125,000	14,370
FY 1988	$5,027,442,000	14,442
FY 1987	$5,364,092,000	13,442
FY 1986	$3,663,841,000	12,892
FY 1985	$4,353,655,000	12,410
FY 1984	$4,067,000,000	11,420
FY 1983	$3,688,688,000	10,832
FY 1982	$3,676,013,000	11,402

(continued)

Table 7.4 (continued)

Federal fiscal year	Enacted budget	Workforce
FY 1981	$3,030,669,000	12,667
FY 1980	$4,669,415,000	13,078
FY 1979	$5,402,561,000	12,160
FY 1978	$5,498,635,000	11,986
FY 1977	$2,763,745,000	11,315
FY 1976	$771,695,000	9,481
FY 1975	$698,835,000	10,438
FY 1974	$518,348,000	9,743
FY 1973	$2,377,226,000	9,077
FY 1972	$2,447,565,000	8,358
FY 1971	$1,288,784,000	5,744
FY 1970	$1,003,984,000	4,084

Source https://www.epa.gov/planandbudget/budget

Administrative Structures and Discretion

There are many factors internal to governmental agencies that affect the implementation of regulations, including bureaucratic processes and structures and the exercise of administrative discretion. Bureaucratic organizations have rigid organizational schemes that can prove less flexible and slower to change than might be ideal for the particular issues the organization confronts. For example, the US EPA and most state environmental protection agencies are still organized largely around pollution areas—air, water (drinking and surface), and waste (hazardous and solid). This organizational scheme coincides with the regulatory regime that was constructed to align with the major environmental statutes, such as the CAA, the CWA, and the Safe Drinking Water Act. Although this arrangement made lots of sense decades ago, it arguably makes less sense today as we have come to understand that environmental issues transcend these traditional boundaries of water, waste, and so forth.

Another significant internal challenge has to do with administrative discretion. Our discussion in this chapter (and also in Chapters 5 and 6) conveys the complexities of taking vague statutory language and translating it into actionable regulations. The steps in the process often remove direct oversight from elected officials. Therefore, governmental administrators are relied upon to ensure successful implementation of the laws without direct oversight. Put differently, when Congress enacts policy, it neither supervises the day-to-day activities of rule-writers in the US EPA or state environmental agencies, nor is Congress out in the field with regulators, ensuring the ongoing compliance with the law.

As a result, these regulators exercise discretion, which has a variety of implications. On the positive side, this discretion allows the expert scientists, engineers, and other civil servants to go about protecting the environment free of the meddlesome nature of Congress. Indeed, Michael Milakovich and Gordon Gordon (2013) remind us that these civil servants are, often, in a better position "to make decisions on the basis of the broader public interest" (94). For example, a regulator may be inspecting a printing facility as part of routine compliance monitoring and she finds one of the collection bins of solvent-soaked rags is uncovered, which is a permit violation. The regulator has discretion about how to respond to the facility's violation. She may elect to immediately write-up the facility and suggest to her supervisor that a NOV be issued so the facility is formally reprimanded. Or she may decide that, as the facility is a model for its environmental stewardship, and of the ten bins, only one is uncovered, to simply draw attention to the problem; if the manager immediately sees the error and corrects it, the regulator then only makes a note of the issue in the inspection report. There are plenty of reasons to justify either course of action and the regulator's decision demonstrates administrative discretion. Of course, there is reason to be concerned about the abuse of power that coincides with the exercise of discretion; in the environmental arena, many of these concerns manifest themselves in debate over regulatory capture.

Concerns of Regulatory Capture

A pervasive fear that a regulator will succumb to the regulated community is the essence of capture. More formally, regulatory capture occurs when regulators become beholden to those they attempt to regulate. Furthermore, a regulatory agency or regulator could succumb to the control of outside influences ranging from the community they are responsible for regulating (Bernstein 1955). In the environmental arena, the now defunct Minerals Management Service in the Department of Interior is thought to have demonstrated some aspects of regulatory capture, which came to light after the 2010 Deepwater Horizon spill. Fears of capture permeate all regulatory arenas, not just environmental policy; however, definitive conclusions about its presence remain elusive. Concerns stem from a host of issues, including worries that a regulator will behave a certain way in the hope of securing a job with industry, or concerns that a regulator is simply complacent and ambivalent about the regulatory apparatus he/she is tasked with enforcing, or even that a regulator is sympathetic to industry (c.f. Makkai and Braithwaite 1992).

Concerns of regulatory capture are not entirely unfounded; however, "in crude terms, the idea of capture is a dramatic overstatement or even simply inaccurate and also an insult that impugns the integrity of many good people who have spent their careers working for public interest in regulatory agencies" (Cooper 2009, 11). James Q. Wilson (1980) and Paul Quirk (1981), among others, argue that regulatory capture is not common, and Toni Makkai and John Braithwaite (1992) find the presence of regulatory capture to be weak and situational. Stephen Croley (2008) not only refutes regulatory capture, but also points to how well the public interest has been served by regulatory bodies and their regulators. In the context of environmental regulation, we, too, raise doubts that capture should be an overriding concern about regulators. To get a better glimpse of the complexities of regulatory implementation and compliance, the following case study discusses a facility in Dayton, Ohio that has had its ups and downs in implementing environmental regulations.

Case Study: Regulatory Realities and Clean Water, Limited

Located in Dayton, Ohio, Clean Water, Limited is an industrial wastewater processor, which means that the company takes commercial wastewater and processes it before the waste can either be sent to a landfill or released back into the sewer and water system. The facility in Dayton has existed for decades and was most recently bought by Clean Water, Limited (CWL), although its problems stem from its previous ownership, when the facility was called Perma-fix. Given the nature of its operations, the facility holds a variety of air and water permits, which means it has to deal with state water regulators and local government air regulators (in Ohio, the implementation of air regulations is delegated to local, regional authorities from the state environmental protection agency).

When CWL took over the facility, it inherited a lot of environmental compliance problems, and most of the environmental staff left the company within a year. Therefore, in many ways, the new facility management was starting from scratch, even though it had a litany of compliance problems. To make matters worse, the facility had a poor, long-standing relationship with its neighbors, a mostly residential, minority community. In addition, the new corporate structure of the facility had to contend with enforcement actions from the US EPA.

Many of the compliance issues surrounding this facility are complex and technical. When a facility such as CWL, or any other facility for that matter, wants to make modifications to its operations, it often has to report its intended changes and wait for approval from environmental regulators before moving forward. Although there are a variety of issues concerning the CWL facility, the crux of the problem were modifications to the facility's operations that required permit modifications, but the facility went ahead with the modifications before receiving approval to make such changes. Facilities have to wait for approval in order to ensure that their modifications do not affect their environmental footprint or put them into a different category of regulatory requirements. However, CWL did not wait. As is the case in so many operations, the facility needs to do what it does, and delays from government agencies can stymie those operations. More recently, the facility's thermal oxidizer, which is used to filter air emissions, did not work for more than a week, which led to citation by the US EPA. The thermal oxidizer and its venting system not working properly is releasing pollutants into the air and causing noxious fumes for nearby residents.

Up until this point, the story may seem rather ordinary—a facility is getting in trouble for polluting the environment—but what makes this diverge from that plot a bit is the ability of the state environmental regulators assigned to CWL to work together to help get the facility on the path toward compliance. First, the community was outraged by the noxious fumes coming from the facility and lawsuits were filed by angry citizens. The regulators were equally upset with the ongoing compliance issues at the facility and were in search of a solution. In a unique effort, regulators from the Ohio EPA and the local air pollution control agency, the Regional Air Pollution

Control Agency (RAPCA), worked together to help get the facility on track toward compliance and educate CWL about its regulatory requirements. These regulators even hosted community meetings in which they met with concerned citizens and officials from CWL to help open communication and rebuild the relationships between all the actors.

Instead of the regulators pursuing a path that simply entailed contentious enforcement activity, the regulators decided a different approach was needed. After all, the ultimate goal is compliance with environmental regulations and NOVs were not fixing the issue. Accordingly, regulators from multiple agencies (Ohio EPA, RAPCA, and Montgomery County public health officials) worked together with the facility and the community to educate all parties and address the ongoing issues at the facility. Although the facility still has challenges and the community is not entirely satisfied, the odors have diminished and appropriate permits are in place and all parties are better able to engage with one another. The cooperation exemplified in this case study helps demonstrate that regulatory interactions do not necessarily have to be confrontational and can be cooperative instead. As we look to the future of environmental regulations, an argument can be made that greater flexibility might allow for enhanced cooperation, which could lead to better regulatory outcomes for everyone involved. The final section of the chapter considers the future of regulation in light of critiques of the traditional command and control structure.

The Next Generation of Environmental Regulation

These discussions of the challenges associated with implementing environmental regulations bring up the broader critique of command and control regulations and a consideration of what the future may hold for environmental regulations. Before we can turn to alternative regulatory strategies that might prove advantageous for environmental protection, we should first consider the common critiques of command and control regulations in this arena.

Criticisms of Command and Control Regulation

An emerging theme in this chapter (and in conjunction with the history of environmental policy discussed in Chapter 2) is that environmental policy is a product of the time in which it was created. In the 1960s and 1970s, when most of the foundational environmental laws were passed, the rules and regulations that built upon those statutes reflected the times. For example, the environmental laws that responded to specific environmental problems were built around particular facets of the environment, notably air, water, and waste. Accordingly, the environmental laws focused independently on air, water, and waste concerns. Since then, we have come to understand better that environmental issues cannot be tackled independently of one another. Put differently, we cannot continue to deal with air quality issues in isolation without considering water or waste issues because progress in dealing with one particular issue might impact efforts in another area of environmental concern. With this media-specific approach, environmental protection agencies were set up based around environmental media; therefore, regulators become experts in particular areas of environmental concern and the regulated community has to interact with regulators from air, water, and waste (as their operations dictate). These organizational implications are significant and make collaboration across media and organizational boundaries challenging at times.

As we just discussed, the foundational environmental laws did much to address the pollution problems as we understood them decades ago. However, during the intervening years following the establishment of these laws, new scientific information has come to light, and we now better understand environmental issues; however, our existing regulatory structure has trouble keeping up with environmental issues today (this is not to say, though, that new scientific knowledge is not reflected in specific requirements or pollution limits; rather it is to say that the broad structures remain in place). For example, much of our regulatory structure is reactive to problems rather than proactive in preventing problems. Regulations have done much to curb pollution, but what about preventing pollution in the first place? Moreover, in the decades since most of these laws were passed, many environmental problems—including climate change and loss of biodiversity—have been identified, and these dated laws struggle to adequately address these contemporary issues.

Another theme that emerges with this regulatory approach is that it stifles innovation and fails to recognize the importance and even necessity of collaboration in environmental protection. As we discussed earlier in this chapter, most command and control regulations do exactly what the name indicates—they tell the regulated community what to do and how to control pollution. These commands may include specific emissions limits or the utilization of a particular pollution control technology. As a result, there is usually little opportunity for the regulated community to innovate and embrace new technologies or processes that might result in better environmental outcomes. Moreover, to devise these regulations, the burden is on the government to figure out the best methods of environmental protection, and there is little formal opportunity for those individuals who work in industry to devise cooperatively broader goals that allow industry to be creative. We have come to see that environmental protection is, frequently, a collaborative endeavor in which government and the regulated community has to work together to protect the environment; however, this regulatory structure can make that difficult, and even outright adversarial (c.f. Eisner 2006; Fiorino 2006; Kettl 2002). There continue to be calls for the regulatory approach to be more collaborative because environmental protection is achieved not by government alone, but through the partnership of government, the regulated community, and other public interests.

These criticisms of command and control regulations are poignant and significant, and further evidenced in growing discussions about the future of command and control regulation. However, moving away from this structure will be challenging, as the preceding conversation makes clear, and because of the polarization of American politics that sees perspectives on environmental protection as a barometer for political ideology overall.

The Future of Environmental Regulation

With these criticisms of the traditional command and control approach to environmental regulation, it becomes apparent that serious conversation about a "next-generation" of environmental regulation is needed. The good news is that this conversation is occurring and there are numerous ideas about how the regulatory structure can and should evolve in order to meet twenty-first century environmental challenges. In the final chapter, we delve into these discussions as we look toward the future of environmental regulation in the US. Innovative regulatory strategies are already being employed in some contexts and include provisions that allow for market-trading instead of command and control provisions, and more collaborative, systems-based approaches such as environmental management systems are proving useful. But that future remains uncertain as we may be experiencing a fundamental shift in the nation's attitudes to environmental protection more broadly. And the future of environmental regulations might be hampered by the judicial branch of government, as the Supreme Court in the summer of 2022 curtailed the EPA's ability to curb emissions through its power under the Clean Air Act in *West Virginia v. EPA*.

CHAPTER WRAP-UP

This chapter has explored how environmental policy is implemented, emphasizing the dominant regulatory tool—command and control regulations. Thousands of pages of regulations enable the implementation of the laws passed by Congress. Implementation also requires an array of regulatory actors—many of who garner little consideration in environmental policy. In particular, the efforts of those individuals on the front-lines of environmental protection, the regulators and the individuals at regulated facilities, are essential. And the interactions between these individuals constitutes environmental protection on a daily basis. Scant attention is often paid to these interactions, but here we explore these interactions and discuss the necessity of cooperation among regulatory actors. As expected, there are challenges in implementing environmental regulation and while this regulatory approach has facilitated significant improvement in the nation's environmental health, its critiques are growing louder.

Challenge Question for the Environmental Policy Classroom

The US EPA has a data tool, EJScreen (https://www.epa.gov/ejs creen/what-ejscreen), that enables users to explore a particular area through demographic and environmental data. Check out EJScreen for a geographical area of interest. What do you observe about the demographic and environmental indicators for that area? Then investigate which environmental regulatory agencies have jurisdiction over that area. With the information about the agencies and your from EJScreen, what would you recommend to the head of one of those regulatory agencies about enforcing existing environmental regulations?

SUGGESTED RESOURCES

Reading and Websites

Durant, Robert F., Daniel J. Fiorino, and Rosemary O'Leary, editors. *Environmental Governance Reconsidered: Challenges, Choices and Opportunities*. 2nd edition. Cambridge: MIT Press, 2017.

Environmental Council of the States. http://www.ecos.org.

Fiorino, Daniel J. *The New Environmental Regulation*. Cambridge: MIT Press, 2006.

Hooper, JoyAnna. *Environmental Agencies in the United States: The Enduring Power of Organizational Design and State Politics*. New York: Lexington, 2020.

Klyza, Christopher McGrory and David Sousa. *American Environmental Policy: Beyond Gridlock*. Cambridge: MIT Press, 2013.

Mintz, Joel A. *Enforcement at the EPA: High Stakes and Hard Choices*. Revised edition. Austin: University of Texas Press, 2013.

Pautz, Michelle C. and Sara R. Rinfret. *The Lilliputians of Environmental Regulation: The Perspective of State Regulators*. New York: Routledge, 2013.

Scheberle, Denise. *Federalism and Environmental Policy: Trust and the Politics of Implementation*. 2nd edition. Washington, DC: Georgetown University Press, 2004.

Van de Walle, Steven and Nadine Raaphorst, editors. *Inspectors and Enforcement at the Front Line of Government*. New York: Palgrave Macmillian, 2019.

Woods, Neal D. Regulatory Competition, Administrative Discretion, and Environmental Policy Implementation. *Review of Policy Research*, 00, 1-26, 2021.

Films and Videos

A Civil Action. Directed by Steven Zaillian. 1998. Touchstone Pictures, Paramount Pictures, Wildwood Enterprises, Scott Rudin Productions. DVD.

Erin Brockovich. Directed by Steven Soderbergh. 2000. Universal Pictures, Columbia Pictures, Jersey Films. DVD.

War on the EPA. Directed by James Jacoby. 2017. PBS Frontline documentary.

References

Andrews, Richard L. *Managing the Environment, Managing Ourselves: A History of American Environmental Policy*. New Haven, CT: Yale University Press, 2006.

Ayers, Ian and John Braithwaite. *Responsive Regulation: Transcending the Deregulation Debate*. New York: Oxford University Press, 1992.

Bardach, Eugene and Robert A. Kagan. *Going by the Book: The Problem of Regulatory Unreasonableness*. New Brunswick, NJ: Transaction Publishers, 2002/1982.

Bernstein, Marver. *Regulating Business through Independent Commission*. Princeton, NJ: Princeton University Press, 1955.

Birkland, Thomas A. *An Introduction to the Policy Process: Theories, Concepts, and Models of Public Policy Making*. 4th edition. Armonk, NY: Routledge, 2016.

Blinder, Alan. "Donald Blankenship Sentence to a Year in Prison in Mine Safety Case." *The New York Times*. (April 6, 2016). http://nyti.ms/207NUCI.

Braithwaite, John. *Corporate Crime in the Pharmaceutical Industry*. Boston: Routledge, 1984.

Braithwaite, John, John Walker, and Peter Grabosky. "An Enforcement Taxonomy of Regulatory Agencies." *Law & Policy* 9 (1987): 323–351.

Center on Budget and Policy Priorities. "Policy Basics: Non-defense Discretionary Programs." April 13, 2020. https://www.cbpp.org/research/federal-budget/non-defense-discretionary-programs.

Coglianese, Cary and Jennifer Nash. *Regulating from the Inside: Can Environmental Management Systems Achieve Policy Goals?* Washington, DC: Resources for the Future, 2001.

Cooper, Philip J. *The War Against Regulation: From Jimmy Carter to George W. Bush*. Lawrence: University Press of Kansas, 2009.

Croley, Steven P. *Regulation and Public Interests: The Possibility of Good Regulatory Government*. Princeton, NJ: Princeton University Press, 2008.

Davies, J. Clarence and Jan Mazurek. *Regulating Pollution: Does the U.S. System Work?* Washington, DC: Resources for the Future, 1997.

Dietz, Thomas and Paul C. Stern. "Exploring New Tools for Environmental Protection." In *New Tools for Environmental Protection: Education, Information, and Voluntary Measures*, edited by Thomas Dietz and Paul C. Stern, 3–15. Washington, DC: National Academy Press, 2002.

Eisner, Marc Allen. *Governing the Environment: The Transformation of Environmental Regulation*. Boulder, CO: Rienner, 2006.

Environmental Council of the States. "Delegation by Environmental Act." Environmental Council of the States. 2010. http://www.ecos.org/section/states/enviro_actlist.

Fineman, Stephen. "Street-Level Bureaucrats and the Social Construction of Environmental Control." *Organization Studies* 19, no. 6 (1998): 953–971.

Fiorino, Daniel J. *The New Environmental Regulation*. Cambridge: MIT Press, 2006.

Gormley, William T. "Regulatory Enforcement Styles." *Political Research Quarterly* 51 (1998): 363–383.

———. "Regulatory Enforcement: Accommodation and Conflict in Four States." *Public Administration Review* 57, no. 4 (July–August 1997): 285–293.

Hawkins, Keith. *Environment and Enforcement: Regulation and the Social Definition of Pollution*. Oxford: Clarendon Press, 1984.

Hawthorne, Fran. *Inside the FDA: The Business and Politics behind the Drugs We Take and the Food We Eat*. New York: John Wiley, 2005.

Hijazi, Jennifer. "Biden EPA Sends Early Signal of Tough Pollution Enforcement." *Bloomberg Law*. May 28, 2021. https://news.bloomberglaw.com/environment-and-energy/biden-epa-sends-early-signal-of-aggressive-pollution-enforcement.

Hoffman, Andrew J. *From Heresy to Dogma: An Institutional History of Corporate Environmentalism*. Expanded edition. Stanford: Stanford University Press, 2001.

Hooper, JoyAnna. *Environmental Agencies in the United States: The Enduring Power of Organizational Design and State Politics*. New York: Lexington, 2020.

Hutter, Bridget M. *Compliance: Regulation and Environment*. Oxford: Clarendon Press, 1997.

———. "Variations in Regulatory Enforcement Styles." *Law & Policy* 11, no. 2 (April 1989): 153–174.

———. *The Reasonable Arm of the Law? The Law Enforcement Procedures of Environmental Health Officers*. Oxford: Clarendon Press, 1988.

Joskow, Paul L. and Roger G. Noll. "Regulation in Theory and Practice: An Overview." In *Studies in Public Regulation*, edited by Gary Fromm, 1–65. Cambridge: MIT Press, 1981.

Kagan, Robert A., Neil Gunningham, and Dorothy Thornton. "Explaining Corporate Environmental Performance: How Does Regulation Matter?" *Law and Society Review* 37 (2003): 51–90.

Kamieniecki, Sheldon. *Corporate America and Environmental Policy: How Often Does Business Get Its Way?* Stanford: Stanford University Press, 2006.

Kettl, Donald. *Environmental Governance: A Report on the Next Generation of Environmental Policy*. Washington, DC: The Brookings Institution, 2002.

Klyza, Christopher McGrory and David Sousa. *American Environmental Policy 1990–2006*. Revised and expanded edition. Cambridge: MIT Press, 2013.

Klyza, Christopher McGrory, and David Sousa. *American Environmental Policy 1990–2006*. Cambridge: MIT Press, 2008.

Kraft, Michael E. *Environmental Policy and Politics*. 5th edition. New York: Longman, 2011.

Kraft, Michael E., Mark Stephan, and Troy D. Abel. *Coming Clean: Information Disclosure and Environmental Performance.* Cambridge: MIT Press, 2011.

Kraft, Michael E. and Norman J. Vig. "U.S. Environmental Policy: A Half Century Assessment." In *Environmental Policy: New Directions for the Twenty-First Century.* Norman J. Vig, Michael E. Kraft, and Barry G. Rabe, editors. Thousand Oaks, CA: Sage CQ Press. 3–33.

Laffont, Jean-Jacques and Jean Tirole. "The Politics of Government Decision-Making: A Theory of Regulatory Capture." *The Quarterly Journal of Economics* 106, no. 4 (November 1991): 1089–1127.

Levine, Michael E. and Jennifer L. Forrence. "Regulatory Capture, Public Interest, and the Public Agenda: Toward a Synthesis." *Journal of Law, Economics, & Organization* 6, no. Special Issue (April 1990): 167–1983.

Lipsky, Michael. *Street-level Bureaucracy: Dilemmas of the Individual in Public Services.* New York: Russell Sage Foundation, 1980.

Lipton, Eric and Danielle Ivory. "Under Trump, E.P.A. Has Slowed Actions Against Polluters, and Put Limits on Enforcement Officers. *The New York Times.* (December 10, 2017). http://nyti.ms/2jDgT4c.

Makkai, Toni and John Braithwaite. "In and Out of the Revolving Door: Making Sense of Regulatory Capture." *Journal of Public Policy* 12, no. 1 (January–March 1992): 61–78.

May, Peter J. "Compliance Motivations: Perspective of Farmers, Homebuilders, and Marine Facilities." *Law & Policy* 27, no. 2 (April 2005): 318–347.

May, Peter J. and Raymond J. Burby. "Making Sense Out of Regulatory Enforcement." *Law & Policy* 20, no. 2 (April 1998): 157–182.

May, Peter J. and Robert S. Wood. "At the Regulatory Front Lines: Inspectors' Enforcement Styles and Regulatory Compliance." *Journal of Public Administration Research and Theory* 13, no. 2 (2003): 117–139.

May, Peter J. and Søren Winter. "Reconsidering Styles of Regulatory Enforcement: Patterns in Danish Agro-Environmental Inspection." *Law & Policy* 22, no. 2 (April 2000): 143–173.

Maynard-Moody, Steven and Michael Musheno. *Cops, Teachers, Counselors: Stories from the Front Lines of Public Service.* Ann Arbor: University of Michigan Press, 2003.

McCaffrey, David P., Amy E. Smith, and Ignacio J. Martinez-Moyano. "Then Let's Have a Dialogue: Interdependence and Negotiation in a Cohesive Regulatory System." *Journal of Public Administration Research and Theory* 17, no. 2 (April 2007): 307–334.

Milakovich, Michael E. and George J. Gordon. *Public Administration in America.* New York: Wadsworth, 2013.

Milazzo, Paul Charles. *Unlikely Environmentalists: Congress and Clean Water, 1945–1972.* Lawrence, KS: University Press of Kansas, 2006.

Mintz, Joel A. *Enforcement at the EPA: High Stakes and Hard Choices.* Austin: University of Texas Press, 1995.

Office of Management and Budget, Office of Information and Regulatory Affairs. *2016 Draft Report to Congress on the Benefits and Costs of Federal Regulations and Agency Compliance with the Unfunded Mandates Reform Act* (2016). Available at https://obamawhitehouse.archives.gov/sites/def ault/files/omb/assets/legislative_reports/draft_2016_cost_benefit_report_ 12_14_2016_2.pdf.

Pautz, Michelle C. "Perceptions of the Regulated Community in Environmental Policy: The View from Below." *Review of Policy Research* 26, no. 5 (September 2009): 533–550.

Pautz, Michelle C. and Sara R. Rinfret. *The Lilliputians of Environmental Regulation: The Perspective of State Regulators.* New York: Routledge, 2013.

Pautz, Michelle C. and Carolyn Slott Wamsley. "Pursuing Trust in Environmental Regualtory Interactions: The Significance of Inspectors' Interactions with the Regulated Community." *Administration & Society* 44, 7 (October 2012): 853–884.

Peltzman, Sam. "Toward a More General Theory of Regulation." *Journal of Law and Economics* 19 (1976): 211–240.

Potoski, Matthew and Aseem Prakash. "The Regulation Dilemma: Cooperation and Conflict in Environmental Governance." *Public Administration Review* 64, no. 2 (March/April 2004): 152–163.

Prakash, Asseem. *Greening the Firm.* New York: Cambridge University Press, 2000.

Press, Daniel and Daniel A. Mazmanian. "Toward Sustainable Production: Finding Workable Strategies for Government and Industry." In *In Environmental Policy: New Directions for the 21st Century*, edited by Norman J. Vig and Michael E. Kraf, 230–254. Washington, DC: CQ Press, 2013.

Pressman, Jeffrey L. and Aaron Wildavsky. *Implementation: How Great Expectations in Washington Are Dashed in Oakland.* Los Angeles: University of California Press, 1984.

Quirk, Paul J. *Industry Influence in Federal Regulatory Agencies.* Princeton, NJ: Princeton University Press, 1981.

Rabe, Barry G. "Racing to the Top, the Bottom, or the Middle of the Pack? The Evolving State Government Role in Environmental Protection." In *Environmental Policy: New Directions for the Twenty-First Century*, edited by Norman J. Vig, Michael E. Kraft, and Barry G. Rabe, 35–62. Thousand Oaks: Sage CQ Press, 2022.

Rabe, Barry G. "Power to the States: The Promise and Pitfalls of Decentralization." In *Environmental Policy: New Directions for the Twenty-First Century*, edited by Norman J. Vig and Michael E. Kraft, 34–56. Washington, DC: CQ Press, 2006.

Rabe, Barry G. "Permitting, Prevention, and Integration: Lessons from the States." In *Environmental Governance: A Report on the Next Generation of Environmental Policy*, edited by Donald F. Kettl, 14–57. Washington, DC: The Brookings Institution, 2002.

Reiss, Jr., Albert J. "Selecting Strategies of Social Control over Organizational Life." In *Enforcing Regulation*, edited by Keith Hawkins and John M. Thomas. Boston: Kluwer-Nijhoff Publishing, 1984.

Riccucci, Norma M. *How Management Matters: Street-Level Bureaucrats and Welfare Reform*. Washington, DC: Georgetown University Press, 2005.

Richardson, G. M., A. I. Ogus, and P. Burrows. *Policing Pollution: A Study of Regulation and Enforcement*. Oxford: Clarendon Press, 1983.

Rinfret, Sara. "The Untold Stories: Women on the Front-lines of Environmental Regulation." *Public Integrity*. (2021).

Scheberle, Denise. *Federalism and Environmental Policy: Trust and the Politics of Implementation*. 2nd edition. Washington, DC: Georgetown University Press, 2004.

Scholz, John T. "Cooperative Regulatory Enforcement and the Politics of Administrative Effectiveness." *The American Political Science Review* 85, no. 1 (March 1991): 115–136.

Scholz, John T. and Heng Wei Feng. "Regulatory Enforcement in a Federalist System." *American Political Science Review* 80, no. 4 (December 1986): 1249–1270.

Simpson, Sally S. and Melissa Rorie. 2011. "Motivating Compliance: Economic and Material Motives for Compliance." In *Explaining Compliance: Business Responses to Regulation,* edited by Christine Parker and Vibeke Lehmann Nielsen, 59–77. Northampton, Massachusetts: Edward Elgar.

Smith, Kevin B. and Christopher W. Larimer. *The Public Policy Theory Primer*. 2nd ed. Boulder, CO: Westview Press, 2013.

Stigler, George. "The Theory of Economic Regulation." *Bell Journal of Economics and Management Science* 2 (1971): 3–21.

US Environmental Protection Agency. "Budget and Spending." U.S. Environmental Protection Agency. 2013. http://www2.epa.gov/planandbudget/budget.

US Environmental Protection Agency. *US EPA Our Mission and What We Do.* 2022. https://www.epa.gov/aboutepa/our-mission-and-what-we-do

US Environmental Protection Agency. NPDES State Program Authority. 2021. https://www.epa.gov/npdes/npdes-state-program-authority.

US Environmental Protection Agency. Watershed Assessment, Tracking, and Environmental Results. 2015. http://iaspub.epa.gov/waters10/attains_n ation_cy.control.

US Environmental Protection Agency. "Our Nation's Air: Trends Through 2020." US Environmental Protection Agency. 2021. https://gispub.epa.gov/air/trendsreport/2021/#air_trends.

US Environmental Protection Agency. FY 2022 Budget. https://www.epa.gov/planandbudget/cj. 2022.

US Environmental Protection Agency, Office of the Inspector General. *Studies Addressing EPA's Organizational Structure*. August 26, 2006.

US Environmental Protection Agency. 2017. National Water Quality Inventory: Report to Congress. https://www.epa.gov/sites/production/files/2017-12/documents/305brtc_finalowow_08302017.pdf. 2017.

US Government Accountability Office. "Major Management Challenges and Program Risks: Environmental Protection Agency." US Government Accountability Office. 2003.

Van de Walle, Steven and Nadine Raaphorst. "Introduction: The Social Dynamics of Daily Inspection Work." In *Inspectors and Enforcement at the Front Line of Government, edited by Steven Van de Walle and Nadine Raaphorst*, 1–10. New York: Palgrave Macmillian, 2019.

Viscusi, W. Kip, Joseph E. Harrington, and John M. Vernon. *Economics of Regulation and Antitrust*. 4th edition. Cambridge: MIT Press, 2005.

Wilson, James Q. *The Politics of Regulation*. New York : Basic Books, Inc., 1980.

Wisconsin Department of Natural Resources. "Our Mission." Wisconsin department of Natural Resources. 2013. http://dnr.wi.gov/about/mission.html.

CHAPTER 8

Is It Working? Evaluating Environmental Policy

With Jeffrey J. Cook

Introductory Story: Energy and the Race Reckoning? Bringing Energy Justice to the US DOE

Shalanda Baker has been committed to developing, implementing, and evaluating environmental policy during her entire career in the public and private sector. Though Baker has not always been a public servant, she has had a strong commitment to environmental justice, or the equitable distribution of environmental harms, asserting: "The problems of environmental injustice and the problems of energy injustice are pervasive in this country" (DOE 2021a). Furthermore, she has linked these issues with the racial reckoning stating "in many ways, the energy system is complicit in the structural violence that is routinely experienced by people of color in this country" (Brady 2021). In particular, she notes that black and brown families are often energy insecure, where they struggle to pay for electricity, gasoline, and other energy-related necessities. As a result, these families are more likely to have to decide between paying for energy and paying for other household necessities like food, medicine, and shelter. This is personal for Deputy Director Baker, given she recalls in her mother's home, they "used the oven to warm our apartment" (Brady 2021).

S. R. Rinfret and M. C. Pautz, *US Environmental Policy in Action*,
https://doi.org/10.1007/978-3-031-17503-9_8

That is why she believes "that the technical terrain of energy policy should be the next domain to advance civil rights" (Brady 2021).

Baker has put this philosophy in action through her effort to establish the Initiative for Energy Justice in 2018, which is an organization focused on supporting disadvantaged and minority communities on the front-lines of climate change (DOE, n.d.). Most recently, Baker joined the US Department of Energy (DOE) as the first ever Deputy Director for Energy Justice and Secretarial Advisor on Equity in 2021 (DOE 2021b).

Under Deputy Director Baker's leadership, the DOE has developed the first-of-its-kind Energy Justice Dashboard that is updated monthly and identifies how DOE programs are implementing the Biden administration's Justice40 Initiative ensuring that at least 40% of federal clean energy and energy efficiency investments benefit disadvantaged communities (DOE 2021a).

Furthermore, she has sought to bring underrepresented communities into DOE decisionmaking processes and program development directly. She argues that historically energy policy discussions have not incorporated citizen perspectives and for energy policy to become more equitable "those voices [need] to be heard in the energy policy-making space" (Brady 2021). Here, the DOE has subsequently conducted a crowd-source campaign targeted to underrepresented groups to identify barriers they face in working with the federal government. The department has also established new outreach relationships with media outlets that serve underrepresented groups (DOE 2022).

Deputy Director Baker's commitment to environmental justice and her subsequent actions requiring the DOE to evaluate and assess environmental justice issues in each policy are reflective of a broader and vital component of environmental policy, policy analysis, and evaluation. The goal is to determine how policy works and most importantly how it can be improved to achieve objectives more *effectively* and/or *equitably*. No two people may come to agreement on what constitutes "effective" or "equitable" and this is an ongoing challenge. This introductory story helps to situate the chapter's focus is on how scholars and practitioners assess the performance of environmental policy in the twenty-first century.

POLICY ANALYSIS AND EVALUATION

Policymakers and practitioners have regularly assessed the effectiveness of all major environmental laws to ensure that they are achieving their goals, whether it is clean air, water, or environmental justice. As a result, an entire field—policy analysis—has been dedicated to the evaluation of policy (Dunn 2008; Lasswell 1971; Quade 1989). Although definitions of policy analysis vary, for the purpose of this chapter, we suggest policy evaluation is simply the act of critically examining a policy, or as Michael Kraft and Scott Furlong (2013) succinctly suggest, "[a]nalysis means deconstructing an object of study–that is, breaking it down into basic elements to understand it better" (8).

Policy evaluation is a profession conducted by policy analysts or program evaluators. These individuals have varying skills, expertise, and educational backgrounds depending upon the policy they study (Bardach 2004). More specifically, in the environmental arena, policy analysts may have backgrounds in biology, ecology, political science, economics, or sociology, among other fields. In addition, policy analysts are employed by consulting firms, private corporations, public agencies, trade associations, and a host of other entities.

Just as these analysts' backgrounds may differ, the types of policy evaluation they conduct can also vary. For example, an analyst could take a macro approach to evaluate the cost and benefit of all environmental regulation published by the EPA, which means that this analyst would examine each air, water, and land regulation's impact on overall environmental quality in the US. In turn, an analyst might approach the evaluation of environmental regulation through a micro lens. Here, an analyst might evaluate the impact of one regulation to measure its impact in relation to costs. For instance, under this guise, a policy evaluator could examine the EPA's regulation of greenhouse gas (GHG) emissions from passenger vehicles and light trucks to assess its impact on climate change. The purpose of this brief comparison is to illustrate that policy analysts have a variety approaches at their disposal to assess environmental policy, which is the focus of this chapter.

Accordingly, this chapter begins with a discussion of why policy evaluation is necessary, the theoretical underpinnings that structure its processes, and a discussion of how it occurs in practice. Second, we address some of the issues associated with how policy evaluation is employed and the difficulties of examining one evaluative criterion: environmental justice. Third, we provide an assessment of the overall record of environmental policy in achieving environmental outcomes to date, and what is needed to improve these assessments for the future. Lastly, the chapter concludes with a discussion of the evolution of coal ash policy and the role environmental justice played in shaping this arena.

The goal of this chapter is to provide a basic understanding of the promise and pitfalls of policy evaluation within an environmental context. Therefore, after reading this chapter, the reader should be able to take away a few important lessons. The first lesson is that policy evaluation or analysis is essential to understanding if environmental laws or policies are indeed, working. Making this determination is not without its challenges, given that stakeholders may view the goals and related performance of programs differently. This challenge is like those associated with problem definition as outlined in Chapter 2. If a given policy is "working," the second lesson is for policymakers and the public to pay attention to how benefits are distributed. Cases of environmental justice demonstrate that it may not be enough to show improved national outcomes when local conditions may stagnate or decline. Third, policy analysis often names winners or losers—and those pronouncements have consequences. Therefore, we need to pay attention to who is conducting the evaluation or who is funding it.

THE PURPOSE OF POLICY EVALUATION

Environmental policy can be costly, and how programs are implemented and achieve their goals is important to understand. Although there is significant agreement that environmental policy should be evaluated frequently, there is far less agreement on the best approach to evaluate these policies. For instance, there is some acceptance of the US Government Accountability Office (GAO) and the National Academy of Sciences (NAS) assessments of policy as sources of unbiased and accurate analyses: however, these are not the only entities that provide policy evaluation (Kraft 2018, 272–277). There is a whole host of other federal agencies, think tanks, trade associations, environmental interests, and other entities that provide policy evaluations, and the results of these analyses can vary.

For example, when the EPA developed its GHG emission regulations for passenger vehicles and light trucks from 2017–2025, the agency found the regulation's benefits outweighed the costs by more than $450 billion dollars (EPA 2012). As a result, the EPA argued that the rulemaking was justified to improve environmental quality. This determination was not supported by all stakeholders. At the time, the US Chamber of Commerce (2014), a business trade association, concluded that the cost of passenger vehicle regulation exceeded total benefits by nearly $10 billion. The

Trump administration then entered office and the EPA began to roll-back these regulations, ultimately publishing a far less stringent rule that they argued would save over $100 billion dollars in regulatory costs and make new cars more affordable for consumers (EPA 2020). These claims were largely unsubstantiated and highly criticized outside the administration, though the rule was adopted anyway (Davenport 2020). The Biden administration ultimately reversed the Trump decision and found that its new rule (largely reinstating the Obama standards) would deliver a net $16 billion in benefits relative to the Trump rule (DOT 2022). In short, four different evaluations of drastically different regulatory approaches to the same problem all ostensibly showed benefits.

Some of the differences in the assessments of passenger vehicle regulations could be the result of a biased policy evaluator—the analyst responsible for conducting the evaluation. However, any policy analyst will tell you, the goal is for an analyst to remain value neutral and not to insert biases into the evaluation of the policy or program. More specifically, a policy analyst is not supposed to inject their values or beliefs into the analysis. This allows the evaluator to provide an evidence-based policy analysis that includes all relevant factors so that policymakers can make changes or modifications based upon that objective information (Dunn 2008).

It is more likely that the aforementioned differences in policy evaluation actually stem from variation in policy evaluation design. The act of policy evaluation is not simple (Dunn 2008; Lindblom 1959; Lindblom 1979; Ostrom 1990; Rhoads 1985; Weimer and Vining 2011). Policy analysts do not have unlimited resources to acquire data regarding a policy problem; thus, they cannot identify all the factors that impact a program or policy (Weimer and Vining 2011). Accordingly, how an evaluator structures analyses may elevate some priorities over others based upon necessity, or blatant or latent political, ideological, or ethical grounds (Dunn 2008). Finally, the supporter of the evaluation (the person funding the project) may also sway the overall outcome of the analysis based upon his own values (Bardach 2004; Weimer and Vining 2011). For instance, if a member of city council, who believes renewable energy is costly and unreliable, pays a private firm with an interest in fossil-fuels to conduct an evaluation of a community's 100% renewable energy program it is possible the results from this evaluation will support his original perspective. Despite these challenges, the overall goal of these and other policy evaluations is to suggest that a policy or program is either working, should be improved, or is no longer needed (Dunn 2008).

THE STAGES OF POLICY EVALUATION

Although judgements may be superimposed on evaluations, analysts follow a set process that is designed to help standardize analyses. This process includes (see Fig. 8.1): (1) identifying policy or program goals, (2) selecting evaluative criteria, (3) producing recommendations, and (4) disseminating the final product (Bardach 2004; Weimer and Vining 2011). Evaluators' decisions at each step in the process can influence the results and this section provides an overview of what occurs within each stage.

First, policy evaluation begins by identifying the original intent of the policy or program (Bardach 2004). At this stage in the process, policy analysts examine the specific goals of the policy or program. Let us assume the City of Burlington, Vermont has implemented a program to achieve 100% renewable energy consumption citywide and the city's stated goal of the program was to provide residents and businesses with clean, reliable, and low-cost renewable electricity. After an analyst has confirmed the goals of a given policy, the analyst then must determine what happened after the policy was adopted. Simply stated, what are the outcomes of the program? For our Burlington example, the evaluator might compare how much electricity is served by renewable energy sources after the program was implemented versus before the program. The evaluator might also review how the cost of electricity compares to previous rates with lower renewable energy content or improvements in public health resulting from lower electricity-related emissions.

In order to determine whether the outcomes of the program actually achieved the goals of the program, an analyst may use a number of evaluative criteria—effectiveness, efficiency, equity, responsiveness, and appropriateness—which drive the second stage of the process (Bardach 2004; Dunn 2008). Each one of these criteria answers a different question regarding how well a policy is achieving its goals. First, effectiveness assesses whether a program has resulted in a valued outcome; basically, has the policy worked, and in our example, does the city consume 100% renewable electricity? The efficiency criterion evaluates how much effort, or, commonly, how much money was required to achieve a valued outcome. For Burlington, the city might be interested in how electricity

Fig. 8.1 Stages of environmental policy evaluation

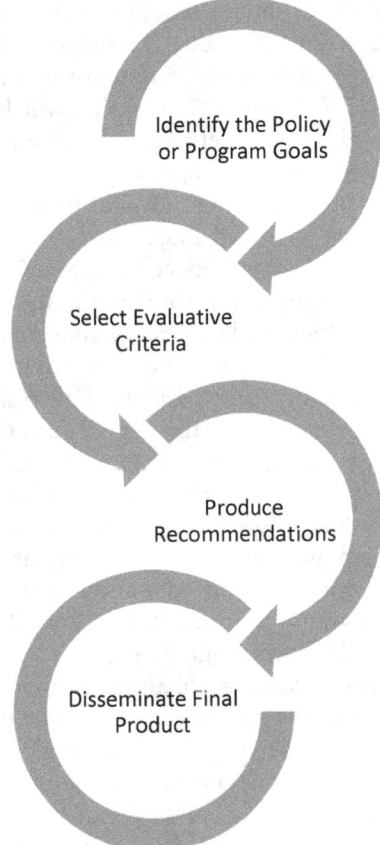

costs differ as compared to before they implemented the 100% renewable program. Are costs comparable or lower than what the city used to pay for fossil fuel-generated electricity? Equity assesses how the desired outcomes are distributed between groups (e.g., do impacts vary by race, gender, income group). Burlington policymakers may be interested in how differences in electricity rates benefit or harm certain constituents based on income. Responsiveness, then, determines whether the documented outcomes are actually valued by the public. More succinctly, does the public want their electricity to come from renewable energy? Finally, appropriateness is related to responsiveness in some ways, as it assesses whether the objectives or valued outcomes are, in fact, useful or important (Dunn 2008). In short, is low-cost, clean electricity good for the city? Each of the evaluative criteria is often referred to as the lifeblood of policy evaluation, which will be discussed in more detail in the next section of this chapter (Kraft and Furlong 2013).

The result of applying these evaluative criteria to a policy are analyzed to understand the overall impact of that action and next steps. This is where the third stage, policy recommendations, comes in. Policy analysts provide pros and cons associated with a policy. Our policy analysts in Burlington, Vermont might suggest the program achieved its objective of achieving 100% renewable energy consumption, with some additional cost than would have occurred absent the policy. They may find that this negatively affects low-income residents who pay disproportionally more on energy bills than more affluent residents. They might also suggest developing a new fund, paid by all electricity customers to help offset low-income resident's energy bills. However, it is up to local policymakers to determine the best course of action based upon the evidence provided by policy analysts. Therefore, at this stage, policymakers may take this information and adjust, terminate, or continue to support the policy or program (Bardach 2004; Dunn 2008).

The overall goal of policy evaluation is an assessment of how well various laws, regulations, and programs are achieving the objectives set out by their architects (such as legislators and rule-writers). Thus, if policy analysts determine that a policy or program is not achieving the valued outcomes, or simply that the problem does not exist anymore, it is up to analysts to disseminate that information to policymakers and the public. Policymakers can take this information and use it to redirect resources toward other problems. As a result, evaluation is critically important in the policymaking process in assessing how well programs achieve their objectives, but it is critical that the evaluation is credible. Overall, policy analysis is not a strictly scientific field, and value judgments can permeate the process. These value judgements are often most pronounced in the selection and application of evaluative criteria. The next section outlines the methods used by evaluators to apply these criteria and the controversies that can occur.

EVALUATIVE CRITERIA: THE LIFE
BLOOD OF POLICY EVALUATION

In theory, policy analysts would apply all the available evaluative criteria (effectiveness, efficiency, equity, responsiveness, and appropriateness) to a policy (Weimer and Vining 2011). However, evaluators are constrained with the type of analysis they can conduct due to limits on time and resources. We spend the following pages examining the pros and cons associated with the most frequently applied evaluative criteria— effectiveness, efficiency, and equity (Bardach 2004; Weimer and Vining 2011).

Assessing Effectiveness and Efficiency

Of all the available criteria, effectiveness is, often, the most straightforward. Recall that the effectiveness criterion is used to determine whether a policy has achieved the intended outcome. As a new example, a policy analyst might evaluate the performance of the Clean Water Act (CWA) by assessing its effectiveness in improving water quality. The analyst could evaluate pollutant levels, such as heavy metal content, and track improvement over time. However, the effectiveness criteria may not always be so straightforward. One could attempt to assess the effectiveness of the CWA in improving ecosystem health, where the outcomes of the program are much more difficult to determine. This is because scientists and practitioners have not agreed upon metrics to determine the health of ecosystems (Kraft 2018, 273).

By way of comparison, no criterion has been subject to more controversy than the efficiency criterion. This controversy generally revolves around how benefits of environmental programs are quantified. The cost of environmental programs can be high, and these expenses are generally easy to add up. For example, the cost to purchase and install pollution control equipment and the cost of managing and operating that equipment are usually easy to locate, record, and forecast into the future. In some cases, virtually anyone with an Internet connection, and a significant amount of free time, could come up with these costs. However, assessing, compiling, and quantifying benefits of environmental programs are far more complex. As a result, practitioners use several methods to determine these benefits and compare them to costs, with the two most common methods—Cost-Effectiveness Analysis (CEA) and Cost–Benefit

Table 8.1 Comparing cost-effectiveness and cost–benefit analyses

Cost-effectiveness analysis characteristics	Cost–benefit analysis characteristics
• Used infrequently in environmental policy • Comparison between cost and effectiveness • Useful when used to compare competing policies or programs • Typically used for transportation or criminal justice policy analysis	• Used frequently in environmental policy • Comparison between costs and benefits across all policies or programs • Can be controversial due to scientific uncertainties • Difficult to use as a single measurement to determine the effectiveness of a program

Analysis (CBA) (Weimer and Vining 2011). Table 8.1 offers a comparison of the two different approaches.

Typically, a CEA compares monetary cost against effectiveness in achieving a given outcome (Boardman et al. 2018). For example, what is the cost of adding a new pollution control technology to a facility, and how does this compare to the benefit accrued in terms of reduced pollution from that technology? If evaluators have this information, they can provide a per unit ratio of costs to benefits. This is useful when, for instance, comparing one specific pollution abatement technology with another. Typically, this type of analysis has been employed for criminal justice, transportation, health, and defense policy (Dunn 2008). However, the common criticism of CEAs is the inability of analysts to compare across policy areas because the metrics and ratios are inherently different because they are using different units of measure (Boardman et al. 2018).

In comparison, CBA is the most common method to evaluate policy within the environmental policy arena. For instance, administrative agencies must employ CBA as a component of their Regulatory Impact Assessments (RIAs) for all significant rules. This is because CBA has been mandated by policymakers (mostly, presidents) because it provides analysts with the ability to evaluate *all* costs and benefits within one common unit of value—the dollar (Boardman et al. 2018). The goal of CBA is to determine if a program is providing a net benefit to society.

Because CBA is such an integral component of governmental policy evaluations, it is relevant to discuss how it is conducted. CBA unfolds throughout five stages: (1) identifying the costs and benefits of a program, (2) applying values to those benefits and costs, (3) discounting those values to present dollars, (4) conducting sensitivity analyses on the data, and (5) subtracting costs from benefits to determine the benefits to society. Although it seems straightforward, each step is complex and fraught with uncertainty.

The uncertainty starts at the outset of the process when analysts must determine all the costs and benefits of a program. As one might think, this is difficult to do in practice, but scholars have outlined a structure to determine these values. First, evaluators must set boundaries around a problem area, or what a program does, and who it affects (Boardman et al. 2018). Then, analysts determine what the internal and external costs are of a given program, along with the external costs and benefits. Internal costs and benefits refer to those that are included within the market setting (e.g., cost of a program's implementation). External costs and benefits then refer to those values that are not included in the internal costs; these can be either negative harms or positive benefits to society that are not accounted for in the market price (Dunn 2008). These negative external costs are often present in the environmental arena, as air, water, and land pollution impacts.

After determining what costs and benefits exist both internally and externally, analysts must determine which are directly and indirectly measurable. More specifically, directly measureable values refer to the tangible costs and benefits that have a market price (e.g., pollution control equipment), whereas indirectly measurable values are those that are intangible and do not have a definitive market price (e.g., clean air; see Dunn 2008).

One presumption in the preceding discussion is that an analyst can make several assumptions during a CBA that could lead to significant differences in determining the efficiency of a program. This may help explain why the EPA under three separate administrations, and the US Chamber of Commerce-supported analyses provided such varied results on the cost and benefits of vehicle emission regulations. In the context of environmental regulation, analyst decisions relating to the benefit from lives saved, GHG emissions avoided, and the inclusion of co-benefits often contribute to the dramatic differences in CBAs. The following pages provide a snapshot of the controversies that are associated with these components of a CBA.

Environmental regulation can save lives, by reducing citizen exposure to hazardous pollution. Though this much is clear, policy analysts have struggled to quantify this value for inclusion in CBA. A variety of methods have been proposed to monetize lives. The two most common methods are the Value of Statistical Life Years Saved (VSLYS) and Quality-Adjusted Life Years (QALY). These methods are similar. The VSLYS method places a value on 1 year of life and multiples that by the number of life years saved. The QALY method is similar to the VSLYS, but makes one adjustment—value is placed upon how old the individual is, as a younger individual would likely have more quality life years left than an elderly person (Cooney 2003).

The Bush administration attempted to adjust how the federal government valued human life, through briefly applying the QALY method. This effort was criticized and nicknamed the "senior death discount" (Cooney 2003; Seelye and Tierney 2003). The administration swiftly returned to using the VSLYS, but controversy around the value of a life saved persisted. Subsequent administrations have apparently learned from this political firestorm. Federal agencies under the Obama administration regularly increased the VSLYS, while the Trump administration did not seek to reduce these values (Appelbaum 2011; Bastasch 2016; Merrill 2017). Currently, many federal agencies estimate the value of a human life at approximately $10 million (Merrill 2017; Frankel 2020; Gonzalez 2020).

Although it is politically unpopular to reduce the estimated value of a human life, questions remain regarding whether $10 million is overvaluing or undervaluing human life. This is critically important, given it is an essential input when evaluating the benefits of a regulatory action (Merrill 2017). Existing literature suggests that the most appropriate "value" may be anywhere from $1 million to $24.5 million (Merrill 2017). This wide range in potential values can result in significant differences in a given regulation's benefits depending on which value the policy analyst uses. Thus, decisions made applying VSLYS have significant impacts on overall costs and benefits and can go unnoticed absent careful review of a CBA's methodology.

Another area of controversy relates to whether CBA's should consider benefits associated with avoided GHG emissions. The analyst, and more likely the funder, must believe that climate change is a real environmental problem that negatively effects the public before including it in a CBA. If, as in most cases, the benefit of avoided GHG emissions is included, policy analysts must still determine how to value these avoided emissions. In 2010, the Obama administration introduced the social cost of carbon (SCC) as the means for agencies to quantify the climate change benefit of regulatory actions (Interagency Working Group on Social Cost of Carbon 2010). The SCC offered a range of costs that could be incorporated into CBAs and the Obama administration periodically updated, and increased, the SCC. The administration defended these increases, arguing that the costs of climate change were increasing (Cook and Rinfret 2013; Interagency Working Group on Social Cost of Greenhouse Gases 2016).

Upon entering office, President Trump's administration swiftly reduced the SCC from an inflation adjusted $45 per ton in 2020 to between $1 and $6 per ton in 2020 (Mooney 2017). The Trump administration supported the move, arguing that the Obama era SCC estimated global climate benefits associated with regulatory actions, rather than domestic impacts. Subsequently, the Biden administration entered office with a commitment to reduce carbon emissions, and immediately increased the value to $51 per ton, which was more aligned with the SCC under the Obama administration (Eilperin and Dennis 2021). The Biden administration is further considering increasing the value to $125 per ton given the impacts of climate change are already present in the United States and expected to get worse soon (Eilperin and Dennis 2021). Initially, a federal judge blocked the Biden administration's use of the higher social cost of carbon for federal regulations, but an appeals court overturned the previous decision and reinstated the higher SCC (Guillen 2022). Here again, depending on which metric is used, the benefit of regulations that reduce GHG emissions vary substantially.

In addition to considering the benefit of avoided GHG emissions, policy analysts might also include co-benefits in their CBA. Co-benefits, in the environmental context, refer to benefits from the reduction of pollutants not directly subject to regulation that will also decline from the application of certain control technologies. The controversy surrounding this variable in a CBA is best illustrated by the EPA's adoption of the Mercury and Air Toxic Standards (MATS) for power plants in 2011. The EPA argued that the MATS would result in $90 billion in annual benefits, as compared to $10 billion in costs (The Economist 2012). The clear majority of these benefits are not associated with reducing mercury, which was the subject of the regulation, but rather associated with reduced particulate matter. Critics of the MATS have argued that the efficiency of the regulation designed to reduce mercury, should not be based on the value generated from the co-benefits of the action. Assessing the rule in this context, may suggest it provides more costs than benefits. Others might argue that the goal of the rule is to improve environmental quality, and as such co-benefits including reductions in particulate matter should be included. The Obama administration believed this, but the Trump administration did not. The Trump administration rolled back the regulation suggesting that quantifying these co-benefits was misguided, even though most companies had installed technology necessary for compliance with the Obama standards (Walton 2017). Subsequently, the Biden administration has aligned with the Obama era perspective to incorporate these co-benefits in their effort to restore the MATS rule (Davenport 2022).

These three examples demonstrate that quantifying benefits is not a simple task, nor is it apolitical. Fundamentally, policy analysts need to decide what benefits to include and a metric to quantify them. These questions can be philosophical, as they deal with individual values and ethics, making it difficult for bureaucrats—or anyone, for that matter—to agree on a standardized value. Given this challenge, most policy analysts attempt to incorporate a range of values to subsequently provide a range of benefits. Even so, two well-meaning policy analysts may produce widely different CBA results. Scholars are aware of this challenge and thus argue that CBA alone should not be used to determine whether an individual policy is useful or valuable (Boardman et al. 2018; Kraft 2018; Weimer and Vining 2011; Olmstead 2018).

Assessing Equity

Effectiveness and efficiency are the two most common criteria to assess environmental policy; however, the incorporation of equity has become more prevalent, and we turn to examples of environmental justice to understand why. Much like efficiency, this criterion is subject to significant controversy. Overall, the argument is that the benefits of environmental policy decisions as well as the harms should be evenly distributed across society.

Consideration of environmental fairness and justice concerns emerged in the 1980s amid protest by a predominantly African-American community in Warren County, North Carolina, which was designated for a hazardous waste landfill. The National Association for the Advancement of Colored People (NAACP) held a protest against the designation, and it garnered significant media attention when 500 individuals were arrested (Department of Energy 2013). This protest, along with others, led politicians to request a report from the GAO to determine if low-income and minority communities were disproportionately targeted for these facilities. The GAO found that three of the four hazardous waste landfills it analyzed were sited in minority communities, and all four were sited in locations where at least 26% of the population was below the poverty line (GAO 1983). Several other studies in the 1980s and early 1990s confirmed these results: the poor and minorities are more likely to have increased rates of exposure to toxic chemicals and other environmental harms (Bryant and Mohai 1992; Hill 2014; UCC 1987; US EPA 1992).

As a result, in 1994, President Clinton issued Executive Order 12,898 titled *Federal Actions to Address Environmental Justice in Minority Populations and Low-Income Populations.* Executive Order 12,898 required that each:

> federal agency shall make achieving environmental justice part of its mission by identifying and addressing, as appropriate, disproportionately high and adverse human health or environmental effects of its programs, policies, and activities on minority populations and low-income populations in the United States.

This Executive Order put the EPA in charge of overseeing the implementation of this directive. As noted, the EPA has subsequently defined environmental justice as "the fair treatment and meaningful involvement of all people regardless of race, color, national origin, or income with respect to the development, implementation, and enforcement of environmental laws, regulations, and policies" (EPA 2022b). Ultimately, the Office of Environmental Justice within the EPA is in charge of integrating these principles into the operations of the agency.

Though environmental justice has had a home at the EPA since the 1990s, incorporating this concept into federal decisionmaking has been challenging. GAO published a report in 2011 suggesting that the EPA should do more to address environmental justice concerns when creating rules. More specifically, the GAO (2011) recommended that the agency develop a strategy to define key terms in order to establish a "consistent and transparent approach for identifying potential communities with environmental justice concerns" (32). Furthermore, the GAO (2011) suggested that the EPA needed to assess the resources needed to carry out its goals, and develop a plan for how the agency will measure its performance in achieving those goals.

During the Obama administration, the EPA took a number of steps to address these concerns. First, the EPA developed EJ 2014, which the agency considered a roadmap to integrating environmental justice into the activities of the agency (EPA 2013). Second, the EPA launched EJSCREEN in 2015 a web-based tool that identifies areas with minority and low-income populations, along with environmental quality issues that are greater than usual (2016).

In contrast, the Trump administration was less supportive of environmental justice considerations. In line with the administration's broader deregulatory agenda, the administration sought to disband the EPA's Environmental Justice Office entirely (Perls 2020). Though this effort failed, the administration was successful in reducing the grants and other environmental justice investments the federal government made during the Trump presidency (Perls 2020).

Since entering office, President Biden has addressed his campaign promises to implement a variety of new programs centered around the Justice40 Initiative (The White House 2022). This unprecedented initiative is designed to ensure that 40% of overall benefits of climate, energy, housing, and other investments are directed to underserved communities (Fears 2022). The Biden administration is further investing in a new version of the EJScreen tool that expands its scope and capabilities, while also ensuring that all federal activities across the government consider environmental justice and not just those at the EPA (The White House 2022). Despite this significant commitment and related activities, remaking the federal government with an emphasis on environmental justice has been very difficult and requires significantly more resources than have been allocated (Fears 2022). Overall, it is too soon to determine how impactful these activities have or will be, in mitigating environmental justice issues.

Even with the benefit of time, effectively evaluating the Biden administration's performance will be challenging given environmental justice and adequate mitigation or restitution for confirmed cases has not been explained. For example, there is likely to be some variation in the distribution of benefits and harms nationwide. The EPA and other federal agencies have not answered what distribution is acceptable or expected making it difficult for policy analysts to incorporate a standardized metric into their analyses. Even so, the development of EJSCREEN and its upcoming predecessor is likely to increase citizen awareness of environmental justice communities and subsequent calls for including an analysis of equity in policy evaluation going forward.

EVALUATING PROGRAMS AND ACHIEVING GOALS

As indicated throughout this chapter, most evaluations assess specific aspects rather than a holistic discussion of the environment. More specifically, analysts have evaluated the effectiveness of implementing laws like the Clean Air Act (CAA), the CWA, and the Endangered Species Act (ESA) to provide some insight into how the US is doing in achieving its most important environmental goals. Thus, in this section, we provide a brief overview of how the nation is doing in achieving these goals.

We begin with a discussion of the implementation of the CAA. Since the law was enacted in 1970, the six most common air pollutants including particulate matter, sulfur dioxide, nitrogen oxides, volatile organic compounds, carbon monoxide, and lead have dropped 78% (EPA 2021). Meanwhile, gross domestic product, a metric of economic growth, has increased 272% and population has increased 61%. Despite these impressive improvements, GHG emissions have increased 21% (EPA 2021). During the Obama administration, the EPA took steps to address these emissions, then the Trump administration dialed back regulations (Eilperin and Dennis 2018). Currently, the Biden administration plans to again address these emissions (The White House 2021), but it is yet to be determined whether these efforts will be effective.

The EPA has been less successful in implementing the water quality goals of the CWA. This is in part because water pollution is generated by a wide variety of sources. For example, the nutrients from misapplied lawn fertilizers can run-off and pollute waterways after rain events. Though this pollution may be negligible on a per home basis, collectively it can result in dead zones in rivers and streams. For example, nutrient pollution from the Mississippi River has resulted in an estimated 5,000 square mile dead zone in the Gulf of Mexico (EPA 2022a). Even so, regulating homeowner's lawn care practices may not be practical, which will impact agency performance on improving water quality. Overall, the EPA (2017) concludes that 46% of rivers and streams are in poor biological condition. In comparison, 32% of wetlands, 21% of lakes, and 18% of coastal waters are in poor condition. Although there has been improvement in these numbers over time, emerging challenges in urban water pollution and drinking water quality are rising as exemplified by lead-poisoning in Flint, Michigan (Vig and Kraft 2018; Blakely 2021).

In addition to air and water quality, land protection is also an important area for investigation. The assessment of improved land quality has historically been based on the amount of land that has been set aside for protection (WSTB 2004). Under this measure, the United States has been quite successful. Land set aside for national parks, wilderness areas, and the national wildlife refuge system has increased since the 1970s (Kraft and Vig 2013). However, this is an insufficient metric to determine the value of natural resource conservation (Jenkins et al. 2015). Jenkins et al. (2015) map conserved land to areas of threatened biodiversity and conclude that the United States is not protecting the land, predominantly in the southeast, where biodiversity is most threatened. Therefore, more may need to be done to protect unique land.

Accordingly, what may be more indicative of US protection of natural resources is an assessment of US efforts to protect endangered species and biodiversity under the ESA. The US Fish and Wildlife Service (USFWS) (2022), which implements the ESA, lists 1,670 species as endangered (1,268) or threatened (402). Since the ESA was passed, many species that have been listed are still endangered and the agency continues to add species to the list. Even so, 54 species have been delisted, while 56 have been downgraded from endangered to threatened, while another 60 species may be delisted soon (USFWS 2021). On the other hand, the USFWS recently delisted 23 species that have been confirmed extinct (USFWS 2021). In short, policy evaluators should assess these numbers differently. One could argue that the program has been a success in avoiding species extinction, given relatively few (23 species) of 1,670 on the list have gone extinct. Another could argue that the results are more mixed given that the law has done nothing to improve the status of most species on the list, while some have gone extinct despite protection.

Ultimately, policy analysts can come to different conclusions regarding environmental policy effectiveness in reducing air, land, and water pollution. Perhaps, an even stronger argument can be made regarding whether they have been efficient. Although the United States has reduced air pollution, scholars argue that these environmental benefits, associated predominately with command and control regulation, may have come at a much higher cost than necessary (Portney 1994; Freeman 2006; Fiorino 2009; Olmstead 2018).

POLICY EVALUATION IN THE TWENTY-FIRST CENTURY

This chapter has defined and documented the various pros and cons associated with policy evaluation, the tools or methods associated with it, and overall environmental performance. However, for the future of environmental policy, policy evaluation must improve. First, a fundamental component of environmental policy evaluation is efficiency. CBA is often used to examine this element, and this chapter has demonstrated that policy analysts can come to widely different conclusions about the efficiency of programs using this tool. One factor of this variation is the lack of agreed upon environmental indicators or cost and benefit values for ecological services. This disagreement sheds doubt on the objectivity of the field. To solve this problem, researchers have diligently attempted to identify and quantify environmental benefits. If these values can be developed, and agreed upon, policy evaluation's most controversial component, the CBA, may actually be the objective tool its supporters suggest it is. Though these efforts could be valuable, it is important to bound optimism. Having accurate and consistent costs and benefits, may not be enough to push policymakers to act. For example, researchers suggest that pollinators, including bumblebees, contributed $15–$29 billion to the US economy (Ramanujan 2012; FDA 2018). Yet, in 2021 about 45% of the nation's honeybee colonies died up from one third in 2016 (Rossman, 2017; Sigafoos and Bilinski 2021). Having a better understanding of the value of pollinators did not result in a subsequent policy designed to protect these species. Ultimately, policy evaluation may show significant *societal* benefits of action, but policymakers will still need to be convinced that these benefits outweigh near-term likely negative impacts on constituents.

Second, most policy evaluation is conducted in a media-specific, piecemeal fashion. For example, policy evaluators might argue that emission control equipment at power plants is quite successful in reducing heavy metal concentrations released to the air because they are precipitated out as physical waste. The evaluation typically ends there and does not consider the impacts associated with that physical waste. If poorly handled, this waste may have more significant, negative impacts on land and water quality. This problem is in part a function of the media-specific legislative design of the environmental policy framework in the United States. The focus of each law is on reducing pollution from the air, land, OR water and not necessarily all three (Bryner and Duffy 2012).

The problem then is that individual policy evaluations might show an improvement, but a holistic analysis may not. Solving this problem may require legislative action and there are some regulatory efforts to integrate policies in the US absent legislative activity (Duffy and Cook 2018). Additional research evaluating the performance of these integrated policies and comparing that performance to typical media-specific approaches is essential to provide more holistic assessments of environmental policy performance.

Finally, if environmental justice is going to become an integral evaluative tool in terms of assessing environmental policy, it is critical that experts come to a consensus on which groups are most negatively impacted, and how to address the identified environmental injustice. First, researchers need to identify which groups have been disproportionally impacted. Historically, most environmental justice research has focused on race and socioeconomic status as indicators of communities suffering from environmental injustices. More recently, scholars have argued that these indicators are too blunt (Faber et al. 2021). They have applied concepts from gender analysis and critical race theory to point out that individuals of the same race and/or socioeconomic status can be more negatively impacted than another individual of the same race and/or socioeconomic status given their varied gender, sexuality and/or societal status among other factors. For example, a poor, black female who identifies as a lesbian, belongs to more than one disadvantaged community, as compared to an affluent, straight black man. These scholars would argue that those individuals that experience multiple forms of exploitation are least likely to be able to avoid environmental harms and mitigating these impacts should be prioritized (Faber et al. 2021). Once impacted communities are identified, then decisionmakers must decide how to act upon this finding. Should certain facilities be prohibited from locating in environmental justice communities and rather be in more affluent communities? What economic impacts might this have on environmental justice communities that already may lack economic growth opportunities? Alternatively, should more affluent communities compensate environmental justice communities for the additional harm they are subjected too? Answering these questions requires quantifying the cost of environmental injustices, which will face similar challenges to those debated in the efficiency arena. Inevitably, there are real environmental justice concerns and our chapter's case study makes this point.

Case Study: Understanding Environmental Justice: Lessons for the Future

As noted, the poor and minority communities are more likely to be exposed to environmental harms than more affluent, white communities. Environmental justice advocates have long argued this is because these communities have been targeted for the siting of significant polluters. For these individuals, policy should be adopted to correct these imbalances. Meanwhile, others have contended that these injustices have not resulted from vindictive actions. Rather, the poor and minorities have chosen to locate in areas near these pollution sources because they offer lower costs of living. From this perspective, no policy change is necessary, because the poor and minorities willingly moved to these locations. This disagreement has persisted for decades because there was limited research into environmental justice claims and variation in methodological assumptions resulted in conflicting conclusions (Niles and Lubell 2012; Mohai and Saha 2015).

In 2015, Mohai and Saha conducted a seminal, nationwide study of commercial hazardous waste facilities sited from 1966–1995 to address this debate. They show that new hazardous waste facilities were located in areas that already had higher concentrations of poor and minority communities. These concentrations then increased after these facilities located in the community. The authors argue that this shows a pattern of commercial facilities searching for the path of least resistance, when siting new facilities. The goal of these companies is to find communities that are less likely to generate a protracted battle to receive approval and construct the facility. For these scholars, this explains why minority communities compose more than 50% of all people living within 3 km of a hazardous waste facility. These conclusions support the perspective of environmental justice advocates that the poor and minorities have been targeted for these facilities and have thus been disproportionally impacted by environmental harms. Subsequent research has confirmed this finding in other related environmental injustice areas, including disparities in drinking water, higher exposure to air pollutants, and enforcement of existing air and water regulatory enforcement (Konisky et al. 2021).

Another area that has been identified as a potential environmental justice issue is the transportation and storage of coal ash. Coal ash is generated from burning coal for electricity production. According to the EPA (2018), coal ash it is one of the largest sources of industrial waste with over 110 million tons of ash produced in 2012. About half of this ash is beneficially reused as a strengthening agent in cement for roads and bridges, while the other half is often laced with heavy metals (e.g., arsenic, mercury, and selenium) and is stored in large shallow ponds near coal plants (Dilts 2014). These ponds went largely unnoticed until December 22, 2008 when a dike failed at the Tennessee Valley Authority's Kingston coal-fired power plant. This failure released 5.4 million cubic yards of toxic coal ash into the nearby Emory and Clinch River's in Tennessee (Gang 2013). TVA spent $1 billion to clean up the ash, buy impacted property, develop new parks, and monitor wildlife (Gang 2013). In addition, TVA stopped holding coal ash in ponds on-site and began transporting it to a landfill in Alabama.

Though the Kingston spill spurred concern, policy change was slow to follow. After this spill, 200 coal ash sites were associated with subsequent air and water pollution including the Dan River spill in 2014 where 27 million gallons of coal ash contaminated waste water was released in North Carolina (Bienkowski 2016). Significant discharges like that at Dan River are noticeable and negatively affect the entire watershed. However, smaller discharges near coal ash ponds may go unnoticed. This is most problematic for those individuals that live closest to these facilities, including an estimated 1.5 million people of color. In response to the growing concerns about coal ash pits, the EPA promulgated new rules in 2014 that required groundwater monitoring near pits, stronger pit liners, and limits on coal ash discharges into rivers (Bienkowski 2016). In response to regulation and spills, some utilities have taken the approach of TVA and have started to transport their coal ash to landfills. This represents a victory for the individuals living closest to coal plants, as they may face fewer risks of air and water pollution.

If the case study ended here, this story might be considered an environmental justice success. Yet, the conclusion to this story is more complicated. Returning to TVA's Kingston spill. TVA began to ship the coal ash to the Arrowhead Landfill, near Uniontown Alabama (Dewan 2009). The town is about 90% black with a median income 74% below the national average as compared to Kingston a predominantly white, middle-class town (Bienkowski 2016). Local politicians supported the agreement citing the $3 million that would be added to the county's $4.5 million budget, and the addition of 30 local jobs (Dewan 2009). From the beginning, residents voiced concerns about the safety of the project, the honesty of their elected officials, and the intimidation tactics of the landfill owners that has included defamation lawsuits (Cerullo 2018; Milman 2018). Since the landfill began accepting coal ash, residents have complained of a host of illnesses including nosebleeds and cancers that have not yet been studied for potential links to coal ash (Milman 2018). In addition, residents are concerned with the impacts of the landfill on an adjacent unmanaged cemetery, where land, owned by the landfill, had been cleared making it difficult for some to locate their ancestral remains (Pillion 2015). The residents of Uniontown filed a complaint against the project to the EPA under Title VI of the Civil Rights Act in 2013. The EPA held hearings on the issue in 2016 and has since closed the case arguing there was "insufficient evidence" that authorities in Alabama breached the Civil Rights Act in allowing the facility to locate in the town (Milman 2018). The EPA decision in this, and other Trump-era environmental justice cases has been criticized as partisan, given the Trump administration's interest in deregulating industry and coal ash ponds in particular (Milman 2017). Whether or not political motives were at play in this case, the EPA has received 100's of claims since the mid 1990s and has only once ruled in favor of those bringing the suit (The Associated Press 2021). Some suggest that this is by design given it is almost impossible to deliver the proof required for the EPA to rule in the favor of those asserting harm. With the Biden administration's emphasis on environmental justice, some have called for changes in how the EPA carries out these assessments (The Associated Press 2021).

Even with a revised process, it is unclear the EPA would have come to a different decision. That is because environmental justice cases are often not cut and dry. The complicated outcome associated with cleaning up the coal ash pit in Kingston illustrates two key questions worth discussing in more detail (1) what constitutes an environmental justice issue and (2) what should be done about identified or potential cases? Clearly, this case demonstrates that waste was moved from one, more affluent community to a poorer one. In addition, the waste can cause public health impacts if handled improperly. As a result, there is a risk that the Alabama residents will be negatively impacted from the transfer of waste. The question is has this occurred and resulted in an environmental justice concern? For Uniontown, there have not been studies of the impact that this waste has had on the community making it difficult to assess injustice. It is possible that the landfill has not caused increased public health problems, suggesting there is no impact as landfill supporters might suggest. Alternatively, it could be causing yet-to-be-seen health complications, suggesting that the community is a toxic experiment. Understandably, residents may not be comfortable waiting to see which result is accurate. Nevertheless, future analysis addressing these claims is necessary to determine if an injustice has occurred in Alabama.

If these residents do face disproportionate risks, what should be done? In Uniontown, the community is benefiting from compensation from accepting the waste. In addition, many more people may be benefitting from the fact that fewer coal ash ponds are being breached nationwide. However, it is unclear whether the compensation for this individual community is enough to offset potential environmental harms. Moreover, once the landfill is full the facility will no longer receive compensation which could make it difficult to mitigate future environmental and public health problems should they arise. As a result, it is unclear whether the town's current compensation adequately matches the risk they are assuming. Ultimately, the residents of Uniontown might have argued that more research needed to be done before the facility was built to assess these risks and determine compensation. Though this would have been valuable, in reality, most communities will have to make decisions with limited information as new technology and associated environmental challenges are just emerging. This is not lost on environmental justice advocates, who counter that even in situations with limited information community members need to be informed of the potential risks they face and be included in decisionmaking processes. In the case of Uniontown, many residents felt that they had been excluded from this process, generating mistrust from the start. Determining just how to include community members in decisionmaking processes and provide the relevant information to make decisions that mitigate environmental justice impacts will be an ongoing challenge.

Overall, this coal ash case study demonstrates that minorities and the poor are more likely to be exposed to environmental harms. Determining whether an individual claim is justified and warrants remediation is challenging, which helps explain why incorporating environmental justice into policy evaluation and broader policy processes has been challenging. This case also illustrates the fundamental role policymakers must play in answering the question: how much environmental harm is too much, and what should be done to address it.

Chapter Wrap-Up

This chapter provides four key insights. First, policy evaluation is a valuable component of the environmental policymaking process because it provides policymakers and practitioners with data regarding how effective policies are in achieving outcomes. Moreover, these analyses are useful when Congress and agencies must make difficult decisions about how to prioritize resources. Because of these inherent values, in theory, evaluation is supported by virtually all players in the environmental policy arena.

Second, we cannot forget that policy evaluation often suffers because experts do not agree about policy performance. These challenges are compounded by the fact that asking questions such as how much is a life worth or how much environmental harm is too much, are value-laden questions that are difficult to answer, no matter the circumstances. Therefore, attempts to apply CBA, in particular, have been criticized as thin veils over political activities.

Third, despite these concerns, policy evaluations have shown that the environment has improved in the US. The air, water, and land are cleaner than they were in the 1970s. However, for policy evaluation in the environmental arena to shed the controversy surrounding it, more scientific consensus is necessary on measuring policy outcomes, as well as more definitive determinations on the values of those outcomes to society.

Lastly, this chapter demonstrates that the policy evaluation field is robust and evolving. There are many opportunities to join this field conducting evaluations, quantifying environmental services, or critiquing results. If this sounds appealing, becoming a policy evaluator may be the most rewarding career for you. After all, understanding whether a policy is effective is essential to the future of environmental policymaking in the US.

Challenge Question for the Environmental Policy Classroom

Research and define gender analysis and critical race analysis. Which federal environmental agencies adopt either policy analysis tool in their evaluations? What adopting these policy analysis approaches more widely lead to different outcomes than CBA? Why or why not?

SUGGESTED RESOURCES

Readings and Websites

Ackerman, Frank and Lisa Heinzerling. "Pricing the Priceless: Cost-Benefit Analysis of Environmental Protection." *University of Pennsylvania Law Review* 150 (2002). Accessed May 4, 2022. https://scholarship.law.upenn.edu/cgi/viewcontent.cgi?article=3277c&context=penn_law_review.

Bullock, Claire, Kerry ARd, and Grace Saalman. "Measuring the Relationship between State Environmental Justice Action and Air Pollution Inequality, 1990–2009." *Review of Policy Research* 35, no. 3 (2018). Accessed May 4, 2022. https://onlinelibrary.wiley.com/doi/full/10.1111/ropr.12292.

Cole, Luke W. and Sheila R. Foster. *From the Ground Up: Environmental Racism and the Rise of the Environmental Justice Movement*. New York: New York University Press, 2000.

GAO. Natural Resources and Environment. Accessed May 4, 2022. https://www.gao.gov/topics/natural-resources-and-environment.

Hill, Barry E. *Environmental Justice: Legal Theory and Practice*. Washington, DC: Environmental Law Institute, 2014.

Ihab, Mikati, Adam, F. Benson, Thomas J. Luben, Jason D. Sacks, and Jennifer Richmond-Bryant. "Disparities in Distribution of Particulate Matter Emission Sources by Race and Poverty Status." *American Journal of Public Health*

(2018). Accessed May 4, 2022. https://ajph.aphapublications.org/doi/pdf/10.2105/AJPH.2017.304297
US EPA Toxics Release Inventory (TRI) Program. Accessed April 1, 2022. https://www.epa.gov/toxics-release-inventory-tri-program.
US EPA EJSCREEN. Accessed April 1, 2022. https://www.epa.gov/ejscreen.

Films and Videos

Erin Brockovich. Directed by Steven Soderbergh. 2000.Universal Pictures. DVD.
Coal Country a New Civil War. Directed by MariLynn Evans and Phylis Geller. 2009. Evening Star Productions. DVD.
Flint's Deadly Water. Directed by Abby Ellis, Kayle Ruble, Jacob Carah, Sarah Childress, and Frank Koughan. 2019. Frontline. https://www.pbs.org/wgbh/frontline/film/flints-deadly-water/.
"Environmental Racism." *Last Week Tonight*. Directed by Joe Perota, Christopher Werner, Jim Hoskinson, Paul Pennolino, and Bruce Leddyliver. 2022. HBO.

REFERENCES

The Associated Press. "Biden Administration Promises Focus on Environmental Justice, Like Uniontown's 2013 Coal Ash Claim." *AL*. 2021. https://www.al.com/news/2021/02/biden-administration-promises-focus-on-environmental-justice-like-uniontowns-2013-coal-ash-claim.html.
Appelbaum, Binyamin. "As US Agencies Put More Value on a Life, Businesses Fret." *New York Times*. 2011. Accessed May 4, 2018. https://www.nytimes.com/2011/02/17/business/economy/17regulation.html.
Bardach, Eugene. *Practical Guide for Policy Analysis: The Eightfold Path to More Effective Problem Solving*. 2nd edition. Washington, DC: CQ Press, 2004.
Bastasch. Michael. "Rep. Chaffetz Worries EPA is Fudging The Numbers To Justify Costlier Regs. *The Daily Caller*. 2016. http://dailycaller.com/2016/07/15/rep-chaffetz-worries-epa-is-fudging-the-numbers-to-justify-costlier-regs/.
Bienkowski, Brian. 2016. "Toxic Coal Ash Hits Poor and Minority Communities Hardest." *Scientific American*. Accessed May 4, 2018. https://www.scientificamerican.com/article/toxic-coal-ash-hits-poor-and-minority-communities-hardest/.
Blakely, Natasha. 2021. "Seven Years On: The Flint water crisis has yet to conclude." Great Lakes Now. https://www.greatlakesnow.org/2021/10/seven-years-flint-water-crisis/.

Boardman, Anthony, David Greenberg, Aidan Vining, and David Weimer. *Cost-Benefit Analysis*. 4th edition reissued. Upper Saddle River, NJ: Prentice Hall, 2018.

Brady, Jeff. "'Energy Justice' Nominee Brings Activist Voice To Biden's Climate Plans." 2021. *NPR*. Accessed June 8, 2022. https://www.npr.org/2021/06/08/1004059950/energy-justice-nominee-brings-activist-voice-to-bidens-climate-plans.

Bryant, Bunyan and Paul Mohai. *Race and the Incidence of Environmental Hazards: A Time for Discourse*. Boulder, CO: Westview Press, 1992.

Bryner, Gary C., and Robert J. Duffy. *Integrating climate, energy, and air pollution policies*. Cambridge, MA: MIT Press. 2012.

Cerullo, Megan. 2018. "Alabama Residents Blast EPA for Allowing Massive Coal Ash Landfill to Operate Nearby Largely Black Town." *NY Daily News*. Accessed May 4, 2018. http://www.nydailynews.com/news/national/alabamians-blast-epa-coal-ash-landfill-poor-black-town-article-1.3858923.

Cook, Jeffrey J. and Sara Rinfret. "Adjusting the Social Cost of Carbon: A Commonsense Revision." *The Regulatory Review*. 2013. Accessed May 4, 2018. https://www.theregreview.org/2013/08/20/20-cook-rinfret-scc/.

Cooney, Catherine M. "Gauging the Price of Good Health." *Environmental Science and Technology. American Chemical Society* (2003): 365A–368A.

Davenport. Coral. 2020. "Trump's Path to Weaker Fuel Efficiency Rules May Lead to a Dead End." *The New York Times*. https://www.nytimes.com/2020/02/13/climate/trump-fuel-economy-rollback.html.

———. 2022. "Biden Administration to Reinstate Mercury Pollution Rules Weakened Under Trump." *The New York Times*. https://www.nytimes.com/2022/01/31/climate/epa-mercury-pollution-coal.html.

Department of Energy (DOE). 2013. "Environmental Justice History." Accessed May 4, 2018. http://energy.gov/lm/services/environmental-justice/environmental-justice-history.

Department of Transportation (DOT). 2022. *Corporate Average Fuel Economy Standards for Model Years 2024–2026 Passenger Cars and Light Trucks*. https://www.nhtsa.gov/sites/nhtsa.gov/files/2022-04/Final-Rule-Preamble_CAFE-MY-2024-2026.pdf.

Dewan, Shaila. 2009. "Clash in Alabama Over Tennessee Coal Ash." *The New York Times*. Accessed May 4, 2018. https://www.nytimes.com/2009/08/30/us/30ash.html.

Dilts, Elizabeth. "After North Carolina Spill, Coal Ash Ponds Face Extinction." *Reuters*. 2014. Accessed May 4, 2018. https://www.reuters.com/article/us-usa-coal-spill-regs-analysis/after-north-carolina-spill-coal-ash-ponds-face-extinction-idUSBREA2D1G720140314.

DOE. *Shalanda H. Baker Secretarial Advisor on Equity and Deputy Director for Energy Justice.* No Date. Accessed June 8, 2022. https://www.energy.gov/diversity/person/shalanda-h-baker.

———. *Baker Details Ambitious Effort to Remedy Environmental, Energy Injustice.* 2021a. Accessed June 8, 2022. https://www.energy.gov/em/articles/baker-details-ambitious-effort-remedy-environmental-energy-injustice.

———. *Department of Energy Announces New Senior Leaders.* 2021b. Accessed June 8, 2022. https://www.energy.gov/articles/department-energy-announces-new-senior-leaders.

———. *US Department of Energy's Equity Action Plan Agency Lead: Shalanda H. Baker, Secretarial Advisor on Equity.* 2022. Accessed June 8, 2022. https://www.energy.gov/sites/default/files/2022-04/DOE%20Equity%20Action%20Plan_Letterhead.pdf.

Duffy, Robert and Jeffrey J. Cook. "Overcoming Bureaucratic Silos? Environmental Policy Integration in the Obama Administration." *Environmental Politics.* 2018. https://www.tandfonline.com/doi/abs/10.1080/09644016.2018.1511074?journalCode=fenp20.

Dunn, William N. *Public Policy Analysis: An Introduction.* 4th edition. Upper Saddle River, NJ: Pearson Prentice Hall, 2008.

Eilperin, Juliet and Brady Dennis. "EPA to Roll Back Car Emissions Standards, Handing Automakers a Big Win." *The Washington Post.* 2018. Accessed May 18, 2018. https://www.washingtonpost.com/national/health-science/epa-to-roll-back-car-emissions-standards/2018/04/02/b720f0b6-36a6-11e8-acd5-35eac230e514_story.html?utm_term=.2d4872114329.

———. "Biden Is Hiking the Cost of Carbon. It Will Change How the US Tackles Global Warming." *The Washington Post.* 2021. https://www.washingtonpost.com/climate-environment/2021/02/26/biden-cost-climate-change/.

EPA. *Regulatory Impact Analysis: Final Rulemaking for 2017–2025 Light Duty Vehicle Greenhouse Gas Emission Standards and Corporate Average Fuel Economy Standards.* 2012. Accessed May 4, 2018. https://nepis.epa.gov/Exe/ZyPURL.cgi?Dockey=P100EZI1.TXT.

———. "Plan EJ 2014." 2013. Accessed May 4, 2018. https://www.epa.gov/environmentaljustice/plan-ej-2014.

———. "Plan EJ 2020." 2016. Accessed May 4, 2018. https://www.epa.gov/environmentaljustice/about-ej-2020#goals.

———. *National Water Quality Inventory: Report to Congress.* 2017. Accessed May 4, 2018. https://www.epa.gov/sites/production/files/2017-12/documents/305brtc_finalowow_08302017.pdf.

———. "Coal Ash (Cola Combustion Residuals, or CCR)." 2018. Accessed May 4, 2018. https://www.epa.gov/coalash.

———. *US DOT and EPA Put Safety and American Families First with Final Rule on Fuel Economy Standards.* 2020. https://www.epa.gov/newsreleases/us-dot-and-epa-put-safety-and-american-families-first-final-rule-fuel-economy-standards.

———. *Our Nation's Air Trends Through 2020.* 2021. https://gispub.epa.gov/air/trendsreport/2021/.

———. *Northern Gulf of Mexico Hypoxic Zone.* 2022a. https://www.epa.gov/ms-htf/northern-gulf-mexico-hypoxic-zone#:~:text=The%202017%20%E2%80%9CDead%20Zone%E2%80%9D%20measured,of%20the%20large%20zone%20measurement.

———. *Environmental Justice.* 2022b. https://www.epa.gov/environmentaljustice.

EPA, Office of Policy, Planning, and Evaluation. "Environmental Equity: Reducing Risk for All Communities." *EPA 1992* 2. Washington, DC: GPO, 1992.

Faber, Daniel, Benjamin Levy, and Christina Schlegel. 2021. Not all People Are Polluted Equally in Capitalist Society: An Eco-Socialist Commentary on Liberal Environmental Justice Theory. *Capitalism, Nature Socialism.* https://www.tandfonline.com/doi/full/10.1080/10455752.2021.2009640.

FDA. *Helping Agriculture's Helpful Honey Bees.* 2018. https://www.fda.gov/animal-veterinary/animal-health-literacy/helping-agricultures-helpful-honey-bees.

Fears, Darryl. "Biden's Focus on Environmental Justice Led to a Year of Progress—And Burnout." *The Washington Post.* 2022. https://www.washingtonpost.com/climate-environment/2022/01/27/environmental-justice-biden-cecilia-martinez/.

Fiorino, Daniel. "Regulating for the Future: A New Approach for Environmental Governance." In *Toward Sustainable Communities: Transformations and Transition in Environmental Policy,* edited by Michael E. Kraft and Daniel A. Mazmanian, Cambridge: MIT Press, 2009.

Frankel, Todd C. "The Government Has Spent Decades Studying What a Life Is Worth. It Hasn't Made a Difference in the Covid-19 Crisis." *Washington Post.* https://www.washingtonpost.com/business/2020/05/23/government-has-spent-decades-studying-what-life-is-worth-it-hasnt-made-difference-covid-19-crisis/.

Freeman, Myrick A. "Economics, Incentives, and Environmental Regulation." In *Environmental Policy,* edited by Norman E. Vig and Michael E. Kraft. Washington, DC: CQ Press, 2006.

Gang, Duane W. "5 Years After Coal-Ash Spill, Little Has Changed." *USA Today.* 2013. Accessed May 4, 2018. https://www.usatoday.com/story/news/nation/2013/12/22/coal-ash-spill/4143995/.

Golfarb, Ben. "An Advocate in Pursuit of Environmental Justice at the EPA." *Yale Environment 360*. 2013. https://e360.yale.edu/features/interv iew_with_epa_environmental_justice_director_matthew_tejada.

Gonzalez, Sarah. "How Government Agencies Determine the Dollar Value of Human Life." *NPR*. 2020. https://www.npr.org/2020/04/23/843310 123/how-government-agencies-determine-the-dollar-value-of-human-life.

Government Accountability Office (GAO). *Siting of Hazardous Waste Landfills And Their Correlation With Racial And Economic Status of Surrounding Communities*. 1983. Accessed August 11, 2013. http://archive.gao.gov/d48 t13/121648.pdf.

———. "Environmental Justice: EPA Needs to Take Additional Actions to Help Ensure Effective Implementation." 2011. Accessed August 11, 2013. http:// www.gao.gov/new.items/d1277.pdf.

Gullien, Alex. "Appeals Court Revives Key Climate Measure Rejected by Trump Judge." *Politico*. 2022. https://www.politico.com/news/2022/03/16/app eals-court-social-cost-carbon-biden-trump-00017986.

Interagency Working Group on Social Cost of Carbon. *Technical Support Document: Social Cost of Carbon for Regulatory Impact Analysis—Under Executive Order 12866*. 2010. Accessed May 4, 2018. https://obamawhiteho use.archives.gov/sites/default/files/omb/inforeg/for-agencies/Social-Cost-of-Carbon-for-RIA.pdf.

Interagency Working Group on Social Cost of Greenhouse Gases. *Technical Support Document: Technical Update of the Social Cost of Carbon for Regulatory Impact Analysis Under Executive Order 12866*. 2016. Accessed May 4, 2018. https://www.epa.gov/sites/production/files/2016-12/doc uments/sc_co2_tsd_august_2016.pdf.

Jenkins, Clinton N., Kyle S. Van Houtan, Stuart L. Pimm, and Joseph O. Sexton. "US Protected Lands Mismatch Biodiversity Priorities." *Proceedings of the National Academy of Sciences of the United States of America*. 2015. Accessed May 4, 2018. https://www.ncbi.nlm.nih.gov/pmc/articles/PMC4413281/ .

Konisky, David, Christopher Reenock, and Shannon Conley. "Environmental Injustice in Clean Water Act Enforcement: Racial and Income Disparities in Inspection Time." *Environmental Research Letters* 16, no. 8 (2021). https:// iopscience.iop.org/article/10.1088/1748-9326/ac1225.

Kraft, Michael E. and Scott R. Furlong. *Public Policy: Politics, Analysis, and Alternatives*. 4th edition. Washington, DC: CQ Press, 2013.

Kraft, Michael E. *Environmental Policy and Politics*. 7th edition. New York: Routledge, 2018.

Kraft, Michael E. and Norman Vig. "Environmental Policy over Four Decades Achievements and New Directions." In *Environmental Policy*, edited by

Norman J. Vig and Michael E. Kraft, 206–229. Washington, DC: CQ Press, 2013.

Lasswell, Harold D. *A Pre-view of Policy Sciences*. New York: American Elsevier Publishing, 1971.

Lindblom, C. E. "The Science of 'Muddling Through'." *Public Administration Review* 19, no. 2 (Spring 1959): 79–88.

———. "Still Muddling, Not Yet Through." *Public Administration Review* 39, no. 6 (1979): 517–526.

Milman, Oliver. "A Civil Rights 'Emergency': Justice, Clean Air and Water in the Age of Trump." *The Guardian*. 2017. Accessed May 4, 2018. https://www.theguardian.com/us-news/2017/nov/20/environmental-justice-in-the-age-of-trump.

———. "Environmental Racism Case: EPA Rejects Alabama Town's Claim Over Toxic Landfill." *The Guardian*. 2018. Accessed May 4, 2018. https://www.theguardian.com/us-news/2018/mar/06/environmental-racism-alabama-landfill-civil-rights.

Merrill, Dave. "No One Values Your Life More Than the Federal Government." *Bloomberg*. 2017. https://www.bloomberg.com/graphics/2017-value-of-life/.

Mohai, Paul and Robin Saha. "Which Came First, People or Pollution? A Review of Theory and Evidence from Longitudinal Environmental Justice Studies." *Environmental Research Letters* 10, no. 12 (2015): 1–9.

Mooney, Chris. "New EPA Document Reveals Sharply Lower Estimate of Cost of Climate Change." *The Washington Post*. 2017. Accessed May 4, 2018. https://www.washingtonpost.com/news/energy-environment/wp/2017/10/11/new-epa-document-reveals-sharply-lower-estimate-of-the-cost-of-climate-change/?utm_term=.03cbade750e8.

National Academy of Public Administration. *Transforming Environmental Protection for the 21st Century*. Washington, DC: National Academy of Public Administration, 2000.

Niles, Meredith T. and Mark Lubell. "Integrative Frontiers in Environmental Policy Theory and Research." *The Policy Studies Journal* 40, no. S1 (2012): 41–64.

Office of Management and Budget (OMB). *2017 Draft Report to Congress on the Benefits and Costs of Federal Regulations and Agency Compliance with the Unfunded Mandates Reform Act*. 2017. Accessed May 4, 2018. https://www.whitehouse.gov/wp-content/uploads/2017/12/draft_2017_cost_benefit_report.pdf.

Olmstead, Sheila M. "Applying Market Principles to Environmental Policy." In *Environmental Policy*, edited by Norman J. Vig and Michael E. Kraft, 245–268. Washington, DC: CQ Press, 2018.

Ostrom, Elinor. *Governing the Commons: The Evolution of Institutions for Collective Action.* Cambridge, MA: Cambridge University Press, 1990.

Perls, Hannah. *EPA Undermines its Own Environmental Justice Programs.* 2020. https://eelp.law.harvard.edu/2020/11/epa-undermines-its-own-environme ntal-justice-programs/.

Pillion, Dennis. "Cemetery Dispute the Latest Conflict Between Arrowhead Landfill, Uniontown Residents." *Al.com.* 2015. Accessed May 4, 2018. https://www.al.com/news/index.ssf/2015/12/arrowhead_landfill_ uniontown_r.html.

Portney, Paul R. "Does Environmental Policy Conflict with Economic Growth?" *Resources* 115 (1994): 21–23.

Quade, Edward S. *Analysis for Public Discourse.* 3rd edition. New York: North Holland Publishing, 1989.

Ramanujan. Krishna. "Insect Pollinators Contribute $29 Billion to US Farm Income." *Cornell Chronicle.* 2012. http://news.cornell.edu/stories/2012/ 05/insect-pollinators-contribute-29b-us-farm-income.

Rhoads, Steven E. *The Economist's View of the World.* Cambridge, MA: Cambridge University Press, 1985.

Rossman, Sean. 2017. "A Third of the Nation's Honeybee Colonies Died Last Year. Why You Should Care." *USA Today.* 2017. Accessed May 4, 2018. https://www.usatoday.com/story/news/nation-now/2017/05/26/third-nations-honeybee-colonies-died-last-year-why-you-should-care/348418001/.

Schwartz, John. "Decline of Pollinators Poses Threat to World Food Supply, Report Says." *The New York Times.* 2016. Accessed May 4, 2018. https:// www.nytimes.com/2016/02/27/science/decline-of-species-that-pollinate-poses-a-threat-to-global-food-supply-report-warns.html?hp&action=click& pgtype=Homepage&clickSource=story-heading&module=second-column-reg ion&region=top-news&WT.nav=top-news&_r=0.

Seelye, Katharine Q. and John Tierney. "E.P.A. Drops Age-Based Cost Studies." *New York Times.* 2003. Accessed May 4, 2018. http://globalag.igc.org/eld errights/us/seniordiscount.htm.

Sigafoos, Stephanie and Molly Bilinski. "Are Honeybees Dying Off? It Depends on Whom You Ask." *AP.* 2021. https://apnews.com/article/technology-bus iness-science-bees-4539519fb935484e017861a0c0cec79a.

The Economist. "The Rule of More." *The Economist.* 2012. Accessed May 4, 2018. https://www.economist.com/node/21547772.

The White House. *FACT SHEET: President Biden Sets 2030 Greenhouse Gas Pollution Reduction Target Aimed at Creating Good-Paying Union Jobs and*

Securing US Leadership on Clean Energy Technologies. 2021. https://www.whitehouse.gov/briefing-room/statements-releases/2021/04/22/fact-sheet-president-biden-sets-2030-greenhouse-gas-pollution-reduction-target-aimed-at-creating-good-paying-union-jobs-and-securing-u-s-leadership-on-clean-energy-technologies/.

———. *Fact Sheet: A Year Advancing Environmental Justice*. 2022. https://www.whitehouse.gov/briefing-room/statements-releases/2022/01/26/fact-sheet-a-year-advancing-environmental-justice/.

UCC. *Toxic Wastes and Race in the United States*. New York: United Church of Christ Commission for Racial Justice, 1987.

US Chamber of Commerce. "Charting Federal Costs and Benefits." 2014. Accessed May 4, 2018. https://www.uschamber.com/sites/default/files/021615_fed_regs_costs_benefits_2014reportrevise_jrp_fin_1.pdf.

USFWS. *Listed Species Summary (Boxscore)*. 2022. https://ecos.fws.gov/ecp/report/boxscore.

USFWS. *U.S. Fish and Wildlife Service Proposes Delisting 23 Species from Endangered Species Act Due to Extinction*. 2021. https://www.doi.gov/pressreleases/us-fish-and-wildlife-service-proposes-delisting-23-species-endangered-species-act-due.

Vig, Norman J. and Michael E. Kraft. Environmental Policy: New Direction for the 21st Century. Washington, DC: CQ Press, 2018.

Walton, Robert. "EPA to Review MATS Rule Limiting Mercury Emissions from Coal Plants. *Utility Dive*. 2017. Accessed May 4, 2018. https://www.utilitydive.com/news/epa-to-review-mats-rule-limiting-mercury-emissions-from-coal-plants/440850/.

Weimer, David L. and Aidan R. Vining. *Policy Analysis*. 5th edition. Boston, MA: Longman Pearson Ltd., 2011.

WSTB. *Valuing Ecosystem Services: Toward Better Environmental Decision-Making*. Washington, DC: National Academies Press, 2004.

CHAPTER 9

The Intersection of Natural Resource and Energy Policy

Introductory Story: Leading a Top Federal Agency & Breaking Glass Ceilings

The American West's picturesque landscapes and vast blue skies are unforgettable. The grandeur of Wyoming's Grand Teton National Park or the "Big Sky Country" of Montana are memorable. To promote westward expansion and to protect the splendor of the West, President Theodore (Teddy) Roosevelt set aside much of these lands as federal public lands—meaning the government owns and manages them.

The managers of public lands in the US are a number of federal agencies, including the United States Fish and Wildlife Service (USFWS), the United States Forest Service (USFS), the National Park Service (NPS), and the Bureau of Land Management (BLM). The majority of the land management agencies are housed within the Department of the Interior, this includes USFWS, NPS, and BLM. The U.S. Department of Agriculture houses the USFS. Overseeing public lands is not an easy endeavor because it requires the supervision of multiple uses of those lands, and those multiple uses often conflict with one another. The National Park Service, for example, simultaneously manages land for multiple objectives: preservation, extraction, and recreation. Within a park, a manager could be tasked with preserving an endangered species while determining

© The Author(s), under exclusive license to Springer Nature
Switzerland AG 2023
S. R. Rinfret and M. C. Pautz, *US Environmental Policy in Action*,
https://doi.org/10.1007/978-3-031-17503-9_9

how snowmobiles affects its habitat, for instance. In addition, conversations around who should have a say in public land management and how to ensure representation of those voices leads to more complexity for management.

The importance of the Department of Interior for federal public land management is vast and the secretary, a position appointed by the president, provides overall direction and vision for the department. In 2021, President Biden appointed Deb Haaland to become the first Native American to serve as cabinet secretary (DOI 2021). Haaland is a member of the Pueblo of Laguna and a 35th generation New Mexican (DOI 2021). Her journey to this position is noteworthy and exemplary of how women can break glass ceilings. Haaland commitment to public service and protecting public lands began with the Pueblo of Laguna community where she served on the Board of Directors for the Laguna Development Corporation (DOI 2021). In this role, she was the first female board member and advocated for environmentally friendly business practices (DOI 2021).

Her political career began as a volunteer, working to increase voter turnout among Native Americans (NIGA 2021), working with President Obama's reelection campaign in 2012, which spurred her to run for New Mexico Lieutenant Governor in 2014 (NIGA 2021). While her campaign was unsuccessful, Haaland became the Chair of the New Mexico Democratic Party and eventually was elected to the House of Representatives in 2016 (NIGA 2021). As a Congresswoman, Haaland served as Vice-Chair of the Committee on Natural Resources and Chair of the Subcommittee on National Parks, Forests, and Public Lands, in addition to her role as Co-Chair of the Native American Caucus (NIGA 2021). Haaland is known for advocating for climate change policies, environmental justice, and issues relating to the missing and murdered indigenous women epidemic (Kerns 2019).

The management of federal lands has historically excluded its original land owners, Native Americans. Yet, tribal communities are often at the front-lines of the intersection between environmental justice, public lands, and extractive industry. With Haaland's appointment to secretary of the Department of Interior, a Native American voice will influence its decision-making. This signifies an effort to change the way public lands have been managed in the past to recognize its original land managers. As we finish writing the pages of our 3rd edition, Secretary Haaland allocated $1.7 billion for tribal water rights, to help build water infrastructure so that tribes can access the water they have rights to (Heinsius 2022). Haaland's work only begins to unpack federal land management policies with a very long and complicated history.

Secretary Haaland's historic appointment also serves as an important reminder about her day job—it illuminates the interconnectedness of public lands, natural resource, and energy policy. Most importantly, natural resource policy is guided by multi-use laws by which federal managers must reconcile how to best use the land, preserve the land for future generations, and the land for economic benefits. At the crux of this debate is the protection of public lands versus the advancement of extractive resource industries. This is a simplistic explanation and this chapter investigates the complexities of these issues and the multiple layers of government and actors that are involved. In, this chapter, we begin with an overview of the topic, defining public lands and exploring the four central agencies for managing these lands—United States Fish and Wildlife Service (USFWS), the National Park Service (NPS), the United States Bureau of Land Management (BLM), and the United States Forest Service (USFS). Within this context, we delve into some of the multi-use natural resource policies that provide broader linkages to US energy policy. We conclude by considering issues and concerns, such as water scarcity in the American West. Readers of this chapter will be able to convey the myriad of actors involved (institutional and non-institutional) that define how we manage the use of natural resources on public land. Simply put, the way in which we manage our public land affects the future of our environment. By no means can we cover every single topic related to natural resource and energy policy and this chapter serves as an introduction.

Defining the Intersection

As we have noted throughout this text, environmental policy is complex, involving multiple layers. How we use natural resources on public lands helps us understand the driving components of energy policy—the building blocks to the messy nature of environmental policymaking. As *The Lorax* depicts in Chapter 1, the decisions we make about the use of our public lands affect all of us. If we decide to open the Grand Canyon National Park to uranium mining, its impacts are far-reaching.

Here is a plausible list of environmental consequences of such action in this particular national park:

1. Contamination of the Havasupai Tribe's travertine waterfalls and drinking water supply;
2. Tusayan, Arizona (community outside of the South Rim, Grand Canyon) local economy plummets because Grand Canyon National Park visitation decreases due to mining activity; and/or
3. Uranium mining tailings contaminate the Colorado River, a drinking water source for seven states—Colorado, Arizona, New Mexico, California, Utah, Wyoming, and Nevada.

Uranium mining is just one example of the connections between natural resource and energy policy in the US. We begin our discussion of defining this natural resource and energy policy intersection through the lens of public lands in the US.

Public lands are designated lands for the use and enjoyment of the American people and are managed by the federal government. However, over time, the concept of public lands has shifted from selling the land to preservation of the land. As Jacqueline Vaughn (2007) defines, "When the US was at its infancy "public lands" referred to the area between the Appalachian Mountains and the Mississippi River that were held by seven of the original 13 colonies – the land claim states" (111). As payment for fighting in the Revolutionary War, soldiers were compensated with land to raise revenue for the US. By 1842, up to 160 acres of land would be provided if a person would be willing to fight Indians in Florida or couples could settle the Oregon Territory, receiving 640-acre parcels (Vaughn 2007).

The American Antiquities Act of 1906 changed the direction of the federal government's approach from selling land for a profit to conservation of the land. Under the Act, the president of the US can designate land as a national monument to protect the land for scientific, cultural, or archeological purposes, to name a few reasons. Catalysts for this legislation were related to the writings from Henry David Thoreau and Ralph Waldo Emerson. Both poets, Thoreau and Emerson wrote about the beauty of the natural landscape of the Western US and did not want a future where the commodification of the land would deplete all of its resources, stifling future enjoyment of the land's magnificence (Andrews 2006).

Roughly, 640 million acres, or 28%, of all the land in the US are federal public lands. The vast majority of this land resides in the Western US because much of this land was undeveloped during the origins of the US since, "[m]any mountainous, arid and difficult-to-reach tracts of land in the West simply weren't attractive to farmers. Colonizers claimed the few valleys where farming was feasible and built towns. The only thing most of the remaining land was good for was grazing, but cattle ranchers and sheep herders needed large tracts of land to feed their livestock, not the smaller parcels they could claim through homestead policies" (Quoctoring and Sanger-Katz 2016, n.pn).

Table 9.1 uses a few state examples to differentiate the amount of federal public land per state. Alabama's landmass includes 22 million acres and 2.7% is federal public lands (867,360 acres). Idaho, in contrast, has approximately 4.9 million acres, and 61.6% of this is federal public lands.

America's public lands encompass many different categories, including national parks, national forests, national conversation areas, national wildlife refuges, national monuments, national historical areas, wilderness areas, national recreation areas, national battlefields, national seashores and lakeshores, scenic areas, and national trails (US Department of Interior 2016). We compare a few of these land types to convey some of the differences. A national park (e.g., Grand Canyon, Yellowstone) is land designated by the federal government to preserve this land and the future enjoyment of its environment. A national forest, by way of comparison, is also land designated by the federal government but contains many uses—timber harvesting, recreation, wildlife, or fishing. A national battlefield is designated to commemorate historical point in US history.

Table 9.1 Public lands in the US

State	Total federal acreage	Percent of state
Alabama	867,360	2.7
New York	188,537	0.6
Ohio	307,180	1.2
Montana	27,049,302	29
Wyoming	30,183,609	48.4
Idaho	32,623,376	61.6

Source https://fas.org/sgp/crs/misc/R42346.pdf

Public lands contain natural resources—renewable and non-renewable. A renewable natural resource is replaceable by nature or human intervention (e.g., trees, water, soil, wildlife). In comparison, a nonrenewable resource has a set amount available, which cannot be replenished (e.g., coal, petroleum, natural gas). Public lands in the US are inevitably a unique treasure and an envy of the world (Davis 2018). These lands are managed in a variety of ways and serve multiple purposes. As Davis (2018) notes,

> They provide critical and otherwise unavailable habitats for precious biodiversity. They churn out trillions of dollars of ecological services, generally unpriced yet vital to life. They provide recreation and aesthetic wonders that undergird entire global economies. They provide stable access to such resources as timber, minerals, energy, and pasture that also support local economies. They also provide untold intangible benefits: wonder, reverence, solitude, psychological and physical health, history, national and community pride, connections to land and place, and intergenerational continuity in an increasingly turbulent and confusing world. (209)

Creating public lands does not come without conflict and controversy. For example, do you allow for the creation of a new natural gas power plant or protect the habitat of an endangered species? Nevertheless, the management of federal lands is not an easy undertaking. The estimated cost to oversee these lands is approximately the same price for one hundred F-35 fighter jets (Davis 2018). We examine the four largest managers of public lands to understand some of the difficulties involved.

THE FEDERAL LANDLORDS

As we learned in Chapter 6, Congress delegates its authority to the bureaucracy for the interpretation and implementation of environmental laws. Ninety-six percent of federal public lands are managed by four federal agencies, which fall under the US Department of Interior, (except the US Forest Service, which is within the US Department of Agriculture): the Bureau of Land Management (BLM), the United States Fish and Wildlife Service (USFWS), the United States Forest Service (USFS), and the National Park Service (NPS). Each of these agencies must reconcile multiple use on federal public lands—recreation, preservation, and development of natural resources. As stated previously, multiple use simply means that the land has been designated by the federal government for a variety of purposes (see explanation of national forests above).

Bureau of Land Management: The BLM, the youngest of the federal land agencies, oversees the largest amount of federal public lands—248 million acres. This acreage is primarily within eleven Western states in arid rangeland or desert. In 1946, the BLM was created through the merger of two existing agencies—the Grazing Service and the General Land Office. The permanent protection of these lands occurred in 1976 with the passage of the Federal Land Management Policy Act (FLPMA).

The Taylor Grazing Act of 1934 and Public Lands Rangeland Improvement Act of 1978 are two essential pieces of legislation that BLM agency officials grapple with. Under these Acts, BLM officials oversee grazing districts whereby western ranchers rent the land for their cattle to graze. Concerns about rangeland management and overuse is a constant concern for the BLM to reconcile with ranching and environmental interests (Andrews 2008). The approach taken is animal unit month (AUM) which is the carrying capacity for forage on a pasture. More specifically, an AUM means an animal unit (AU) is a mature cow weighing approximately 1,000 pounds that requires 26 pounds of dry matter or food per day (DM). This is a system to standardize the forage (hay, grass) needs of cattle (or other grazing animals—sheep, horses) and the forage available. The BLM manages approximately 18,000 leases for cattle ranchers to graze on public lands. The grazing fee for 2018 is $1.41 per AUM (US Department of Interior 2018).

In 2014, Cliven Bundy, a longtime Nevada rancher declared war against the federal government, noting he should not have to pay for his cattle to graze on public lands. After three ignored court orders, the BLM impounded his cattle due to failure to pay. This led to an armed standoff between Bundy, his militia supporters, and federal officials (Childress 2018). Several court case attempts were made to hold Bundy accountable, but none have been successful. It is estimated that Bundy owes over $1 million dollars in grazing fees to the US government (Childress 2018). Movements like this are not uncommon and were also attempted by individuals during the Reagan administration Sagebrush Rebellion—during the 1980s a group of individuals in the American West organized and argued to have more state and local control over federal lands.

United States Fish and Wildlife Service: The origins of the USFWS date back to two federal agencies established in the early nineteenth century. The intent of each agency was to oversee the nation's fish and wildlife supplies, respectively. The Commissioner of Fish and Fisheries studied the supply of coastal and lake fisheries, which later become the Bureau of Fisheries in the Department of Commerce. In 1905, the Bureau of Biological Survey in the Department of Agriculture was established, with the stated mission of studying birds and mammals in the US (Loomis 1993). By 1939, the Bureau of Fisheries and the Bureau of Biological Survey were consolidated, which created the USFWS.

The primary responsibilities of USFWS are to manage migratory birds, develop hunting regulations, acquire/protect habitat, and enforce international treaties that protect migratory birds. The broadest sources of statutory authority for the USFWS are the National Environmental Policy Act (NEPA) of 1969, and the Endangered Species Act (ESA) of 1973. NEPA serves as a formal vehicle for USFWS to analyze the impact of projects on all types of fish and wildlife through environmental assessments. The other key directive for USFWS came in 1973, with the passage of the ESA to protect endangered or threatened plants and animals. Under the ESA, USFWS, along with the Department of Commerce, is responsible for carrying out this law through rulemaking processes (see Chapters 6 and 7 for more detail). The language of the ESA directs USFWS to use only the best scientific data to list a species, develop a recovery plan, and designate critical habitats once a species goes through the rulemaking process and is listed as endangered or threatened. In 2017, the USFWS decided to delist the grizzly bear as an endangered species, changing its classification to threatened in the Greater Yellowstone Ecosystem. Lawsuits from numerous environmental groups claimed that the USFWS did not use the best available science to make this de-listing and in 2018, a US District Judge ruled in favor of the environmental groups, restoring the protection for Yellowstone Ecosystem grizzly bears (Miller 2017 ; NPS 2020).

The United States Forest Service: Created in 1905, the USFS oversees our national forests and grasslands. The origins of the USFWS are rooted in the ideals of Gifford Pinchot (former governor of Pennsylvania, forester, and first administrator of the USFS) who viewed the forest through a utilitarian lens. Simply put, the forest would be used for multiple uses—resource extraction, recreation, or wildlife (Davis 2018).

The Multiple Use Sustained Yield Act (MUYSA) of 1960 serves as a prominent legislative directive for the USFS. MUYSA mandates that the agency not only mange the forest but also produce sustained yield—total amount of timber which can be removed from any forest at any time

(Davis 2018). Recall from Chapter 5, Daniel McGowan ardently opposed USFS practices, used violent protest mechanisms, and as a result, classified as ecoterrorism.

Although USFS is often criticized for its approach to multiple use, there are additional concerns. The USFS continues to struggle with wildland fire management. Some critics contend that the development of national forests (e.g., timber) coupled with climate change has led to record seasons of wildland fires. Over the summer of 2021, there were 58,985 wildfires with 18 fires that each individually burned over 40,000 acres (National Interagency Fire Center 2021). The Dixie fire in California burnt nearly 1 million acres (National Interagency Fire Center 2021). The USFS often spends fifty percent of its budget fighting fires and does not have enough resources for prevention; as a result, under President Trump the USFS developed new management approaches through the Agriculture Improvement Act of 2018, often referred to as the 2018 Farm Bill. These additions expanded the agency's abilities to work closely with states, counties, and tribes to manage wildfire cooperatively and across jurisdictional boundaries (USFS 2018). The agency's new strategy is termed Shared Stewardship which focuses on a state or tribe working with the USFS on a collaborative management plan. Since its adoption, the agency has entered into 28 Shared Stewardship Agreements with state governments (USFS 2021). Some question whether the USFS should be in the firefighting business or if forests should naturally burn. Christopher Stone's (USC law professor) famous 1972 law review article—*Should Trees Have Standing*—goes one-step further—asking the question who really speaks for the trees. Stone stresses that trees are indeed objects and should have standing to sue. Supreme Court Justice Douglas even cited his argument in one of his dissenting opinions (*Sierra Club v. Morton*).

The National Park Service: In 1916, the NPS was created as part of the Organic Act—often referred to as a dual mandate. This dual mandate provides that the NPS is designated by Congress to provide recreational enjoyment for the people as well as preservation of the land. The NPS maintains 79.7 million acres of national parks, preserves, monuments, battlefields, lakeshores, and historic sites (Davis 2018). Much like the USFWS, the NPS uses NEPA and the ESA for guidance for species protections within park boundaries.

However, the Antiquities Act provides US presidents authority over the designation and creation of national monuments, often increasing the amount of management for NPS officials. Presidents can designate national monuments through executive orders under the Antiquities Act of 1906. President Obama was classified as the "monument man" for creating the most national monuments since President Teddy Roosevelt under one administration—1.65 additional acres. In 2017, the Trump administration decreased the size of Bears Ears and Grand Staircase-Escalante national monuments; however, President Biden restored the boundaries in 2021 (Shivaram 2021).

The aforementioned history provides basic background information about the origins of the four federal landlords and some issues each confronts. Inextricably, these federal landlords confront a deluge of issues. Certainly, answers to how best to use natural resources on public lands is complex and involves numerous institutional and non-institutional actors. We could fill pages of several chapters about the management approaches for each respective public lands agency. Nevertheless, our purpose here is simple—to introduce the reader and to investigate one of the larger nuances that federal public land manager's face—reconciling energy development and preservation. Much like the opening pages of this chapter, and Chapter 1, how do we reconcile preservation of public lands while providing energy for Americans?

Energy Policy and Public Lands

Energy development is at the epicenter of the public lands debate. Much like with management of public lands, an essential piece of energy policy is how do we effectively manage the land under multiple use mandates? Energy policy concerns the management and use of the nation's energy resources, both renewable sources (e.g., solar or wind power) and non-renewable (e.g., coal, natural gas, petroleum) sources of energy. Public lands are one of *the* sources of non-renewable resources of energy.

The federal government manages public lands. Energy policy, by way of comparison, refers to government action or inaction that deals with issues related to the production, distribution, transportation, and consumption of energy (Rinfret et al. 2018). However, energy resources are located on public lands, as is the case with uranium deposits in the Grand Canyon. Additionally, energy is at the forefront of Americans' minds because it affects our daily lives—from filling up our car with gasoline, to paying our monthly energy bill, to receiving a tax credit for the solar panels on your rooftop.

Energy production, as Fig. 9.1 illustrates, is an economic driver for several state economies. Wyoming, Colorado, and North Dakota are all within the top 10 energy producers for the US. These same states contain a significant portion of federal public land.

In addition to energy production, we also need to consider our consumption. We can use information from the US Energy Information Administration (EIA), which tracks our energy consumption over time. In 2021, according to the US EIA, we consumed 97.3 quadrillion Btus. This consumption is driven by electric power (38%); transportation (29%); industry (22%), residential (6%), and commercial (4%) (US Energy Information Administration 2017). By way of comparison, consumption of renewable energy (e.g., wind, solar) has more than doubled since 2008

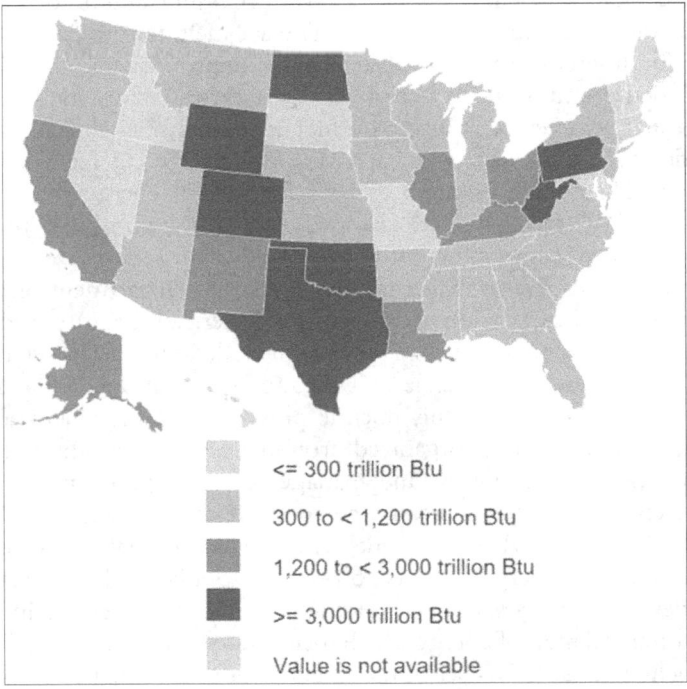

Fig. 9.1 Total energy production per state (*Source* https://www.eia.gov/state/rankings/?sid=US#/series/101)

(Morton 2018). It remains to be seen if this will be affected by Biden's Inflation Reduction Act and investments in renewable energy.

Federal Energy Managers

Although we have already extensively discussed the federal public land managers, these same individuals often work with individuals within energy agencies or commissions to determine the relevancy of energy production on public lands or its impact on species. Two of the key guiding policies for federal energy managers include the Energy Policy Act of 2005 and the Energy Independence and Security Act of 2007. The Energy Policy Act of 2005 was the result of an energy task force, headed by Vice President Dick Cheney. The focus is to find ways to increase domestic sources of energy, such as coal, providing grants for development of various energy technologies. The act includes provisions for tax credits for homeowners who make energy improvements. The Energy Independence and Security Act of 2007 promotes energy independence from foreign sources by focusing on fuel economy, biofuel development, fuel efficiency of vehicles, and improving the energy efficiency of public buildings. These policies serve as laws for federal energy managers to implement. We consider a few energy agency and commission to better understand their intersection with public land managers.

Department of Energy: Most notably is the US Department of Energy (DOE). Its agency mission is "to ensure America's security and prosperity by addressing its energy, environmental, and nuclear challenges through transformative science and technology solutions." The agency implements policies involving nuclear power, fossil fuels, and alternative energy sources. It is organized around three major offices: nuclear security, science and energy, and management and performance and it is overseen by a cabinet secretary, currently Jennifer Granholm (Rinfret et al. 2018). The DOE often works with the BLM regarding placement of solar and wind energy products on western public lands, for example.

Federal Energy Regulatory Commission: FERC manages the interstate sale and transmission of energy which includes the sales, licensing, pricing, and pipeline rates. It is a self-funding entity, meaning that it pays for its operations from the fees it charges the energy industry, which it regulates (Rinfret et al. 2018). In February of 2021, FERC released an Environmental Assessment for the Mountain Valley Pipeline to determine the impacts of the project (FERC 2021). This proposed pipeline would cross public lands in Virginia and West Virginia. After the release of the EA, the BLM and USFS issued permits for the Mountain Valley Pipeline to begin, however, lawsuits from environmental groups brought this project to the federal appeals court which rejected the permits for inadequately considering the impacts of the project (Vogelsong 2022). This is not the end however, and as we write this book the Mountain Valley Pipeline project is still considering next steps.

Nuclear Regulatory Commission: This NRC is responsible for the safe use and environmental security of nuclear energy for non-military purposes. This includes the operation of nuclear reactors, materials, transportation, storage, and disposal of nuclear waste. The NRC is overseen by five commissioners, appointed by the president for fixed terms. This commission was created in 1974 and its headquarters are in Rockville, Maryland with four regional offices throughout the country. Most importantly, the NRC is tasked with the safe storage of radioactive waste which has been a topic surrounding the use of Yucca Mountain, Nevada as a geological repository for nuclear waste. It is yet to be determined if this site will be used to store waste.

Nevertheless, presidential policy directives also define US energy production. These policies can make it difficult for public land management. To provide context, we briefly examine presidential energy policy approaches from 2001 to 2022 as a foundation for our chapter's case study—Keystone Pipeline XL.

National Security, Energy, and Presidential Directives

Post-9/11, energy policy in the US has been defined through the lens of a national security. President George W. Bush framed energy policy as a national security when he charged his Vice President, Dick Cheney, with the responsibility of overseeing an energy taskforce. He wanted his Vice President to investigate environmental regulations that would stifle energy production on public lands. For example, one of the recommendations of the Taskforce was to open the Alaska National Wildlife Refuge to the drilling of oil and gas. The Taskforce underwent scrutiny because its makeup consisted of energy industry representatives without the input from environmental interests (Rinfret et al. 2018). Although the Republican Party maintained control of the U.S. House of Representatives, the US Senate was divided during Bush's tenure. Therefore, many policy directives fell flat (e.g., drilling for oil in ANWR).

President Obama took a different approach toward energy policy on public lands. The American Recovery and Reinvestment Act of 2009 provided tax incentives and favored the use of renewable energy. President Obama's approach was for a clean energy future on public lands. For example, the BLM approved plans for 15,000 megawatts of renewable power (e.g., solar and wind). Additionally, President Obama urged public land agencies to undergo climate change assessments and its effects on management practices. The NPS, for example, did not have a climate program prior to President Obama, but conducted 235 climate assessments out of its 413 parks during his tenure (Shogren 2017).

President Trump's approach to energy policy was to prioritize energy production on all public lands. *Outside Magazine*, in 2018, defined President Trump as the rollback president with energy first and public lands second. To illustrate this label, President Trump repealed regulations that prevented mining companies from dumping their waste into rivers. Most notably, President Trump was successful in opening ANWR to oil and gas development (Outside Editors 2018).

On his first day in office, President Biden canceled the permit for the Keystone XL pipeline and later suspended the leases for the ANWR oil and gas development. In addition, the president signed a memorandum called Consultation and Coordination with Indian Tribal Governments that requires federal agencies to consult with tribal governments on policies that will impact their land and people (Biden 2021a). Some believe that this order will give tribes legal standing to oppose energy projects on public lands.

Public Perceptions in the West

Presidential approaches inherently affect the use of natural resources on public lands, but public opinion matters because voters effect policy change (see Chapter 2). In 2017, Colorado College conducted a telephone survey of voters in seven Western states (Montana, Wyoming, Utah, Colorado, Nevada, Arizona, New Mexico) to assess perspectives about how public lands should be managed. Their findings suggest five overarching findings:

1. More than 67% of respondents want to protect clean water, air, and wildlife habitats on public lands;
2. More than 55% believe that oil and gas development on public lands should be strictly limited;
3. Black, Latino, and Native American respondents more strongly support conservation efforts;
4. 66% of respondents want to completely transition to renewable energy in the next fifteen years; and
5. Respondents are happy with the management of public lands by the four major agencies (Colorado College 2017).

These Western state perspectives are consistent with national trends. In 2022, Pew Research Center found that 69% of Americans support prioritizing the development of alternative energy sources. Comparatively, only 30% want to expand US production of fossil fuel sources of energy development (Tyson et al. 2022).

Now that we have a basic understanding of why energy policy is connected to the use of natural resources and public lands management, it is helpful to contextualize this through the case of Keystone XL Pipeline. This case helps to illuminate the broader connections within this text—institutional and non-institutional actors and how policy is implemented.

Case Study: Keystone XL

Throughout this chapter, natural resources on public lands sits center stage. The Keystone XL Pipeline sheds light on the convergence of institutional and non-institutional actors on the use of a natural resources on public lands and its long-term development effects on the environment. Figure 9.2 depicts the key actors in describing this case.

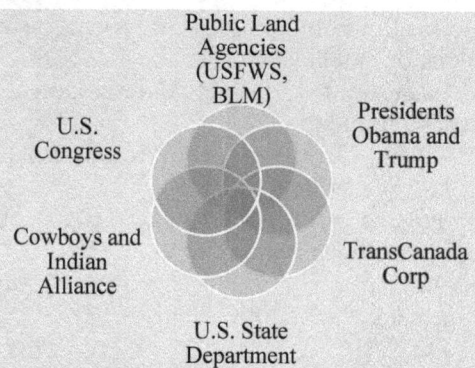

Fig. 9.2 Understanding the players

In 2008, TransCanada Corporation proposed a presidential permit application to the US. Department of State for the construction of a pipeline from Alberta, Canada to Texas to carry hundreds of thousands of oil sands crude oil. This pipeline would traverse Montana, North Dakota, South Dakota, Nebraska, Kansas, Oklahoma, and Texas. As part of the application process, the US Department of State in 2010, conducted an environmental impact assessment under the National Environmental Policy Act to determine environmental effects. Agencies such as the USFWS and BLM conduct assessments to determine impacts on land and species habitats (Canadian Press 2017).

The US Department of State released its environmental assessment in 2011, stating there would be limited impact on the environment. As a result, hundreds of protesters such as Canadian activist Naomi Klein protest for two weeks in front of the White House to prevent the development of the Keystone XL Pipeline. Soon after, additional research from the US Department of State suggests there would be sensitive areas in Nebraska's protected Sandhills and the developers of the pipeline would need to come up with a new route. The TransCanada Corporation agrees to re-route the pipeline. The US Congress passed legislation stating President Obama must decide about the pipeline within 60 days. January 2012, President Obama rejected the Keystone Pipeline proposal arguing there was not enough time to evaluate the re-route proposal and its effects (Canadian Press 2017).

In response, TransCanada stated it would only build the southern leg of the pipeline from Oklahoma to Texas' Gulf Coast. Their argument was that since it does not cross international borders, it no longer needed presidential approval, but submitted a new request to the US Department of State for review. During their review, the US Department of State suggested less greenhouse gases would be emitted through the pipeline as opposed to transporting by truck. April 2014, the Cowboys and Indian Alliance (e.g., ranchers, conservationists, and Tribes), protested outside of the White House to reject the pipeline to protect public land. However, in August 2014, the State Department suspended its review process indefinitely because of a pending lawsuit in Nebraska—the Governor decided to approve the pipeline construction, but opponents sue stating it violated their state constitution (Canadian Press 2017).

December 2014, the Republican Party gained control of the US Congress and passed legislation for the construction of the Keystone Pipeline. On February 24, 2015, President Obama vetoed the legislation. January 2016, TransCanada filed a lawsuit against the Obama administration for exceeding his powers by denying construction of the project. November 2016, Trump elected president. January 2017, President Trump signed a memorandum for the reconsideration of the construction of the pipeline if the company used US steel (Canadian Press 2017). March 2017, the US Department of State, under President Trump issued a permit to TransCanada for the construction of the Keystone XL Pipeline. In November 2018, Judge Brian Morris of the US District Court in Montana blocked the construction of the pipeline, stating the Trump administration failed to provide fact-based evidence for its decision to move forward with construction. January 2021, on President Biden's first day as president, he issued an executive order that revoked the permit for the Keystone XL Pipeline (Biden 2021a). June 2021, TransCanada now known as TC Energy formally called off plans to build the pipeline (Lindwall 2021).

This case occurred over several years and involved numerous actors, but access for energy development on public lands continues to be debated but as of June 2022, this case appears to be complete. As this chapter depicts, public land managers routinely confront how to manage the land, reconciling preservation, recreation, and development. Vague presidential and congressional instruction leaves agency officials interpreting vague statutes from implementation. Therefore, if a spill occurs, it will be up to public land managers to develop approaches to protect species and the environment. This embodies a reactionary approach to the implementation of US environmental policy.

CHALLENGES AND CONSIDERATIONS

Natural resource and energy policy is characterized by how we use and manage our public lands. Although our federal managers confront a host of issues, new concerns are on the horizon and they are tasked with coordinating plausible solutions. We explore four issue areas: the evolution of natural resource economies; devolution of federal public land oversight to state officials; the demographic makeup of public land agencies; and water scarcity in the West.

The Evolving West and Natural Resource Economies

As evidenced throughout this chapter, tradition and natural resource extraction economies (e.g., coal, uranium), often explain American Western communities. After the Revolutionary War, many soldiers, instead of receiving salaries, were provided payment in the form of a Western land parcel. Moreover, homesteaders traveled West in hopes of making it rich through the exploration of gold or uranium.

Families have lived on these lands for generations and are suspect of outsiders. In Montana, for example, you define your family by generation—"I am fifth generation Montanan," which is essential for running for local or statewide office. However, the tribal response would be they are the original and only generation of Montana. Such sentiments were dramatized in Kevin Costner's *Yellowstone* series where a ranching family confronts nearby development. These long-standing family traditions collide as "outsiders" move to rural Western states (e.g., Montana,

Wyoming) with different viewpoints. The "old" West is defined by tradition and the "new" West through the lens of new perspectives on how best to manage the land.

Regardless, as more individuals move to the American West, perspectives about public lands have changed—specifically, how we define natural resource extraction economies. Colorado, for example, contained 1.75 million people in 1960. In 2022, the population has grown to over 5 million. As Kerklivet (2017) suggests, "Old economies are simple and easy to see. A ton of coal is mined, shipped to a power plant, and the miner is paid. New economies are more complex and links between production and payment are less easily seen" (n.pn.). Nonetheless, rural, Western communities are accustomed to extraction producing jobs and monetary support for local communities. However, land is symbolic for conservation efforts and if contaminated it could be destructive for local economies. President Obama's Clean Power Plan Rule challenged the rural West to consider new ways to use the land (e.g., wind and solar) to produce energy. States and federal agencies were tasked with co-creating plans for a new energy future.

The Western US is facing the choice of "old" (economy based upon resource extraction) or "new" (economy based upon clean environment, renewable energy). At the heart of the debate are public land agencies attempting to reconcile these old and new ideals searching for new ways to shepherd bargain and compromise. Arguably, research suggests respecting the long-standing cultural norms without pre-determined solutions (Nie 2009). The most important reminder for public land agencies is, as Wyoming rancher stated, "It's the leanin' against the pickup conversation where you let your guard down because you build up trust, that's where the magic starts. This takes decades of trust building, rather than walking in and telling you what to do" (Partners for Collaboration 2018). Nonetheless, if the American West continues to consider transitioning from coal extraction to wind power, bringing individuals to the table for a discussion could prove fruitful.

State or Federal Control

The Trump administration set forth a movement of federal control and oversight of public lands to states. The idea is that the US Congress would create a land transfer bill. As previously mentioned, this would appease individuals, such as Cliven Bundy, who vehemently oppose federal control of public lands. This is not a new approach and was attempted during the Reagan administration during the Sagebrush Rebellion to devolve more power to state governments to oversee federal public lands.

Proponents of the management transfer of public lands use the Constitution as their guide—that federal ownership of land is a prohibited activity. However, opponents of transfer from federal to state authority use the Constitution's Property Clause to articulate that the federal government can own and control land (Davis 2018). Regardless of perspective, if states were transferred control of all federal public lands, who has access and who pays for the management?

Another component in this conversation are Native American groups. As Davis (2018) succinctly states, "Despite losing their ancestral homes to the establishment of public domain, many Native Americans are steadfast opponents of privatization, as public lands, at their best, can act to protect sacred sites, resources, landscapes, with at least some accountability and accessibility for tribes" (197). Regardless, if you are a proponent or opponent, if management shifts from federal to state control, what role do the BLM, USFWS, USFS, and NPS play in its future? As noted previously, Colorado College's survey of the American West stresses the desire for respondents is to maintain federal oversight of their public lands (Weigel 2017).

Water Scarcity

Many of us might not realize this, but there is a looming water crisis in the American West. The Great Salt Lake in Utah and Lake Powell in Arizona are at historic lows. Another important example is from Lori Paup, resident of Sulphur Springs Valley, Arizona. Lori and her family moved to Arizona in 2014 from Pennsylvania. The home they purchased contained a well—something that most individuals have in rural parts of the Midwestern US. However, on numerous occasions (laundry, bath time), Lori's water was cloudy or did not contain a steady flow of water. Her family had their well inspected to investigate. The well inspector concluded, "you are running out of water" (Shannon 2018, n.pn.).

Homeowners and farmers began to confront one another—who was using all of the water resources. The alternative—drill deeper water wells for the hefty price of $15,000–30,000. However, since 1915, cattle ranchers and homesteaders adopted the oil industry's approach to extract oil from the ground using turbine pumps to extract water to irrigate farmland using Aquifer water across the American West (Shannon 2018).

Due to less rain and snowmelt reaching the floor of dry, arid Western lands, public land managers are now confronting a new term—groundwater mining—water withdrawal exceeds the rate of replenishment (Shannon 2018). Presumably, water in the American West is becoming a semi-renewable infinite resource. Because of this, public land managers, states, and vested interests need to design collective solutions. Finding new water sources is not easy or cheap. Moreover, conservation mechanisms are troubling for individuals accustomed to providing water supplies for cattle and agricultural practices. Experts are considering measures such as toilet to tap (recycle wastewater for consumption) or the construction of desalination plants (remove salt from sea water for and make it drinkable).

The underlining question is who owns water on federal public lands. In 2016, Colorado passed the Colorado Water Rights Protection Act, which reaffirms their right to water on federal land. Legislation defining water on federal public lands has yet to pass the US Congress (Kaufman 2018). This leaves federal public landowners at the eye of yet another storm.

Demographic Makeup of Public Land Agencies

In our final example for issues and concerns for consideration surrounds the makeup of those within public land agencies. Even before the #MeToo Movement, the USFS and NPS have been under investigation for discriminatory behavior against women. Kathryn Joyce (2018) from *Outside Magazine* spotlighted the stories of Bush and Szydlo.

Bush was an established forester with nineteen years of service for the USFS. In 2011, Bush accepted a position as an engine captain for Sequoia National Forest. Within this position, she was responsible for engine maintenance and physical training (e.g., hiking or running). When Bush became pregnant with twins, she declined to take the fitness test required for training. This test included a three-mile hike with a 45-pound load to be completed within 45 minutes. She asked her boss for a transfer of assignment until post-pregnancy. Reportedly, Bush's boss stated she was useless for the position. This remains a pending class action lawsuit against the USDA, under the Equal Employment Opportunity Commission (EEOC).

NPS practices are also of concern. Szydlo, a biologist, was selected to conduct field research for the Grand Canyon National Park. However, she shares a story of sexual harassment from 2006 while on the Colorado River. Her story describes a series of sexual advances from a colleague, the boatman on the river—guiding her from one spot to the next. She recounts countless sexual advances from this individual and concerned sexual assault would ensue. Joyce (2007), in an interview with Szydlo, describes a specific example, "Loeffler slowed the motorboat to a crawl, stopping at nearly every beach. Finally, in the middle of a channel, she heard the motor go quiet. Loeffler came up behind her, grabbed her shoulders and asked her to describe her sexual fantasies so he could act them out" (Joyce 2007, n.pn.). Syzdlo documented her experiences, with countless other women, which led to a full investigation of the Grand Canyon's practices.

There is a much deeper story here that far surpasses discriminatory behavior in the USFS and sexual harassment in the NPS. It is about the treatment of individuals within public land agencies. These are the agencies responsible for reconciling preservation, recreation, and development on our federal lands. These individuals are on the front-lines of implementing policy that affect the future of our environment. If agencies are ill equipped to ensure fairness within an agency, how can we tackle any of the aforementioned issues and concerns that confront the future of US environmental policy? Joyce reminds us, "Ever since the US created institutions to protect its wilderness, those agencies have been bound up with a particular image of masculinity. The first park rangers in the US were former cavalrymen, assigned to protect preserves like Yellowstone and Yosemite from poachers and fire. The public quickly became enamored by these rugged, solitary figures" (n.pn.).

These four issues have broader consequences for US environmental policy. Consider the consequences the devolution of federal oversight of public lands to states—would this mean that we would eliminate agencies such as the BLM, USFWS, NPS, and USFS. If we did this, would states have the monetary resources to manage the vast amount of federal land in their state? Moreover, if the American Southwest runs out of water— would we then have an extreme case of environmental justice, as discussed in Chapter 8? Regardless, each captures stories across the American West. The "doers" within our public land management agencies are charged with tackling such issues for our future.

CHAPTER WRAP-UP

Our natural resource policies lead to the management practices of public lands. The way in which we use public lands at the heart of the debate. This chapter provides three broader themes. First, the use of public lands in the American West is riddled with conflict. At the crossroads, are public land managers within the BLM, USFS, USFWS, and NPS tasked with the interpretation of dated congressional statutes and ever-changing presidential directives. Second, and by design, our public land agencies have dual or multiple mandates by Congress—manage for the future enjoyment of the public while preserving species and be open to energy extraction. Finding a balance across these elements have evolved over time. President Obama sounded the environmental alarm, asking public land agencies to extensively study their practices in the era of a changing environment. President Trump in a dramatic rollback set energy development as the premiere purpose of our public lands. Presumably, President Biden returns to his campaign promises of an environmental protection agenda, but with increased gas prices and a global pandemic will these promises continue.

Often missing from these conversations is the "public" in public lands. As evidenced throughout this chapter, public opinion polls suggest strong support to conserve our public lands so future generations can enjoy. As Secretary Haaland breaks glass ceilings as serving as the first woman to oversee the DOI, can she steward a new approach for the management of public lands to protect our natural environment?

Challenge Question for the Environmental Policy Classroom

We discussed throughout this chapter the who "owns" federal public lands. Further examine how Congress has defined the purpose of the federal public land agencies within this chapter—do these promote a sense of diversity, equity, and belonging? Why or why not?

SUGGESTED RESOURCES

Readings and Websites

Andrews, Richard L. *Managing the Environment, Managing Ourselves: A History of American Environmental Policy.* New Haven, CT: Yale University Press, 2006.

Childress, Sarah. "The Battle of Bunkerville." 2018. https://www.pbs.org/wgbh/frontline/article/the-battle-over-bunkerville/.

Davis, Chuck. *Western Public Lands and Environmental Politics.* Westview Press, 2001.

NASA. Fire and Smoke. https://www.nasa.gov/mission_pages/fires/main/index.html

Rasband, James, Salzman, James, and Mark Squillance. *Natural Resources Law and Policy.* New York: Foundation Press, 2009.

Vaughn, Jacqueline. *The Public Land Debate.* Belmont, CA: Thomson Wadsworth, 2007.

Nie, Martin. *The Governance of Western Public Lands: Mapping the Present and Future.* University of Kansas Press, 2009.

Films or Videos

Yellowstone. Directed by Taylor Sheridan. 2018. Paramount. American Drama Series.

The National Parks: America's Best Idea. Directed by Ken Burns. 2009. Public Broadcasting Service. DVD.

Promise Land. Directed by Gus Van Sant. 2013. DVD.

REFERENCES

Andrews, Richard L. *Managing the Environment, Managing Ourselves: A History of American Environmental Policy.* New Haven, CT: Yale University Press, 2006.

Andrews, Richard L. 2008. https://www.amazon.com/Managing-Environment-Ourselves-American-Environmental/dp/030011124X.

Biden, Joseph. "Executive Order on Protecting Public Health and the Environment and Restoring Science to Tackle the Climate Crisis". *The White House.* 2021a, January 20. https://www.whitehouse.gov/briefing-room/presidential-actions/2021a/01/20/executive-order-protecting-public-health-and-environment-and-restoring-science-to-tackle-climate-crisis/.

———. "Memorandum on Tribal Consultation and Strengthening Nation-to-Nation Relationships." *The White House.* 2021b, January 26. https://www.whitehouse.gov/briefing-room/presidential-actions/2021/01/26/memorandum-on-tribal-consultation-and-strengthening-nation-to-nation-relationships/.

Boyle, Lisa Kass. "Earth and the Balance of Power What the Citizens United Ruling Means for the Environment." *Huffington Post*, 2010, February 6. http://www.huff-ingtonpost.com/.

Canadian Press. 2017. https://www.cbc.ca/news/politics/keystone-xl-pipeline-timeline-1.3950156

Colorado College. 2017. https://www.coloradocollege.edu/other/stateofthero
ckies/conservationinthewest/2022/CC%20Poll%20National%20Release%202
022.pdf.

Congressional Research Service. Federal Land Management Overview: Data.
2017. https://fas.org/sgp/crs/misc/R42346.pdf.

Conservation in the West Poll. 2017. https://www.coloradocollege.edu/other/
stateoftherockies/conservationinthewest/2017/2017SORPollReleasePresen
tation.pdf.

Ebbs, Stephanie. "Trump Administration to Take a Smarter, More Aggressive
Approach to Prevent Wildfires." https://abcnews.go.com/Politics/trump-
administration-smarter-aggressive-approach-prevent-wildfires/story?id=572
18357.

Davis, Steven. *In Defense of Public Lands: The Case Against Privatization and
Transfer.* Philadelphia, PA: Temple University Press, 2018.

FERC. "Environmental Assessment for the Mountain Valley Pipeline Amendment Project." 2021. https://www.ferc.gov/environmental-assessment-mou
ntain-valley-pipeline-amendment-project docket no-cp21-57-000.

Grand Canyon National Park. Culture and History. September 1, 2018. https://
www.nps.gov/grca/learn/historyculture/index.htm.

Grajvila, Raul. https://grijalva.house.gov/protecting-the-grand-canyon/.

———. 2016. https://www.sierraclub.org/sierra/2016-4-july-august/last-
words/us-representative-ra-l-grijalva-where-he-found-his-passion-for.

Heinsius, Ryan. "Interior Department Allocates $1.7 Billion for Tribal Water
Rights Settlements". *Arizona Public Radio.* 2022. https://www.knau.org/
knau-and-arizona-news/2022-02-22/interior-department-allocates-1-7-bil
lion-for-tribal-water-rights-settlements.

Javier, Carla. "A Timeline of the Year of Resistance at Standing Rock".
Splinter News. 2016. https://splinternews.com/a-timeline-of-the-year-of-res
istance-at-standing-rock-1794269727.

Joyce, Kathryn. 2007. https://highline.huffingtonpost.com/articles/en/park-
rangers/.

———. 2018. https://www.outsideonline.com/2334781/forest-service-silenc
ing-women-harassment-discrimination?utm_source=facebook&utm_medium=
social&utm_campaign=facebookpos.

Kaufman, Rachel. "Water Crisis in the West." 2018.
library.cqpress.com/cqresearcher/document.php?id=cqresrre2018051100.

Kerklivet, Joe. 2017. https://www.journals.uchicago.edu/doi/10.1093/reep/
rex026

Kerns, Keegan. "Secretary Deb Haaland's Appointment to the Cabinet
Earlier This Year Provides Important Representation for Native Americans." *Enspire.* 2019. https://enspiremag.com/2021/11/deb-haaland-pro
vides-important-representation-as-secretary-of-the-interior/.

Lindwell, Courtney. "The Unlikely Takedown of Keystone XL". *NRDC*. June 29, 2021. https://www.nrdc.org/stories/unlikely-takedown-keystone-xl.

Loomis, John. 1993. https://www.amazon.com/Integrated-Public-Lands-Man agement-Loomis/dp/0231124449/ref=sr_1_1?crid=2BAE4SB4AJYME&key words=loomis+bureau+of+land+management&qid=1668784613&sprefix=loo mis+bureau+of+land+managemen%2Caps%2C112&sr=8-1.

McKinnon, Taylor. *New Scientist* 210, no. 2807 (September 4, 2011): 28–29, 2 p.

Miller, Kathryn. "Legal Developments in the ESA Status of the Grizzly Bear." 2017. http://wildlife.org/legal-developments-in-the-esa-status-of-the-grizzly-bear/.

Morton, Victor. "Judge Brian Morris Blocks Keystone Pipeline." *Washington Times*. November 8, 2018. https://www.washingtontimes.com/news/ 2018/nov/8/judge-brian-morris-blocks-keystone-pipeline/#:~:text=Judge% 20Brian%20Morris%20blocks%20Keystone%20pipeline%20-%20Washing ton,administration%20hadn%27t%20justified%20changing%20President%20O bama%27s%20earlier%20rulings.

National Indian Gaming Association (NIGA). "National Indian Gaming Asso- ciation Applauds Biden Nomination of Deb Haaland as DOI Secretary." 2021. http://www.indiangaming.org/news/national-indian-gaming-associ ation-applauds-biden-nomination-of-deb-haaland-as-doi-secretary#:~:text= Haaland%20began%20her%20career%20in%20politics%20as%20a,as%20Chair% 20of%20the%20New%20Mexico%20Democratic%20Party.

National Interagency Coordination Center. "Wildland Fire Summary and Statis- tics Annual Report 2021." 2021. https://www.predictiveservices.nifc.gov/int elligence/2021_statssumm/intro_summary21.pdf.

National Park Service. "Grizzly Bears & the Endangered Species Ac." 2020. https://www.nps.gov/yell/learn/nature/bearesa.htm.

Outside Editors. "A Timeline of President Trump's War on Public Lands." https://www.outsideonline.com/2277446/public-lands-war-timeline.

Partners for Collaboration. 2018. https://www.partnersforconservation.org/les sons-learned-from-the-greater-sage-grouse-collaboration/.

QUOCTRUNG BUI and MARGOT SANGER-KATZ. "Why the Government Owns So Much Land in the West." *The New York Times*. January 6, 2016 Wednesday. Retrieved from Nexis Uni.

Rinfret, Sara, Scheberle, Denise, and Michelle Pautz. *Public Policy: A Concise Introduction*. CQ Press, 2018.

Shannon, Noah Gallagher. 2018. https://www.nytimes.com/2018/07/19/mag azine/the-water-wars-of-arizona.html?smid=fb-nytimes&smtyp=cur.

Shivaram, Deepa. "Biden Restores Protections for Bears Ears Monument, 4 Years After Trump Downsized It." October 8, 2021. https://www.npr.org/2021/ 10/07/1044039889/bears-ears-monument-protection-restored-biden.

Shogren, Elizabeth. https://www.wired.com/2017/01/obamas-energy-legacy-west-outlast-trump-administration/.

Stone, Christopher. "Should Trees Have Standing? Towards Legal Rights for National Objects." Southern California Law Review 45 (1972): 450–501.

Tyson, A., C. Funk, and B. Kennedy. "Americans Largely Favor US Taking Steps to Become Carbon Neutral by 2050". Pew Research Center. March 1, 2022. https://www.pewresearch.org/science/2022/03/01/americans-lar gely-favor-u-s-taking-steps-to-become-carbon-neutral-by-2050/.

US Department of Interior. Public Lands Explained. 2016. https://www.doi. gov/blog/americas-public-lands-explained.

———. Livestock Grazing. 2018. https://www.blm.gov/programs/natural-res ources/rangelands-and-grazing/livestock-grazing.

———. Deb Haaland. 2021. https://www.doi.gov/deb-haaland.

US Energy Information Administration. 2017. https://www.eia.gov/

US Forest Service. The Agriculture Improvement Act of 2018 (2018 Farm Bill). 2018. https://www.fs.usda.gov/managing-land/farm-bill.

———. Shared Stewardship. 2021. https://www.fs.usda.gov/working with us/ shared-stewardship.

Vogelsong, Sarah. "Federal Court Again Yanks Two Mountain Valley Pipeline Approvals." Virginia Mercury. January 25, 2022. https://www.virginiam ercury.com/2022/01/25/federal-court-again-yanks-two-mountain-valley-pip eline-approvals/.

Weigel, Lori. 2017. https://www.coloradocollege.edu/other/stateoftherockies/ conservationinthewest/2018/release/18002%202018%20SOR%20Poll%20P resentation%20FINAL.pdf.

"What Is the New West versus the Old West Economy?" https://newwest.net/ city/article/what_is_a_new_west_vs_old_west_economy/C396/L396/.

CHAPTER 10

The Politics and Policies of Food

> **Introductory Story: A Partnership to Address Food Deserts in West Virginia**
>
> Across the US, people face food insecurity every day because they do not know where or when they will get their next meal. Compounding factors of geographic location, income, and access to transportation impact a person's ability to find food (Dutko et al. 2012). Areas of the country where people have limited access to healthy and affordable food, particularly fruits and vegetables, are called food deserts. In 2021, 13.5 million people were reported to be living in food deserts according to census data (USDA 2021d). Often, food deserts are thought of as rural areas where people might have to travel hours to get to the nearest grocery store. But this problem exists in urban areas too, particularly in low-income and minority communities where people might have access to a convenience store, but the food is predominantly processed and packaged options that lack essential nutrients (Dutko et al. 2012). In addition, with less options for stores nearby, food prices can be very high.
>
> In 2018, a network of students at West Virginia University (WVU) within the Business School's Supply Chain Management program set out to tackle the problem of food deserts in their state. Through a partnership with Grow Ohio Valley (GrowOV), a nonprofit focused on building a local food system with farming operations across the city, the two groups

© The Author(s), under exclusive license to Springer Nature Switzerland AG 2023
S. R. Rinfret and M. C. Pautz, *US Environmental Policy in Action*,
https://doi.org/10.1007/978-3-031-17503-9_10

launched a project to open a market within a transportation terminal in the City of Wheeling, West Virginia (Gregg 2018). Wheeling was once bustling from the coal and steel industries but has experienced years of disinvestment and a declining economy (Board 2014). The location for the Public Market was right in the middle of a food desert in downtown Wheeling with convenient access to public transportation (GrowOV 2021). The students from WVU utilized their supply chain knowledge to set up the materials handling, production processes, demand management, retail offerings, and information management system, to get this project off the ground and ready to run year-round to serve the community (Gregg 2018).

Since the initial startup of the Public Market, GrowOV has tackled initiatives to invest in the community and increase access to affordable, fresh food. One important change was to adopt a policy for people utilizing the Supplemental Nutrition Assistance Program (SNAP) to receive fifty percent off their purchases (GrowOV 2021). Also, in an effort to increase access outside of Wheeling, the nonprofit started a mobile markets and farm stands program to travel to communities needing convenient, healthy food (GrowOV 2021).

The City of Wheeling and the larger area that GrowOV serves is one of the successful stories of transforming a local food system. Many communities across the US face similar issues with a decline in economic activity, low-income residents, lack of access to transportation, and most importantly, few opportunities for healthy food. These problems are not always an easy fix and require whole system approaches. Shifting to locally owned food systems, like the example here, could solve many problems in the US, but as you will read in this chapter, the agricultural sector is complicated.

On first glance, a chapter on food may seem out of place in a book devoted to environmental policy, but a closer examination quickly reveals how intertwined food is with the environment. The health and the well-being of the natural environment are critical for the production of food that humans need to grow and flourish—indeed, the two are inextricably linked. Growing and producing food humans need impacts the environment, often in a negative way due to modern agricultural practice (e.g., use of fertilizers and non-point-source pollution). Accordingly, this chapter will investigate the intersection of environmental concerns with the food system in the US. To do so, we start at the foundation and examine what we mean by food policy and politics, and then, we discuss the agricultural sector in the US to not only understand the direct effects on the environment but also to get a sense of the scope and scale of agriculture. From there, we explore patterns of food consumption, nutrition, and public health so that we can grapple with food safety and nutrition assistance. The final section of the chapter turns our attention to culture and food as the role of the public is instrumental in investigating food policy.

Food Policy and Politics

Food policy refers to the decisions and actions surrounding food taken by, or instigated by the government. These steps may include laws, regulations, and actions by government agencies that affect the growth, production, distribution, and consumption of food. Often, these decisions incorporate political, economic, and cultural dimensions. Food politics is a term that incorporates the dilemmas and tensions associated with these decisions about food, and to paraphrase Theodore Lowi, food politics is about who gets what, when, and how regarding food. Both food policies and food politics encompass the food industry, which includes all the organizations and "...companies that produce, process, manufacture, sell, and serve food, beverages, and dietary supplements" (Nestle 2002, 11).

The size and scale of the food industry in the US are massive. Just over half of one percent of the nation's Gross Domestic Product (GDP) comes from the output of American farms, or about $134.7 billion annually (USDA 2022b). According to the U.S. Department of Agriculture, the food service industry prior to the Covid-19 pandemic, which encapsulates restaurants and operations that sell or provide food, as worth approximately $1.79 trillion dollars (USDA 2022a). After the onset of the pandemic, that sector, however, saw steep declines (USDA 2022a). Nearly 20 million jobs, both full-time and part-time, come from the agriculture and food sectors, representing about ten percent of total US employment (USDA 2022b). Americans spend about 12% of their household budgets on food, which is lower than the majority of nations in the world (USDA 2022b, Bosso and Tichenor 2015). In other words, most Americans spend a much smaller portion of their money on food than people in other nations, indicating that food is comparatively cheap for Americans. At the beginning of the 1900s, Americans spent around 40 percent of their budgets on food, indicating that food was nearly four times as expensive then as it is today (Paarlberg 36). Furthermore, crops and food products play a major role in the nation's trade, both imports and exports. The economic dimensions of the food system in the US should be sufficient to compel attention to this complex policy area, but with our primary focus on the natural environment, the connections to the environment are significant.

Connections Between Food and Environmental Issues

The environment plays a central role in the nation's food system because without the physical environment—meaning the air, water, and land—we would not be able to grow crops. Without the health of grasslands, corn would not grow, which is a common part of animal diets and the key ingredient in many processed foods. And the impacts of agricultural practices on the environment are significant; approximately seven percent of the greenhouse gas emissions in the US come from agriculture, and this does not include the emissions that result from the processing, transportation, and distribution of the food products (Wilde 48). This means that growing and producing food has a substantial impact on the climate change. Additionally, runoff from agricultural fields is a major contributor to non-point-source pollution. As we will see in the coming pages, the centrality of the environment in food policy and politics is very clear, and examination of environmental issues has to involve food politics and policy.

THE AGRICULTURAL SECTOR IN THE US: ITS SIZE, SCOPE, AND ENVIRONMENTAL IMPACT

Discussions of farming and its role in society often gravitate to idyllic notions of a farmer and his family working hard on their small plot of land to grow crops and raise animals. Although there are still small farms throughout the nation, most farming is tied to the enormous agriculture industry and small farms are often tied to large corporations. Therefore, to explore the agricultural sector in the US and grapple with its connections with the environment, we start by considering the scope of the sector and farming in the nation.

The majority of farms today are large operations that employ the latest technologies to cultivate the crops we eat. The U.S. Department of Agriculture reports that in 2020 there were just over two million farms nationwide (USDA 2021, 4). By way of comparison, in 1935, there were about six and a half million farms in the US (Bosso and Tichenor

2015). Approximately 896 million acres are farmed in the US with the average farm more than 444 acres (USDA 2021, 4). As the number of farms has been declining steadily for years, the average size of farms has grown (USDA 2021, 7). Around four percent of farms account for two-thirds of farm products in the market; in other words, a small handful of farms produce about two-thirds of the agricultural products (Bosso and Tichenor 2015). These figures offer the evidence that small, family run farms are not the principle type of farm used to produce the nation's food. Moreover, these large farms do not necessarily employ legions of workers to run as technology is increasingly relied on in agriculture. Around one percent of the American workforce today is involved in farming whereas in 30 years ago that figure was about three percent, down dramatically from 50 percent in 1870 (Paarlberg 3).

There are many different ways to categorize farms, including by area of the country, type of farm, or industry group. The Heartland, as labeled by the U.S. Department of Agriculture, comprises Iowa, Illinois, Indiana, and Missouri and it is the most productive region of the nation for farming. Broadly, there are two major types of farms: farms that produce crops (e.g., grains, feed for animals, vegetables) and farms that produce livestock (e.g., dairy, poultry, cattle). In terms of value, the biggest sectors are in cash grains and soybeans and other high value crops, like fruits and vegetables (Park et al. 2011, 10). Figure 10.1 breaks down farm income by commodity.

Another way to consider the different types of farms is by industry groups: grain and oilseeds, fruits and vegetables, cattle, dairy, and hogs, poultry, and eggs. Grain and oilseeds include corn, which is most often used for animal feed, and soybeans which is also used in animal feed, vegetable oil, and manufactured foods. This is the industry sector that receives the largest share of farm subsidies and most of the production in this sector comes from America's Heartland (Wilde 18–19). Fruits and vegetables represent the smallest percentage of farmland in the US, but the harvest is very valuable. This sector includes crops such as grapes, oranges, apples, almost, strawberries, lettuce, and potatoes. Most of these crops come from California and Arizona, along with Idaho for potatoes. The cattle sector is found in areas in the western US where the land is not as ideal for growing crops, but land is plentiful since raising cows requires a lot of land—indeed, 40 percent of the agricultural land in the country is used for cattle (Wilde 20). There are two primary types of cattle farm: farms where cows are born and farms called feedlots, where cows

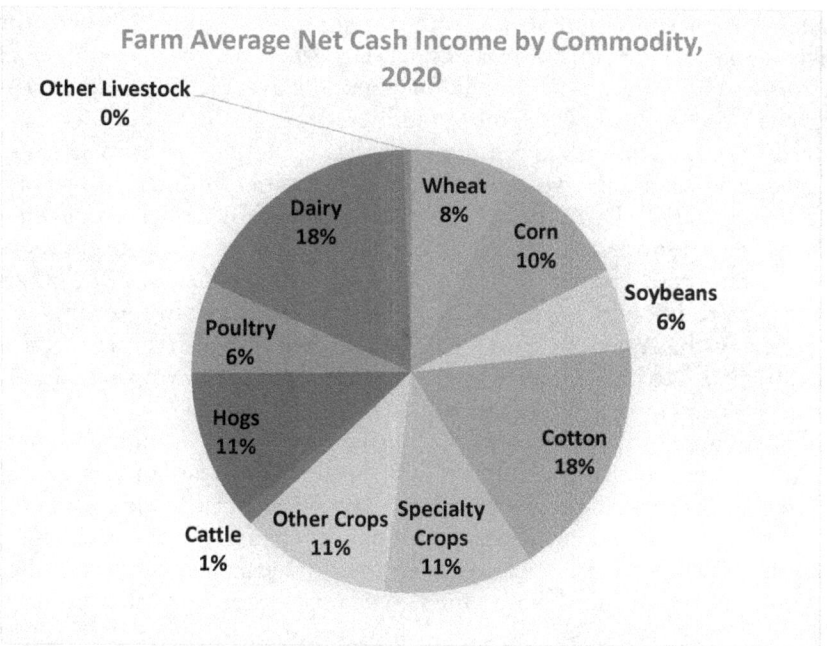

Fig. 10.1 US Net Farm Income by Farm Production Specialty (*Source* Adapted from USDA Economic Research Service, Farm Business Average Net Cash Income Data. Accessed 29 March 2022. https://data.ers.usda.gov/reports.aspx? ID=17840)

are fattened up for slaughter. Dairy farms are found mostly in Wisconsin, Minnesota, and New York (Wilde 20). The primary function of this sector is to turn animal products into cheese, milk, and butter. Finally, the hogs, poultry, and eggs sector is largely found in the Heartland, but North Carolina has seen dramatic growth in this sector. This agricultural sector in particular has seen increasing control by large corporations and food manufacturers, such as Tyson, Smithfield, and Perdue. And this sector has experienced rapid technological innovations in recent decades.

Much more could be said about the modern agricultural sector in the US today, but in keeping with our focus on the intersection of food and environmental policy, this brief overview enables us to grasp the scale of the sector and recognize that farming in reality may not comport with the images we have about farming. To that end, consider some of the summary points Bosso and Tichenor (2015) offer about today's agricultural sector: efficiency, specialization, technologized, energy dependent, and globalized. Agriculture is well developed, harnessing technological innovations to enable it to efficiently and economically produce for its customers. These improvements in farming have enabled Americans to see the portion of their budgets they have to spend on food drop dramatically. However, the effects of agriculture and food production on the natural environment are significant. In fact, in some areas, agriculture is the biggest contributor to environmental degradation, from non-point-source pollution to methane emissions from farms. And this sector of the economy uses a lot of energy.

Environmental Impacts of Agriculture

The sheer size of the agricultural sector alone helps us start to grasp the potential environmental impact of this sector. With approximately 900 million acres utilized for farming in the US, the connection with the natural environment is apparent. More specifically, food production impacts the following environmental resources: water, air, land and soil quality, and native species. The use of chemicals and the generation of waste have additional environmental implications. Agriculture uses more than 70 percent of the planet's freshwater—and more than 90 percent in some areas of the western US (Anderson 2015, 59). More specifically, the agricultural activities that impact water quality include: tillage and plowing, fertilization, spreading manure, raising animals in feedlots, applying pesticides, irrigating, and aquaculture. Much of the contamination of groundwater and surface water is a result of agriculture (Anderson 61).

As we have seen in previous chapters, the US has an array of laws that deal with water quality. The Clean Water Act addresses point-source pollution, which means water contamination that is attributable to particular source (e.g., a pipe draining into a waterway). When it comes to agriculture, though, the water contamination issues stem from runoff, which is a non-point-source of pollution. This means it is difficult to pinpoint a specific pollutant and level of contamination from an individual source; therefore, it can be difficult to use the Clean Water Act to address water quality concerns from agriculture (Angelo and Choate 2013). The primary means the CWA addresses water quality is through the issuance of National Pollutant Discharge Elimination Systems (NPDES) permits and agriculture is not subject to these permits. In fact, most agricultural practices are exempt from water quality protections. Runoff from agriculture however can be addressed through Total Maximum Daily Loads (TMDLs) that are established for a given waterway, but TMDLs only specify how much of a particular pollutant a waterway can handle and then requires states to take action to meet water quality standards. This is not to imply that there are no government efforts addressing water quality concerns and runoff from agriculture, however. Various provisions of the farm bill provide subsidies for farmers to restore habitats, prevent erosion, and utilize best management practices for addressing runoff.

Air quality is another concern when it comes to agriculture. In 2019, ten percent of all US greenhouse gas emissions were attributable to agriculture (EPA 2021). Worldwide, farming accounts for about 18.4 percent of all GHGs (Ritchie 2020). Livestock production, along with farming equipment, generates significant amounts of air pollution. Additionally, application of fertilizers can contribute to air pollution along with the release of particular matter into the atmosphere from soil tiling and erosion. Confined Animal Feeding Operations (CAFOs) are a concentrated source of air pollutants, generated from animal waste, that range from ammonia, hydrogen sulfide, particulate matter, volatile organic compounds (VOCs), hazardous air pollutants (HAPs), and odor. The Clean Air Act regulates these pollutants, but most of the regulations focus on "major" sources of air pollution and often, farms, even large industrial ones, do not meet the threshold standards for major sources, according to the US EPA (Clemmer 2013, 163).

Although the EPA has been somewhat reluctant to regulate farms as stringently as other industries under the Clean Air Act, some states have taken steps to address air pollution from agriculture (Clemmer 176). A handful of states, including Colorado, Missouri, and Illinois, have implemented odor standards for factory farms and some have also specified construction standards as well as operational requirements (Clemmer 181). The EPA continues to face pressure to regulate more stringently factory farms that have been exempted from air laws (and the Emergency Planning and Right-to-Know Act as well) as part of a consent agreement in place since the George W. Bush administration.

Growing crops and raising livestock can degrade the land's quality. Soil degradation can come from a range of agricultural activities from deforestation and tilling to excessive vehicle and equipment traffic, too much irrigation, and application of fertilizers. The use of chemicals in farming can fall under the Federal Insecticide, Fungicide, and Rodenticide Act, but FIFRA only applies to the manufacturing of chemicals and not their use or application on land. Further, animal waste can pose a significant environmental impact, particularly massive amounts of waste in Confined Animal Feeding Operations (CAFOs). However, unlike waste we generate in our households and hazardous wastes, there are not environmental statutes that tackle mountains of animal manure, for example, and address the environmental impacts of its generation. Agriculture and food production have effects on every facet of the natural environment and contribute to the majority of environmental issues we contend with today, from climate change to biodiversity loss.

There are a number of ways that the government is involved with agriculture that do not directly pertain to environmental concerns. The nation has long provided price supports for farmers and their crops (e.g., subsidies) and helped to control the supply in order to make farming feasible for those in the industry and make food affordable. The federal government has also been very involved in providing insurance to farmers as their livelihoods are often at the mercy of weather patterns and pests.

A number of additional pieces of legislation that merit mention here as they pertain to agriculture, which can impact the environment. The farm bill,[1] which is the term for a collection of laws passed by Congress every five or so years, deals with many facets of agriculture. The first farm bill was first passed in 1933 and called the Agriculture Adjustment Act as part of Franklin D. Roosevelt's New Deal. The farm bill covers a range of agricultural issues from subsidies for the industry to research to international trade and environmental conservation. Up until recent years, the passage of the farm bill has been largely noncontroversial and enjoyed bipartisan support—after all, the nation thinks well of its idyllic farms. The farm bill has engendered controversy in recent iterations as provisions were included to make changes to the food stamp program (more on that program is in the next section) as well as the sheer size of the bill and its cost. The last farm bill, the Agriculture Improvement Act, was passed in 2018 and runs through 2023 (c.f. Blevins 2021).

---

[1] Various names have been used for specific farm bills, including the Food, Conservation, and Energy Act of 2008 or the Agricultural Adjustment Act of 1938. The term "farm bill" refers to a category of legislation that is the primary means of federal government policy surrounding agriculture and food.

Besides the farm bills, a number of laws have been passed that may not seem directly relevant, but do have implications for the agricultural sector. The 2007 Energy Independence and Security Act may not seem relevant to farming, but a provision in this law has major implications for the industry. The law, which was passed during the George W. Bush administration, was an effort to make the US more reliant on domestic sources of energy rather than relying on energy imported from around the world, including volatile places such as the Middle East. Part of the law promotes alternative energy sources other than fossil fuels and requires the increased use of ethanol, which is made from corn, which has agricultural and environmental implications. While ethanol is a fuel source that is not a traditional fossil fuel, it requires a lot of fossil fuels to produce. Corn farmers are understandably thrilled with mandates for a larger share of the nation's energy to come from their product, but many other interests are less enthusiastic, from environmentalists to the renewable energy sector.

In response to the outbreak of Covid-19, a number of relief bills were also passed, including the Coronavirus Aid, Relief, and Economic Security (CARES) Act and in the American Rescue Plan Act of 2021. The CARES Act allocated nearly $50 billion for the agriculture and food industries through small business loans, increases in food assistance programs, among other efforts. And over $10 billion was allocated in the American Rescue Plan to strengthen agriculture and the food supply chain, including purchasing and distributing commodities and assistance to farmers through direct payments and loan forgiveness.

Agricultural practices can have significant impacts on the environment, notably pertaining to air quality, water quality, land quality, and the generation of waste. Most environmental laws in the US do not address agricultural practices and their impact on the environment directly, and as mentioned previously, much of the sector is exempt from environmental regulatory provisions. Regardless of one's perspective on farming, it is important to recognize there is a direct and substantial impact on the environment, but addressing those concerns are not easy given the centrality of food to human well-being. These considerations do not address the environmental impacts that result from transportation crops and animals nor do they address the environmental inputs needed to process and manufacture the food products that we buy, cook, and consumed daily.

FOOD CONSUMPTION, NUTRITION, AND PUBLIC HEALTH

The evolution of agriculture in the US and the increased mechanization of it supported urbanization, thereby contributing to a host of environmental issues as the population shifted. No longer did people have to spend most of their time growing and preparing food to survive as those activities could be done by a smaller and smaller percentage of the population more efficiently and economically. With American involvement in both world wars, more and more people left agricultural fields for other types of work, so foods that were convenient were increasingly necessary. Women entered the workforce in large numbers during World War II in particular and this led to the rise of Betty Crocker's cake mixes and Swanson's TV dinners (Wilde 87). Food had to be more convenient and have a longer shelf life. And these changes had major implications for agricultural practices, nutrition and health, and the environment. Accordingly, the food system in the US grew in size and complexity and while it became more convenient for people as less time was required to prepare food, important health and environmental implications resulted from these changes in consumption patterns. And these implications help explain the role of government in these topics. As we will see in this section, the role of government—from legislation to rulemaking and implementation—is significant and complex.

Dietary Guidance from the Government

In the US, and elsewhere, there is widespread public confusion about nutrition and the government plays a role in all of this. But we do know that in the US, Americans are eating more calories than they did generations ago. Forty years ago, Americans averaged around 1875 cal per day and that figure has climbed to nearly 2100 cal (Moshfegh 2015, 379). And more of those calories are coming from carbohydrates while we consume less calories from fats.

The US government has long been concerned with nutrition and dietary guidance. In 1862, the U.S. Department of Agriculture was created to ensure a sufficient and reliable food supply and to provide information to the nation on agricultural matters (Nestle 2002, 33). By the early 1900s, the government became particularly worried about nutritional deficiencies and the disorders that resulted. The USDA issued its first dietary recommendations in 1917 in a 14-page booklet entitled *How to Select Foods* and offered five food groups during the 1920s (Nestle 34). In the following decade, the USDA identified some "protective" foods that offered important vitamins and nutrients. Then, in 1941, the Food and Nutrition Board offered Recommended Dietary Allowances. The four basic food groups—milk, meat, fruits and vegetables, and breads and cereals—were introduced in the 1950s along with recommended dietary allowances for each group. The 1960s saw the government make its first statements that some foods might be "bad" or "unwise"; these included foods that were high in fat, cholesterol, salt, sugar, and calories.

Since the 1970s, the federal government has regularly updated its dietary guidance for Americans. In 1977, the *Dietary Goals for the US* encouraged increased consumption of carbohydrates but decreased consumption of fats. This guidance was greeted with outrage from various sectors, including cattle ranchers, dairy farmers, and egg producers among others, because they viewed the government's guidance as telling Americans that their products were bad. Similar politics were involved in the guidance released in 1980. The *Dietary Guidelines for Americans* recommended that people eat a variety of foods, maintain their ideal weight, and avoid too much fat, cholesterol, sugar, and sodium. Initially, these guidelines included phrases such as "eat less" but that wording was not politically palatable, so language was amended to encourage Americans to avoid too much (Nestle 2002, 46). Revisions to these guidelines and wordsmithing continued throughout the 1980s.

It was during the aforementioned decade that work began on a symbol of healthy eating that you are probably familiar with: the food pyramid (see Fig. 10.2).

First released in 1991, and updated several times since then, the food pyramid reflected the government's efforts to encourage healthy eating by helping Americans make sense of all the messages around nutrition and health guidance. Controversy surrounded the release of the pyramid because various food producers were upset that the government would seemingly convey an endorsement of certain food sectors over others. So, in 1992, a revised *Food Guide Pyramid* was released by the USDA. Language was changed to appease the food industry, especially Kraft Foods, and "eating right" became "food guide" (Nestle 2002, 64). Instead of telling Americans to eat two to three servings of a particular food category, the language was updated to say "at least" two to three servings. More updates followed about every five years.

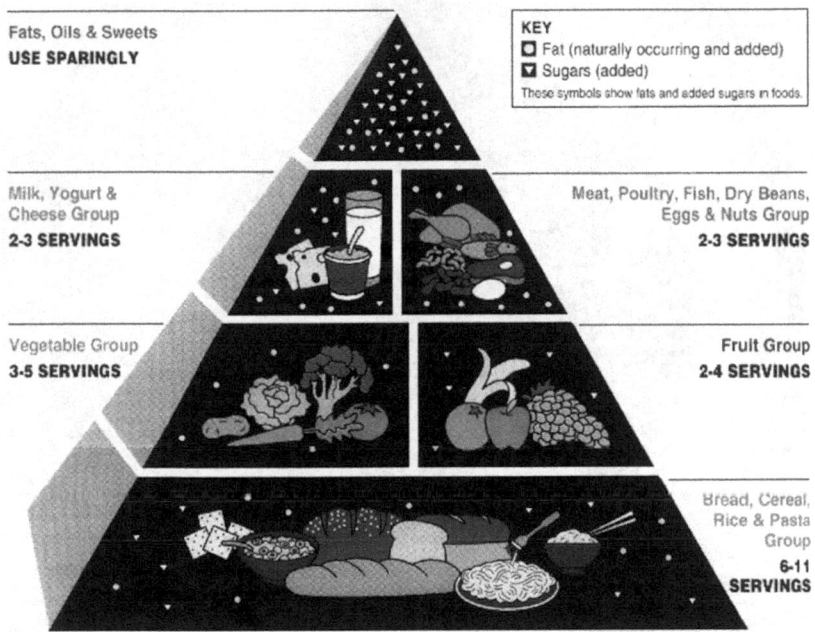

Fig. 10.2 Food guide pyramid (*Source* https://www.cnpp.usda.gov/food-guide-pyramid-graphic-resources)

Alas, in 2011, the Pyramid was replaced by MyPlate (see Fig. 10.3). The MyPlate initiative from the USDA was an effort to convey better nutrition information in a more visually appealing manner—via a place setting. According to the USDA, "MyPlate is designed to remind Americans to eat healthfully, and is not intended to change consumer behavior alone" (USDA 2018a). Note the careful language from the agency about its aim; undoubtedly, the language was deliberate in an effort to be mindful of past controversies around federal government nutrition and dietary guidance.

This is unlikely to be the federal government's last effort in providing dietary and nutrition guidance, especially given the government's interest in the overall health of the general public.

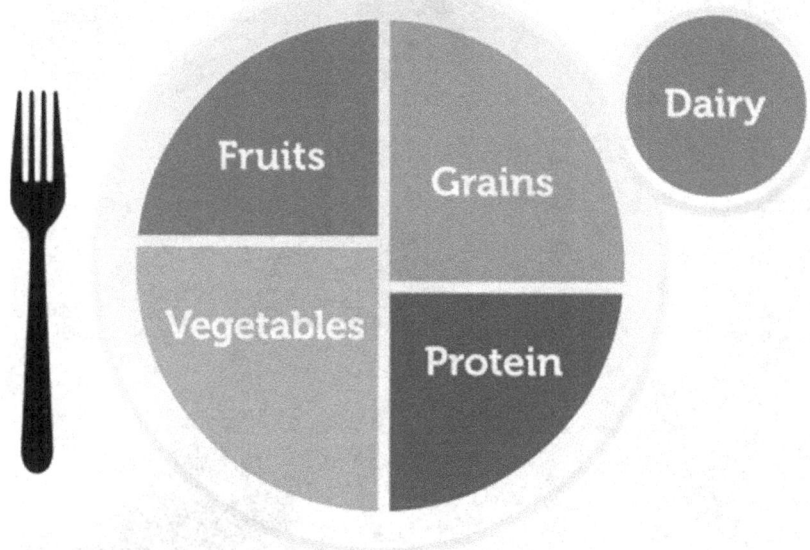

Fig. 10.3   MyPlate (https://www.myplate.gov/)

Public Health

At this point, you might be wondering why the government would even engage in such efforts surrounding dietary guidance if it raises so much ire from the food industry. These efforts stem from concern over the health of Americans. During the first part of the twentieth century, the government was very concerned about malnutrition and conditions that resulted from nutrient deficiencies. These worries grew as the government had challenges recruiting people for the military. Today, the concern is less about lack of nutrients and more about the excessive intake of food as diet is linked to four of the top ten leading causes of death in the US (heart disease, cancer, stroke, and diabetes) (Paarlberg 81–82). Thirty-six percent of American adults were obese in 2010, which is double the percentage from 1971 (Paarlberg 82). By 2018, that figure grew to 42.4 percent (CDC 2021a). More than two-thirds of Americans are either overweight or obese (NIDDK 2018).

Another mechanism that the government employs to encourage healthy food choices is food labeling. Various pieces of legislation—and subsequent rulemaking—require country-of-origin labeling and the listing of potential allergens. The Nutrition Facts Panel, or the nutrition information label, adorns most packaged food in the US to help Americans understand what is in the food they are eating. The first labels of this kind appeared in 1990 under direction of the U.S. Food and Drug Administration and have undergone a variety of updates. The most recent rules came about in 2016 and include revisions to the serving size to make it a better reflection of how much a person might consume and additional information about any sugars that were added to the food during the production process. Unsurprisingly, there was strong objection to these revisions, particularly the updates about sugar additions (see Fig. 10.4 for the original and revised nutrition label).

Beyond the government's role in providing Americans information about the food they eat and helping clarify the best science of nutrition guidance, the government is also very involved in ensuring the safety of the food we eat and ensuring access to food for those individuals who may otherwise go hungry. The next section investigates government programs and regulations surrounding food safety and hunger.

THE ROLE OF GOVERNMENT IN FOOD SAFETY AND NUTRITION ASSISTANCE

Since the government is concerned about the health and well-being of its citizens, there are two specific policy areas to explore: food safety and nutrition assistance programs.

Food Safety

The federal government estimates that every year, there are approximately 48 million cases of food poisoning or one in every six Americans will become sick from eating contaminated food (Food Safety.gov 2022). Each year, about 128,000 people will be hospitalized because of food-borne illnesses, and approximately 3,000 Americans die every year as a result of contaminated food, resulting in costs of more than $15 billion dollars annually (CDC 2018, 2021b). There are more than 250 food-borne diseases that result from a variety of bacteria, viruses, and pathogens

Nutrition Facts

Serving Size 2/3 cup (55g)
Servings Per Container About 8

Amount Per Serving

Calories 230   Calories from Fat 40

	% Daily Value*
Total Fat 8g	**12%**
Saturated Fat 1g	**5%**
Trans Fat 0g	
Cholesterol 0mg	**0%**
Sodium 160mg	**7%**
Total Carbohydrate 37g	**12%**
Dietary Fiber 4g	**16%**
Sugars 1g	
Protein 3g	

Vitamin A	10%
Vitamin C	8%
Calcium	20%
Iron	45%

* Percent Daily Values are based on a 2,000 calorie diet.
Your daily value may be higher or lower depending on
your calorie needs.

	Calories:	2,000	2,500
Total Fat	Less than	65g	80g
Sat Fat	Less than	20g	25g
Cholesterol	Less than	300mg	300mg
Sodium	Less than	2,400mg	2,400mg
Total Carbohydrate		300g	375g
Dietary Fiber		25g	30g

Nutrition Facts

8 servings per container
Serving size   2/3 cup (55g)

Amount per serving

Calories   230

	% Daily Value*
Total Fat 8g	**10%**
Saturated Fat 1g	**5%**
Trans Fat 0g	
Cholesterol 0mg	**0%**
Sodium 160mg	**7%**
Total Carbohydrate 37g	**13%**
Dietary Fiber 4g	**14%**
Total Sugars 12g	
Includes 10g Added Sugars	**20%**
Protein 3g	

Vitamin D 2mcg	10%
Calcium 260mg	20%
Iron 8mg	45%
Potassium 235mg	6%

* The % Daily Value (DV) tells you how much a nutrient in
a serving of food contributes to a daily diet. 2,000 calories
a day is used for general nutrition advice.

Fig. 10.4 Original and revised nutrition labels (*Source* https://en.wikipedia.org/wiki/Nutrition_facts_label)

including *salmonella, listeria, clostridium perfringens,* and *e. coli.* It is difficult to monitor and measure the exact figures since most Americans have likely experienced some form of food poisoning and they may or may not have sought professional medical care and had their illness tracked. It is also complicated by a web of actors who are involved in food safety from growers and producers to local health departments and medical professionals to the CDC and USDA.

In today's world, food is far safer with than it used to be even a century ago as sanitary practices, safer packaging, and refrigeration are mainstays of food production and consumption. But as the statistics above indicate, food contamination is still common as food can be contaminated at numerous points from production and transportation to cooking and consumption. In the production process, contaminants can be introduced in slaughterhouses, through insufficient manufacturing processes and monitoring and the adulteration processes of many manufactured foods, and even in agricultural fields. Common sources of contamination in food preparation include unwashed hands and cutting boards as well as poor refrigeration and insufficiently cooked meats. The US Department of Health and Human Services (DHHS) maintains a website (http://www.foodsafety.gov) in which current recalls and food safety alerts are updated continuously. At the time of writing, a review of this site indicates recalls on "Happy Face Cookies," peanut butter, dried sweetened strawberries, enoki mushrooms, and buttermilk pancake and waffle mix. Most of these recalls garner little converge in the news media, but there are notable examples of major, nationwide recalls. In 2022, over 160,000 pounds of Skippy Peanut Butter was recalled because of steel pieces in it. A number of different prepackaged salads prompted recalls in 2021 over *listeria* contamination which led to a handful of deaths. In 2009, the Peanut Corporation of America recalled more than 2100 products made by 200 companies in 43 states because of tainted peanuts. Nestle recalled 300,000 cases of premade cookie dough in the same year because of *e. coli*. In 2008, Hallmark Beef recalled 143 million pounds of beef and Cargill pulled 36 million pounds of ground turkey in 2011. The FDA maintains an active Twitter presence informing the public of the latest food safety recalls (among other means of notifying the public).

The government has a long history of trying to mitigate these episodes and there are some notable pieces of federal legislation that address food safety. In 1906, the Pure Food and Drug Act was the first of its kind and required accurate labeling of food and drug products and created the Food and Drug Administration. During the same year, the Meat Inspection Act was passed focusing on the processing of meat. Mandatory factory inspections by the government came in 1938 with the Federal, Food, Drug, and Cosmetic Act after more than 100 people were killed from a toxic product. The 2004 Food Allergy Labeling and Consumer Protection Act requires foods to be labeled if they contain or may contain common allergens. And the Food Safety Modernization Act passed in 2010 gives the FDA additional authority to regulate how foods are grown and processed, and came about after many of the food safety recalls mentioned earlier. This was the first major legislation since 1938 to address food safety.

To implement these laws and ensure the safety of the nation's food supply, numerous government agencies are involved at multiple levels of government. At the federal level, the Department of Health and Human Services houses the Food and Drug Administration and the Centers for Disease Control. The FDA is primarily responsible for the safety of most food products, with the exception of meat, poultry, and processed eggs. And the CDC monitors and investigates foodborne illnesses. The U.S. Department of Agriculture (USDA) includes the Food Safety Inspection Service (FSIS), the Animal Plant Health Inspection Service, and the Agricultural Marketing Service. The FSIS is responsible for the safety of meat, poultry, and processed eggs. Here, it is important to underscore that two major and distinct federal agencies are responsible for food safety and each agency—the USDA and DHHS—has a very different mission from the other. The Agricultural Marketing Service establishes the quality and marketing grades and standards for dairy products, fruits, vegetables, and meats. In addition to these agencies, the EPA is involved in food safety as it regulates the pesticides that are used in agriculture and the National Oceanographic and Atmospheric Administration within the U.S. Department of Commerce oversees the voluntary seafood safety and quality inspection services. And US Customs and Border Protection within the Department of Homeland Security inspects food products that are imported from other countries. In addition to the work of these federal-level agencies, state and local government agencies are involved, especially public health entities. Needless to say, there are a lot of organizations involved just from the government side of food safety without even enumerating the food manufacturers, retailers, associations, and interest groups that are also concerned with food safety.

Hunger and Food Insecurity

With all of this investigation of food and worry about keeping it safe, it is imperative to note that significant numbers of Americans suffer from hunger and food insecurity. Hunger can be defined as "the uneasy or painful sensation caused by a lack of food," according to the Life Sciences Research Office of the Federation of American Societies for Experimental Biology (as quoted in Christaldi and Castellanos 2018, 16). And hunger is often used to reference chronic undernutrition, which is the long-term condition that includes deficiencies in diet (Paarlberg 31).

Food insecurity, according to the USDA, encompasses "households [that] were uncertain of having, or unable to acquire, enough food to meet the needs of all their members because they had insufficient money or other resources for food" (USDA 2018b). Among those households that are food insecure, there are additional delineations of low food security and very low food insecurity. In 2020, 10.5 percent of American households, or 13.8 million households, were food insecure, which is roughly the same figure from the previous year (USDA 2021c). Put differently, 38.3 million people in the US were food insecure and 6.1 million children live in food insecure households (USDA 2021c). The consequences of food insecurity can be profound, including adverse psychosocial and health effects (Christaldi and Castellanos 19). Stress, anxiety, and depression are common with food insecurity, and for children, this can mean poor performance in school, higher rates of absenteeism, and altered social skills (Christaldi and Castellanos).

Historically, hunger and food insecurity garnered attention as the nation transitions from an agrarian society to an industrial one. And then during the Great Depression, hunger again became a prominent societal concern and the New Deal included federal government efforts to curb hunger. As the nation became embroiled in World War II, the nation was again focused on hunger as 40 percent of potential draftees were rejected by the military because of malnutrition (Christaldi and Castellanos 17). Later in the twentieth century, a CBS documentary on *Hunger in America* focused the nation's attention on malnutrition when it first aired in May of 1968. Viewers were astonished to see the problem of hunger rampant in their own nation, as many assumed hunger to be a problem that beset other nations, and demanded the government take action to alleviate the issue. Each of these historical circumstances resulted in policy action about hunger, ranging from school food programs that started in the 1940s to nutrition assistance programs in the 1960s. In reviewing this history, it is important to note that American society continues to face challenges ensuring that people have enough to eat and that the food available is nutritious. During this time in American history, the wealth and prominence of the country have continued to grow, but a sizeable portion of Americans still do have reliable access to food, especially as the economic implications of the Covid-19 pandemic persist.

A Spring 2021 Gallup Poll found that concerns about hunger in America are rising. When asked if they worry about hunger and homelessness in the US, 55 percent of respondents to the poll said they worried a great deal, marking the highest point in 20 years of measurement and concern is up dramatically from 35 percent of respondents expressing the same concern in 2004 (Brenan 2021).

Americans' worry about hunger has historically led to a variety of federal government programs to combat hunger. During the Great Depression, the first federal government food assistance program was created, known as food stamps. The program started in the Department of Agriculture and recipients got orange or blue stamps that could be used to buy food and lasted for just a few years. In 1964, the Food Stamp Act was passed by Congress as part of President Lyndon B. Johnson's "War on Poverty." Essentially, the modern food stamp program was a federal aid program run by the Department of Agriculture that helped those individuals and families with no or low incomes buy food with "stamps" or "coupons" at local grocery stores and markets. Since the 1960s, the program has gone through a variety of revisions, including eligibility requirements and the process to determine eligibility. The program has seen varying levels of support and cuts over the decades. Significant changes came in the 1990s when welfare programs, including food stamps, saw alterations including changes in requirements to receive aid and the conversion of the books of stamps to an electronic benefits transfer (EBT) card that looks and acts much like an ATM card. The 2008 farm bill renamed the food stamps program the Supplemental Nutrition Assistance Program (SNAP).

The program is still administered by the Food and Nutrition Service in the U.S. Department of Agriculture today; however, the benefits are distributed to state governments who in turn administer the program within the state. To qualify for SNAP benefits, individuals and households must earn 130 percent or less of the federal poverty limit. This means that an individual with a monthly income less than $1,396 per month or a household of three with a monthly income of $2,379 or less would qualify for SNAP. There are restrictions about what SNAP recipients can and cannot buy with their EBT cards. For example, paper towels and napkins cannot be purchased under SNAP nor can alcoholic beverages.

In 2021, approximately 41.5 million people received SNAP benefits, up slightly from the previous year (SNAP 2022). The average household received $416.72 a month in SNAP benefits (SNAP 2022). Another program that is similar in some ways is the Special Supplemental Nutrition Program for Women, Infants, and Children, better known as WIC. This program provides similar benefits to women who are pregnant and women who have children under the age of five. In 2020, approximately 6.3 million people participated in this program, receiving about $38 a month (Hayes et al. 2021). Like SNAP, WIC is overseen by the USDA but administered through state governments.

The school lunch and breakfast programs represent other government efforts to ensure children have access to food. The National School Lunch Program (NSLP) was created during Harry Truman's administration to provide food for kids and, perhaps more importantly, to help the nation's farmers with their surplus crops. Passed in 1946, the National School Lunch Act was a fascinating compromise between those politicians who were concerned about nutrition and children and those politicians concerned about the state of agriculture in the U.S (Levine 2008, 72). Farmers were experiencing dropping prices and an excess supply of crops and, at the same time, there were growing concerns about childhood nutrition. So the school lunch program was born in an effort to help the agricultural sector by having a customer for their excess crops and to provide some price stability while also providing food to school kids. This explains why the program was then and is still run out of the U.S. Department of Agriculture, rather than health or education-focused agencies. In the 1960s, the school breakfast program was added.

These programs provide free or reduced priced meals to school children. In 2020, school cafeterias served more than 12 million kids under this program, a decrease from recent years attributed to the irregularity of in-person schooling during the pandemic (USDA 2021b). As with the SNAP and WIC programs, the USDA oversees the program, but it is administered at the state level. Schools, both public and private, participate in the program and receive cash subsidies to provide meals to children as well as the ability to obtain food from the USDA Foods program (which distributes agricultural surplus foods). Schools are reimbursed at various rates for the meals they serve; they receive between $2.83 and $3.06 for a reduced priced lunch and between $3.23 and $3.46 for a free lunch. The point here is that a school has to figure out how to serve a meal that meets nutritional guidance set by the government that is also appealing a child that costs just a few dollars! Children whose families have incomes at or below 130 percent of the federal poverty level are eligible for free meals and children whose families have incomes between

185 and 130 percent of the federal poverty level are eligible for meals at reduced prices of no more than forty cents.

In 2010, the Healthy Hunger-Free Kids Act was passed by Congress that reauthorized these programs. For the first time since 1995, the USDA updated the nutritional standards of the meals served in these programs, doubling the amount of fruits and vegetables required—now there is a weekly requirement for a dark green, a red or orange vegetable, and beans and peas. Also required are whole grains and a reduction of sodium and elimination of trans fats from meals. Additional nutritional guidelines came in 2012. These programs were under scrutiny with the Trump administration. In December 2017, the Trump administration announced that it was not going to pursue additional reductions in salt in school lunches that the Obama administration put in place (c.f. Rutledge 2021). In 2022, the Biden administration took actions to undo the reduced nutritional standards from the Trump administration. The USDA released nutritional standards for milk, whole grains, and sodium that give school cafeterias two years to transition to healthier meals from pandemic operations, economic challenges, and prior standards (USDA 2022c). Longer-term nutritional standards are expected to be in place for the 2024–25 academic year. These programs are some of the major avenues that the federal government is involved in reducing hunger and food insecurity in the US.

Worry about the food Americans eat and the access they have to that food has been and will continue to be a concern of the government. And we have seen from the discussion in this section that determining and disseminating nutritional information about food is complex, just as making sure that the food is safe to eat and available to those individuals and families who suffer from food insecurity is as well. The role of government in these pursuits is long-standing and that history brings many actors into the process, making it complex. Not only are there environmental implications to the growing and production of the food we eat, but there are implications for the work of federal, state, and local governments and the other public sector organizations that work alongside the government.

Case Study: Sodium Requirements from the FDA

The Food and Drug Administration (FDA) is responsible for protecting the public health and when it comes to food and drugs, this means setting guidance, standards, and regulations. One topic that has been on the agenda of health agencies in the US for many years is sodium. Sodium is a concern for public health because it can lead to high blood pressure, heart disease, and stroke, which are leading causes of death in the U.S. (FDA 2021b). Because these chronic health diseases are often diet-related, improving nutrition is a top priority for the federal government (FDA 2022a). Americans consume nearly 50 percent more sodium than the federally recommended amount per day for individuals over the age of 14 (FDA 2021b). In addition, the health implications disproportionately affect marginalized populations. Statistics show that four in ten American adults have high blood pressure and that increases to six in ten for non-Hispanic Black adults (FDA 2021b). The majority of sodium in people's diets come from processed, packaged, and prepared foods, not additional salt added by the consumer (FDA 2022a). This means that sodium is often hidden in foods as many people do not read nutrition labels at the grocery stores and as discussed in preceding section on food deserts, many people do not have access to healthy, nutritional food. For these reasons, reducing sodium falls largely on food producers.

Actions to reduce sodium content in the food industry have been underway since 2016 when the FDA first released a draft guidance (FDA 2022a). These recommendations targeted the food industry to voluntarily reduce sodium in their products. Although other health departments have developed sodium requirements, this is the first time an agency with regulating authority has developed its own requirements (Roeder 2021). The approach has remained consistent throughout the past six years with a focus on incremental reduction and voluntary guidance (FDA 2022a). In the fall of 2021, the FDA passed the final rule which sets sodium reduction targets over the next 2.5 years (FDA 2022a). Although industries are not required to reduce sodium in their products, the FDA is planning to revisit these recommendations after the 2.5 years to see the changes and determine if more stringent measures are necessary (Roeder 2021).

Following the FDA's action, the USDA issued a final rule for school nutrition standards. This rule establishes transitional standards for schools to work toward reducing sodium in lunches by ten percent in the school year 2023–24 (USDA 2022c). The USDA intends to propose a long-term rule for nutrition standards within the next year. These examples of sodium reduction point to a common theme we continue to see with the Biden administration, a full government approach toward addressing large-scale issues. The Covid-19 pandemic exposed many chronic inequities in the US, particularly relating to health. By creating a healthier food supply through a reduction in sodium, the US can help to improve health equity.

FOOD AND CULTURE

A discussion of food policy and politics would be incomplete if we did not consider the role of culture on our food consumption. As we have seen already in this chapter, Americans' concerns about food and nutrition have changed quite a bit since the 1800s along with the availability of food items. Our nation is more concerned now with overconsumption of foods, particularly foods that have limited nutritional value, than we were in the early twentieth century. Part of the overconsumption of food stems from the fact that there is also far more variety and choice of foods at the ready, at least for Americans who do not live in food deserts (recall the discussion of food deserts at the beginning of the chapter). In the second decade of the twenty-first century, supermarkets carry an average of 42,000 different items, which represents a significant increase from the roughly 14,000 items they carried in 1980 (Moshfegh 2015, 376). And with this increase in choice, food comprises a smaller percentage of our household spending than it did just a few decades ago for many Americans. But with all of these changes, we must wonder about our food literacy. The Food Literacy Center defines food literacy "as an understanding of the impact of food choices on health, the environment, and [one's] community" (as quoted in Jones 232). Keep in mind this concept as we explore various facets of food in our society.

As the lifestyle of so many Americans seems to get busier, the convenience of food is increasingly important. Just think about the availability of foods that are single serve, easy to consume, and equally easy when it comes to disposal. Keurig's single-cup coffee makers, or K-cups, have transformed access to coffee (and other hot beverages). Approximately one in three American homes has a single-serve coffee machine, and in 2014, 9 billion K-cups were sold (Hamblin 2015). And those figures only soared during the first years of the Covid-19 pandemic, bringing the number of households with a single-serve coffee maker to 33 million (Perelmutter 2021). While exceedingly convenient in offices and homes alike, the waste generated from those seemingly small, single-serve cups is significant as they are not recyclable or biodegradable.

Along these lines, consider the growing sector of "fast causal" restaurants that offer convenience and purportedly better food than fast-food franchises, such as McDonald's, without the table-service one would find in a restaurant. Examples of this type of dining option include Panera Bread, Chipotle Mexican Grill, Five Guys Burgers & Fries, and Boston Market. If you have eaten at any one of these, or similar, establishments, consider the disposable, single use nature of the plates, wrappers, and other dining items you find there. And then think about the nutritional value of what you ordered (or perhaps not!).

It was not too long ago when most families, most of the time, ate all their meals at home. Families cooked food together from scratch. There was little in the way of premade meals that enabled a few, quick steps to produce a healthy, tasty meal for all. Growing numbers of Americans do not even know how to cook or prepare the simplest of meals. According to a Harris Poll, fourteen percent of Americans do not like to cook, seven percent do not cook at all and only forty-one percent of Americans prepare home cooked meals five or more times a week (Jones 231). In the mid-1960s, approximately 112 min a day was spent cooking, and in the early twenty-first century, that figure is down to 66 min (Jones 231). When we think about food in today's society, we increasingly think about convenience.

The emphasis on convenience may stem from the mixed messages we receive about food and nutrition. The research and information about food, what we should and should not eat and in what amounts evolve, and it can be difficult to stay abreast of that information. This is a major motivation behind the government's efforts to provide Americans nutritional guidance and other information. However, as we have seen, that information is not always the summation of the most up-to-date information as politics can and does play a role in providing that guidance. And, as Marion Nestle (2002) argues, the food industry would prefer the public to stay confused about what they should and should not eat. The marketing and advertising of food and related products is big business and the industry would rather provide their own messages to consumers. Have you ever stopped and thought about the placement of products on supermarket shelves? Most of us have not, but it is big business and manufacturers pay not inconsequential sums of money for their product to be eye level of kids shopping with the adults in their lives for their products that are marketed to kids.

Beginning in the 1990s, food manufacturers have also taken to fortifying foods with additional supplements in an effort to add to the nutritional benefits you may receive by eating their products. But these additions may or may not be substantiated by science. Often called "functional foods," these food products are foods that "...tempt consumers with a variety of health and welfare claims from the prevention of heart disease to better gastrointestinal health to cancer prevention. The producers who design and market them seek to capture consumer dollars, and if the claims made by functional food proponents are to be believed, these products create a new bridge, lucrative both to the corporations that produce them and beneficial to the people who consume them, between food and health" (Thomas 2018, 94). The first two decades of "functional foods" saw many food products enhanced with specific nutrients, such as high fiber chicken or omega-3 yogurts; most of these products failed (Thomas 95). More recently, a second generation of functional foods tries to emphasize what consumers want with "naturally functional" foods, such as probiotic yogurts, which make sense while probiotic pizza does not (Thomas 95). Ultimately, the efforts by food producers and manufacturers are focused on giving consumers what they want and making a profit at the same time. The challenge lies in whether or not the advertising claims are based on sound science and data and what, if anything, the government should do regarding the claims made. Current guidelines from the Food and Drug Administration permit the labeling of a product as a whole grain food if it has 51 percent or more whole grain ingredients by weight and a whole grain food may let consumers know that "diets rich in whole-grain foods and other plant foods and low in total fat, saturated fat, and cholesterol, may help reduce the risk of heart disease and certain cancers" (Thomas 93). Of course, it is up to the manufacturer the font sizes and graphics used to convey this health information.

Interest in health and nutrition has fueled various diet trends and movements in the US Different fads in diets, whether it is the no carbohydrate diets or the diets predicated on only raw foods, impact food consumption patterns, and the products provided by food manufacturers. And, in turn, there are policy implications as well as environmental impacts. It is difficult to track the number of individuals who are vegetarians or vegans and whether or not more Americans embrace diets without animal products is about the same or growing over time, but restaurants and grocery stores are increasingly hospitable to those dietary patterns. And food manufacturers are offering more and more products that align with these consumption patterns.

One aspect of food preferences and trends that has seen government take action on is the organic food movement. Organic foods are foods that are produced without any human made fertilizers, pesticides, or preservatives. This movement began in Europe in the early twentieth century and has become firmly established in the US (Paarlberg 167). If an individual wants to make choices about food that does not have any of these additives or chemicals in the production process, that individual needs to know information that the typical consumer is unlikely to have. As a result, the federal government has taken steps to ensure that claims made around organic foods are not erroneous. In 1990, the Organic Foods Production Act was passed and stipulated that the USDA create the National Organic Program to set standards regarding organic labeling. According to studies from the Mayo Clinic, there is no conclusive evidence that organic food is safer or more nutritious, and there are some positive benefits for the environment as well as some additional burdens in organic farming (Paarlberg 173). More research is needed to determine the benefits and costs associated with organic foods, but the government is increasingly getting involved in this dimension of food policy.

Without a doubt, the cultural dimension of food is significant. What we value in our food choices and what we demand of food manufacturers will drive much of the actions of the industry and the government around food. And these demands have implications for the natural environment. This section offers a mere introduction to the complexity of food and culture topics. And the discussion thus far has focused largely on these topics generally without exploring the socioeconomic dimensions of them. For example, the ability of an individual to pursue organic foods and make dietary choices based on the social responsibility (or perceived responsibility) of a manufacturer has much to do with that individual's income and wealth. And, if someone wants to ensure that the food she eats is grown organically and fair trade practices are followed, having a Whole Foods Market nearby might be advantageous. She may not realize that there is a large and growing percentage of Americans that do not have easy access to any grocery store, let alone a Whole Foods. As a reminder, a food desert is an area that has limited access to affordable and healthy foods, particularly fresh fruits and vegetables. Food desserts are particularly common in low-income areas. In 2010, more than 18 million Americans live in food deserts according to the USDA (Lee 2017).

Ultimately, the choices we make about food are a function of many dimensions, from health and nutrition to income and access to convenience and culture. For some of us, the choices are manifold and growing while for some of us those choices are limited and perhaps even diminishing. And policy decisions about food have environmental ramifications. When you started reading this section, you might not have thought much about the cultural dimensions of food, but they are varied and many.

CHALLENGES AND CONSIDERATIONS FOR THE FUTURE

As we consider the many dimensions of food policy and politics, there are a number of dimensions facing citizens and politicians alike, including: the multitude of stakeholders and interest areas; the consumption of scientific information, continually evolving cultural and societal norms about food and the inequalities in the American food system.

Multitude of Interests

Food policy and politics encompass a huge range of stakeholders and interest areas that make a single chapter a meager introduction. Starting with the growing of crops and the raising of livestock, there are many individuals and organizations that are involved in food production, including farmers, ranchers, and associations including the American Farm Bureau and the National Cattlemen's Beef Association, as examples. Then, there are the individuals and companies that produce the supplies farmers and ranchers need from animal feed to pesticides and fertilizers. Once crops are grown and animals raised, transportation companies help facilitate the production of food along with the food manufacturers. Once food products are ready for consumers, they have to be transported to grocery stores and restaurants, for individuals to purchase and consume the food. Throughout this entire journey, waste is produced that requires disposal. All of these actors represent a wide range of interests when it comes to food policy and politics. This list does not include nutritionists and public health officials, school kids and cafeteria food service directors, or chefs and food celebrities. These stakeholders have varying interests that elected leaders in Congress and state legislatures and civil servants in government agencies from local health departments to the FDA have to contend with as they strive to create and maintain a coherent approach to food policy in the US. The point is that something as seemingly uncontroversial as food becomes exceedingly complicated with this number of stakeholders and their various interests.

Understanding and Conveying Scientific Information

Complicating matters further is how Americans consume scientific and technical information. Picking up on some of the discussion in Chapter 2, the methodical and incremental nature of scientific research often has difficulty aligning with the media environment of twenty-first-century America. More specifically, it takes lots of time and scientists make incremental steps in their efforts to understand the world around us. Figuring out what is and is not nutritious, for example, is not a one study endeavor; rather, it requires lots of studies that explore all facets of a particular nutrient and how it may affect the human body. Researchers are unlikely to definitively conclude something is good for everyone or something is bad for everyone, yet the media often engage their viewers and readers with headlines touting the latest research conclusions that chocolate is good for us or chocolate is bad for us. How many of us actually track down the scientific journal article that the news is reporting on? Few, if any of us. But many of us rely on the news media and perhaps a medical professional for dietary advice. Ultimately, researchers, the media, and citizens have a responsibility to understand what we understand about health and food and to use that information to make decisions.

Evolving Cultural Values Around Food

Our decisionmaking around food has a lot to do with our values and the culture in which we live in, and these values and notions are constantly evolving. As we discussed previously, consider the rise in popularity of single-serve coffee pods that make coffee—as well as caffeine, and other sugary beverages—all the more convenient and accessible. This creates more and waste than brewing coffee or hot chocolate in more conventional ways. Additionally, the dramatic growth of food services such as Blue Apron and other mail order meal kits are increasingly popular—at least among those demographics that can afford to have food delivered to their home daily or weekly in pre-portioned ingredients to make cooking quick and easy. This is important as fewer and fewer Americans have the time or inclination to cook or even prepare ingredients to make a meal. These manifestations of cultural values will shape the kinds of foods that are grown, prepared, and manufactured for us to consume and it remains to be seen what the health or environmental impacts might be; however, suffice it to say, these trends toward convenience do tell a lot about values and priorities around food. Additionally, the portions of food the average American eats at any given meal has grown and grown. Portion size has implications for the health and the environment. Time will help us better understand the true implications. Seemingly our culture values convenience.

Inequities in the American Food System

Throughout the discussion of the system that produces food for Americans' consumption, a common thread is the inequities in that system. In considering the agricultural sector and its environmental impact, there are disproportionate impacts and burdens. Fewer and fewer farms are run by African Americans, down from 14 percent in 1920 to less than two percent today (Tabuchi and Popovich 2021). Arguments abound about the systemic racism in the sector and reinforced by the federal government programs (c.f. Episode 5 of the 1619 Podcast from *The New York Times*). The environmental impacts of agricultural operations can disproportionately burden communities of color, as discussed in a preceding chapter detailing environmental justice. For example, environmental justice movements in rural eastern North Carolina counties are combatting the environmental impacts of large hog CAFOs. Further, public health outcomes stand in sharp contrast between communities of color and white communities, which has implications for the government's role in promoting health. Access to healthy food is not evenly distributed, as our opening story about food deserts describes, and minority populations are disproportionately affected by food deserts, particularly in urban areas (c.f. Khalil and Mendelson 2017). The Covid-19 pandemic has heightened awareness of the racial inequalities in the school lunch and breakfast programs. This brief mention of the inequities in the food system is simply meant to acknowledge the deeply rooted social justice issues embedded in our food system and note that this challenge needs more focused attention in the future.

All of these considerations must be taken in context of the ever-changing political environment of the nation. As we have seen in this chapter, the politics of food are more than the implementation of food programs for school-aged children or the research surrounding the latest health and dietary information. These initiatives and policy steps have to take place in the broader political environment. This includes political control of state legislatures and Congress, as well as the occupants of these offices. At the outset of the chapter, one may have thought that food could hardly be controversial—after all, everyone needs to eat and food is not about saving the whales, for instance. But as we have seen, these issues are fraught with political tensions and controversies and will likely be for the foreseeable future, especially with the lingering effects of the Covid-19 pandemic.

CHAPTER WRAP-UP

In this chapter, we have explored an area of policy that might seem out of place in a book devoted to environmental policy and an area of policy that might not appear as an area of policy and politics at all—food. The growing, production, and transportation of food have significant implications for the health and well-being of the natural environment. These areas of public policy are not as coordinated as one might expect to find them, thereby compounding challenges to address real problems, such as hunger and food insecurity in the US, and to move forward in a coherent manner to think more holistically about the food system in the country and its effects on the natural environment.

Challenge Question for the Environmental Policy Classroom

The US Department of Agriculture's Economic Research Service has the Food Access Research Atlas (https://www.ers.usda.gov/data-products/food-access-research-atlas/) which enables users to look at food access indicators along with other census tract data. Go to the Atlas and look up your community or a community of interest. What do you conclude about that community's access to food based on various income and demographic factors? Perhaps go a step further and look at the Food Environment Atlas (https://www.ers.usda.gov/data-products/food-env ironment-atlas/) to examine that same community's access to food choices and diet quality. Again, what do you conclude about that community and how does it compare to the choices and dietary quality of other communities?

SUGGESTED RESOURCES

Angelo, Mary Jane, Jason J. Czarnezki, and William S. Eubanks. *Food, Agriculture, and Environmental Law.* Washington, D.C.: ELI Press, 2013.

Blevins, Brent. "How the Farm Bill Underpins US Nutrition Policy". In *Administering and Managing the US Food System*, edited by A. Bryce Hoflund, John C. Jones, and Michelle C. Pautz, 11–24. Lanham, MD: Lexington, 2021.

Bosso, Christopher. *Framing the Farm Bill: Interests, Ideology, and the Agricultural Act of 2014.* Lawrence, Kans.: University Press of Kansas, 2014.

Contois, Emily J. H. *Diners, Dudes, and Diets: How Gender and Power collide in Food Media and Culture.* Chapel Hill, N.C.: The University of North Carolina Press, 2020.

Food, Inc. Directed by Robert Kenner. Magnolia Pictures, Participant Media, River Road Entertainment, 2008.

Levine, Susan. *School Lunch Politics: The Surprising History of America's Favorite Welfare Program.* Princeton, NJ: Princeton University Press, 2008.

Neff, Roni, ed. *Introduction to the US Food System: Public Health, Environment, and Equity.* San Francisco: Jossey-Bass, 2015.

Pollan, Michael. *The Omnivore's Dilemma: A Natural History of Four Meals.* New York: Penguin, 2007.

REFERENCES

Anderson, E.N. *Everyone Eats: Understanding Food and Culture.* New York: New York University Press, 2005.

Anderson, Molly. "Ecological Threats to and From Food Systems." In *Introduction to the US Food System: Public Health, Environment, and Equity,* edited by Roni Neff, 51–78. San Francisco, CA: Jossey-Bass, 2015.

Angelo, Mary Jane and James F. Choate. "Agriculture and the Clean Water Act." In *Food, Agriculture, and Environmental Law,* edited by Mary Jane Angelo, Jason J. Czarnezki, and William S. Eubanks, 147–161. Washington, D.C.: ELI Press, 2013.

Blevins, Brent. "How the Farm Bill Underpins US Nutrition Policy". In *Administering and Managing the US Food System,* edited by A. Bryce Hoflund, John C. Jones, and Michelle C. Pautz, 11–24. Lanham, MD: Lexington, 2021.

Board, Glynis. 2014. "Reclaiming the Abandoned: Ohio Valley Grows Local Food Economy." *West Virginia Public Broadcasting.* Accessed March 16, 2022. https://www.wvpublic.org/news/2014-06-12/reclaiming-the-abandoned-ohio-valley-grows-local-food-economy.

Bosso, Christopher J. and Nicole E. Tichenor. "Eating and the Environment: Ecological Impacts of Food Production." In *Environmental Policy: New Directions for the 21st Century,* edited by Norman J. Vig and Michael E. Kraft, 194–214. Washington, D.C.: CQ Press Sage, 2015.

Brenan, Megan. "Record-High Worry in US About Hunger, Race Relations". *Gallup Poll,* 2021. Accessed March 15, 2022https://news.gallup.com/poll/341954/record-high-worry-hunger-race-relations.aspx.

CDC. 2018. Available at https://www.cdc.gov/foodborneburden/questions-and-answers.html. Accessed April 4, 2022.

CDC. 2021a. Available at https://www.cdc.gov/obesity/data/adult.html. Accessed March 15, 2022.

CDC. 2021b. Available at https://www.cdc.gov/foodsafety/cdc-and-food-safety.html. Accessed April 4, 2022.

Christaldi, Joanne and Diana Cuy Castellanos. "Child and adult food insecurity in the US." In *The Intersection of Food and Public Health: Current Policy Challenges and Solutions,* edited by A. Bryce Hoflund, John C. Jones, and Michelle C. Pautz, 15–31. New York: Routledge, 2018.

Clemmer, Teresa B. "Agriculture and the Clean Air Act." In *Food, Agriculture, and Environmental Law,* edited by Mary Jane Angelo, Jason J. Czarnezki, and William S. Eubanks, 163–184. Washington, D.C.: ELI Press, 2013.

Dutko, P., Ver Ploeg, M. and Farrigan, T. "Characteristics and Influential Factors of Food Deserts". *US Department of Agriculture, Economic Research Service,* 2012, 1–36. https://www.ers.usda.gov/webdocs/publications/45014/30940_err140.pdf.

Ebdon, Carol and Can Chen. "School Food Services Privatization." In *The Intersection of Food and Public Health: Current Policy Challenges and Solutions*, edited by A. Bryce Hoflund, John C. Jones, and Michelle C. Pautz, 291–305. New York: Routledge, 2018.

EPA. Sources of Greenhouse Gas Emissions. 2021. Available at https://www.epa.gov/ghgemissions/sources-greenhouse-gas-emissions. Accessed March 15, 2022.

Evich, Helena Bottemiller. 2016. Michelle Obama Sets Her Garden in Stone. *Politico*. October 5. Available at https://www.politico.com/story/2016/10/michelle-obama-garden-changes-white-house-229204. Accessed December 4, 2017.

FDA. 2021a. Available at https://www.fda.gov/news-events/press-announcem ents/improve-nutrition-and-reduce-burden-disease-fda-issues-food-industry-guidance-voluntarily-reducing. Accessed March 15, 2022.

FDA. 2021b. Available at https://www.fda.gov/food/food-additives-petitions/sodium-reduction#:~:text=Americans%20now%20consume%20on%20aver age%20about%203%2C400%20milligrams,children%2013%20years%20and%20younger%20are%20even%20lower. Accessed March 15, 2022.

FDA. 2022. Available at https://www.fda.gov/news-events/press-announcem ents/fda-sodium-reduction-efforts-underscored-usdas-transitional-nutrition-standards-school-meals. Accessed March 15, 2022.

FoodSafety.gov. 2002. Food Poisoning. https://www.foodsafety.gov/food-poi soning. Accessed April 4, 2022.

Gregg, Patrick. 2018. "WVU Supply Chain Students Tackle State Food Desert." *WV Press*. Available at https://www.wvpress.org/breaking-news/wvu-sup ply-chain-students-tackle-state-food-desert/#:~:text=Supply%20chain%20stud ents%20at%20the%20John%20Chambers%20College,on%20a%20project%20a imed%20at%20reducing%20food%20deserts. Accessed March 16, 2022.

Grow Ohio Valley. 2021. Available at https://www.growov.org/approach. Accessed March 16, 2022.

Hayes, Tara and Williams, Alexis. 2021. "PRIMER: The Special Supplemental Nutrition Program for Women, Infants, and Children (WIC)". *American Action Forum*. Available at https://www.americanactionforum.org/research/primer-the-special-supplemental-nutrition-program-for-women-infants-and-children-wic/#:~:text=In%202020%2C%201.5%20million%20women%2C%201.6%20million%20infants%2C,but%20dropping%20to%20just%2025%20p ercent%20of%20four-year-olds. Accessed March 15, 2022.

Hamblin, James. 2015. "A Brewing Problem: What's the Healthiest Way to Keep Everyone Caffeinated?" *The Atlantic*. March 2. Available at https://www.theatlantic.com/technology/archive/2015/03/the-abomin able-k-cup-coffee-pod-environment-problem/386501/. Accessed February 23, 2018.

Jones, Georgia. "Food Literacy: What Is It and Why Does It Matter?" In *The Intersection of Food and Public Health: Current Policy Challenges and Solutions*, edited by A. Bryce Hoflund, John C. Jones, and Michelle C. Pautz, 231–242. New York: Routledge, 2018.

Khalil, Hanna and Ryan Mendelson. 2017. "Food Deserts: Where Nutrition Meets Inequality." Washington University Political Review. 19 December. https://www.wupr.org/2017/12/19/food-deserts-where-nutrition-meets-inequality/. Accessed April 4, 2022.

Lee, Courtney Hall. 2017. "Grocery Store Inequity: Why Fresh Food is Often a Scarce Commodity for Low-Income People." *Sojourners*. April. Available at https://sojo.net/magazine/april-2017/grocery-store-inequity. Accessed February 23, 2018.

Levine, Susan. *School Lunch Politics: The Surprising History of America's Favorite Welfare Program*. Princeton, NJ: Princeton University Press, 2008.

Moshfegh, Alanna. "Food Consumption in the US." In *Introduction to the US Food System: Public Health, Environment, and Equity*, edited by Roni Neff, 373–398. San Francisco, CA: Jossey-Bass, 2015.

Nestle, Marion. *Safe Food: The Politics of Food Safety*. Updated and expanded edition. Berkeley: University of California Press, 2010.

Nestle, Marion. 2002. *Food Politics: How the Food Industry Influences Nutrition and Health*. Berkeley: University of California Press.

NIDDK. 2018. Available at https://www.niddk.nih.gov/health-information/health-statistics/overweight-obesity. Accessed February 13, 2018.

NPR Staff. 2012. "The First Lady Cultivates 'American Grown' Gardening." National Public Radio. May 29. Available at: https://www.npr.org/2012/05/29/153705721/the-first-lady-cultivates-american-grown-gardening. Accessed December 4, 2017.

Paarlberg, Robert. *Food Politics: What Everyone Needs to Know*. 2nd edition. New York: Oxford University Press, 2013.

Park, Timothy, Mary Ahearn, Ted Covey, Kenneth Erickson, J. Michael Harris, Jennifer Ifft, Chris McGath, Mitch Morehart, Stephen Vogel, Jeremy Weber, and Robert Williams. 2011. *Agricultural Income and Finance Outlook*. A Report from the Economic Research Service, US Department of Agriculture. (December). Available at https://www.ers.usda.gov/webdocs/publications/35822/12822_ais-91_3-1-12.pdf?v=41055. Accessed February 7, 2018.

Perelmutter, Sydney. 2021. How many US Households Became Keurig Users During the Pandemic? XTalks. March 2. Available at https://xtalks.com/how-many-us-households-became-keurig-users-during-the-pandemic-2613/. Accessed April 4, 2022.

Poppendieck, Janet. *Free For All: Fixing School Food in America*. Berkeley: University of California Press, 2010.

Reilly, Katie. 2017. "Melania Trump Plans to Preserve Michelle Obama's Vegetable Garden." *Time*. Available at http://time.com/4668035/melania-trump-michelle-obama-vegetable-garden/. Accessed December 4, 2017.

Ritchie, Hannah. 2020. "Sector by Sector: Where Do Global Greenhouse Gas Emissions Come From?" *Our World Data*. https://ourworldindata.org/ghg-emissions-by-sector. Accessed March 15, 2022.

Roeder, Amy. 2021. "FDA's New Sodium-Reduction Goals a 'Really Good Move' for Heart Health". *Harvard School of Public Health*. https://www.hsph.harvard.edu/news/features/fdas-sodium-reduction-heart-health/. Accessed March 15, 2022.

Rutledge, Jennifer Geist. "Hating Healthy Meals: Policy Rollbacks and School Meals". In *Administering and Managing the US Food System*, edited by A. Bryce Hoflund, John C. Jones, and Michelle C Pautz, 61–75. Lanham, MD: Lexington, 2021.

SNAP. 2022. Available at https://fns-prod.azureedge.net/sites/default/files/resource-files/34SNAPmonthly-2.pdf. Accessed March 15, 2022.

Tabuchi, Hiroko and Nadja Popovich. 2021. "Two Biden Priorities, Climate and Inequality, Meet Black-Owned Farms." *New York Times*. January 31. https://www.nytimes.com/2021/01/31/climate/black-farmers-discrimination-agriculture.html. Accessed April 4, 2022.

Thomas, Courtney I. P. "When is Food (Not) Functional?" In *The Intersection of Food and Public Health: Current Policy Challenges and Solutions*, edited by A. Bryce Hoflund, John C. Jones, and Michelle C. Pautz, 93–106. New York: Routledge, 2018.

Thomas, Courtney I. P. *In Food We Trust: The Politics of Purity in American Food Regulation*. Lincoln, Nebraska: University of Nebraska Press, 2014.

US Department of Agriculture. 2018a. Available at https://www.cnpp.usda.gov/myplate. Accessed February 13, 2018.

US Department of Agriculture. 2018b. Available at https://www.ers.usda.gov/topics/food-nutrition-assistance/food-security-in-the-us/key-statistics-graphics.aspx. Accessed February 16, 2018.

US Department of Agriculture. 2022a. Available at https://www.ers.usda.gov/topics/food-markets-prices/food-service-industry/market-segments.aspx Accessed March 21, 2022.

US Department of Agriculture. 2022b. Available at https://www.ers.usda.gov/data-products/ag-and-food-statistics-charting-the-essentials/ag-and-food-sectors-and-the-economy/. Accessed March 21, 2022.

US Department of Agriculture. 2021. *Farms and Land in Farms 2020 Summary*. (February). https://downloads.usda.library.cornell.edu/usda-esmis/files/5712m6524/tq57pj927/rx914h75j/fnlo0221.pdf . Accessed March 21, 2022.

USDA Economic Research Service. 2022. Farm Business Average Net Cash Income. https://data.ers.usda.gov/reports.aspx?ID=17840. Accessed March 29, 2022.

USDA. 2021a. Available at https://www.ers.usda.gov/topics/food-nutrition-assistance/food-security-in-the-u-s/key-statistics-graphics/. Accessed March 15, 2022.

USDA. 2021b. Available at https://www.ers.usda.gov/topics/food-nutrition-assistance/child-nutrition-programs/school-breakfast-program/. Accessed March 15, 2022.

USDA. 2021c. Food Security in the US https://www.ers.usda.gov/topics/food-nutrition-assistance/food-security-in-the-u-s/key-statistics-graphics/. Accessed April 4, 2022.

USDA. 2021d. Available at https://www.usda.gov/media/blog/2011/05/03/interactive-web-tool-maps-food-deserts-provides-key-data. Accessed March 16, 2022.

USDA. 2022a. Available at https://www.usda.gov/media/press-releases/2022/02/04/usda-helps-schools-build-back better issues-transitional-nutrition. Accessed March 15, 2022.

USDA. 2022b. Available at https://www.ers.usda.gov/data-products/ag-and-food-statistics-charting-the-essentials/farming-and-farm-income/. Accessed March 5, 2022.

USDA. 2022c. USDA Helps Schools Build Back Better, Issues Transitional Nutrition Standards for Coming School Years. https://www.fns.usda.gov/news-item/usda-0037.22. Accessed April 4, 2022.

Wilde, Parke. *Food Policy in the US: An Introduction*. New York: Routledge, 2013.

Winne, Mark. *Closing the Food Gap: Resetting the Table in the Land of Plenty*. Boston: Beacon Press, 2008.

CHAPTER 11

Environmental Policy in Action: Past, Present, and Future

Our approach to environmental policy goes beyond discussions of the politics of making policy decisions to emphasize how those decisions are implemented. It is this approach that necessitates moving beyond the role of politicians and political institutions and examining the work of regulators, activists, and members of the regulated community. The efforts of all of these actors—official and unofficial—constitute environmental policy in action and these efforts signal what we want and what we do not want when it comes to the role of government in environmental matters.

As we have seen throughout this volume, where we are today and where we head tomorrow is a function of learning from our past. In our final chapter, we consider environmental policy past, present, and future. By appreciating the historical evolution of environmental policy, we come to know and grapple with environmental policy of the present, thereby enabling us to look to the future of US environmental policy. This structure affords us the space to ponder some of the normative questions associated with environmental policy in the twenty-first century.

ENVIRONMENTAL POLICY PAST

A good portion of the preceding pages has been devoted to understanding environmental policy and its implementation in the past. Without a knowledge of the history of major environmental laws or

S. R. Rinfret and M. C. Pautz, *US Environmental Policy in Action*, https://doi.org/10.1007/978-3-031-17503-9_11

the actions of previous presidential administrations, it is difficult to comprehend present-day environmental policy. Our experience with environmental policy is dominated by the few dozen major environmental laws passed in the 1960s and 1970s, and these laws have generally achieved laudable results. As discussed earlier, these laws have brought about major reductions in air pollution and improved air quality, for instance. The nation's rivers do not catch on fire, and typically, toxic waste is not intentionally dumped with little regard for the environmental impacts. Although these achievements should not be diminished, they are widely considered low-hanging fruit. In other words, these are the efforts that are the easiest to accomplish, and the simplest situations to realize. Devising procedures for disposal of hazardous waste took time, for example, but the challenges of these issues pale in comparison with the environmental issues we face today, such as climate change.

Our environmental laws are generally reactive, meaning they largely deal with pollution after it has happened and, often, only pollution that is traceable to a particular source (point-source pollution). Now, we have come to understand that point-source pollution is only part of the issue, and pollution with less discernible sources (non-point pollution) is significant. For example, the pollution coming from a waste pipe at a plant is easily noted; however, the runoff from agricultural fields and from parking lots into the nation's streams and waterways is harder to trace, although the effects are no less significant. This reminder of where we have been leads to the first of three summary points about our past: we have made significant progress in the US addressing environmental issues, but much of that work has been reactive rather than proactive. Put differently, our approach to environmental problems has been to deal with it after it happens. By contrast, a more proactive approach would entail preventing pollution from happening in the first place.

Second, the creation, passage, and implementation of these environmental laws that have achieved the results we discussed have built a large regulatory apparatus. Many government agencies at the federal, state, and local levels have been created to implement these regulations. From the rule-writers and environmental compliance inspectors to the work of politicians and interest groups, there is a multitude of actors and organizations involved in environmental policy. The growth of the environmental profession—both in government and in the private sector—has been tremendous. There is an enormous cadre of specially trained professionals, both inside and outside of government, whose work is dedicated to implementing and monitoring compliance with environmental regulations.

The significant number of environmental professionals coincides with thousands and thousands of pages of federal environmental regulations. Although there are only a few dozen major environmental statutes, the corresponding pages of regulations are ever growing. In the more than five decades, the size and scale of government's regulatory structure have become significant. On the one hand, it is impressive that such a structure has been established to ensure environmental protection and realize major environmental achievements. On the other hand, the enormity of government bureaucracy surrounding environmental protection can easily lead to inefficiencies, overlap, inflexibility, and dampen opportunities for innovation. Regardless of one's perspective on the role of government in environmental protection, shifting the course of the governmental structures takes time and is challenging. During the Trump administration, many efforts were initiated to significantly alter the approach to environmental protection and the Biden administration is still working to reverse those actions. Rapid, nimble actions are not easily taken by the environmental bureaucracy, and that has positive and negative implications.

The regulatory structure and the laws it is tasked with implementing are indicative of a third point: in the past, there was widespread agreement that government has a role in protecting the environment. Broadly speaking, mainstream society evolved from a debate over whether the government should be involved in protecting the nation's environment to a general acceptance of the need for government in this policy arena. The debates centered around to what extent the government should have a role in protecting the environment and what level of government (e.g., state or national government) should be in charge. Of course, there has been plenty of debate about the appropriate balance between economic and environmental concerns. However, these were not partisan debates with one political party supporting government's role in environmental protection and the other party not supporting it. Ultimately, government's role—if evidenced by nothing other than the size of the regulatory structure it commands—was clearly established in this policy arena. And there was agreement that the federal government must assume a leadership role in protecting the environment.

It is important at this juncture to emphasize that these are just some of the major characteristics of our environmental policy past. These characteristics are not necessarily positive or negative—as most things are never so easily defined—but they are simply our past. Understanding these attributes of environmental policy helps us explain the present state of environmental policy and enables us to look to the future and what it might entail.

Environmental Policy Present

The characteristics of environmental policy today are quite different than they were even a decade ago. The foundation of some of these characteristics were already in place when the first edition of this volume was written years ago and some have emerged only more recently. We focus here on three characteristics of environmental policy today: (1) hyper-partisanship and polarization, (2) debate over government's role in environmental protection leading to paralysis at the national level, and (3) continued persistence of major environmental issues.

Hyper Partisanship and Political Polarization

As we have discussed at numerous points in previous chapters, action to protect the environment was, at one time, a bipartisan effort that elicited consensus from most sides in the political world. This is no longer the case as positions on environmental issues are now a key litmus test for politicians (c.f. Klyza and Sousa 2013). In the late 1970s and throughout the 1980s, we saw Republicans, in keeping with their conservative principles of a smaller, less intrusive government, wanting to reduce the government's role in environmental protection and, at the very least, give more power over environmental issues to lower levels of governments, notably the states. But those same Republicans saw the need for government to protect the environment.

Today, however, we are witnessing a shift in those tendencies toward a viewpoint that fundamentally questions scientific knowledge and our understanding of environmental issues. More and more Republican politicians and their appointees, including former President Trump and his selections for environmental agency heads, question the science behind climate change (as one example of questioning science). Moreover, vitriol directed toward environmental protection has accelerated as more and more Republicans increasingly question the very existence of environmental problems. Even among Republicans who do acknowledge environmental issues, most are unwilling to advocate action, especially by the federal government. In contrast, Democratic politicians and their appointees argue the government must act decisively to respond to climate change and demand the federal government take an active role in combatting it. However, many Democrats are unwilling to take hardline positions on environmental issues because of the electoral politics associated with such positions. We saw this in Hillary Clinton's presidential campaign, and Joe Biden only talked about climate change in certain circumstances during his, often focusing on environmental issues for select audiences. There also seems to be a growing fault line in the Democratic Party among moderates and those more progressive Democrats advocating for significant environmental efforts. All of these views further complicate the challenges of creating and implementing policy.

Hyper partisanship, or intense devotion to a political party's platform, does not just affect environmental policy, however. And it is not a new phenomenon in American politics, and it will not be the last time the nation experiences such an era that is debilitating for the work of policymakers. In a 2021 Pew Research Center Poll, 90% of Americans noted this growing divide and believed there were strong to very strong conflicts between supporters of different political parties (Silver et al. 2021). As we have mentioned repeatedly, the two major political parties are increasingly standing in opposition to the objectives of the other party. Furthermore, the political parties are seemingly focused on the outcomes of elections and less on building consensus to govern in the interim. Given this entrenchment of views and positions on issues, various stances on key policy issues are surging in importance, including views on science and environmental policy and compounding any action.

Questioning Government's Role in Environmental Protection & Legislative Paralysis

The hyper-partisanship that we have experienced in the country for many years now, exacerbated by the administration of Donald Trump, brought about a debate over the role of government in environmental protection more broadly that is surprising. For the first time since the establishment of our modern environmental laws and regulatory structures to implement those laws, questions swirl over whether or not the government should be involved. Some of this debate may simply be political and fit with former President's Trump rhetorical style of being assertive and desirous of causing a stir—particularly on Twitter. But some of this debate may signal fundamental realignment of the government's—or at least the national government's—role in protecting the environment. Since the creation of the EPA in 1970, there have been presidents of both political parties and their leadership has often had different views on the environment; however, no administration to date has tried to undo so many environmental laws so quickly and to gut the agencies tasked with their implementation and oversight the way President Trump tried to do. President Reagan wanted to curb the federal government's role in environmental protection and was very concerned about the implications for the economy of environmental regulations, but there was not rhetoric that questioned the fundamental need for environmental protection and the agencies tasked with implementation. As a presidential candidate, Trump was asked on Fox News Sunday what agencies he would cut and he named the EPA, calling the agency's actions a "disgrace" (Fox News 2015). When anchor Chris Wallace asked who would protect the environment if the agency was cut, Trump replied "They—we'll be fine with the environment. We can leave a little bit, but you can't destroy businesses" (Fox News 2015). Trump's rhetoric as a candidate was followed up by actions (as chronicled earlier in this volume) as president.

While the Biden administration has repealed many of those actions and is working to undo others (again, as detailed in earlier chapters), the debate over the role of the government—mostly the federal government—in environmental protection seems to persist. Trump's actions and rhetoric as president may have seem an extreme shift for the Republican Party, but we increasingly see political rhetoric from other Republicans (particularly candidates in the 2022 election cycle) espouse such viewpoints. For the moment, it seems the views the Trump administration held on environmental protection and the government's role in it are here to stay.

The federal courts are also pushing back on efforts to protect the environment. In *West Virginia v. EPA* (2022), the EPA's authority to regulate greenhouse gas emissions from power plants was significantly curtailed by the Supreme Court of the US. Chief Justice John Roberts, writing for the Court, noted that "major questions" must be specifically determined by Congress and spelled out in legislation. Writing for the dissenting justices, Justice Elena Kagan wrote that the decision "strips the EPA of the power

Congress gave it to respond to the most pressing environmental challenge of our time." We will see if this ruling is used as precedent to undo other regulations.

Adding this dimension to the debate over government action surrounding the environment further exacerbates the federal government's legislative paralysis. The last four sessions of Congress (the final two years of the Obama administration, the four years of the Trump administration, and now into the Biden administration) have struggled to pass legislation in most policy areas, not to mention on environmental issues. It is worth noting that the Biden administration has seen success, however, at passing one of the largest pieces of legislation in history, the $1.2 trillion dollar infrastructure bill. The Infrastructure Investment and Jobs Act of 2021 encompasses many types of projects, and with regard to environmental policy, this act will support clean drinking water projects, ecosystem restoration, and resiliency projects (H.R. 3684). Democrats wanted to pass this bill alongside the Build Back Better Act (H.R. 5376) which has a heavier focus on climate change mitigation and would provide funding for forest management, wildfire prevention, energy efficiency projects, climate change research, and more. During the summer of 2022, Congress also passed the Inflation Reduction Act that contains significant investments in renewable energy and climate change mitigation. Congress has been unable to do more. And the results of the 2022 midterm elections leave little optimism that things will change.

Some of the inability to pass laws is evidenced in changes to congressional rules and the increased use of the Senate filibuster (or, at the very least, the threat of filibusters), which enables individual members of the Senate to wield sizable power in stopping any legislative action. As a result, cloture votes—those votes that stymie filibusters or the threat of them—are essential to governing these days and require 60 votes, instead of the simple majority that we all associate with Senate procedure (Zeleny and Saenz 2013). During the Biden administration, Democrats in the Senate tried to change the filibuster rules so that legislation could go through, but they lost the votes of two Democrats, Senators Joe Manchin (West Virginia) and Kyrsten Sinema (Arizona), and the effort failed (Healy 2022).

With gridlock in the halls of Congress and the polarization of lawmakers, other avenues of policy action are being sought in policy arenas, including environmental protection. Klyza and Sousa (2008, 2013) coined the term "green drift" to explain the nation's evolving approach to environmental policy. Essentially, as a result of legislative grid-lock, environmental policy is still being made via non-legislative pathways. For example, environmental policymaking is still happening in the halls of administrative agencies as we have repeatedly noted through this book, as well as through the work of civil servants and their exercise of discretion; the courts are still creating environmental policy via their decisions; and state governments are taking an increasingly prominent role in the pursuit of environmental goals.

Political fighting and legislative gridlock only exacerbate a downward spiral of trust in government. Americans continue to express disgust with government, as approval ratings of Congress hover at their lowest recorded levels. This disapproval, coupled with the inability of lawmakers to come together and pass legislation, leave most citizens cynical about the government's ability to accomplish anything and especially deal with issues that are less paramount in the minds of Americans such as environmental concerns. In March 2022, according to a Gallup Poll, 75% of Americans are dissatisfied with the direction of the nation and only 24% are satisfied, which is similar to the way Americans have responded to such questions for years ("Satisfaction with US" 2022). When asked how much confidence Americans have in Congress in a March 2022 Gallup poll, 21% of Americans approve of the way Congress is handling its job and 76% disapprove ("Congress and the Public" 2022).

It is difficult to say what the implications for the polarization and partisanship are, especially when considered alongside the paralysis of federal legislative pathways. Perhaps a reminder of a quote attributed to Thomas Jefferson is appropriate: "The government you elect is the government you deserve." Ultimately, our elected leaders are elected to represent us, so the question becomes are these the views that we have about environmental policy? If they are, then that is the direction for the nation. If they are not, then what should the voters do about that?

Major Environmental Issues Persist

The realities described above about the present state of environmental policy may not be particularly encouraging. And this brings us to another point: while Americans and their elected leaders are struggling to take any significant action on environmental issues, environmental problems persist and in many cases continue to get worse. However, we can address what is happening. Greenhouse gases, for example, continue to pollute the environment and despite the lockdowns worldwide due to Covid-19, the GHG emissions in 2020 set records even though 2020 levels were lower than other years (Neuman 2021). Emissions are only growing as the world emerges from the pandemic. In May 2022, the planet broke a record for carbon dioxide emissions—421 parts per million, which is 50% higher than the preindustrial average (Fountain 2022). Other issues, including biodiversity loss, pollution and waste, raging wildfires, and other challenges continue. The US EPA provides a variety of indicators to track all sorts of environmental conditions (see www.epa.gov/rep ort-environment) which demonstrate that while there has been progress, much work remains. And this work remains while politicians seem increasingly hesitant to make laws addressing the issues, thereby leaving the civil servants in government agencies muddling through.

Not only do we continue to confront environmental issues that fail to remain stagnant—and typically get worse—these issues often have to be confronted by not just nations, but by the world community. This level of collaboration and coordination is difficult to say the least. Just think of all that we have described on these pages of what it takes for the US to act, now multiply those difficulties by the number of nations around the world. But we are seeing action around the world, often precipitated by young people demanding action.

Environmental Policy Future

In light of the present assessment of environmental policy, forecasting the future of environmental policy in the US is difficult. Some of the challenges we face today, including an aging regulatory infrastructure and the very nature and complexity of environmental issues, have been present for some time. And some of the challenges we encounter now are more recent, such as questioning the role of the government in environmental protection and the work of our regulatory agencies. These conditions make discussions of the future hard. The environmental problems the nation—and, indeed, the world—faces in the first part of the twenty-first century are unlike the issues that were a prominent fixture of the environmental agenda more than fifty years ago. Today, climate change and energy concerns dominate much of the discussion. The extent of the changes our climate is undergoing and the effects on humans is at the forefront of much debate. And decades ago, the focus was on cleaning up pollution, whereas now we tend to focus on minimizing pollution before it happens and finding alternative energy sources in an effort to mitigate environmental effects. The differences in these challenges beget changes in our approach to environmental policy.

As we look to the future, two points inform those considerations. First—and as is often the case when we look to the future—uncertainty abounds. The uncertainty is particularly striking with environmental policy because we saw with the Trump administration, significant efforts were made to fundamentally change course of environmental protection, at least at the national level (with spillover effects to subnational governments even less clear). Will the subsequent administrations dismantle decades of environmental regulations and structure, or was this an outlier? Have elected officials and the American public fundamentally changed their views on the environmental protection and the government's role in it? Will Congress ever reclaim their role legislating solutions to environmental problems? How will the courts rule on environmental policy cases and what will the implications of those decisions be? Will the American public reassert their demand for the government to protect the environment, as they did in the 1960s and 1970s? Or will the public leave it to individual decisions and the private sector? Will the contours of international environmental policy fundamentally change given the US's behavior in this policy arena?

Hazarding answers to any of these questions is virtually impossible. As a result, uncertainty and maybe even instability are likely in this policy arena, and this has significant implications for the future. Companies that are subjected to environmental regulations do not know if the regulations are going to go away or be very different from what they are accustomed to—and this makes planning for firms very difficult. Added costs are then likely no matter what happens. State and local governments do not know if the federal government's role will change and what the effects may be for these subunits of government, and especially if and how funding structures will evolve. After all, the federal government provides a lot of the funds state and local governments use to implement environmental regulations. And citizens do not know how environmental protection will change and the effects they may see on their lives. For example, the vehicle emissions standards put in place during the Obama administration, which required average fuel economy to reach 54 miles per gallon by 2025, were altered by the Trump administration to 32 miles per gallon, and then, they were changed by the Biden administration. The Biden administration now is calling for vehicles to achieve 40 miles per gallon by 2026 (Shepardson 2022; Wise 2021).

Second, while it can be frustrating and discouraging to consider what the immediate future of environmental policy might hold, it is important to remember that we have been here before and we made progress. Returning to the history of American environmental policy, we see that we were facing enormous amounts of pollution in the twentieth century and we were able to come together and address it. We were able to do hard things and it is reasonable to conclude that we can do it again, especially with activists and young people pushing for action and change.

Regardless of our assessments of government and its ability to function as we would like, these are the realities that environmental policy—and other areas of policy—must contend with. As we look forward, we identify five needs for environmental policy in the future.

First, more holistic training is needed for environmental professionals. An enduring theme in environmental policy is the sheer complexity of the issues and the interdisciplinary nature of them. Many of our environmental professionals are trained in specific areas of environmental concerns. For example, environmental inspectors, often, have backgrounds in particular areas of the natural sciences or engineering. Then, these individuals become inspectors and spend a career focusing on a particular aspect of environmental regulation such as hazardous waste management (c.f. Pautz and Rinfret 2013). This narrow focus creates a cadre of experts in specific areas, but it hampers efforts to work across environmental media. Moreover, those individuals who pursue careers in advocacy need a more robust background in the various dimensions of environmental concerns—not just the scientific and technical, but the policy, the organization, and the communication of such issues. Many universities offer students environmental studies programs that are multidisciplinary and serve to foster more holistic training, but we would advocate further expansion of such programs even beyond the traditional college environment. Whatever one's predilections about environmental issues may be, a broad and diverse background is essential for effectively understanding and advocating one's viewpoints and deriving solutions.

Second, the public needs to be able to discuss the challenges of various environmental issues effectively. Decades into the information age, the average person has an incredible amount of information available at his/her fingertips because we no longer have to wait for the evening news to hear about the latest current events. However, with the explosion of the Internet and the emergence of numerous forms of information dissemination, including social media, we are frequently overwhelmed with information. As a result, digesting all this information and ascertaining its credibility proves challenging. Instead of engaging a print copy of the newspaper and reading an article from start to finish because there was only a finite amount of news in the daily paper, we now scan and click and read bits and pieces of many more news stories. However, we end up with a much broader knowledge of what is going on without the depth. Just think for a moment about how you scan news stories, Instagram, TikTok, and Twitter: you quickly glance through and read what you deem interesting; however, in many of those formats, algorithms cull what you see and content is distilled down to the fewest possible characters or images. This is not necessarily bad or good, but it begs the question, how do we consume information and how comprehensive is it? Further, anyone with minimal technological skills can post information on the Internet and claim it is accurate. Then, that information only needs to be duplicated, re-posted, or re-tweeted. With the viral nature of information, particularly sensational stories, the vast amount of misinformation is unsurprising.

Given the nature of information dissemination and consumption, understanding of complex social and political issues is distilled to slogans and sound bites. Again, without passing judgment on the merits of information transmission, one does have to reflect on the implications for discussion in the public square of these complex issues. With these technological changes and the dramatic increase in available information, the nature of public debate has changed. The issues for debate in the public square, related to the environment or any number of other pressing matters, are no less complex, but our ability to discuss them in comprehensive ways seems to be waning. Society has much to contend with and the multitude of issues result in a crowding effect, and society's ability to look beyond slogans, especially with the information at its disposal, seems to be absent. Instead, we succumb to slinging slogans that may or may not accurately reflect the facts or represent the complexity of the issue. Ultimately, frustration abounds, but little seems to be done about it.

We urge all citizens to get beyond the slogans and the political rhetoric jostled about and dig deeper to search out facts about issues and then make reasoned arguments about the issues. Public discussion needs to be elevated so we, as a nation, can more productively debate the pressing matters before us and make collective decisions about what should be done. It is easy to blame the politicians for these ills, but we contend that the ultimate responsibility lies with the public and its obligation to check rhetoric that distorts and fails to capture the various sides of any issue. The public needs to hold its leaders responsible for what they say and ensure accountability in that debate. This extends to voting and participating in electoral politics.

Third, more study and information gathering is needed. Aristotle is credited with saying "the more you know, the more you don't know" and this old adage could not be more appropriate in the realm of environmental policy. We have come to understand that environmental issues are usually more complicated than we initially think, and the same could be said for politics. Therefore, although it may seem trite, we need more research and information about any number of environmental issues. A better understanding of the multifaceted nature of the issues is essential, and we must find ways beyond sound bites and slogans to talk about these issues.

Arguably, we have seen the complexity of issues increase whereas our appetite for robust and informed debate seems to be declining. We must rectify the situation because the complexity of issues demands a commensurate level of engagement. Moreover, we need information and research from multiple disciplines, not just science and engineering, but from the health sciences, social sciences, and even the humanities. Our arguments have to be better informed, for example, by the moral and ethical arguments philosophers bring. The desire for information must be balanced with an understanding that decisions must be made and perpetually deferring action in the name of more information is disingenuous and irresponsible. How to strike this balance, though, is invariably the challenge, but it is one we must not shrink from.

Fourth, in an effort to ensure forward momentum in terms of environmental progress, we must recognize that information and solutions can come from all sides in the environmental debate. We must move beyond an "us versus them" mentality when it comes to these concerns. Advocacy groups are not necessarily the good guys, and industry groups are not necessarily the bad guys. Throughout this text, you have seen the complexity of environmental issues and that reductionist views about who is "good" and who is "bad" reflect a cursory understanding of these issues. In every category of actor in this policy arena, there are good guys and bad guys; therefore, it is too simplistic to say simply that it is one side versus the other. Instead, we should move beyond the preconceived notions of "hippie tree-huggers" and "evil, profit-driven corporate executives" and devise ways to see beyond stereotypes and labels in an effort to engage all stakeholders as we strive for solutions for the planet.

Fifth, and finally, we need a regulatory system that fosters collaboration because we are all dependent on the health and the well-being of the environment, and that requires us to work together. As we engage in thoughtful debate about the issues, we must rid ourselves of misinformed stereotypes and be able to work together. This means that environmentalists, governmental regulators, the regulated community, and citizens must come together. Our regulatory system, which was designed to thwart innovation and collaboration due to fears of regulatory shirking, must evolve. Our history with environmental regulation has demonstrated that much of this fear is unfounded—or at least overstated—so, we need to move forward. We need a regulatory system that allows for collaboration and flexibility when appropriate because the best science and information 10 years ago may not be the best information to base a course of action on today. Perhaps, we even need to go so far as embracing, more fully, the next generation of regulatory strategies discussed here.

ACTION IN THE FUTURE

From the preceding discussion, you have likely gleaned that the role the US has played in environmental matters has varied over time. At some points in the history of modern environmental policy, the US has been at the forefront of change and leadership, and at other times, the nation has lagged. Looking to the future, we see a new generation of leaders emerging. With the US's back and forth on environmental policy due to changes in presidential administrations, young people and BIPOC communities are among the most vocal advocates building a movement to compel action on climate change and environmental justice. The Covid-19 pandemic exposed the nation's racial divide and highlighted the interconnectedness of the environment, public health, and communities of color. Racial segregation placed many BIPOC communities in residential areas that are denser and face significantly more environmental hazards from toxic waste, air pollution, unsafe drinking water, and extreme weather events (Fears 2022). The case studies in this text have explored the Flint water crisis and the Standing Rock protest, which are examples of the disparate environmental impacts on communities of color. The Covid-19 pandemic exacerbated these disparities and led to widespread activism in the US The quantity of emerging voices demanding action from government was difficult to ignore and, in response, the Biden administration established the White House Environmental Justice Advisory Council (Joselow 2022). The intention of this body is to ensure that 40% of the federal climate investments benefitted disadvantaged communities; however, as this book goes to print, the Biden administration has adopted a race-neutral approach that environmental justice leaders argue will continue to disadvantage communities of color (Joselow 2022). Remember what we discussed about government action throughout this volume—citizens can and do influence the course of action. Rulemaking requires public notice and comment and citizens and organizations should participate. The courts are available to citizens to compel action or to stop action. And we the people select our elected officials at the federal, state, and local levels.

With our discussion of environmental policy drawing to a close, a few final thoughts on the themes and areas of focus are warranted. As we established from the outset, the focus of this approach to environmental policy has been how this area of policy is actually done on a day-to-day basis and the roles of those on the front-lines. Here, we have conveyed stories of front-line regulators, government rule-writers, activists, and others.

Through our approach, we demonstrated the complexity of environmental issues and the challenges facing government, industry, and society as we enter the third decade of the twenty-first century. If anything, environmental issues are even more involved than we understood them to be just a few decades ago. Not only are environmental issues technically complex and involve a multitude of actors, but also it is often difficult to acquire the necessary information in a time frame that coincides with political realities. The current state of political rhetoric further reduces issues to their least common denominator and slogans that do a disservice to all perspectives on the issue and thwart dialog.

Finally, it is imperative that we remember that inaction is action. Our inability to take steps—whatever those might be—regarding the environment is having, and will continue to have, a significant impact. Environmental problems are not going to wait, and they will only intensify while we choose to debate them or push them aside. The US used to be an environmental leader, but now we lag behind.

The readers of this text constitute the future of environmental action. You will be the environmental professionals, the regulators, the activists, and the citizens who engage these issues. Jobs in this area of the economy continue to hold promise under the heading of green jobs. Furthermore, even if the job is not seemingly related to environmental concerns, the environment touches all facets of life and will, therefore, permeate professions. We hope that you have come to see the complexities of these challenges, the significance of the individuals who work on these issues daily, and the need to continue forward movement.

Challenge Question for the Environmental Policy Classroom

We have completed our whirlwind tour of US environmental policy. At the conclusion of this book, write down 3 bullet points about the relationship between environmental policy and diversity, equity, inclusion, and belonging.

SUGGESTED RESOURCES

Readings and Websites

Klyza, Christopher McGrory and David Sousa. *American Environmental Policy: Beyond Gridlock*. Cambridge: MIT Press, 2013.

Kraft, Michael E., Mark Stephan, and Troy D. Abel.*Coming Clean: Information Disclosure and Environmental Performance*. Cambridge: MIT Press, 2011.

Layzer, Judith. *Open for Business: Conservatives' Opposition to Environmental Regulation*. Cambridge, MA: MIT Press, 2012.

Rabe, Barry G. *Greenhouse Governance: Addressing Climate Change in America*. Washington, DC: The Brookings Institution, 2010.

Films or Videos

Avatar. Directed by James Cameron. 2009. Twentieth Century Fox, Dune Entertainment, Ingenuous Film Partners.

Chinatown. Directed by Roman Polanski. 1974. Paramount Pictures.

Don't Look Up. Directed by Adam McKay. 2021. Hyperobject Industries, Bluegrass Films.

Wall-e. Directed by Andrew Stanton. 2008. Disney.

REFERENCES

"Congress and the Public". Gallup Poll. 2022. Accessed April 15, 2022. https://news.gallup.com/poll/1600/congress-public.aspx?msclkid=00bfb6 9abcd711ec8b17f39c51210189.

Ebbs, Stephanie. "Trump EPA Spends First Year Rolling Back Environmental Regulations." ABC News. 2018. Accessed August 10, 2018. https://abc news.go.com/Politics/trump-epa-spends-year-rolling-back-environmental-reg ulations/story?id=52162794.

EPA. "Proposed Rule and Related Materials for Control of Air Pollution from New Motor Vehicles: Heavy-Duty Engine and Vehicle Standards." Accessed April 15, 2022. https://www.epa.gov/regulations-emissions-vehicles-and-eng ines/proposed-rule-and-related-materials-control-air-1#rule-summary.

Farber, Daniel A. "Trump, EPA, and the Anti-Regulatory State." *The Regulatory Review*. January 24, 2018. Accessed February 6. https://www.theregreview. org/2018/01/24/farber-trump-epa-anti-regulatory-state/.

Fears, Darryl. "Redlining Means 45 Million Americans Are Breathing Dirtier Air, 50 Years After It Ended." March 9, 2022. Accessed April 19, 2022. *Washington Post*. https://www.washingtonpost.com/climate-environment/2022/ 03/09/redlining-pollution-environmental-justice/.

Fountain, Henry. "5 Takeaways from the Major New UN Climate Report." *New York Times*. August 9, 2021. Accessed April 14, 2022. https://www.nytimes.com/2021/08/09/climate/un-climate-report-takeaways.html?searchResultPosition=1.

Fountain, Henry. "Carbon Dioxide Levels Are Highest in Human History." *New York Times*. June 3, 2022. Accessed June 6, 2022. https://www.nytimes. com/2022/06/03/climate/carbon-dioxide-record.html.

Fox News. "Donald Trump Talks Taxes, Trade, 9/11 and Why He Takes Personal Shots at Political Rivals." Fox News Sunday. 2015. Accessed August 10, 2018. http://www.foxnews.com/transcript/2015/10/18/don ald-trump-talks-taxes-trade-11-and-why-takes-personal-shots-at-political.html.

Harvard Law Review. "Juliana v. US." March 10, 2021. Accessed April 15, 2022. https://harvardlawreview.org/2021/03/juliana-v-united-states/? msclkid=031555b3bce511ecb830868927182ca9.

Healy, Jack. "Arizona Democrats Censure Sinema After Filibuster Vote". *New York Times*. January 22, 2022. Accessed April 15, 2022. https://www. nytimes.com/2022/01/22/us/politics/sinema-censure-arizona-democrats. html?searchResultPosition=4.

H.R. 3684—Infrastructure Investment and Jobs Act. https://www.congress. gov/bill/117th-congress/house-bill/3684?msclkid=a4e15c3ebcd111ec8eeb1 ffd9ef0c0f7.

H.R. 5375—Build Back Better Act. https://www.congress.gov/bill/117th-con gress/house-bill/5376.

Joselow, Maxine. "Environmental Justice Leaders Fault White House Race-Neutral Approach." April 13, 2022. Accessed April 19, 2022. *Washington Post.* https://www.washingtonpost.com/politics/2022/04/13/enviro nmental-justice-leaders-fault-white-house-race-neutral-approach/.

Klyza, Christopher McGrory and David Sousa. *American Environmental Policy: Beyond Gridlock.* Updated and Expanded Editions. Cambridge: MIT Press, 2013.

———. *American Environmental Policy 1990–2006.* Cambridge: MIT Press, 2008.

Neuman, Scott. "Greenhouse Gas Levels Reached Record Highs in 2020, Even with Pandemic Lockdowns." *NPR.* October 25, 2021. https://www.npr.org/2021/10/25/1048960283/greenhouse-emissions-reached-record-lev els-in-2020.

Pautz, Michelle C. and Sara R. Rinfret. *The Lilliputians of Environmental Regulation: The Perspective of State Regulators.* New York: Routledge, 2013.

Plumer, Brad. "Trump Officials Link Fuel Economy Rules to Deadly Crashes. Experts are Skeptical." *The New York Times.* August 2, 2018. Accessed August 10, 2018. https://www.nytimes.com/2018/08/02/climate/trump-fuel-eco nomy.html.

"Satisfaction with the US". Gallup Report. 2022. Accessed April 15, 2022. https://news.gallup.com/poll/1669/general-mood-country.aspx?msc lkid=2654d7bdbcd611ec822fa689305a9028.

Shepardson, David. "US Boosts Fuel Efficiency Rules as Biden Reverses Trump Rollback." *Reuters.* April 1, 2022. https://www.reuters.com/business/autos-transportation/biden-administration-finalizes-new-stringent-fuel-eco nomy-rules-2022-04-01/.

Silver, Laura, Fetterolf, Janell, and Connaughton, Aidan. "Diversity and Division in Advanced Economies." Pew Research Center. October 13, 2021. Accessed April 14, 2022. https://www.pewresearch.org/global/2021/10/13/divers ity-and-division-in-advanced-economies/.

White House. "Executive Order on Revocation of Certain Executive Orders Concerning Federal Regulation." January 20, 2021. Accessed April 15, 2022. https://www.whitehouse.gov/briefing-room/presidential-actions/2021/ 01/20/executive-order-revocation-of-certain-executive-orders-concerning-fed eral-regulation/?msclkid=5b0e7d7fbce611ec8489ef8e2307a648.

White House. "FACT SHEET: Biden Administration Releases Agency Climate Adaptation and Resilience Plans from Across Federal Government." October 7, 2021. Accessed April 14, 2022. https://www.whitehouse.gov/briefing-room/statements-releases/2021/10/07/fact-sheet-biden-administration-rel eases-agency-climate-adaptation-and-resilience-plans-from-across-federal-gov ernment/?msclkid=cceea916bc1511ec8a39b8488e6362a0.

Wise, Alana. "EPA Announces Tighter Fuel Economy Standards for Cars and Trucks." *NPR*. December 20, 2021. https://www.npr.org/2021/12/20/1066001919/epa-fuel-economy-standards-cars-trucks.

Zeleny, Jeff and Arlette Saenz. "Senate Goes 'Nuclear,' Changes Nominee Filibuster Rules." ABC News. November 21, 2013. Available online http://abcnews.go.com/Politics/senate-nuclear-filibuster-rules/story?id=20964700. Accessed February 18, 2014.

INDEX

Printed in the USA
CPSIA information can be obtained
at www.ICGtesting.com
LVHW021130050923
757169LV00001B/1